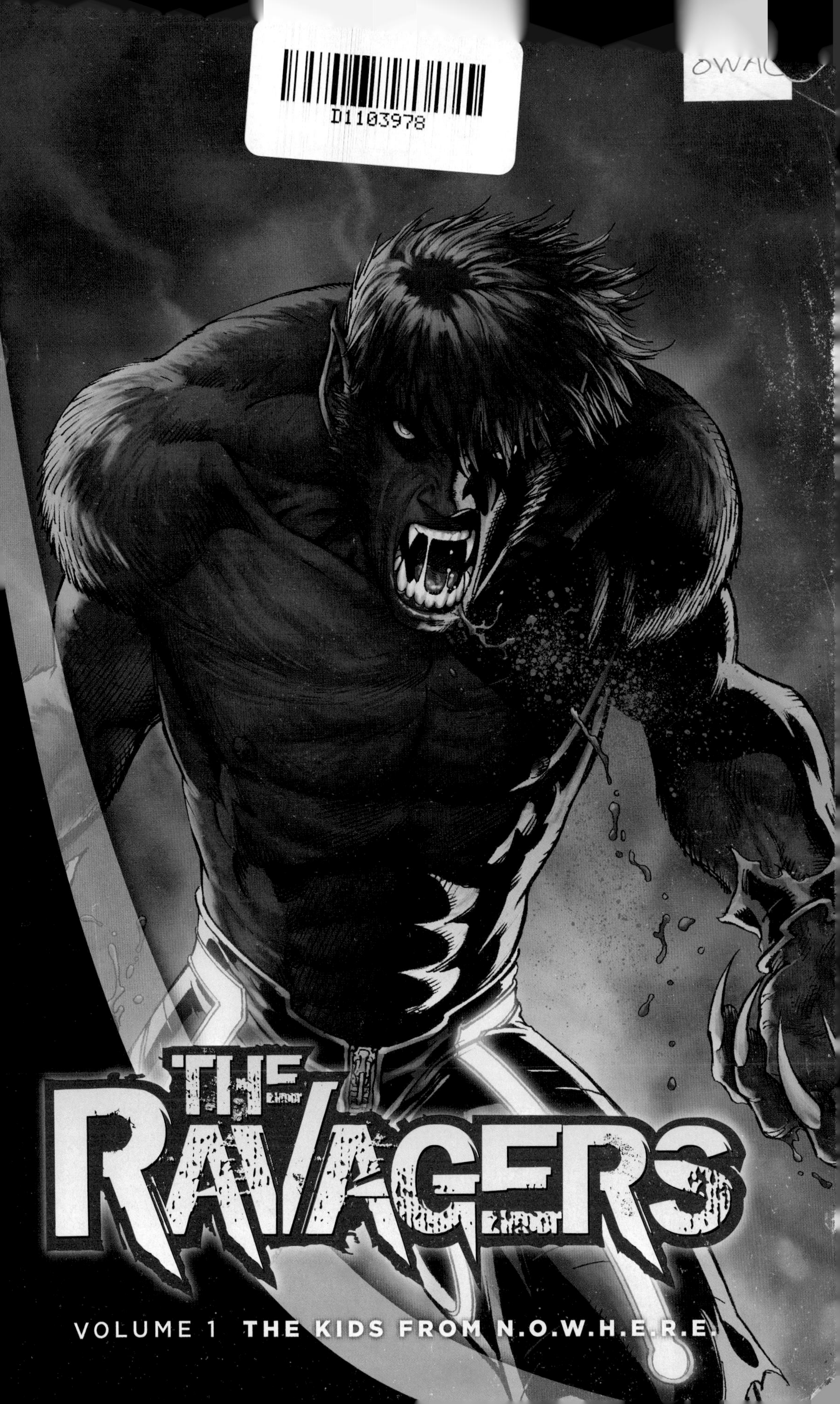

THE RAVAGERS

VOLUME 1 THE KIDS FROM N.O.W.H.E.R.E.

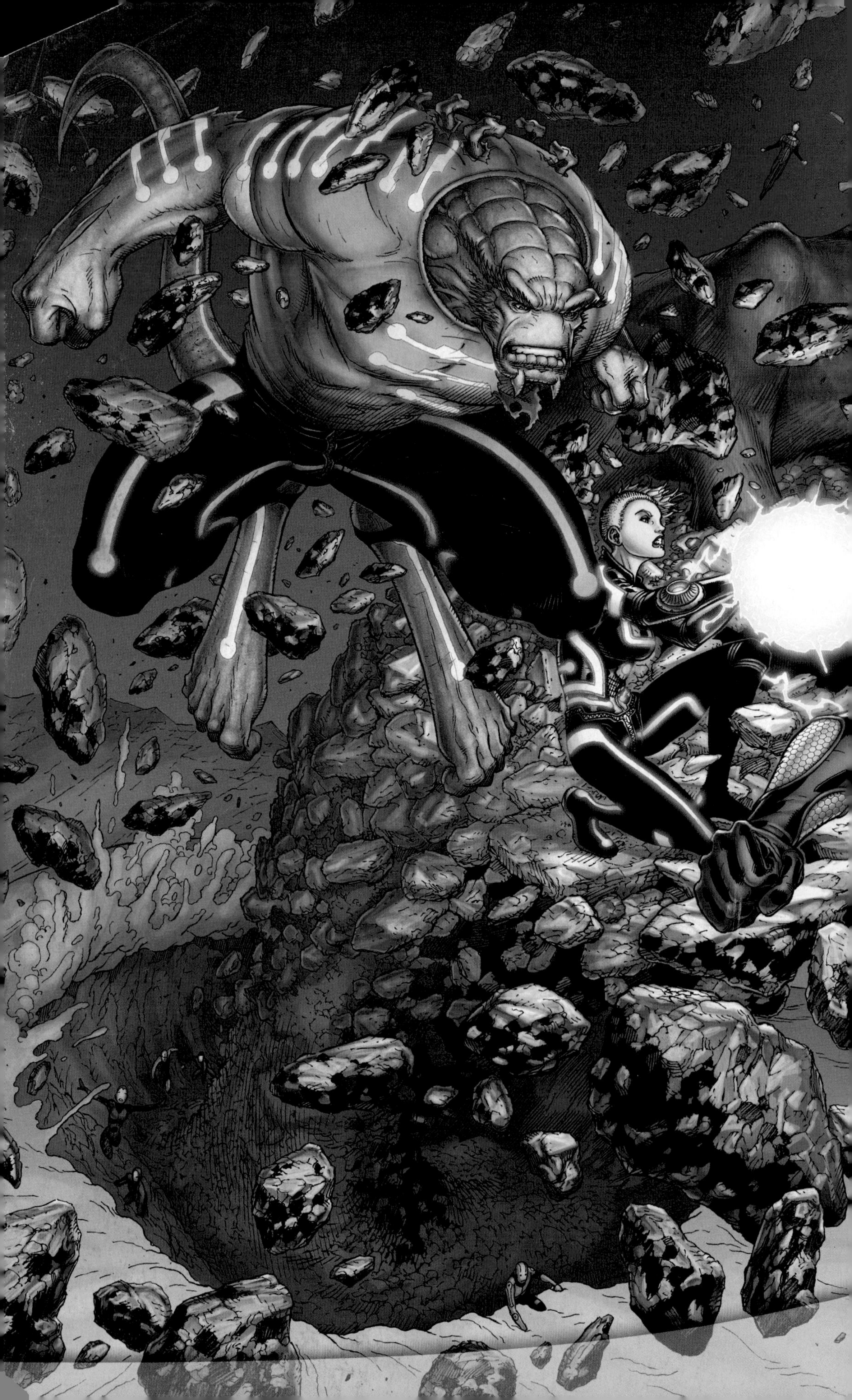

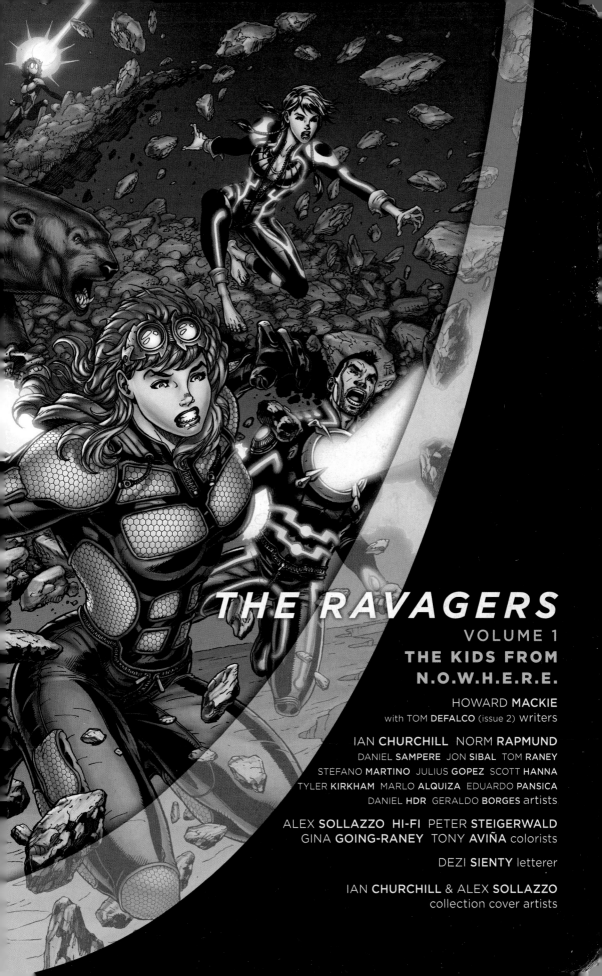

THE RAVAGERS

VOLUME 1
THE KIDS FROM
N.O.W.H.E.R.E.

HOWARD **MACKIE**
with TOM **DEFALCO** (issue 2) writers

IAN **CHURCHILL** NORM **RAPMUND**
DANIEL **SAMPERE** JON **SIBAL** TOM **RANEY**
STEFANO **MARTINO** JULIUS **GOPEZ** SCOTT **HANNA**
TYLER **KIRKHAM** MARLO **ALQUIZA** EDUARDO **PANSICA**
DANIEL **HDR** GERALDO **BORGES** artists

ALEX **SOLLAZZO** HI-FI PETER **STEIGERWALD**
GINA **GOING-RANEY** TONY **AVIÑA** colorists

DEZI **SIENTY** letterer

IAN **CHURCHILL** & ALEX **SOLLAZZO**
collection cover artists

EDDIE BERGANZA PAT McCALLUM Editors – Original Series SEAN MACKIEWICZ DARREN SHAN Assistant Editors – Original Series
RACHEL PINNELAS Editor ROBBIN BROSTERMAN Design Director – Books
ROBBIE BIEDERMAN Publication Design

BOB HARRAS VP – Editor-in-Chief

DIANE NELSON President DAN DIDIO and JIM LEE Co-Publishers GEOFF JOHNS Chief Creative Officer
JOHN ROOD Executive VP – Sales, Marketing and Business Development AMY GENKINS Senior VP – Business and Legal Affairs
NAIRI GARDINER Senior VP – Finance JEFF BOISON VP – Publishing Operations MARK CHIARELLO VP – Art Direction and Design
JOHN CUNNINGHAM VP – Marketing TERRI CUNNINGHAM VP – Talent Relations and Services
ALISON GILL Senior VP – Manufacturing and Operations HANK KANALZ Senior VP – Digital
JAY KOGAN VP – Business and Legal Affairs, Publishing JACK MAHAN VP – Business Affairs, Talent
NICK NAPOLITANO VP – Manufacturing Administration SUE POHJA VP – Book Sales
COURTNEY SIMMONS Senior VP – Publicity BOB WAYNE Senior VP – Sales

THE RAVAGERS VOLUME 1: THE KIDS FROM N.O.W.H.E.R.E.

Published by DC Comics. Cover and compilation Copyright © 2013 DC Comics. All Rights Reserved.

Originally published in single magazine form in THE RAVAGERS 1-7. Copyright © 2012, 2013 DC Comics. All Rights Reserved.
All characters, their distinctive likenesses and related elements featured in this publication are trademarks of DC Comics.
The stories, characters and incidents featured in this publication are entirely fictional.
DC Comics does not read or accept unsolicited ideas, stories or artwork.

DC Comics, 1700 Broadway, New York, NY 10019
A Warner Bros. Entertainment Company.
Printed by RR Donnelley, Salem, VA, USA. 2/22/13. First Printing.

ISBN: 978-1-4012-4091-2

Library of Congress Cataloging-in-Publication Data

Mackie, Howard, author.
The Ravagers. Volume 1, The kids from N.O.W.H.E.R.E. / Howard Mackie, Ian Churchill, Norm Rapmund.
pages cm
"Originally published in single magazine form in The Ravagers 1-7."
ISBN 978-1-4012-4091-2
1. Graphic novels. I. Churchill, Ian, illustrator. II. Rapmund, Norm, illustrator. III. Title. IV. Title: Kids from N.O.W.H.E.R.E.
PN6728.R38M33 2013
741.5'973—dc23
      2012050771

SUSTAINABLE
FORESTRY
INITIATIVE
Certified Chain of Custody
At Least 20% Certified Forest Content
www.sfiprogram.org
SFI-01042
APPLIES TO TEXT STOCK ONLY

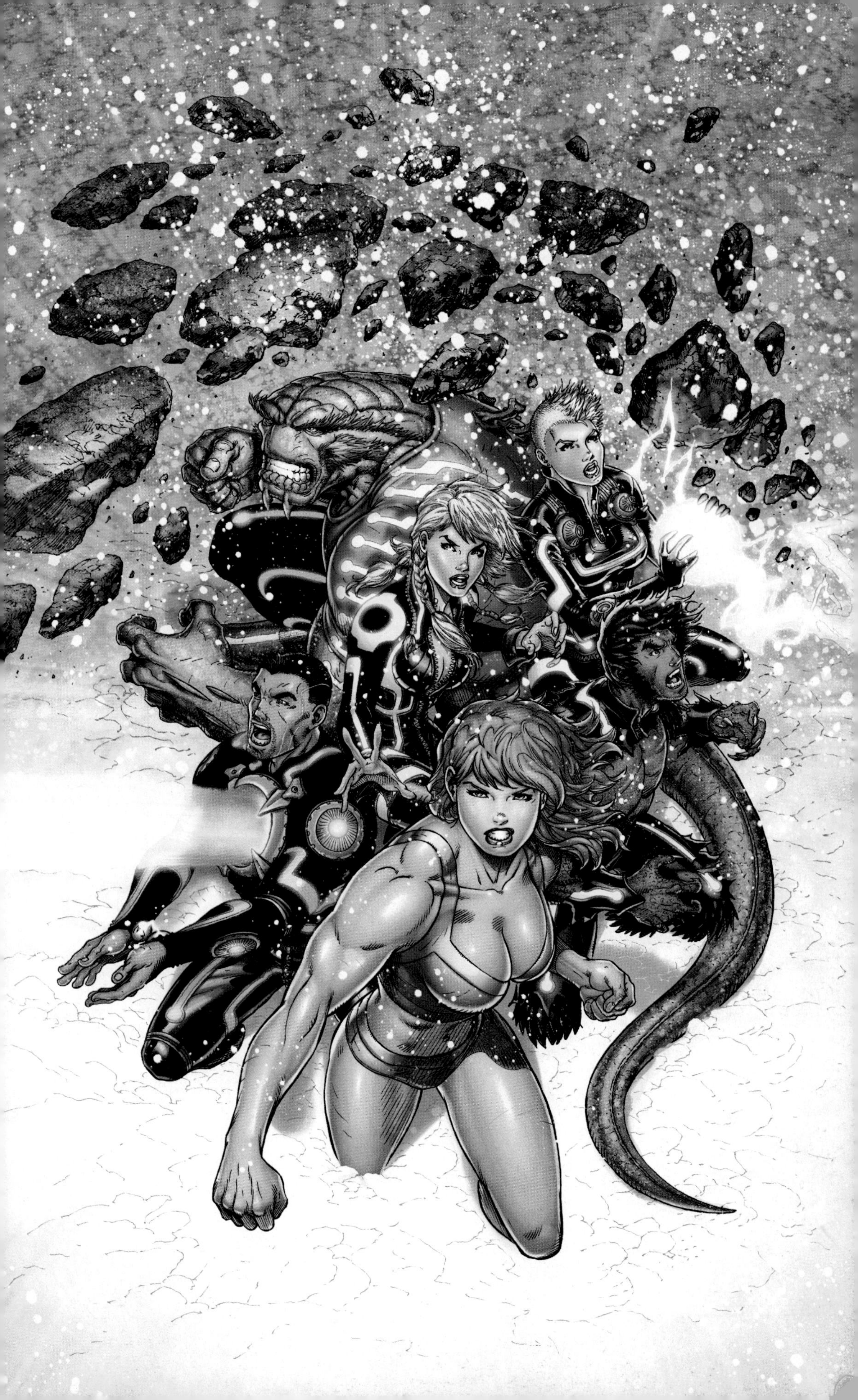

CHILDREN OF DESTINY

HOWARD MACKIE
writer

IAN CHURCHILL
penciller

NORM RAPMUND & IAN CHURCHILL
inkers

cover art by
IAN CHURCHILL & ALEX SOLLAZZO

special thanks to SCOTT LOBDELL

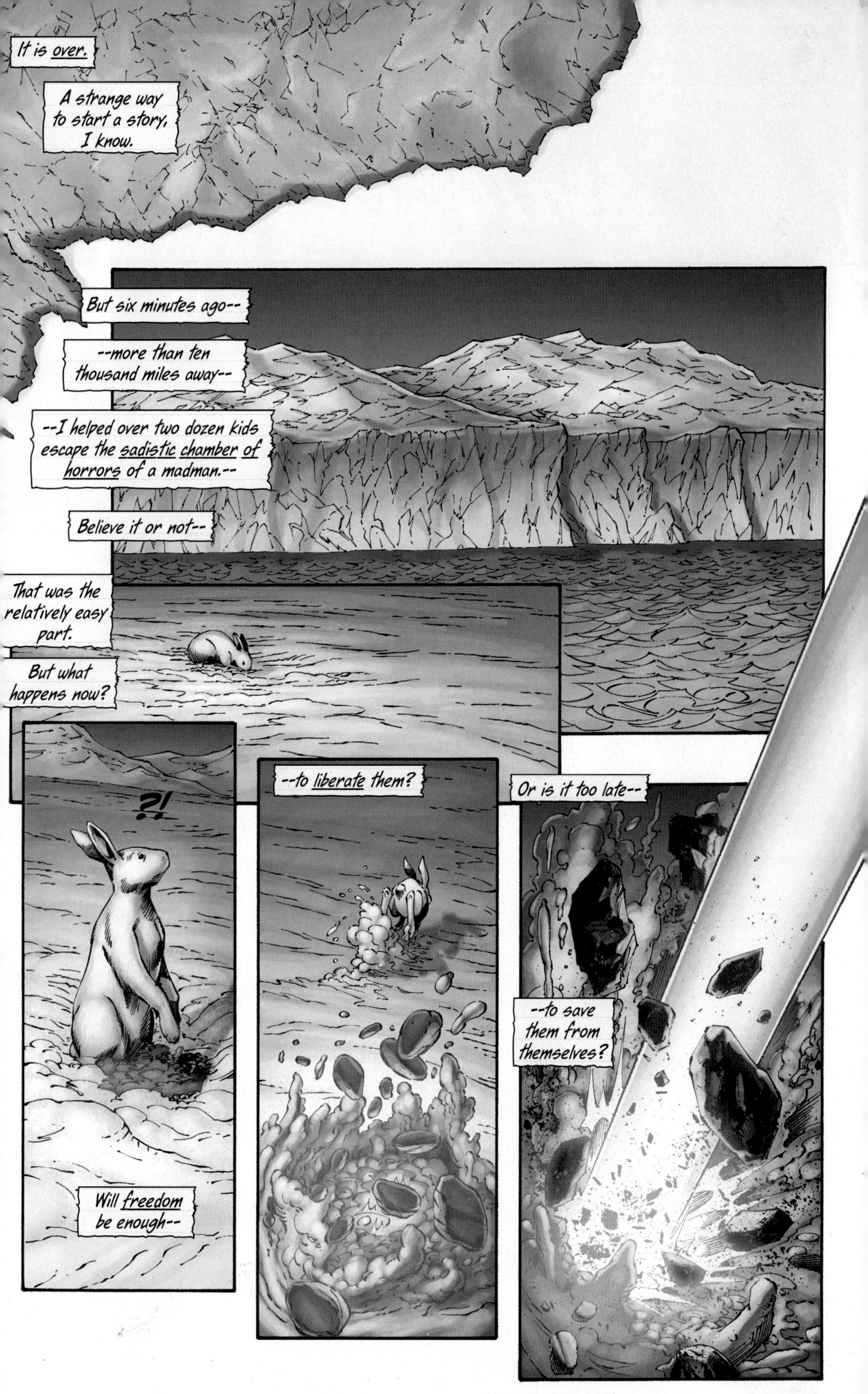
It is over.
A strange way to start a story, I know.
But six minutes ago--
--more than ten thousand miles away--
--I helped over two dozen kids escape the sadistic chamber of horrors of a madman.--
Believe it or not--
That was the relatively easy part.
But what happens now?
?!
Will freedom be enough--
--to liberate them?
Or is it too late--
--to save them from themselves?

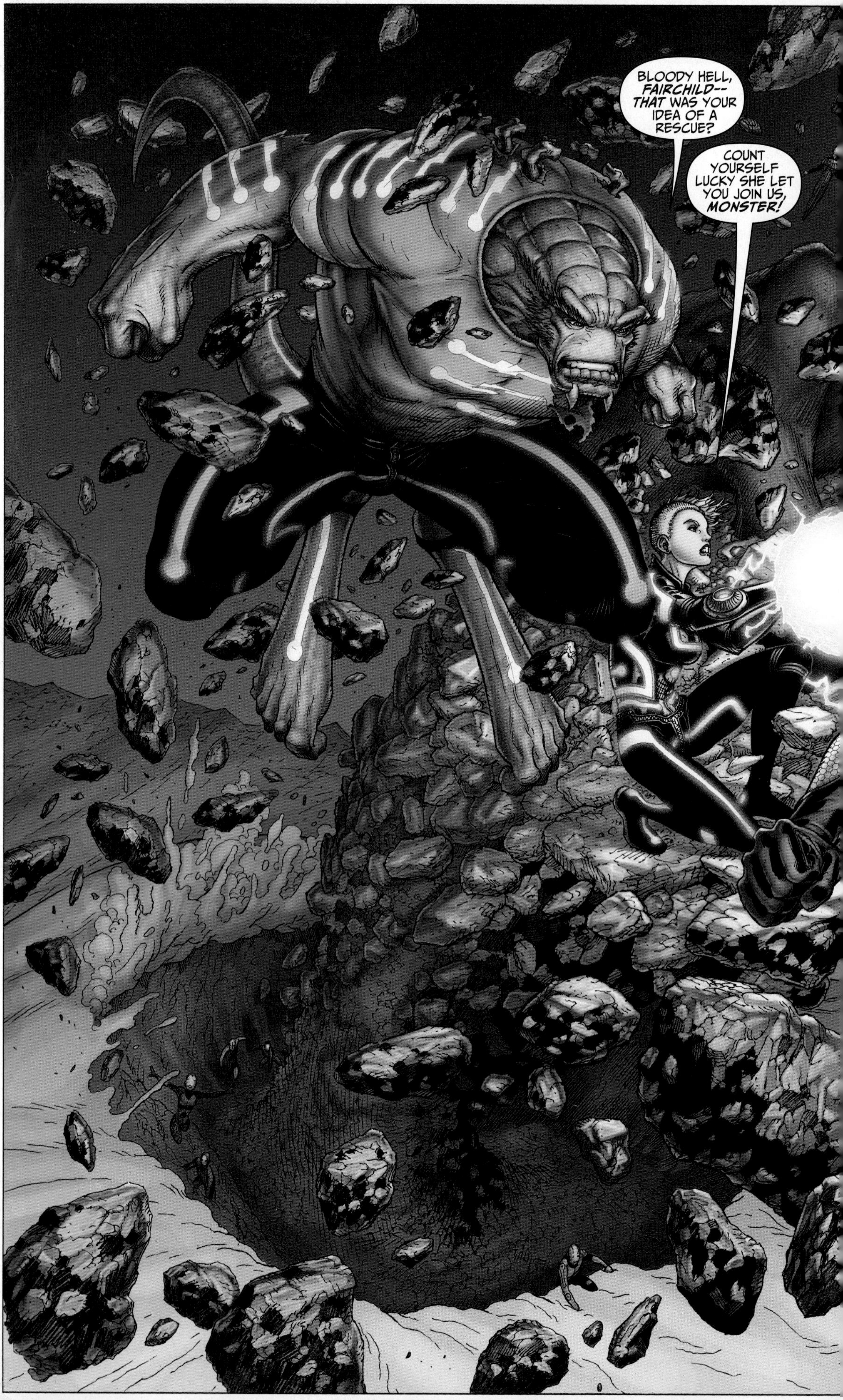
BLOODY HELL, FAIRCHILD-- THAT WAS YOUR IDEA OF A RESCUE?
COUNT YOURSELF LUCKY SHE LET YOU JOIN US, MONSTER!

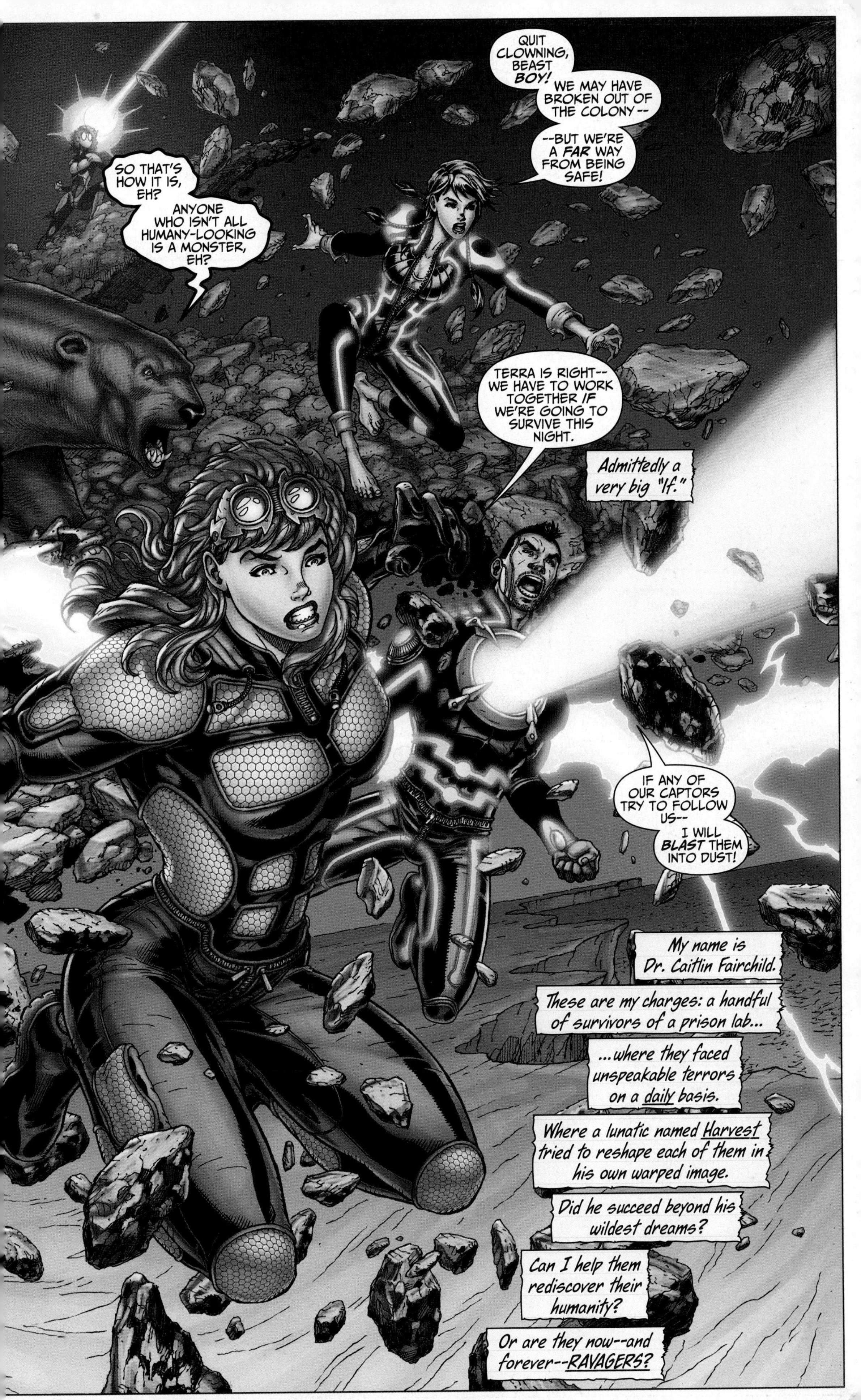
QUIT CLOWNING, BEAST BOY!
WE MAY HAVE BROKEN OUT OF THE COLONY--
--BUT WE'RE A FAR WAY FROM BEING SAFE!
SO THAT'S HOW IT IS, EH?
ANYONE WHO ISN'T ALL HUMANY-LOOKING IS A MONSTER, EH?
TERRA IS RIGHT--WE HAVE TO WORK TOGETHER IF WE'RE GOING TO SURVIVE THIS NIGHT.
Admittedly a very big "If."
IF ANY OF OUR CAPTORS TRY TO FOLLOW US--
I WILL BLAST THEM INTO DUST!
My name is Dr. Caitlin Fairchild.
These are my charges: a handful of survivors of a prison lab...
...where they faced unspeakable terrors on a daily basis.
Where a lunatic named Harvest tried to reshape each of them in his own warped image.
Did he succeed beyond his wildest dreams?
Can I help them rediscover their humanity?
Or are they now--and forever--RAVAGERS?

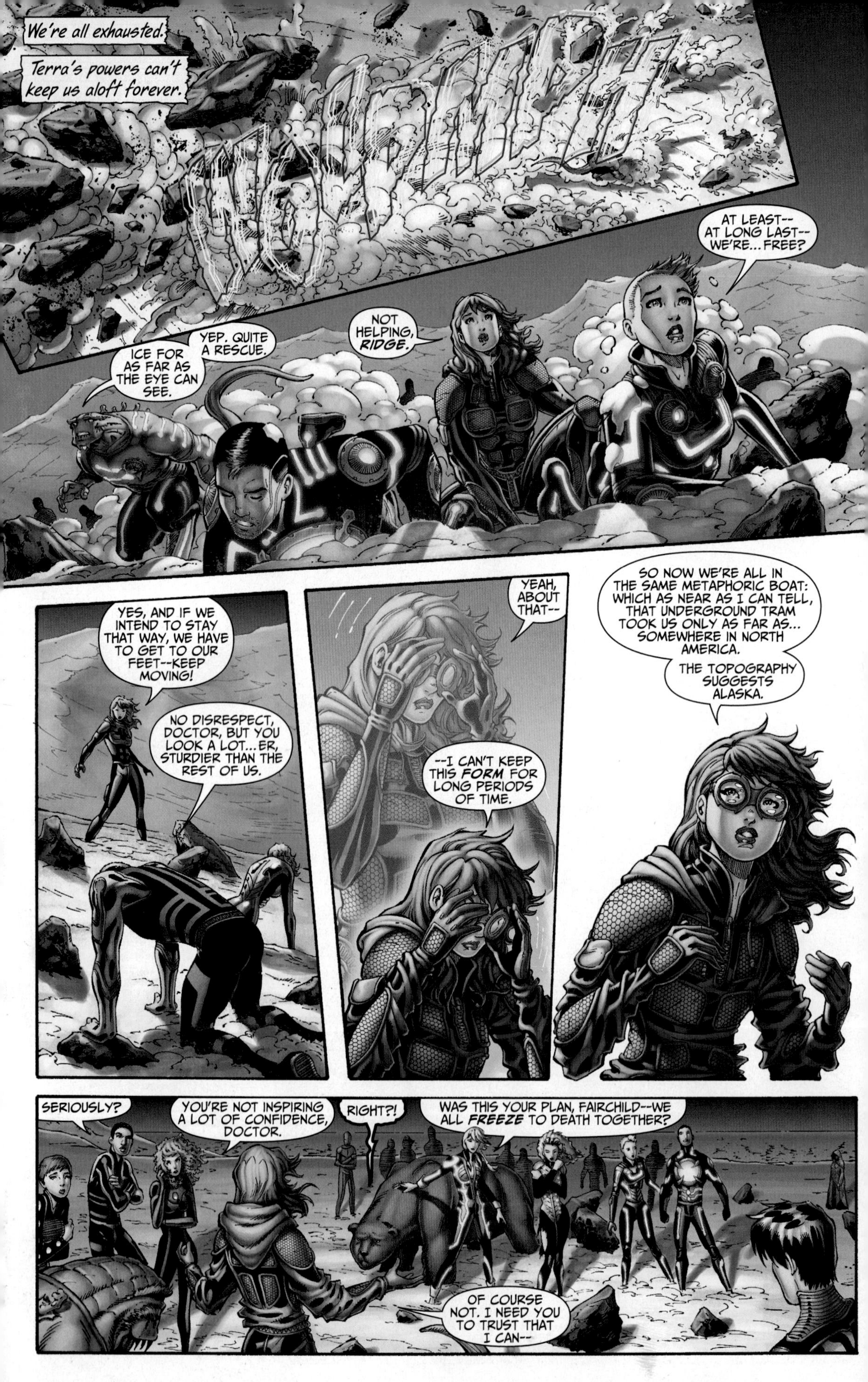
We're all exhausted.
Terra's powers can't keep us aloft forever.
AT LEAST-- AT LONG LAST-- WE'RE... FREE?
NOT HELPING, RIDGE.
YEP. QUITE A RESCUE.
ICE FOR AS FAR AS THE EYE CAN SEE.
YES, AND IF WE INTEND TO STAY THAT WAY, WE HAVE TO GET TO OUR FEET--KEEP MOVING!
NO DISRESPECT, DOCTOR, BUT YOU LOOK A LOT...ER, STURDIER THAN THE REST OF US.
YEAH, ABOUT THAT--
--I CAN'T KEEP THIS FORM FOR LONG PERIODS OF TIME.
SO NOW WE'RE ALL IN THE SAME METAPHORIC BOAT: WHICH AS NEAR AS I CAN TELL, THAT UNDERGROUND TRAM TOOK US ONLY AS FAR AS... SOMEWHERE IN NORTH AMERICA.
THE TOPOGRAPHY SUGGESTS ALASKA.
SERIOUSLY?
YOU'RE NOT INSPIRING A LOT OF CONFIDENCE, DOCTOR.
RIGHT?!
WAS THIS YOUR PLAN, FAIRCHILD--WE ALL FREEZE TO DEATH TOGETHER?
OF COURSE NOT. I NEED YOU TO TRUST THAT I CAN--

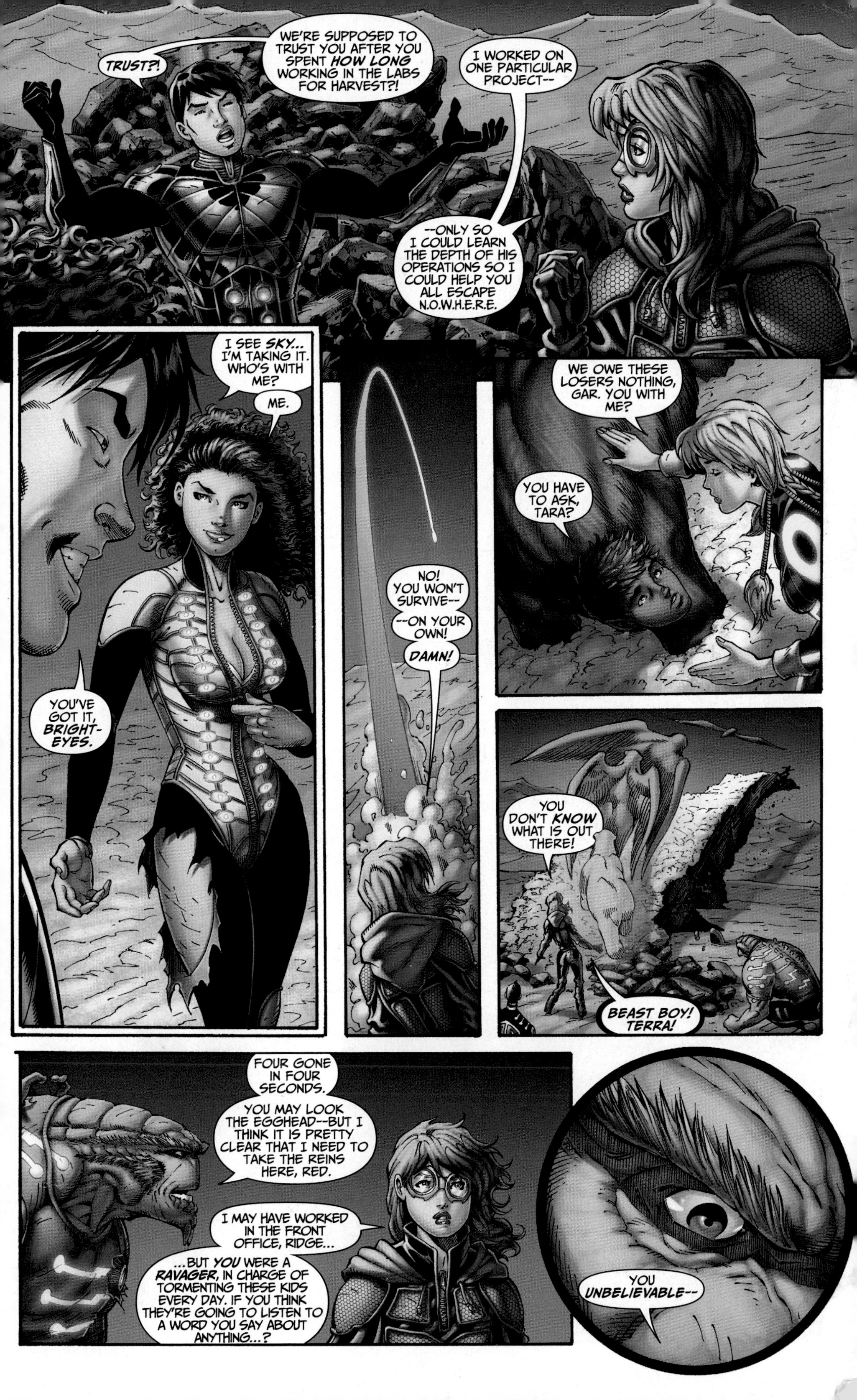
TRUST?!
WE'RE SUPPOSED TO TRUST YOU AFTER YOU SPENT HOW LONG WORKING IN THE LABS FOR HARVEST?!
I WORKED ON ONE PARTICULAR PROJECT--
--ONLY SO I COULD LEARN THE DEPTH OF HIS OPERATIONS SO I COULD HELP YOU ALL ESCAPE N.O.W.H.E.R.E.
I SEE SKY... I'M TAKING IT. WHO'S WITH ME?
ME.
YOU'VE GOT IT, BRIGHT-EYES.
NO! YOU WON'T SURVIVE--
--ON YOUR OWN!
DAMN!
WE OWE THESE LOSERS NOTHING, GAR. YOU WITH ME?
YOU HAVE TO ASK, TARA?
YOU DON'T KNOW WHAT IS OUT THERE!
BEAST BOY! TERRA!
FOUR GONE IN FOUR SECONDS.
YOU MAY LOOK THE EGGHEAD--BUT I THINK IT IS PRETTY CLEAR THAT I NEED TO TAKE THE REINS HERE, RED.
I MAY HAVE WORKED IN THE FRONT OFFICE, RIDGE...
...BUT YOU WERE A RAVAGER, IN CHARGE OF TORMENTING THESE KIDS EVERY DAY. IF YOU THINK THEY'RE GOING TO LISTEN TO A WORD YOU SAY ABOUT ANYTHING...?
YOU UNBELIEVABLE--

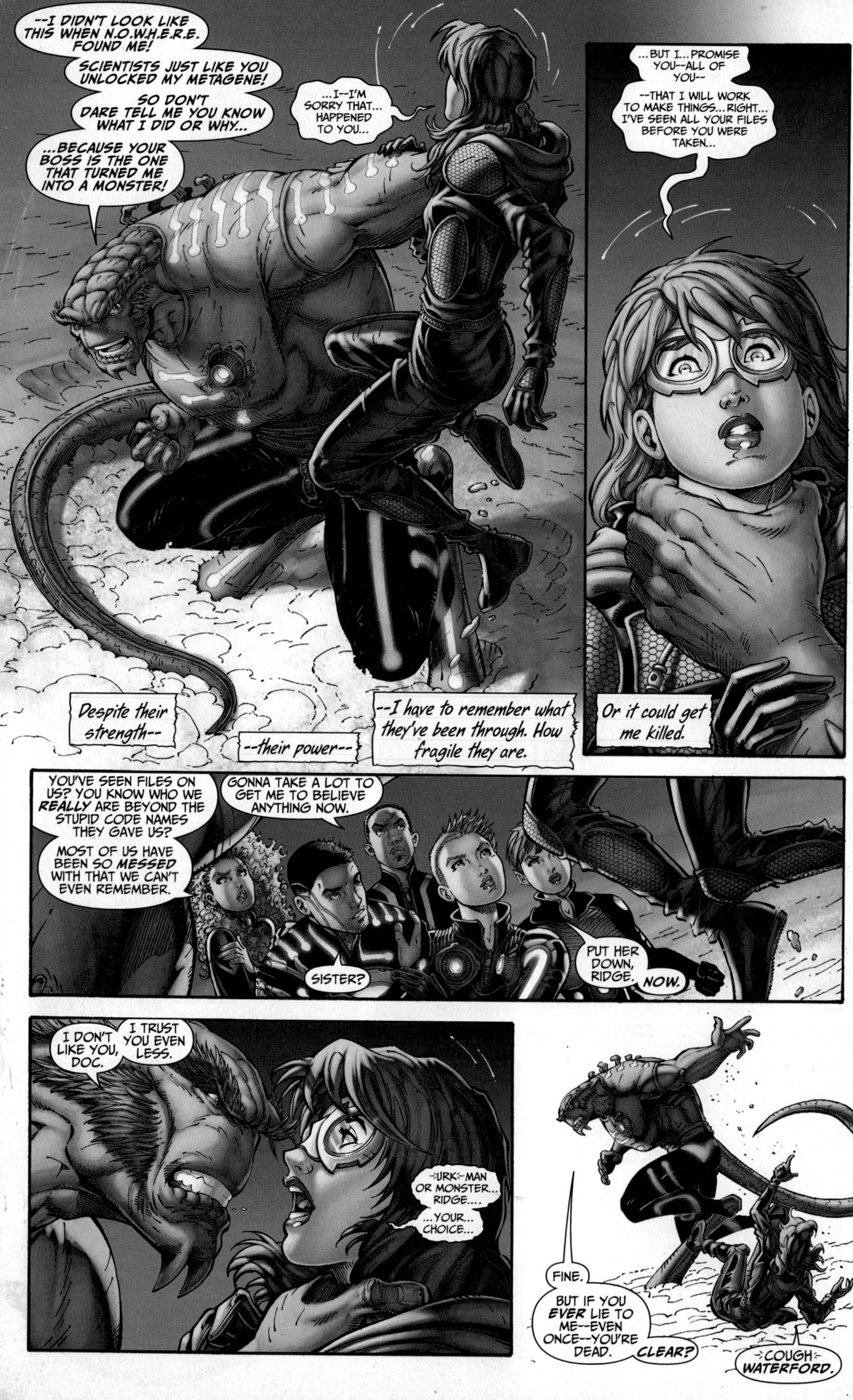
--I DIDN'T LOOK LIKE THIS WHEN N.O.W.H.E.R.E. FOUND ME!
SCIENTISTS JUST LIKE YOU UNLOCKED MY METAGENE!
SO DON'T DARE TELL ME YOU KNOW WHAT I DID OR WHY...
...BECAUSE YOUR BOSS IS THE ONE THAT TURNED ME INTO A MONSTER!
...I--I'M SORRY THAT... HAPPENED TO YOU...
...BUT I...PROMISE YOU--ALL OF YOU--
--THAT I WILL WORK TO MAKE THINGS...RIGHT... I'VE SEEN ALL YOUR FILES BEFORE YOU WERE TAKEN...
Despite their strength--
--their power--
--I have to remember what they've been through. How fragile they are.
Or it could get me killed.
YOU'VE SEEN FILES ON US? YOU KNOW WHO WE REALLY ARE BEYOND THE STUPID CODE NAMES THEY GAVE US?
MOST OF US HAVE BEEN SO MESSED WITH THAT WE CAN'T EVEN REMEMBER.
GONNA TAKE A LOT TO GET ME TO BELIEVE ANYTHING NOW.
SISTER?
PUT HER DOWN, RIDGE. NOW.
I DON'T LIKE YOU, DOC.
I TRUST YOU EVEN LESS.
URK MAN OR MONSTER... RIDGE....
...YOUR... CHOICE...
FINE.
BUT IF YOU EVER LIE TO ME--EVEN ONCE--YOU'RE DEAD.
CLEAR?
COUGH
WATERFORD.

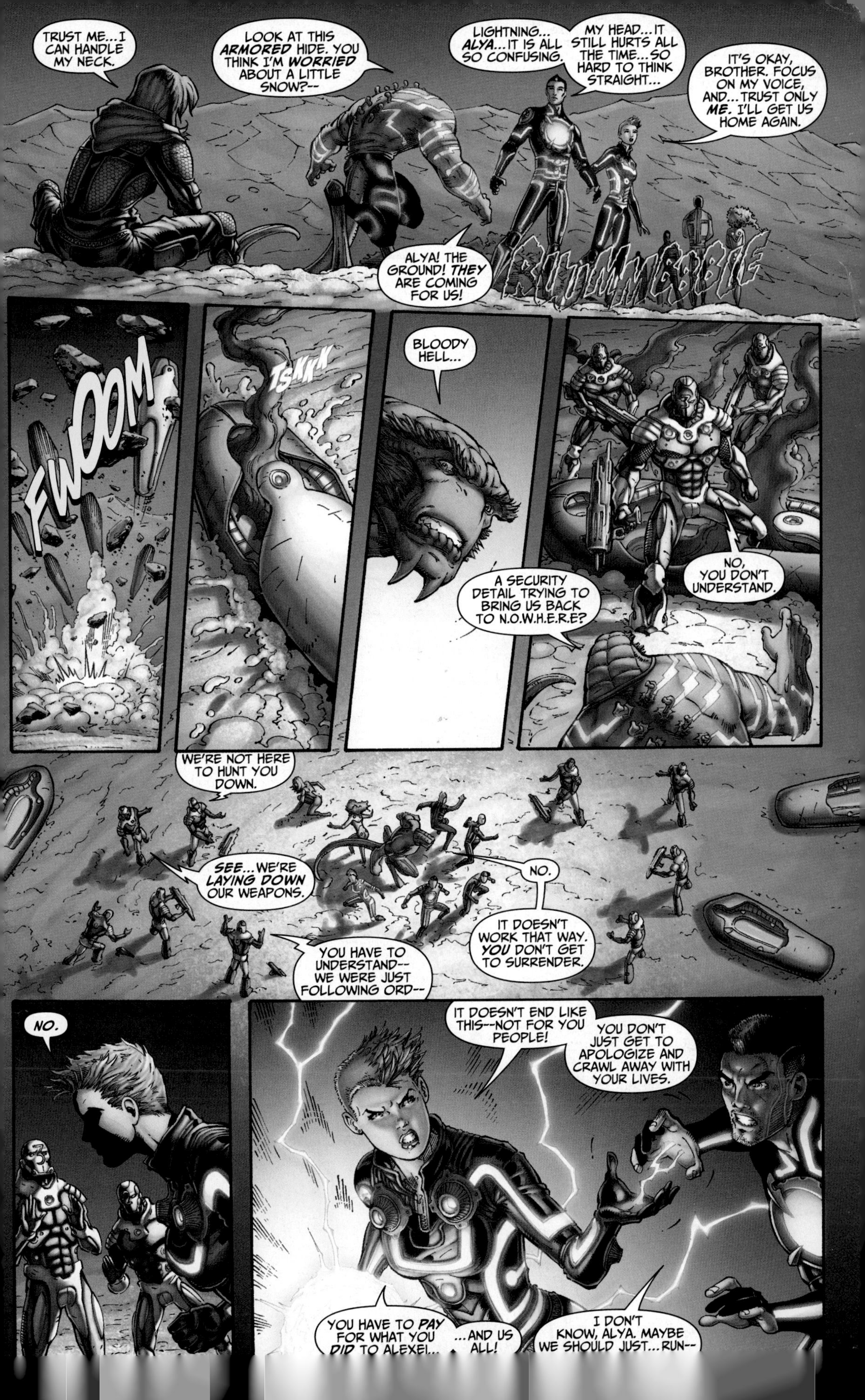
TRUST ME... I CAN HANDLE MY NECK.
LOOK AT THIS ARMORED HIDE. YOU THINK I'M WORRIED ABOUT A LITTLE SNOW?--
LIGHTNING... ALYA... IT IS ALL SO CONFUSING.
MY HEAD... IT STILL HURTS ALL THE TIME... SO HARD TO THINK STRAIGHT...
IT'S OKAY, BROTHER. FOCUS ON MY VOICE, AND... TRUST ONLY ME. I'LL GET US HOME AGAIN.
ALYA! THE GROUND! THEY ARE COMING FOR US!
FWOOM
TSKKK
BLOODY HELL...
NO, YOU DON'T UNDERSTAND.
A SECURITY DETAIL TRYING TO BRING US BACK TO N.O.W.H.E.R.E?
WE'RE NOT HERE TO HUNT YOU DOWN.
SEE... WE'RE LAYING DOWN OUR WEAPONS.
NO.
IT DOESN'T WORK THAT WAY. YOU DON'T GET TO SURRENDER.
YOU HAVE TO UNDERSTAND-- WE WERE JUST FOLLOWING ORD--
NO.
IT DOESN'T END LIKE THIS--NOT FOR YOU PEOPLE!
YOU DON'T JUST GET TO APOLOGIZE AND CRAWL AWAY WITH YOUR LIVES.
YOU HAVE TO PAY FOR WHAT YOU DID TO ALEXEI...
...AND US ALL!
I DON'T KNOW, ALYA. MAYBE WE SHOULD JUST... RUN--

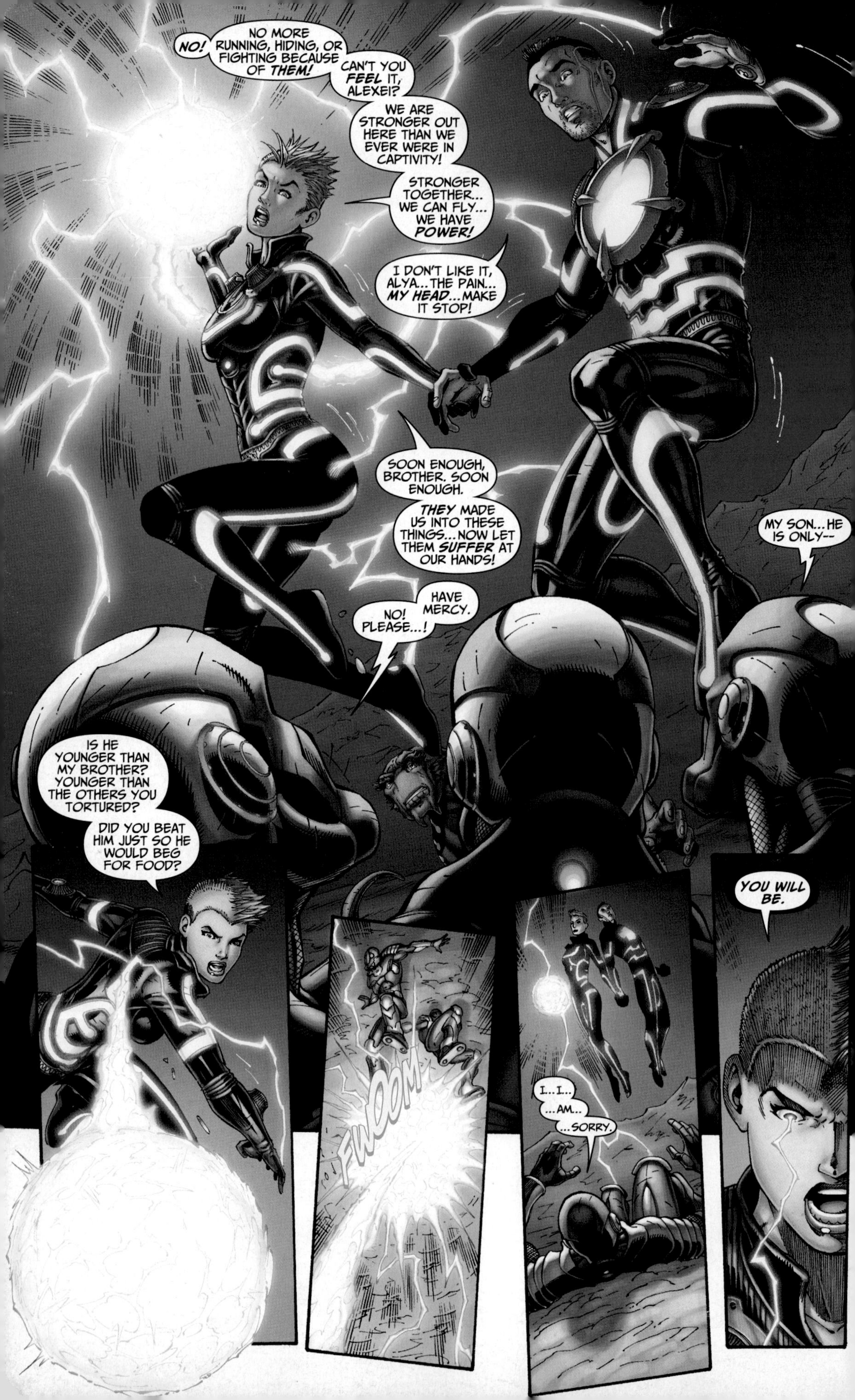
NO!
NO MORE RUNNING, HIDING, OR FIGHTING BECAUSE OF THEM!
CAN'T YOU FEEL IT, ALEXEI?
WE ARE STRONGER OUT HERE THAN WE EVER WERE IN CAPTIVITY!
STRONGER TOGETHER... WE CAN FLY... WE HAVE POWER!
I DON'T LIKE IT, ALYA...THE PAIN... MY HEAD...MAKE IT STOP!
SOON ENOUGH, BROTHER. SOON ENOUGH.
THEY MADE US INTO THESE THINGS...NOW LET THEM SUFFER AT OUR HANDS!
MY SON...HE IS ONLY--
HAVE MERCY.
NO! PLEASE...!
IS HE YOUNGER THAN MY BROTHER? YOUNGER THAN THE OTHERS YOU TORTURED?
DID YOU BEAT HIM JUST SO HE WOULD BEG FOR FOOD?
FWOOM
I...I... ...AM... ...SORRY.
YOU WILL BE.

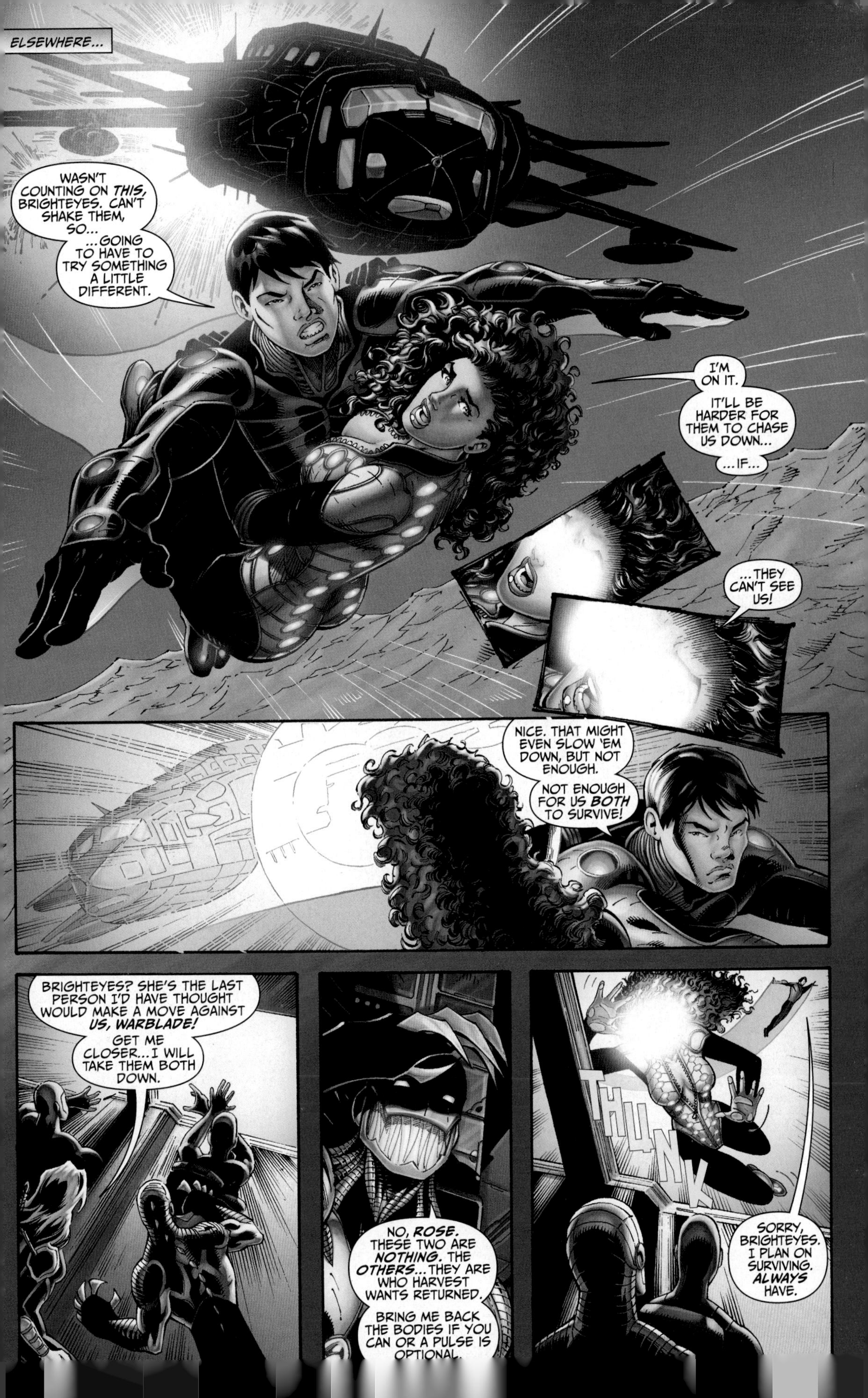
ELSEWHERE...
WASN'T COUNTING ON THIS, BRIGHTEYES. CAN'T SHAKE THEM, SO...
...GOING TO HAVE TO TRY SOMETHING A LITTLE DIFFERENT.
I'M ON IT.
IT'LL BE HARDER FOR THEM TO CHASE US DOWN...
...IF...
...THEY CAN'T SEE US!
NICE. THAT MIGHT EVEN SLOW 'EM DOWN, BUT NOT ENOUGH.
NOT ENOUGH FOR US BOTH TO SURVIVE!
BRIGHTEYES? SHE'S THE LAST PERSON I'D HAVE THOUGHT WOULD MAKE A MOVE AGAINST US, WARBLADE!
GET ME CLOSER...I WILL TAKE THEM BOTH DOWN.
NO, ROSE. THESE TWO ARE NOTHING. THE OTHERS...THEY ARE WHO HARVEST WANTS RETURNED.
BRING ME BACK THE BODIES IF YOU CAN OR A PULSE IS OPTIONAL.
THUNK
SORRY, BRIGHTEYES. I PLAN ON SURVIVING. ALWAYS HAVE.

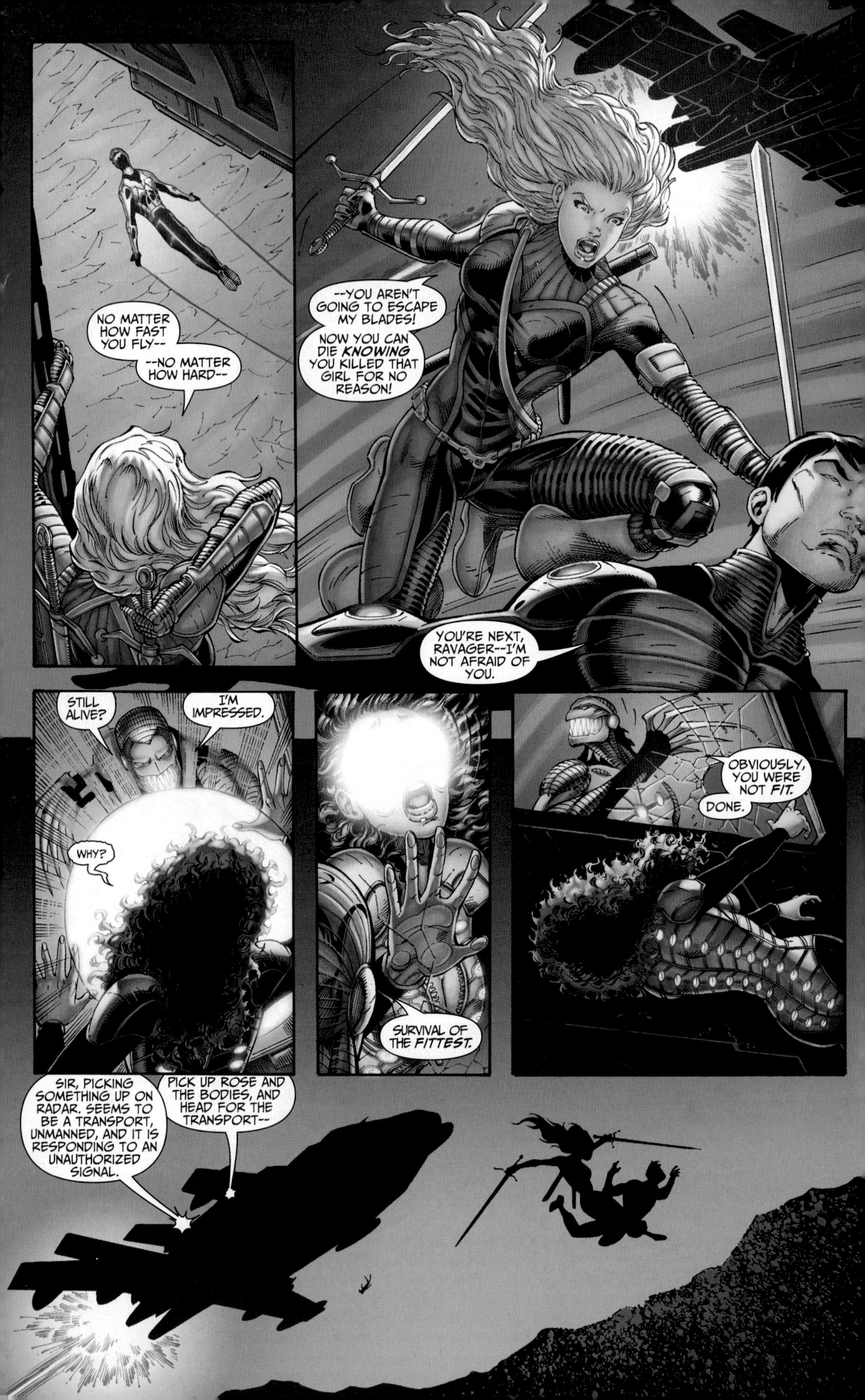
NO MATTER HOW FAST YOU FLY--
--NO MATTER HOW HARD--
--YOU AREN'T GOING TO ESCAPE MY BLADES!
NOW YOU CAN DIE *KNOWING* YOU KILLED THAT GIRL FOR NO REASON!
YOU'RE NEXT, RAVAGER--I'M NOT AFRAID OF YOU.
STILL ALIVE?
I'M IMPRESSED.
WHY?
SURVIVAL OF THE *FITTEST.*
OBVIOUSLY, YOU WERE NOT *FIT.*
DONE.
SIR, PICKING SOMETHING UP ON RADAR. SEEMS TO BE A TRANSPORT, UNMANNED, AND IT IS RESPONDING TO AN UNAUTHORIZED SIGNAL.
PICK UP ROSE AND THE BODIES, AND HEAD FOR THE TRANSPORT--

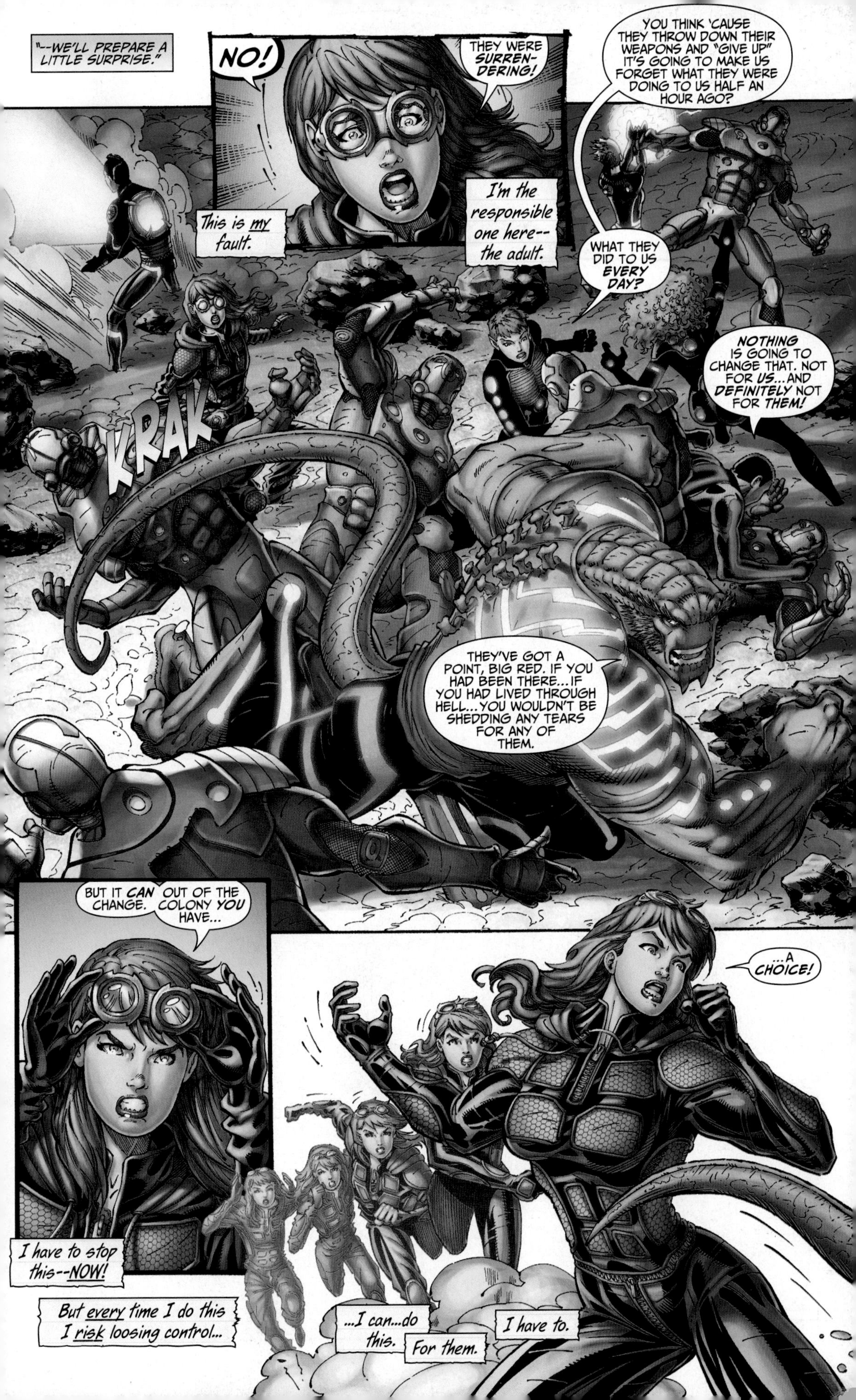
"--WE'LL PREPARE A LITTLE SURPRISE."
NO!
THEY WERE SURREN-DERING!
YOU THINK 'CAUSE THEY THROW DOWN THEIR WEAPONS AND "GIVE UP" IT'S GOING TO MAKE US FORGET WHAT THEY WERE DOING TO US HALF AN HOUR AGO?
This is my fault.
I'm the responsible one here--the adult.
WHAT THEY DID TO US EVERY DAY?
NOTHING IS GOING TO CHANGE THAT. NOT FOR US...AND DEFINITELY NOT FOR THEM!
KRAK
THEY'VE GOT A POINT, BIG RED. IF YOU HAD BEEN THERE...IF YOU HAD LIVED THROUGH HELL...YOU WOULDN'T BE SHEDDING ANY TEARS FOR ANY OF THEM.
BUT IT CAN CHANGE.
OUT OF THE COLONY YOU HAVE...
...A CHOICE!
I have to stop this--NOW!
But every time I do this I risk loosing control...
...I can...do this.
For them.
I have to.

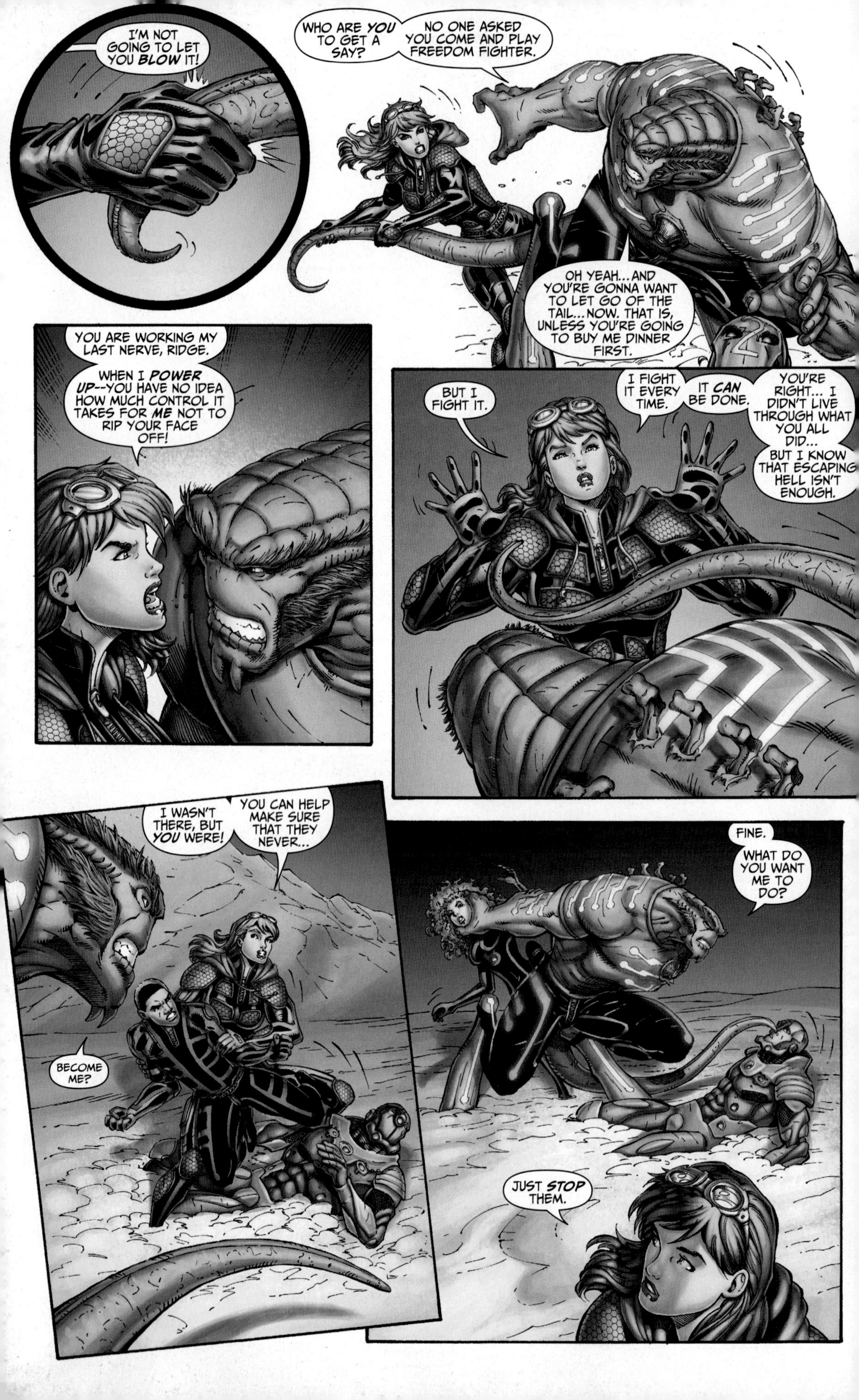
I'M NOT GOING TO LET YOU BLOW IT!
WHO ARE YOU TO GET A SAY?
NO ONE ASKED YOU COME AND PLAY FREEDOM FIGHTER.
OH YEAH...AND YOU'RE GONNA WANT TO LET GO OF THE TAIL...NOW. THAT IS, UNLESS YOU'RE GOING TO BUY ME DINNER FIRST.
YOU ARE WORKING MY LAST NERVE, RIDGE.
WHEN I POWER UP--YOU HAVE NO IDEA HOW MUCH CONTROL IT TAKES FOR ME NOT TO RIP YOUR FACE OFF!
BUT I FIGHT IT.
I FIGHT IT EVERY TIME.
IT CAN BE DONE.
YOU'RE RIGHT... I DIDN'T LIVE THROUGH WHAT YOU ALL DID...
BUT I KNOW THAT ESCAPING HELL ISN'T ENOUGH.
I WASN'T THERE, BUT YOU WERE!
YOU CAN HELP MAKE SURE THAT THEY NEVER...
BECOME ME?
FINE.
WHAT DO YOU WANT ME TO DO?
JUST STOP THEM.

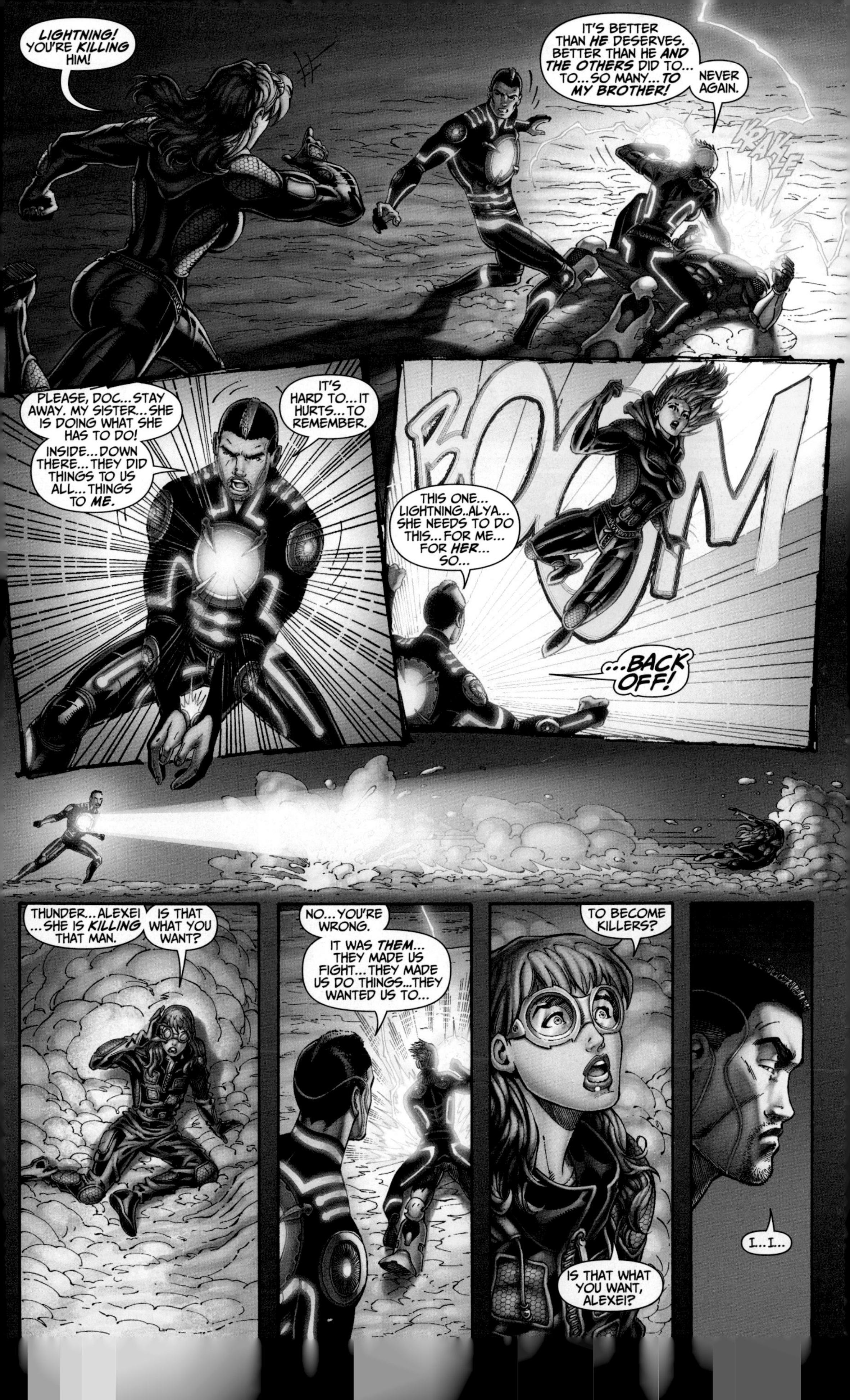
LIGHTNING! YOU'RE KILLING HIM!
IT'S BETTER THAN HE DESERVES. BETTER THAN HE AND THE OTHERS DID TO... TO...SO MANY...TO MY BROTHER!
NEVER AGAIN.
KRAKLE
PLEASE, DOC...STAY AWAY. MY SISTER...SHE IS DOING WHAT SHE HAS TO DO!
INSIDE...DOWN THERE...THEY DID THINGS TO US ALL...THINGS TO ME.
IT'S HARD TO...IT HURTS...TO REMEMBER.
BOOM
THIS ONE... LIGHTNING..ALYA... SHE NEEDS TO DO THIS...FOR ME... FOR HER... SO...
...BACK OFF!
THUNDER...ALEXEI ...SHE IS KILLING THAT MAN.
IS THAT WHAT YOU WANT?
NO...YOU'RE WRONG.
IT WAS THEM... THEY MADE US FIGHT...THEY MADE US DO THINGS...THEY WANTED US TO...
TO BECOME KILLERS?
IS THAT WHAT YOU WANT, ALEXEI?
I...I...

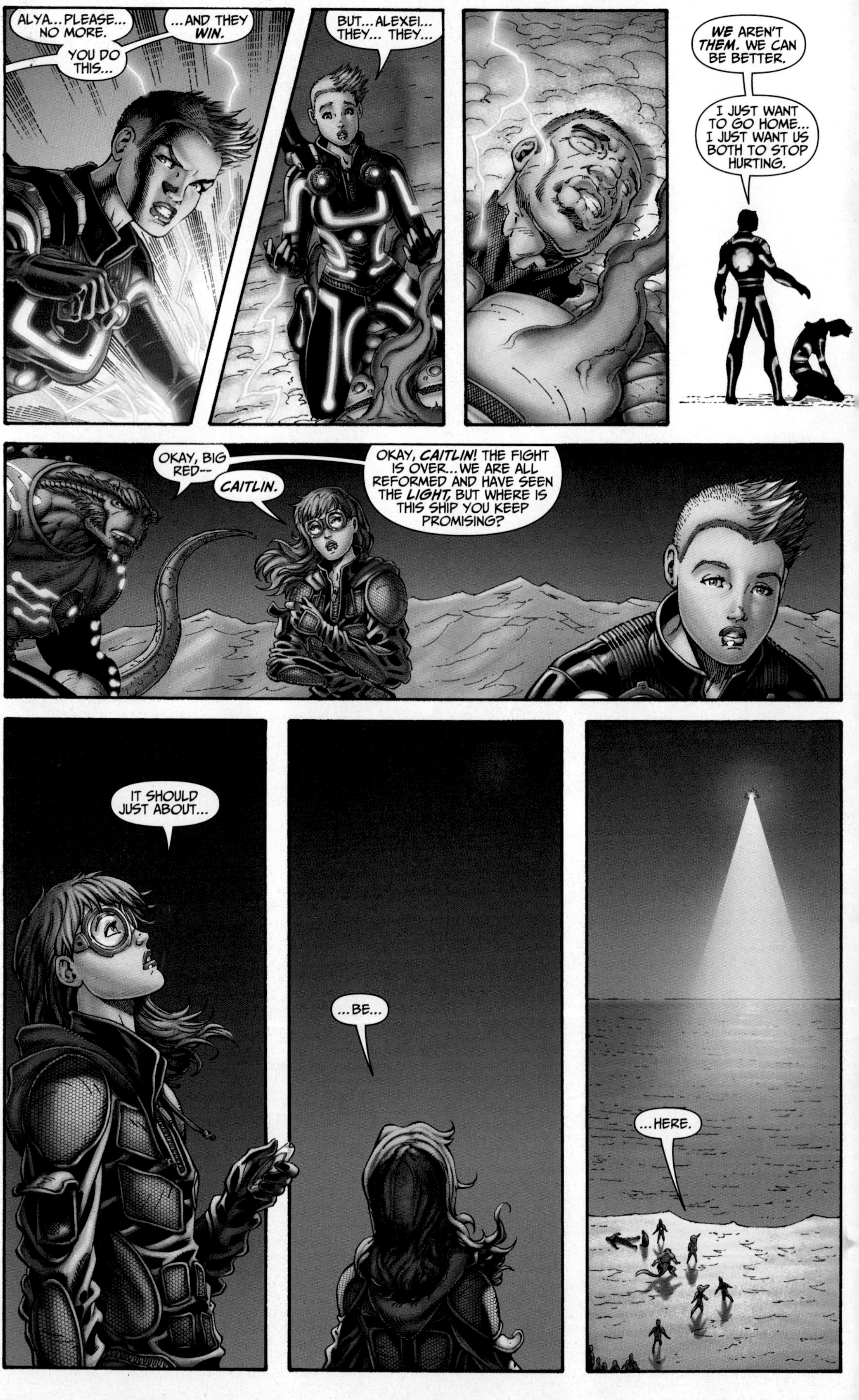
ALYA...PLEASE... NO MORE.
YOU DO THIS...
...AND THEY *WIN.*
BUT...ALEXEI... THEY... THEY...
WE AREN'T *THEM.* WE CAN BE BETTER.
I JUST WANT TO GO HOME... I JUST WANT US BOTH TO STOP HURTING.
OKAY, BIG RED--
CAITLIN.
OKAY, *CAITLIN!* THE FIGHT IS OVER...WE ARE ALL REFORMED AND HAVE SEEN THE *LIGHT,* BUT WHERE IS THIS SHIP YOU KEEP PROMISING?
IT SHOULD JUST ABOUT...
...BE...
...HERE.

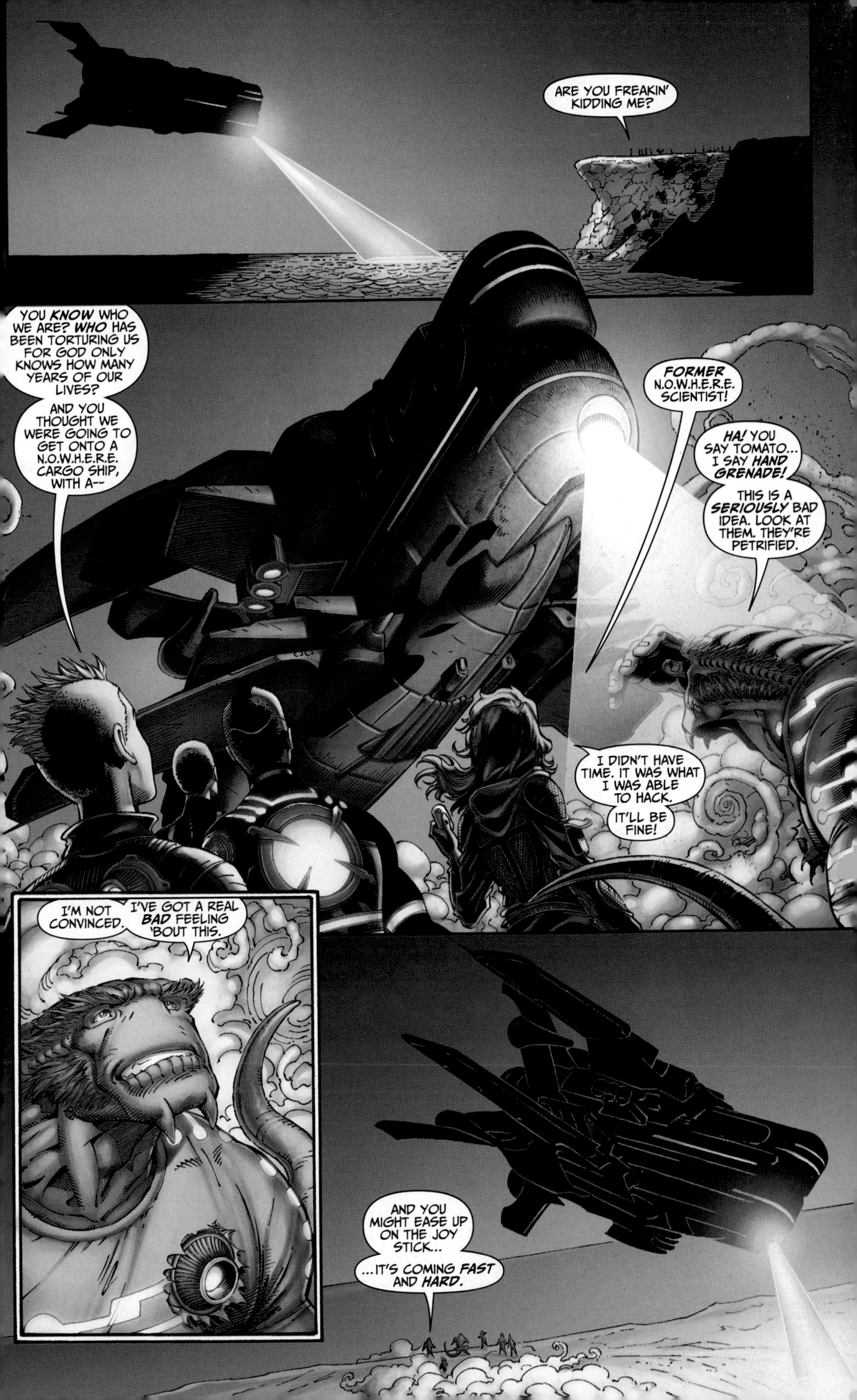
ARE YOU FREAKIN' KIDDING ME?
YOU KNOW WHO WE ARE? WHO HAS BEEN TORTURING US FOR GOD ONLY KNOWS HOW MANY YEARS OF OUR LIVES?
AND YOU THOUGHT WE WERE GOING TO GET ONTO A N.O.W.H.E.R.E. CARGO SHIP, WITH A--
FORMER N.O.W.H.E.R.E. SCIENTIST!
HA! YOU SAY TOMATO... I SAY HAND GRENADE!
THIS IS A SERIOUSLY BAD IDEA. LOOK AT THEM. THEY'RE PETRIFIED.
I DIDN'T HAVE TIME. IT WAS WHAT I WAS ABLE TO HACK.
IT'LL BE FINE!
I'M NOT CONVINCED.
I'VE GOT A REAL BAD FEELING 'BOUT THIS.
AND YOU MIGHT EASE UP ON THE JOY STICK...
...IT'S COMING FAST AND HARD.

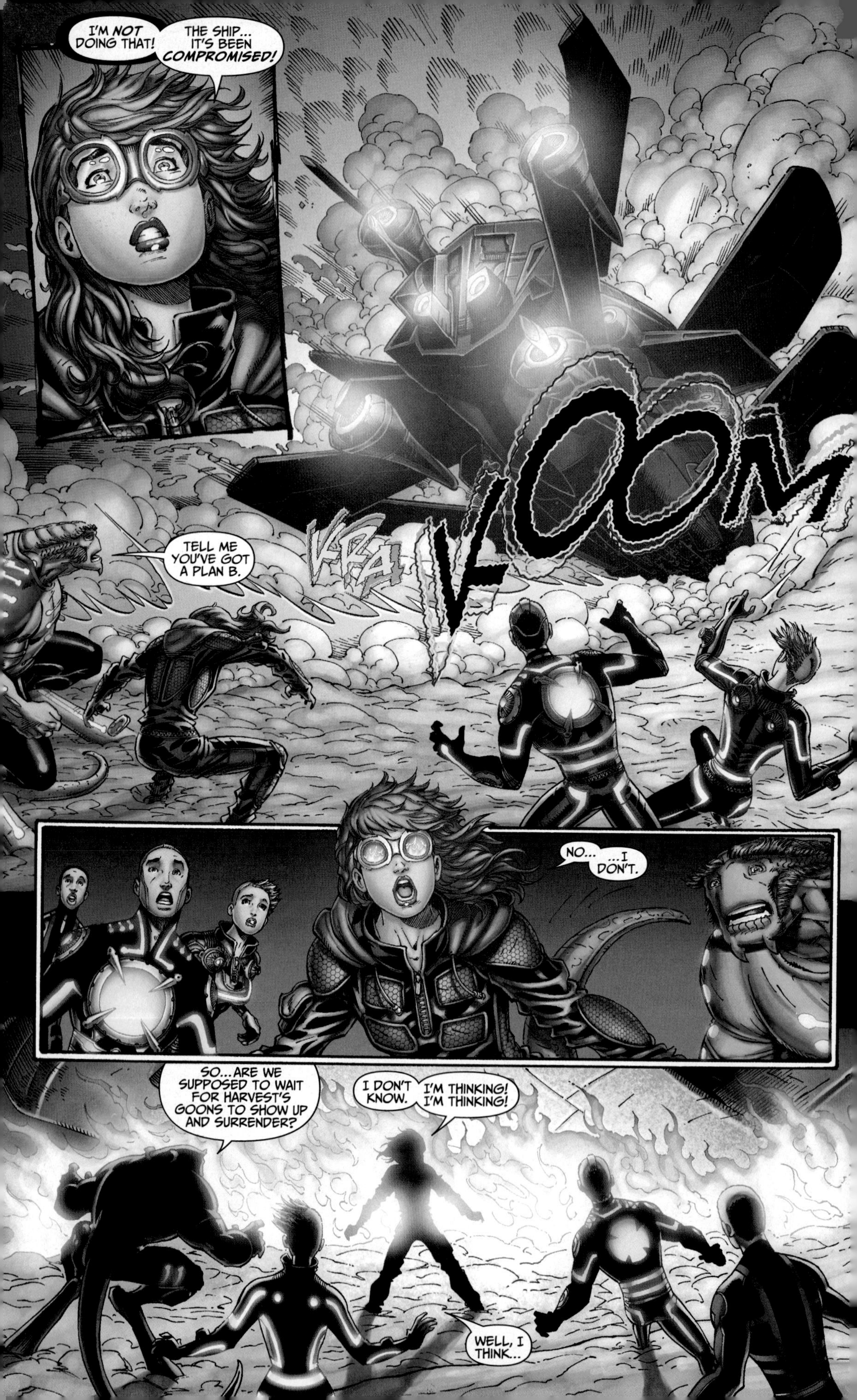

I'M NOT DOING THAT!
THE SHIP... IT'S BEEN COMPROMISED!
TELL ME YOU'VE GOT A PLAN B.
KRA
VOOM
NO... ...I DON'T.
SO...ARE WE SUPPOSED TO WAIT FOR HARVEST'S GOONS TO SHOW UP AND SURRENDER?
I DON'T KNOW.
I'M THINKING! I'M THINKING!
WELL, I THINK...

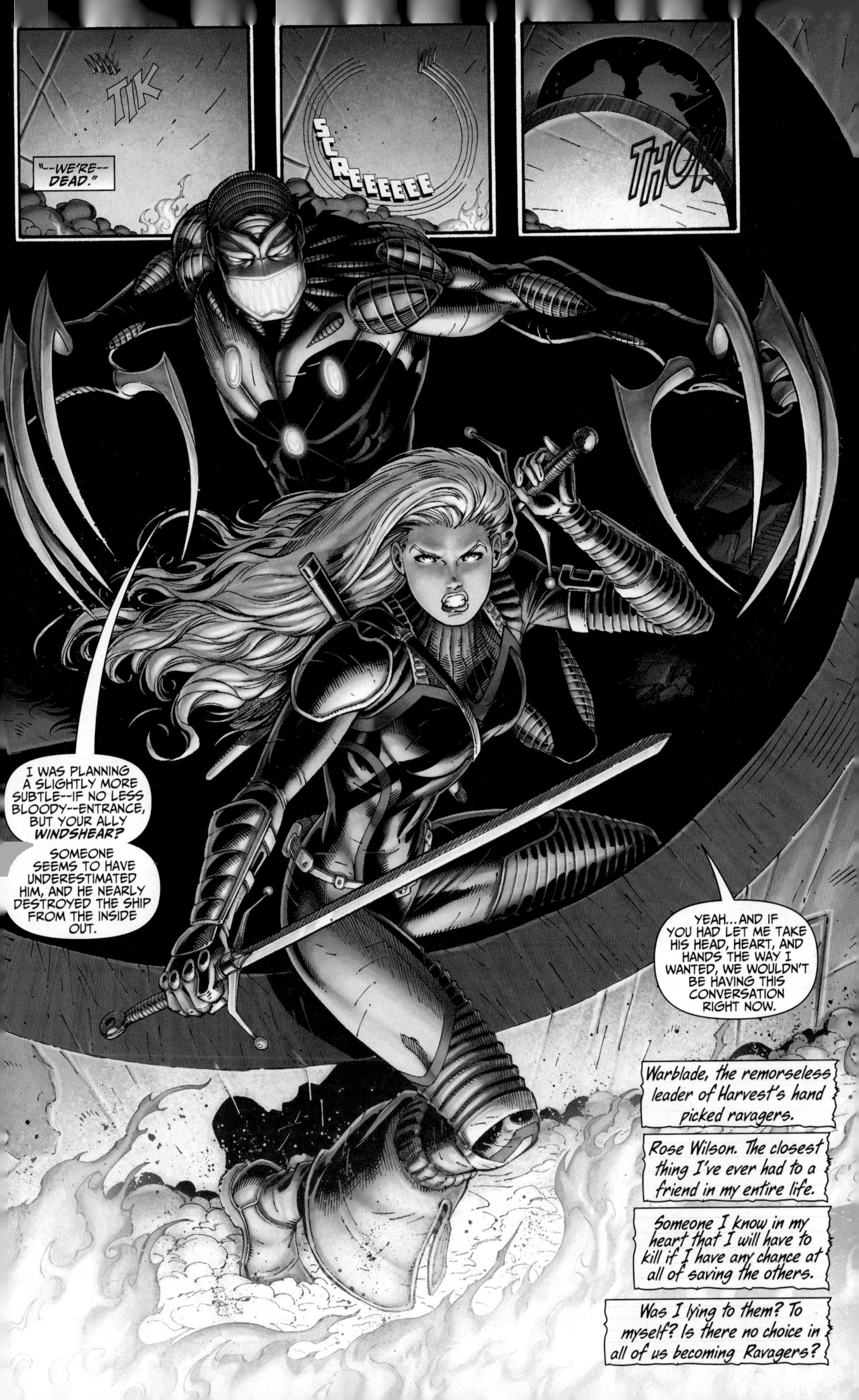
TIK
"--WE'RE--
DEAD."
SCREEEEEEE
THOK
I WAS PLANNING A SLIGHTLY MORE SUBTLE--IF NO LESS BLOODY--ENTRANCE, BUT YOUR ALLY WINDSHEAR?
SOMEONE SEEMS TO HAVE UNDERESTIMATED HIM, AND HE NEARLY DESTROYED THE SHIP FROM THE INSIDE OUT.
YEAH...AND IF YOU HAD LET ME TAKE HIS HEAD, HEART, AND HANDS THE WAY I WANTED, WE WOULDN'T BE HAVING THIS CONVERSATION RIGHT NOW.
Warblade, the remorseless leader of Harvest's hand picked ravagers.
Rose Wilson. The closest thing I've ever had to a friend in my entire life.
Someone I know in my heart that I will have to kill if I have any chance at all of saving the others.
Was I lying to them? To myself? Is there no choice in all of us becoming Ravagers?

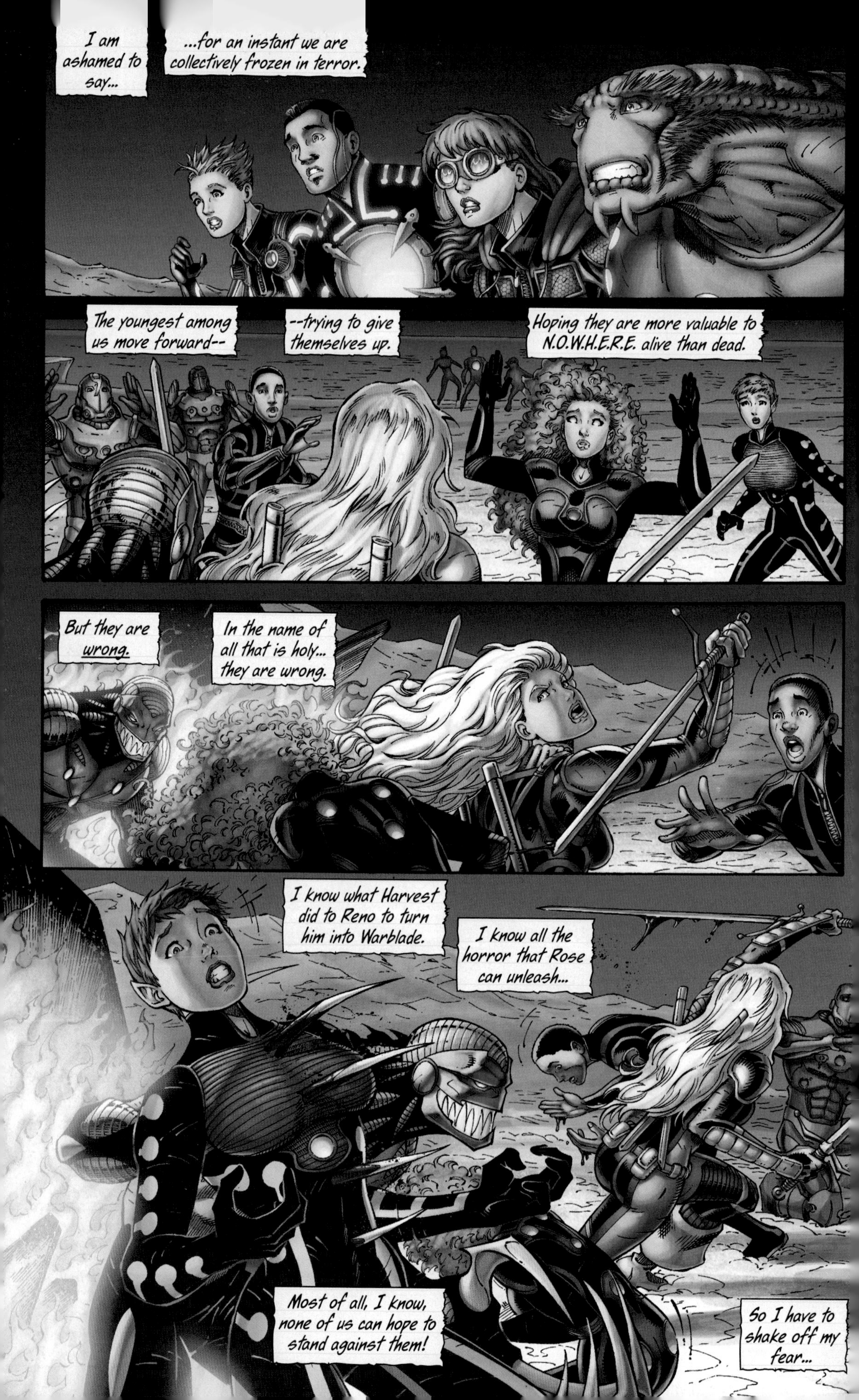
I am ashamed to say...
...for an instant we are collectively frozen in terror.
The youngest among us move forward--
--trying to give themselves up.
Hoping they are more valuable to N.O.W.H.E.R.E. alive than dead.
But they are wrong.
In the name of all that is holy... they are wrong.
I know what Harvest did to Reno to turn him into Warblade.
I know all the horror that Rose can unleash...
Most of all, I know, none of us can hope to stand against them!
So I have to shake off my fear...

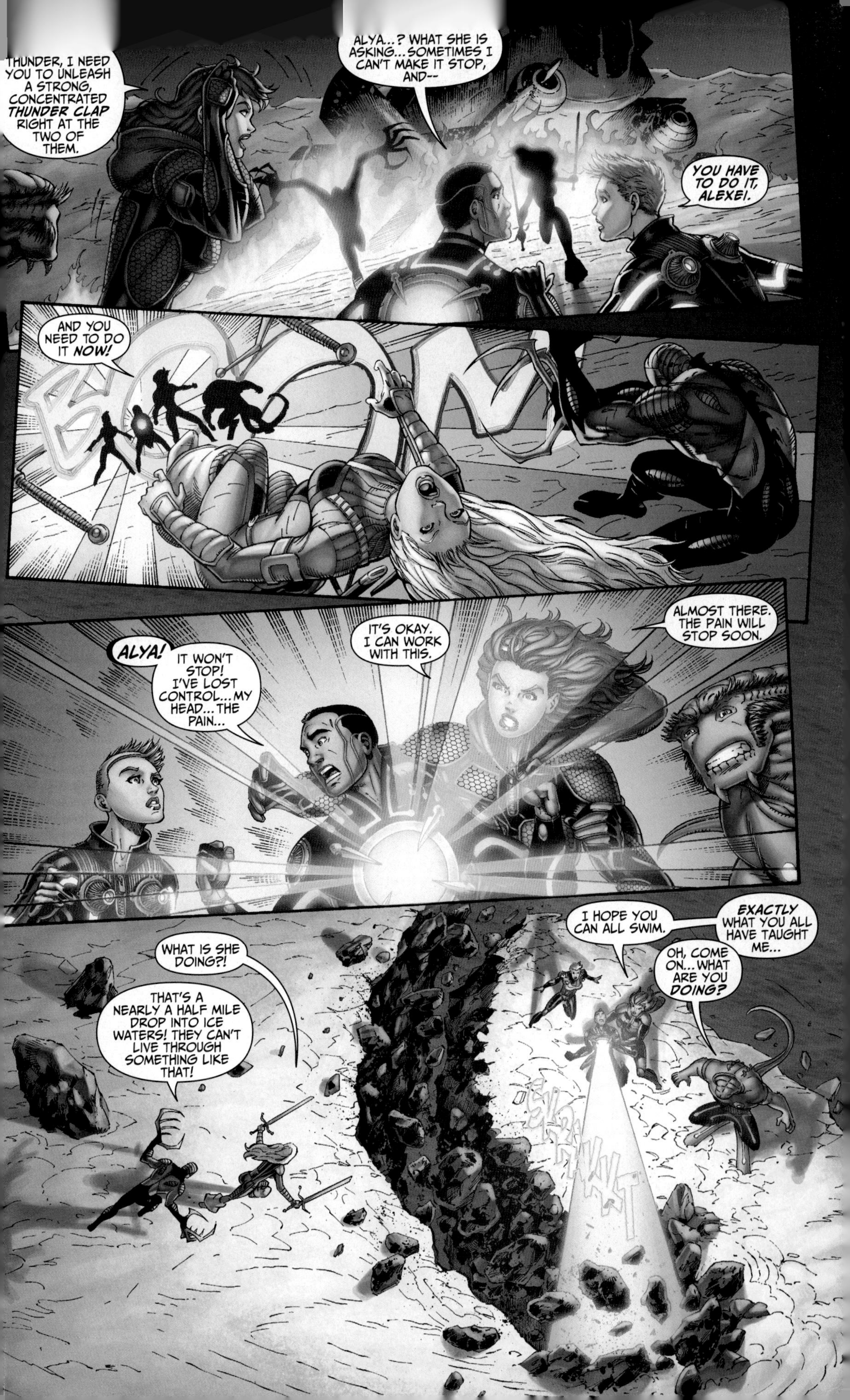
THUNDER, I NEED YOU TO UNLEASH A STRONG, CONCENTRATED THUNDER CLAP RIGHT AT THE TWO OF THEM.
ALYA...? WHAT SHE IS ASKING...SOMETIMES I CAN'T MAKE IT STOP, AND--
YOU HAVE TO DO IT, ALEXEI.
AND YOU NEED TO DO IT NOW!
ALYA!
IT WON'T STOP! I'VE LOST CONTROL...MY HEAD...THE PAIN...
IT'S OKAY. I CAN WORK WITH THIS.
ALMOST THERE. THE PAIN WILL STOP SOON.
WHAT IS SHE DOING?!
THAT'S A NEARLY A HALF MILE DROP INTO ICE WATERS! THEY CAN'T LIVE THROUGH SOMETHING LIKE THAT!
I HOPE YOU CAN ALL SWIM.
EXACTLY WHAT YOU ALL HAVE TAUGHT ME...
OH, COME ON...WHAT ARE YOU DOING?

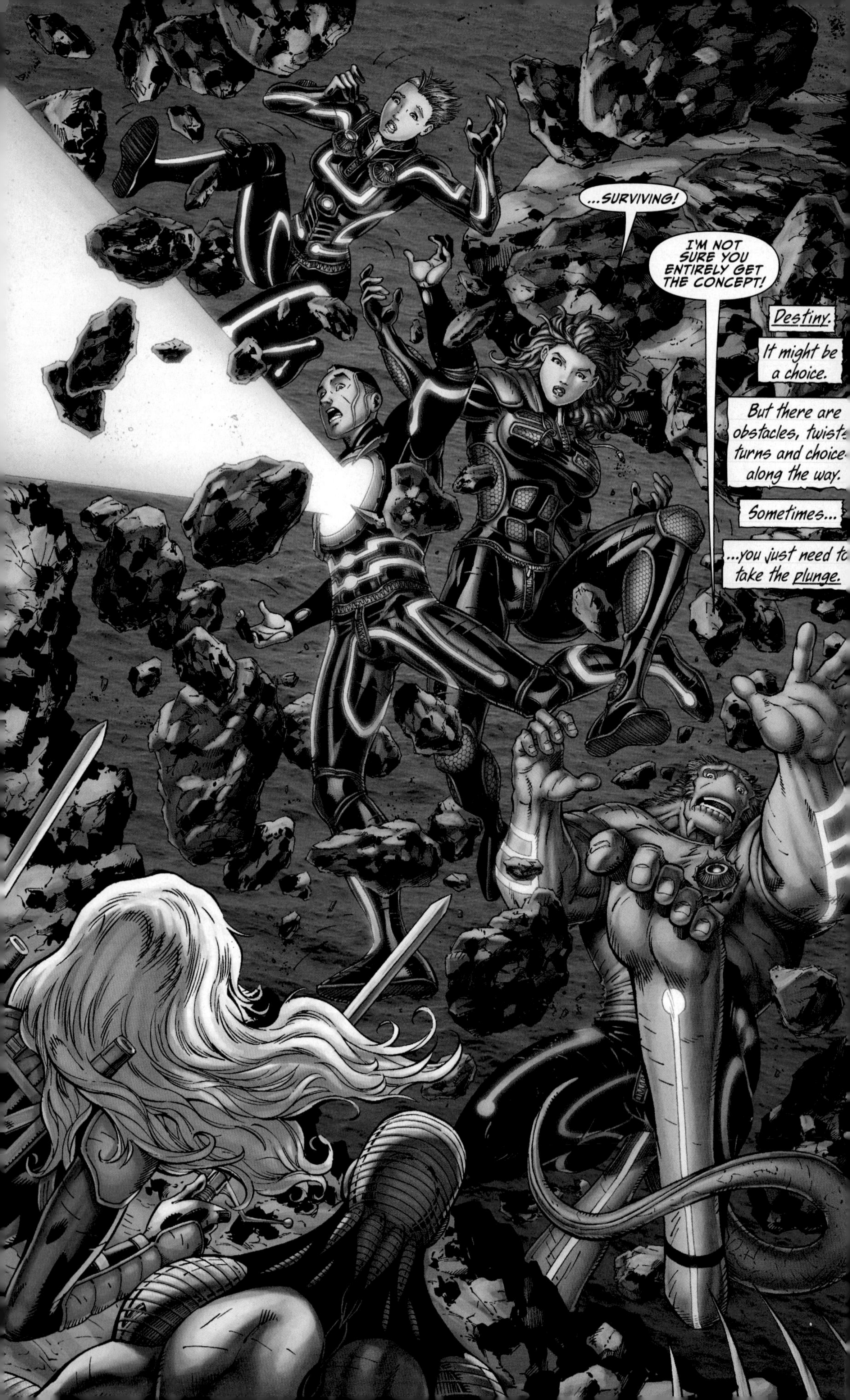
...SURVIVING!
I'M NOT SURE YOU ENTIRELY GET THE CONCEPT!
Destiny.
It might be a choice.
But there are obstacles, twists turns and choices along the way.
Sometimes...
...you just need to take the plunge.

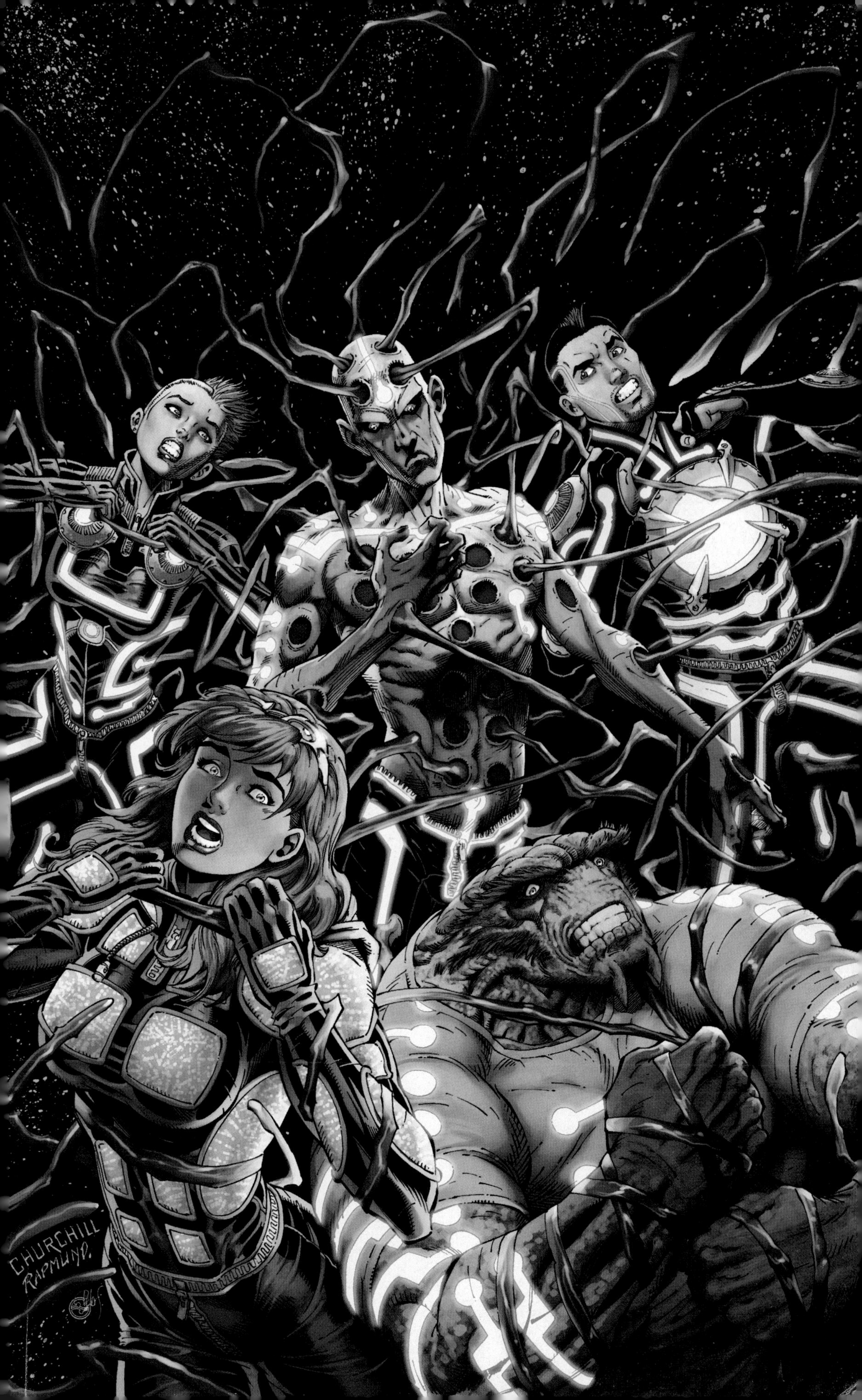
CHURCHILL
RAPMUND

SHADOWS OF THE PAST

HOWARD MACKIE & TOM DEFALCO
writers

IAN CHURCHILL
penciller

NORM RAPMUND
inker

cover art by
IAN CHURCHILL & PETER STEIGERWALD

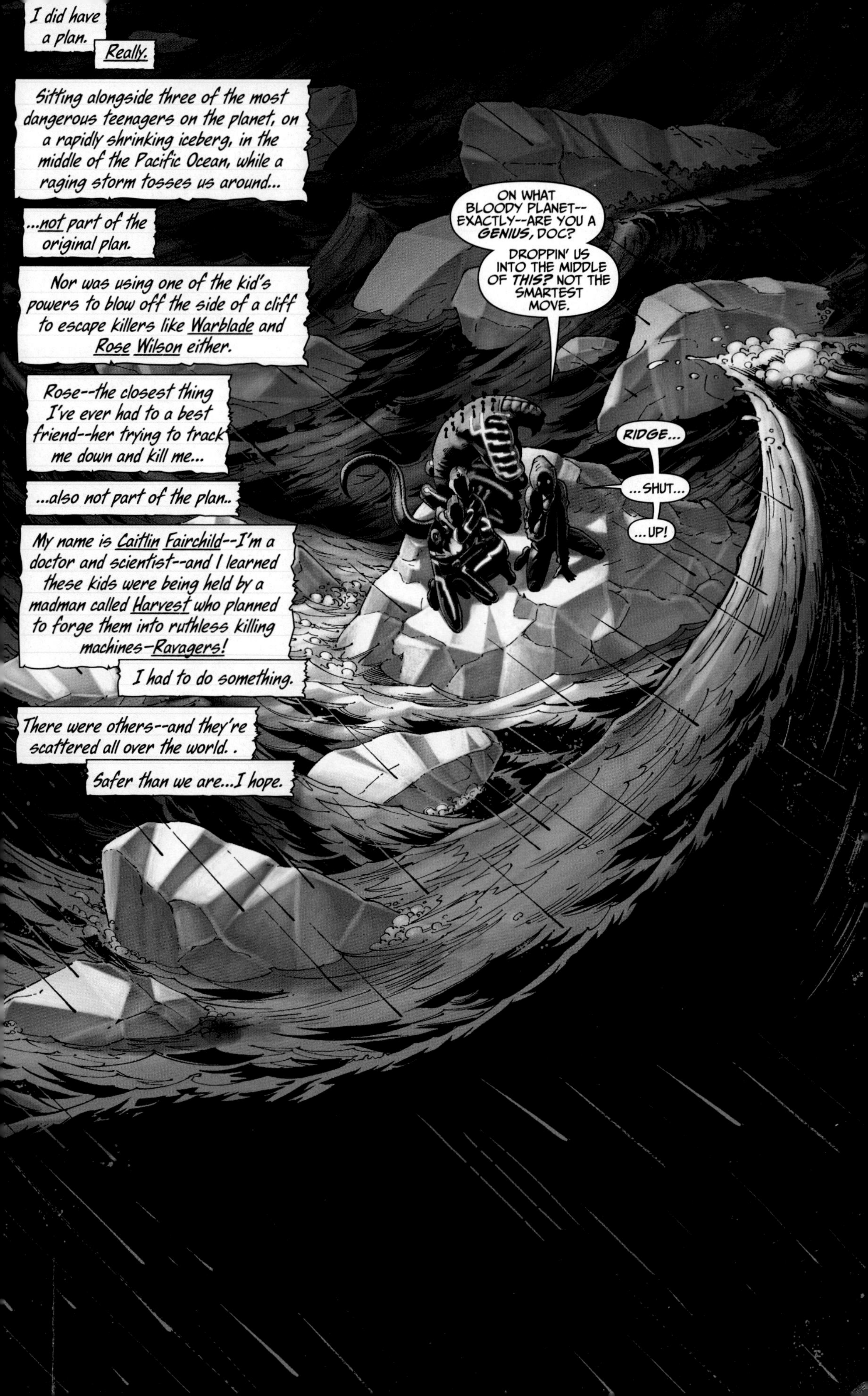
I did have a plan.
Really.
Sitting alongside three of the most dangerous teenagers on the planet, on a rapidly shrinking iceberg, in the middle of the Pacific Ocean, while a raging storm tosses us around...
...not part of the original plan.
Nor was using one of the kid's powers to blow off the side of a cliff to escape killers like Warblade and Rose Wilson either.
Rose--the closest thing I've ever had to a best friend--her trying to track me down and kill me...
...also not part of the plan..
My name is Caitlin Fairchild--I'm a doctor and scientist--and I learned these kids were being held by a madman called Harvest who planned to forge them into ruthless killing machines--Ravagers!
I had to do something.
There were others--and they're scattered all over the world. .
Safer than we are...I hope.
ON WHAT BLOODY PLANET-- EXACTLY--ARE YOU A GENIUS, DOC?
DROPPIN' US INTO THE MIDDLE OF THIS? NOT THE SMARTEST MOVE.
RIDGE...
...SHUT...
...UP!

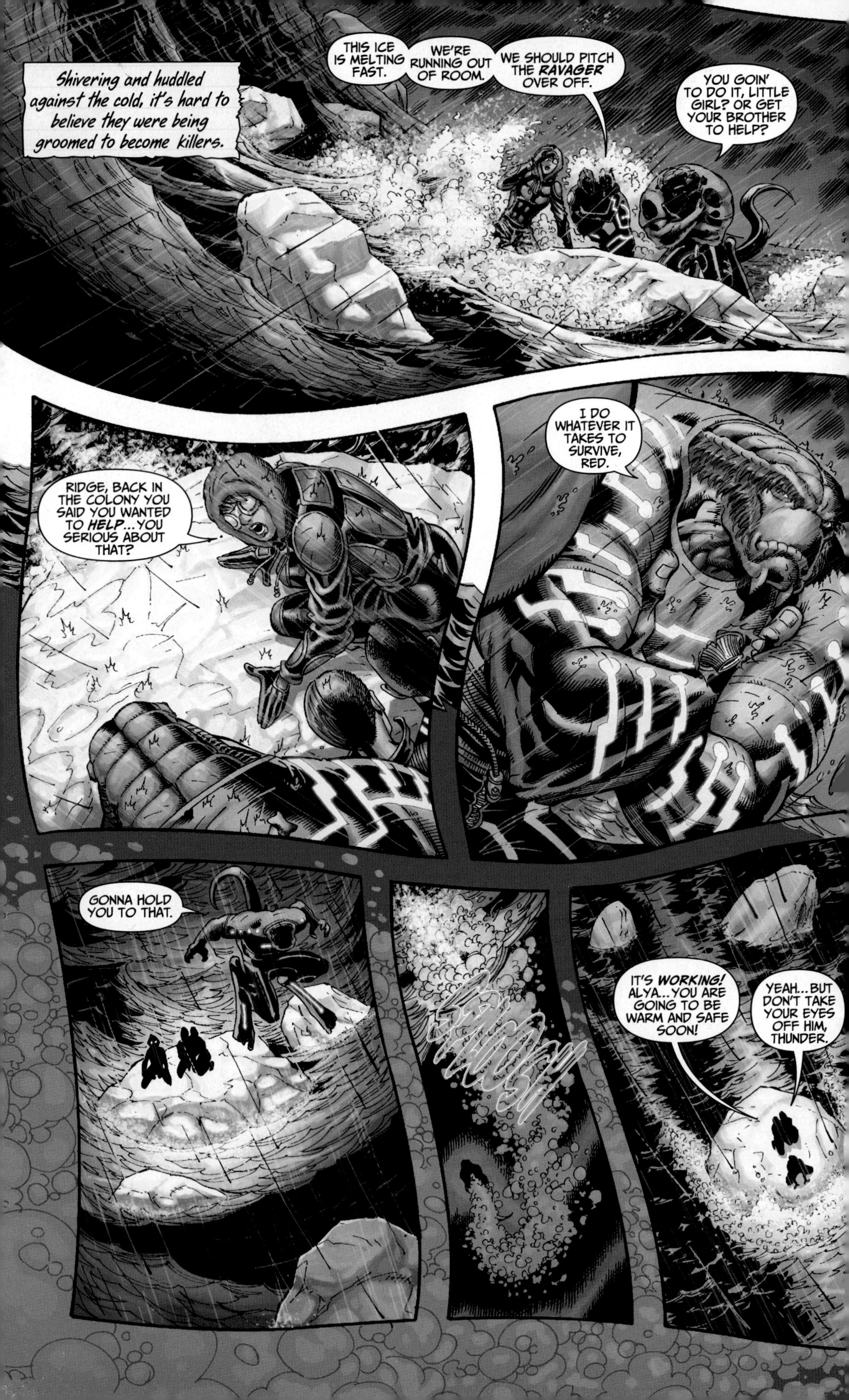
Shivering and huddled against the cold, it's hard to believe they were being groomed to become killers.
THIS ICE IS MELTING FAST.
WE'RE RUNNING OUT OF ROOM.
WE SHOULD PITCH THE RAVAGER OVER OFF.
YOU GOIN' TO DO IT, LITTLE GIRL? OR GET YOUR BROTHER TO HELP?
RIDGE, BACK IN THE COLONY YOU SAID YOU WANTED TO HELP...YOU SERIOUS ABOUT THAT?
I DO WHATEVER IT TAKES TO SURVIVE, RED.
GONNA HOLD YOU TO THAT.
IT'S WORKING! ALYA...YOU ARE GOING TO BE WARM AND SAFE SOON!
YEAH...BUT DON'T TAKE YOUR EYES OFF HIM, THUNDER.

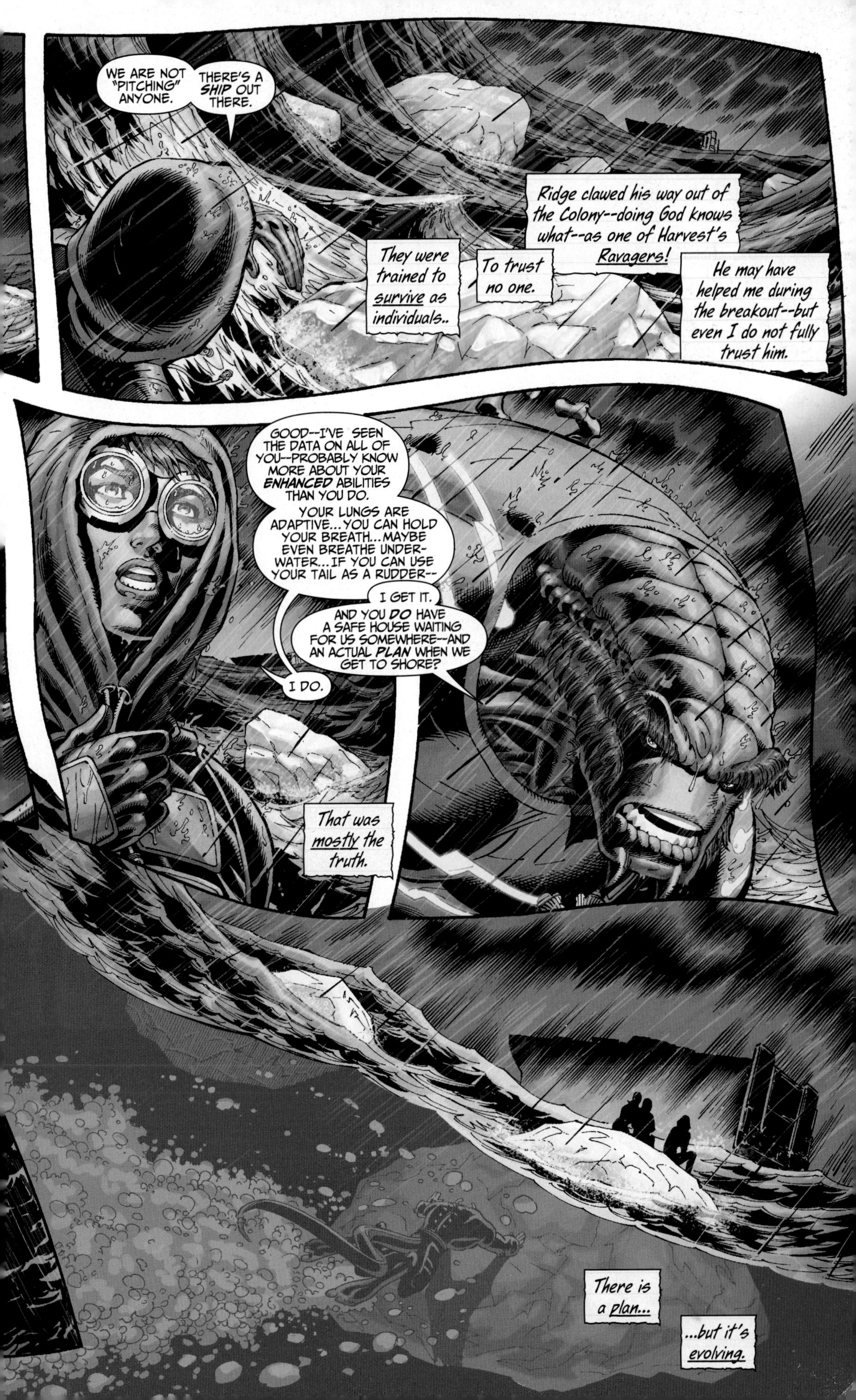

WE ARE NOT "PITCHING" ANYONE.
THERE'S A SHIP OUT THERE.
Ridge clawed his way out of the Colony--doing God knows what--as one of Harvest's Ravagers!
They were trained to survive as individuals..
To trust no one.
He may have helped me during the breakout--but even I do not fully trust him.
GOOD--I'VE SEEN THE DATA ON ALL OF YOU--PROBABLY KNOW MORE ABOUT YOUR ENHANCED ABILITIES THAN YOU DO.
YOUR LUNGS ARE ADAPTIVE...YOU CAN HOLD YOUR BREATH...MAYBE EVEN BREATHE UNDER-WATER...IF YOU CAN USE YOUR TAIL AS A RUDDER--
I GET IT.
AND YOU DO HAVE A SAFE HOUSE WAITING FOR US SOMEWHERE--AND AN ACTUAL PLAN WHEN WE GET TO SHORE?
I DO.
That was mostly the truth.
There is a plan...
...but it's evolving.

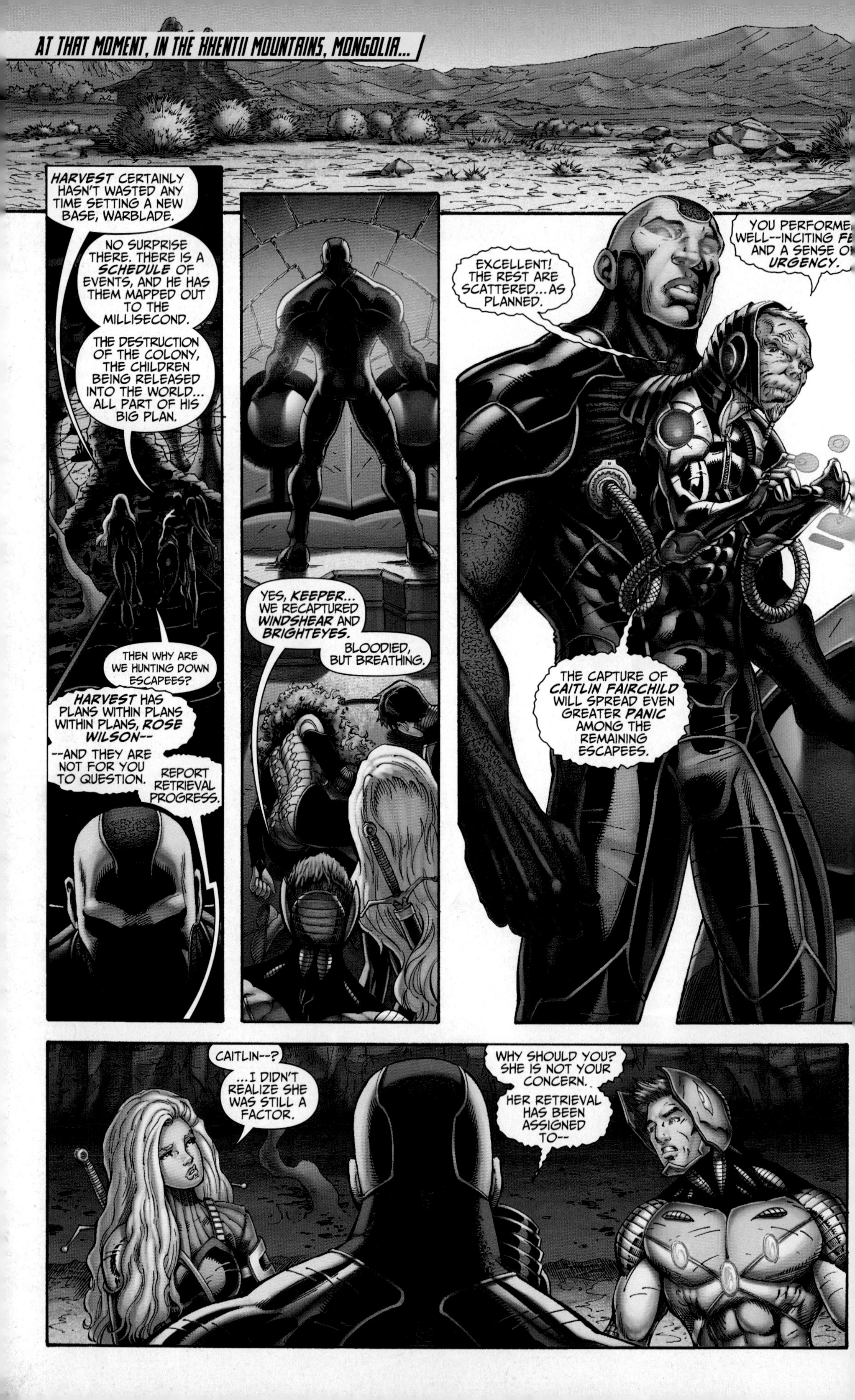
AT THAT MOMENT, IN THE KHENTII MOUNTAINS, MONGOLIA...
HARVEST CERTAINLY HASN'T WASTED ANY TIME SETTING A NEW BASE, WARBLADE.
NO SURPRISE THERE. THERE IS A SCHEDULE OF EVENTS, AND HE HAS THEM MAPPED OUT TO THE MILLISECOND.
THE DESTRUCTION OF THE COLONY, THE CHILDREN BEING RELEASED INTO THE WORLD... ALL PART OF HIS BIG PLAN.
THEN WHY ARE WE HUNTING DOWN ESCAPEES?
HARVEST HAS PLANS WITHIN PLANS WITHIN PLANS, ROSE WILSON--
--AND THEY ARE NOT FOR YOU TO QUESTION.
REPORT RETRIEVAL PROGRESS.
YES, KEEPER... WE RECAPTURED WINDSHEAR AND BRIGHTEYES.
BLOODIED, BUT BREATHING.
EXCELLENT! THE REST ARE SCATTERED... AS PLANNED.
YOU PERFORME WELL--INCITING FE AND A SENSE O URGENCY.
THE CAPTURE OF CAITLIN FAIRCHILD WILL SPREAD EVEN GREATER PANIC AMONG THE REMAINING ESCAPEES.
CAITLIN--?
...I DIDN'T REALIZE SHE WAS STILL A FACTOR.
WHY SHOULD YOU? SHE IS NOT YOUR CONCERN.
HER RETRIEVAL HAS BEEN ASSIGNED TO--

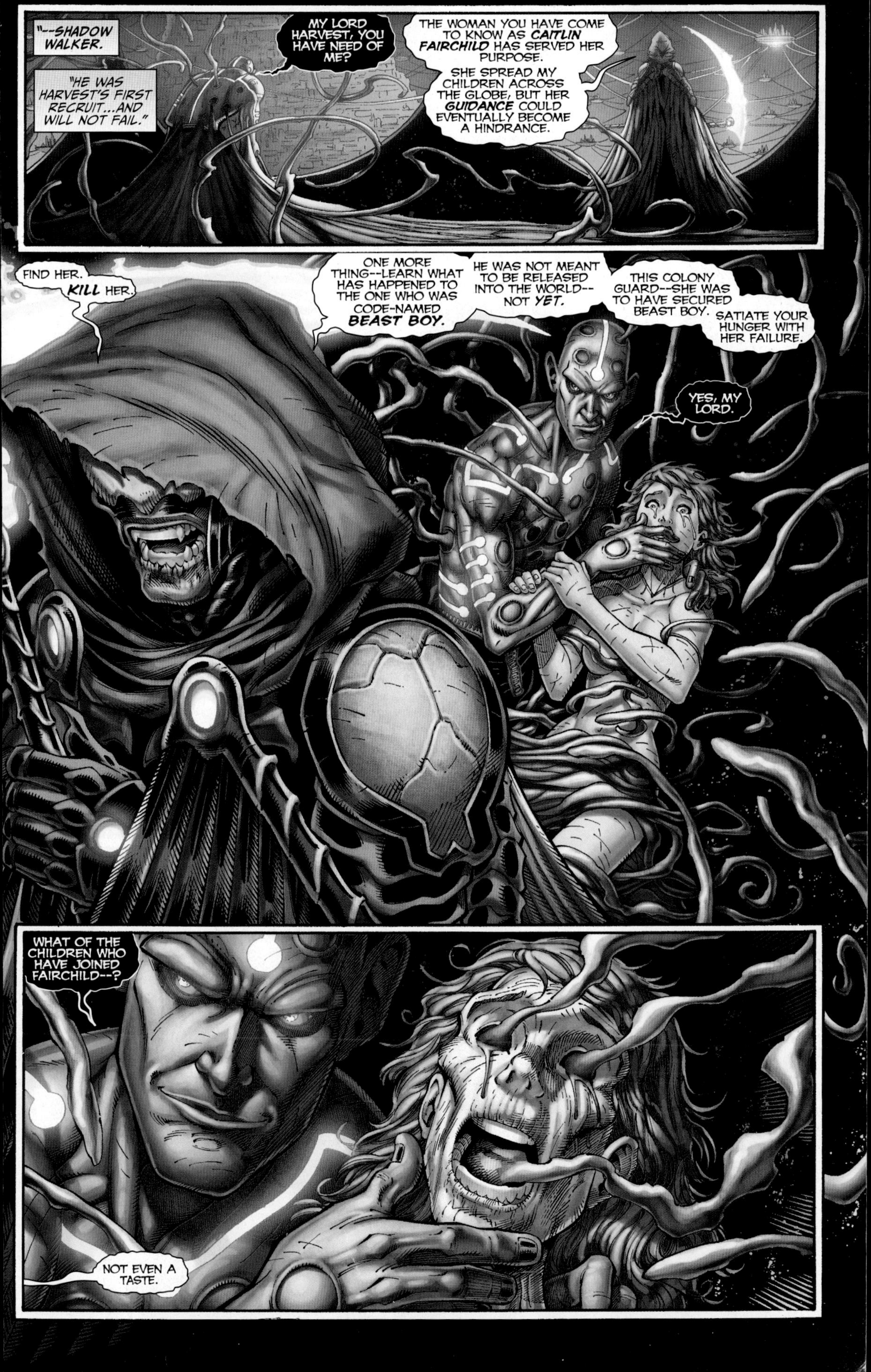
"--SHADOW WALKER.
"HE WAS HARVEST'S FIRST RECRUIT...AND WILL NOT FAIL."
MY LORD HARVEST, YOU HAVE NEED OF ME?
THE WOMAN YOU HAVE COME TO KNOW AS CAITLIN FAIRCHILD HAS SERVED HER PURPOSE.
SHE SPREAD MY CHILDREN ACROSS THE GLOBE, BUT HER GUIDANCE COULD EVENTUALLY BECOME A HINDRANCE.
FIND HER. KILL HER.
ONE MORE THING--LEARN WHAT HAS HAPPENED TO THE ONE WHO WAS CODE-NAMED BEAST BOY.
HE WAS NOT MEANT TO BE RELEASED INTO THE WORLD--NOT YET.
THIS COLONY GUARD--SHE WAS TO HAVE SECURED BEAST BOY.
SATIATE YOUR HUNGER WITH HER FAILURE.
YES, MY LORD.
WHAT OF THE CHILDREN WHO HAVE JOINED FAIRCHILD--?
NOT EVEN A TASTE.

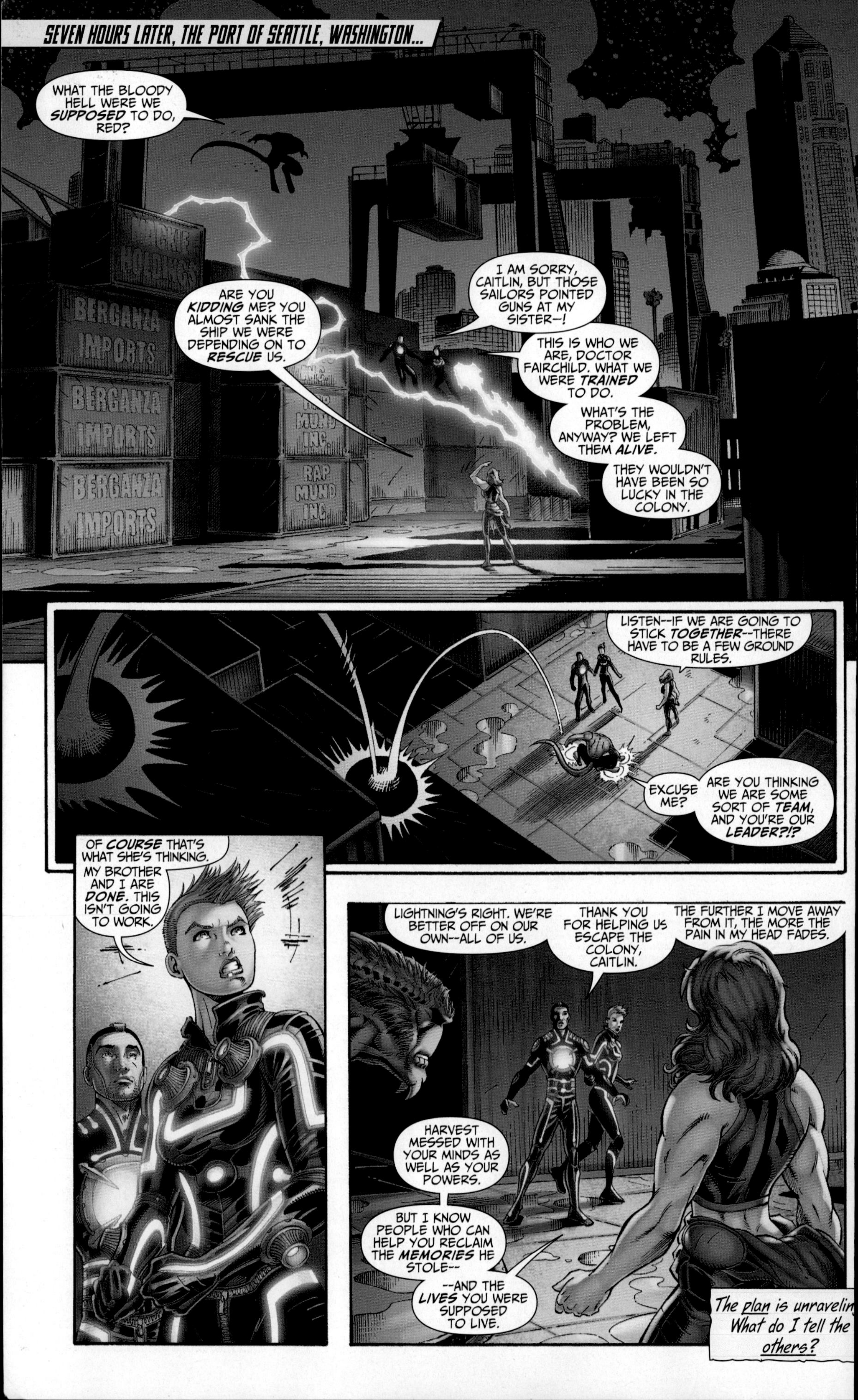
SEVEN HOURS LATER, THE PORT OF SEATTLE, WASHINGTON...
WHAT THE BLOODY HELL WERE WE SUPPOSED TO DO, RED?
ARE YOU KIDDING ME? YOU ALMOST SANK THE SHIP WE WERE DEPENDING ON TO RESCUE US.
I AM SORRY, CAITLIN, BUT THOSE SAILORS POINTED GUNS AT MY SISTER--!
THIS IS WHO WE ARE, DOCTOR FAIRCHILD. WHAT WE WERE TRAINED TO DO.
WHAT'S THE PROBLEM, ANYWAY? WE LEFT THEM ALIVE.
THEY WOULDN'T HAVE BEEN SO LUCKY IN THE COLONY.
MACKIE HOLDINGS
BERGANZA IMPORTS
BERGANZA IMPORTS
BERGANZA IMPORTS
RAP MUND INC.
RAP MUND INC.
LISTEN--IF WE ARE GOING TO STICK TOGETHER--THERE HAVE TO BE A FEW GROUND RULES.
EXCUSE ME?
ARE YOU THINKING WE ARE SOME SORT OF TEAM, AND YOU'RE OUR LEADER?!?
OF COURSE THAT'S WHAT SHE'S THINKING.
MY BROTHER AND I ARE DONE. THIS ISN'T GOING TO WORK.
LIGHTNING'S RIGHT. WE'RE BETTER OFF ON OUR OWN--ALL OF US.
THANK YOU FOR HELPING US ESCAPE THE COLONY, CAITLIN.
THE FURTHER I MOVE AWAY FROM IT, THE MORE THE PAIN IN MY HEAD FADES.
HARVEST MESSED WITH YOUR MINDS AS WELL AS YOUR POWERS.
BUT I KNOW PEOPLE WHO CAN HELP YOU RECLAIM THE MEMORIES HE STOLE--
--AND THE LIVES YOU WERE SUPPOSED TO LIVE.
The plan is unraveling. What do I tell the others?

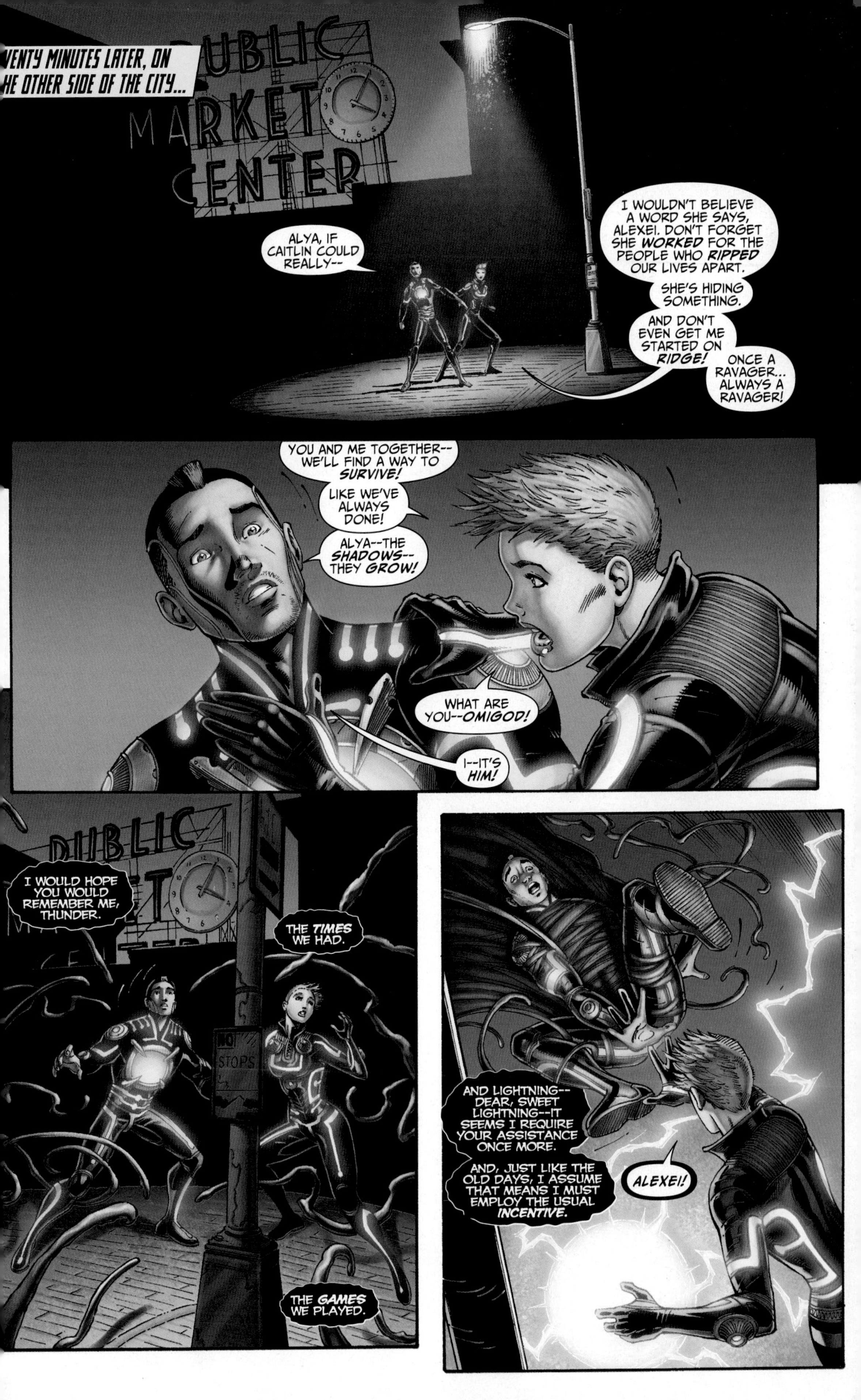

VENTY MINUTES LATER, ON HE OTHER SIDE OF THE CITY...
PUBLIC MARKET CENTER
ALYA, IF CAITLIN COULD REALLY--
I WOULDN'T BELIEVE A WORD SHE SAYS, ALEXEI. DON'T FORGET SHE WORKED FOR THE PEOPLE WHO RIPPED OUR LIVES APART.
SHE'S HIDING SOMETHING.
AND DON'T EVEN GET ME STARTED ON RIDGE!
ONCE A RAVAGER... ALWAYS A RAVAGER!
YOU AND ME TOGETHER-- WE'LL FIND A WAY TO SURVIVE!
LIKE WE'VE ALWAYS DONE!
ALYA--THE SHADOWS-- THEY GROW!
WHAT ARE YOU--OMIGOD!
I--IT'S HIM!
I WOULD HOPE YOU WOULD REMEMBER ME, THUNDER.
THE TIMES WE HAD.
NO STOPS
THE GAMES WE PLAYED.
AND LIGHTNING-- DEAR, SWEET LIGHTNING--IT SEEMS I REQUIRE YOUR ASSISTANCE ONCE MORE.
AND, JUST LIKE THE OLD DAYS, I ASSUME THAT MEANS I MUST EMPLOY THE USUAL INCENTIVE.
ALEXEI!

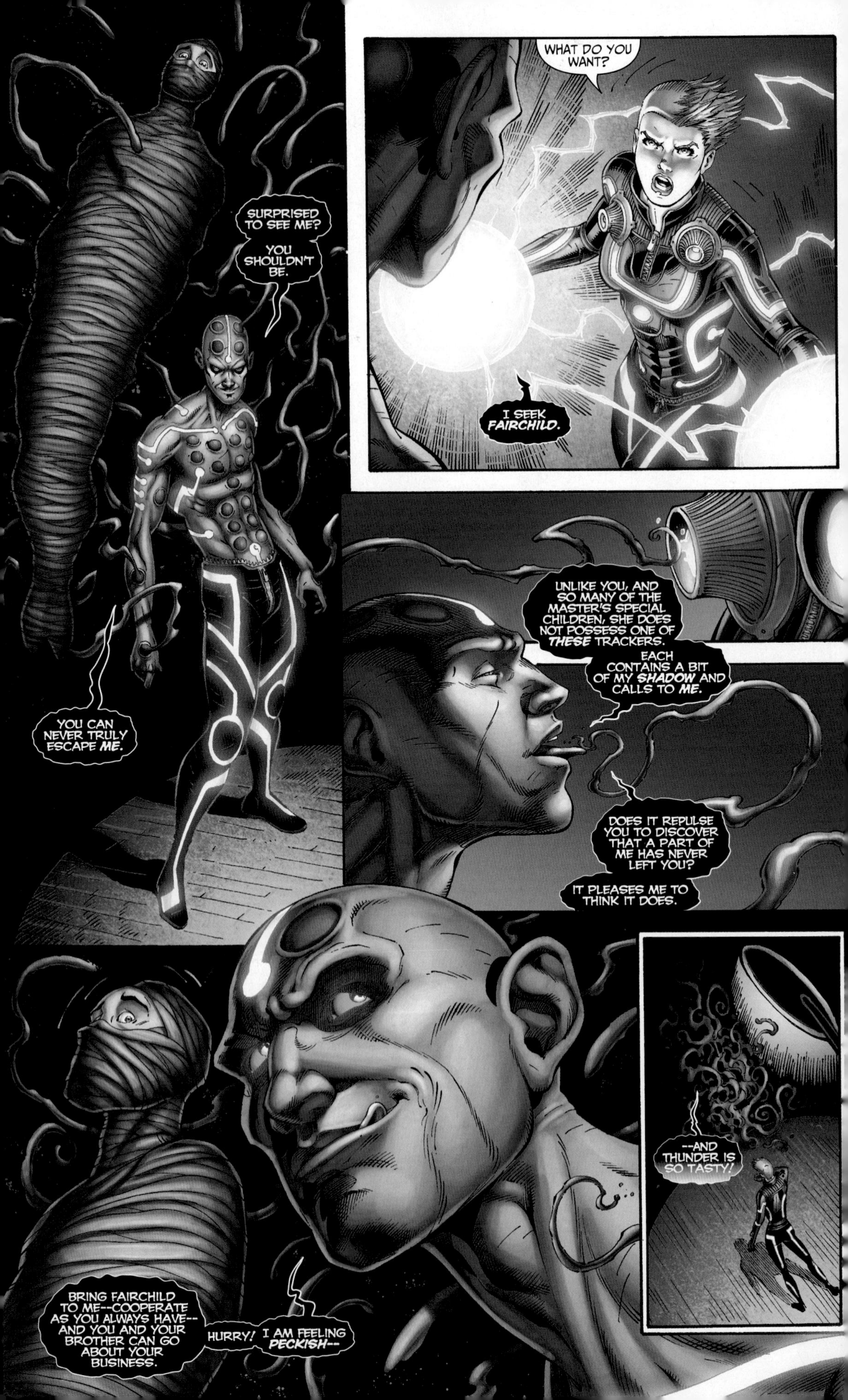
WHAT DO YOU WANT?
I SEEK FAIRCHILD.
SURPRISED TO SEE ME?
YOU SHOULDN'T BE.
YOU CAN NEVER TRULY ESCAPE ME.
UNLIKE YOU, AND SO MANY OF THE MASTER'S SPECIAL CHILDREN, SHE DOES NOT POSSESS ONE OF THESE TRACKERS.
EACH CONTAINS A BIT OF MY SHADOW AND CALLS TO ME.
DOES IT REPULSE YOU TO DISCOVER THAT A PART OF ME HAS NEVER LEFT YOU?
IT PLEASES ME TO THINK IT DOES.
BRING FAIRCHILD TO ME--COOPERATE AS YOU ALWAYS HAVE--AND YOU AND YOUR BROTHER CAN GO ABOUT YOUR BUSINESS.
HURRY! I AM FEELING PECKISH--
--AND THUNDER IS SO TASTY!

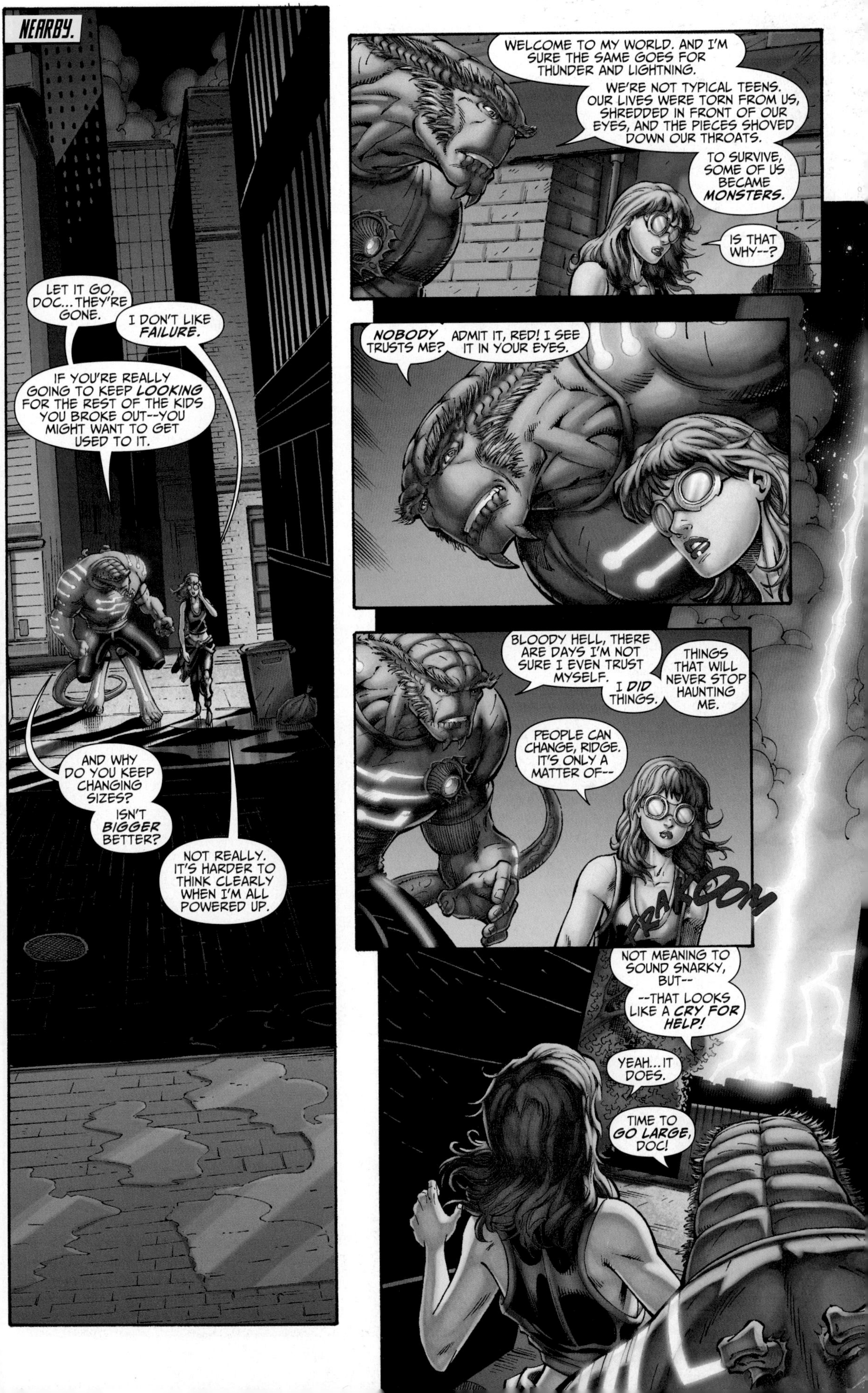
NEARBY.
LET IT GO, DOC...THEY'RE GONE.
I DON'T LIKE FAILURE.
IF YOU'RE REALLY GOING TO KEEP LOOKING FOR THE REST OF THE KIDS YOU BROKE OUT--YOU MIGHT WANT TO GET USED TO IT.
AND WHY DO YOU KEEP CHANGING SIZES?
ISN'T BIGGER BETTER?
NOT REALLY. IT'S HARDER TO THINK CLEARLY WHEN I'M ALL POWERED UP.
WELCOME TO MY WORLD. AND I'M SURE THE SAME GOES FOR THUNDER AND LIGHTNING.
WE'RE NOT TYPICAL TEENS. OUR LIVES WERE TORN FROM US, SHREDDED IN FRONT OF OUR EYES, AND THE PIECES SHOVED DOWN OUR THROATS.
TO SURVIVE, SOME OF US BECAME MONSTERS.
IS THAT WHY--?
NOBODY TRUSTS ME?
ADMIT IT, RED! I SEE IT IN YOUR EYES.
BLOODY HELL, THERE ARE DAYS I'M NOT SURE I EVEN TRUST MYSELF.
I DID THINGS.
THINGS THAT WILL NEVER STOP HAUNTING ME.
PEOPLE CAN CHANGE, RIDGE. IT'S ONLY A MATTER OF--
KRAKOOM
NOT MEANING TO SOUND SNARKY, BUT--
--THAT LOOKS LIKE A CRY FOR HELP!
YEAH...IT DOES.
TIME TO GO LARGE, DOC!

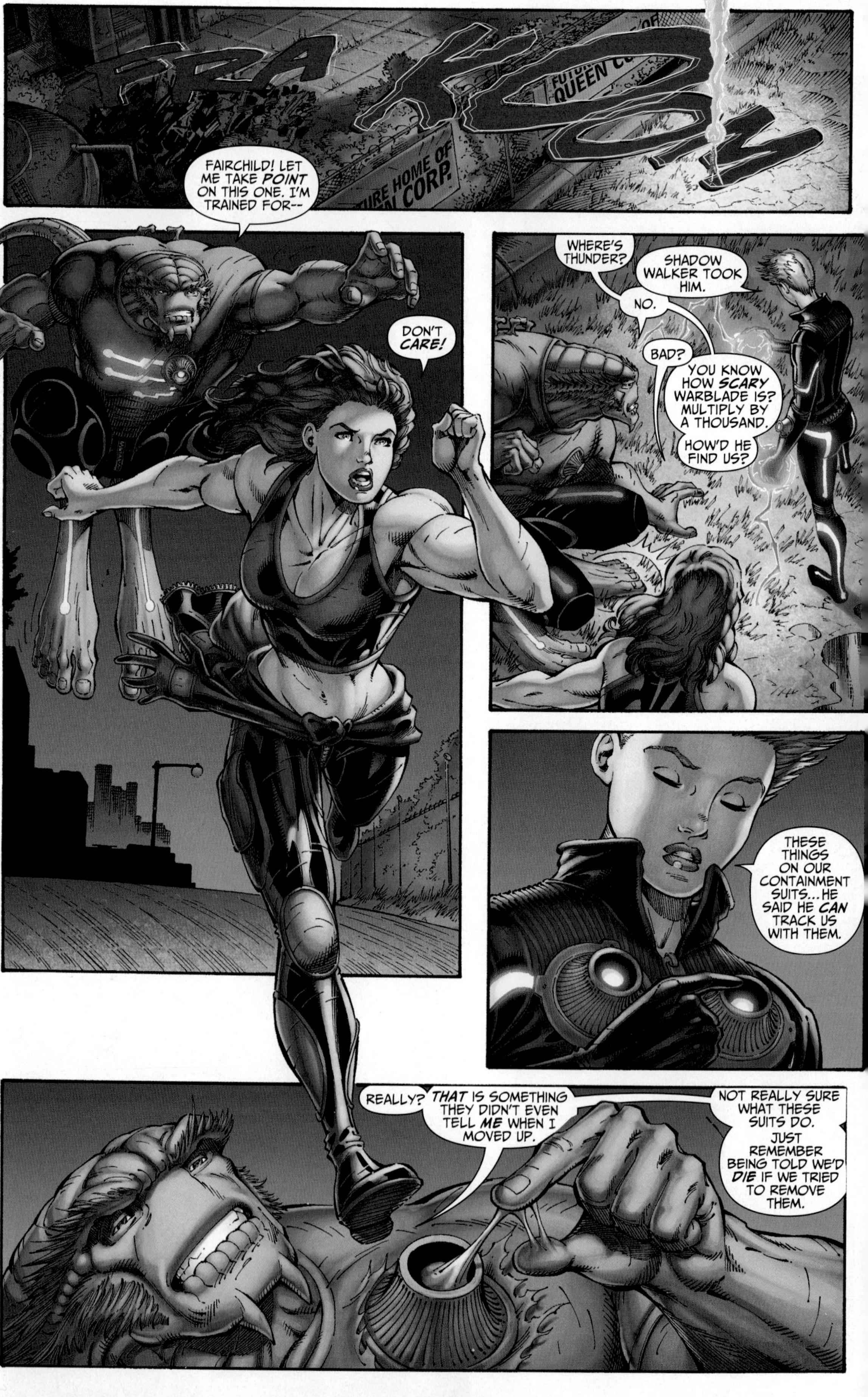

FRAKOOM
FUTURE HOME OF QUEEN CORP.
FAIRCHILD! LET ME TAKE POINT ON THIS ONE. I'M TRAINED FOR--
DON'T CARE!
WHERE'S THUNDER?
SHADOW WALKER TOOK HIM.
NO.
BAD?
YOU KNOW HOW SCARY WARBLADE IS? MULTIPLY BY A THOUSAND.
HOW'D HE FIND US?
THESE THINGS ON OUR CONTAINMENT SUITS...HE SAID HE CAN TRACK US WITH THEM.
REALLY? THAT IS SOMETHING THEY DIDN'T EVEN TELL ME WHEN I MOVED UP.
NOT REALLY SURE WHAT THESE SUITS DO.
JUST REMEMBER BEING TOLD WE'D DIE IF WE TRIED TO REMOVE THEM.

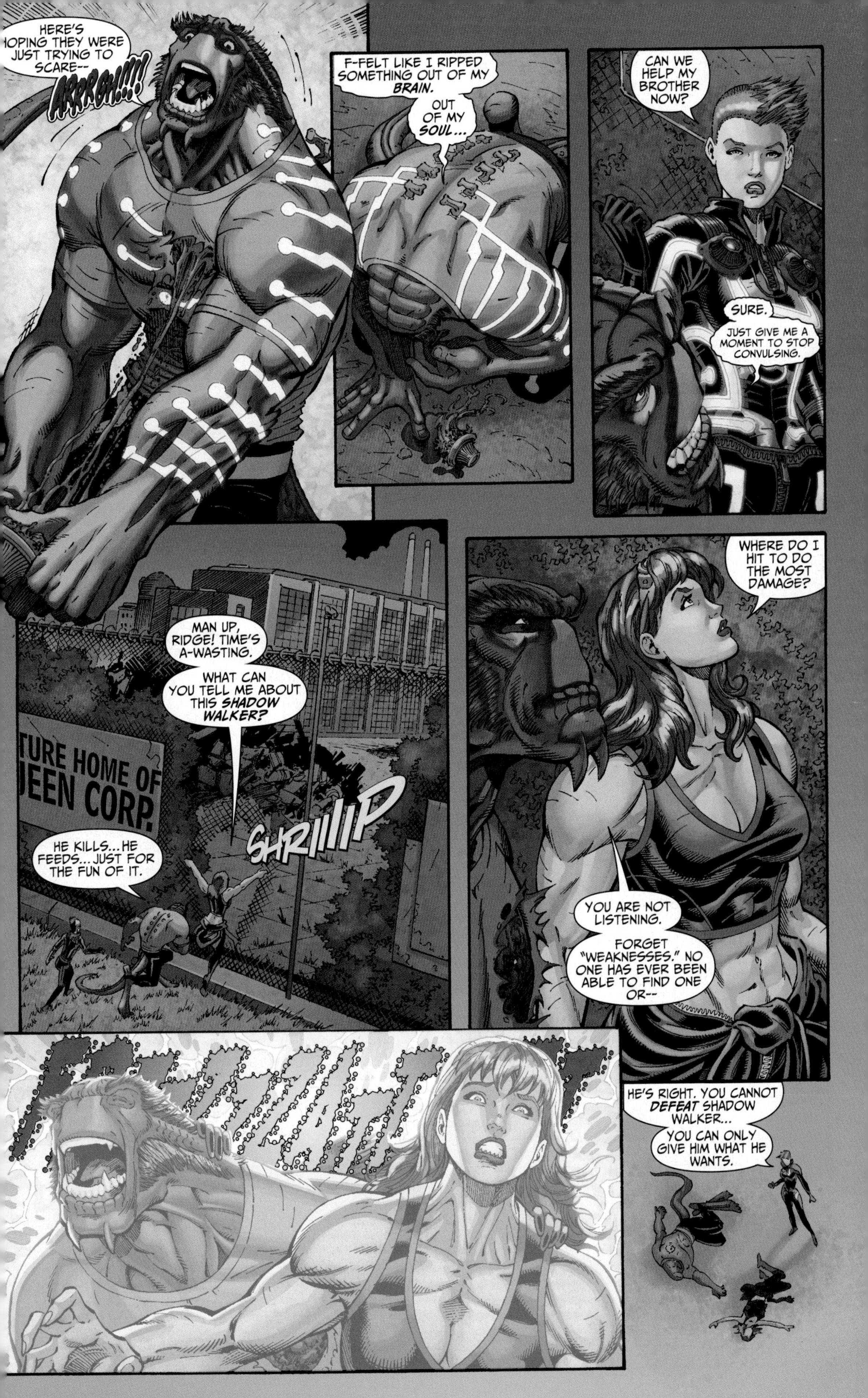

HERE'S HOPING THEY WERE JUST TRYING TO SCARE--
ARRRGH!!!!
F-FELT LIKE I RIPPED SOMETHING OUT OF MY BRAIN.
OUT OF MY SOUL...
CAN WE HELP MY BROTHER NOW?
SURE.
JUST GIVE ME A MOMENT TO STOP CONVULSING.
MAN UP, RIDGE! TIME'S A-WASTING.
WHAT CAN YOU TELL ME ABOUT THIS SHADOW WALKER?
TURE HOME OF
JEEN CORP.
HE KILLS...HE FEEDS...JUST FOR THE FUN OF IT.
SHRIIIIP
WHERE DO I HIT TO DO THE MOST DAMAGE?
YOU ARE NOT LISTENING.
FORGET "WEAKNESSES." NO ONE HAS EVER BEEN ABLE TO FIND ONE OR--
HE'S RIGHT. YOU CANNOT DEFEAT SHADOW WALKER...
YOU CAN ONLY GIVE HIM WHAT HE WANTS.

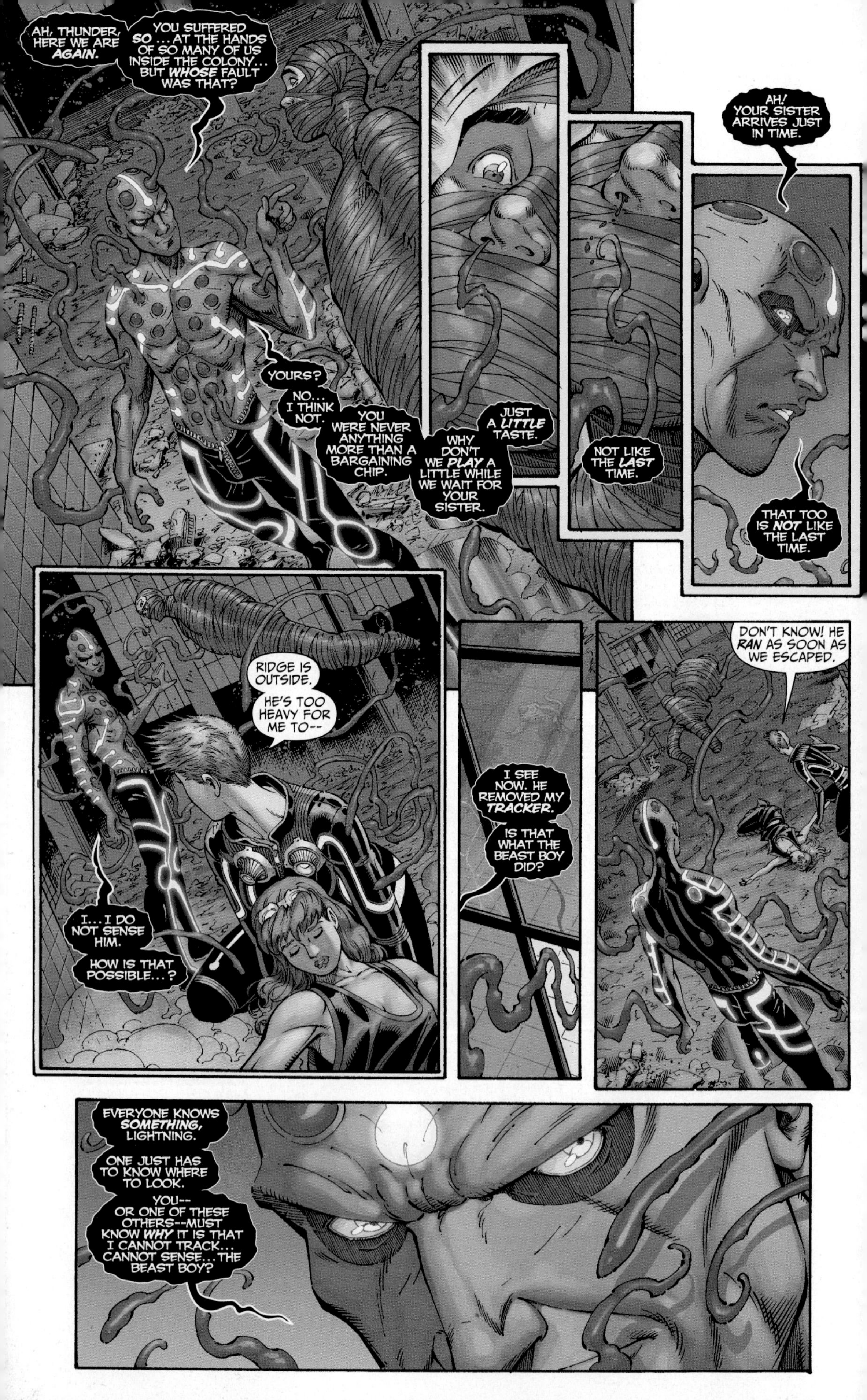
AH, THUNDER, HERE WE ARE AGAIN.
YOU SUFFERED SO... AT THE HANDS OF SO MANY OF US INSIDE THE COLONY... BUT WHOSE FAULT WAS THAT?
YOURS?
NO... I THINK NOT.
YOU WERE NEVER ANYTHING MORE THAN A BARGAINING CHIP.
WHY DON'T WE PLAY A LITTLE WHILE WE WAIT FOR YOUR SISTER.
JUST A LITTLE TASTE.
NOT LIKE THE LAST TIME.
AH! YOUR SISTER ARRIVES JUST IN TIME.
THAT TOO IS NOT LIKE THE LAST TIME.
RIDGE IS OUTSIDE.
HE'S TOO HEAVY FOR ME TO--
I... I DO NOT SENSE HIM.
HOW IS THAT POSSIBLE...?
I SEE NOW. HE REMOVED MY TRACKER.
IS THAT WHAT THE BEAST BOY DID?
DON'T KNOW! HE RAN AS SOON AS WE ESCAPED.
EVERYONE KNOWS SOMETHING, LIGHTNING.
ONE JUST HAS TO KNOW WHERE TO LOOK.
YOU-- OR ONE OF THESE OTHERS--MUST KNOW WHY IT IS THAT I CANNOT TRACK... CANNOT SENSE... THE BEAST BOY?

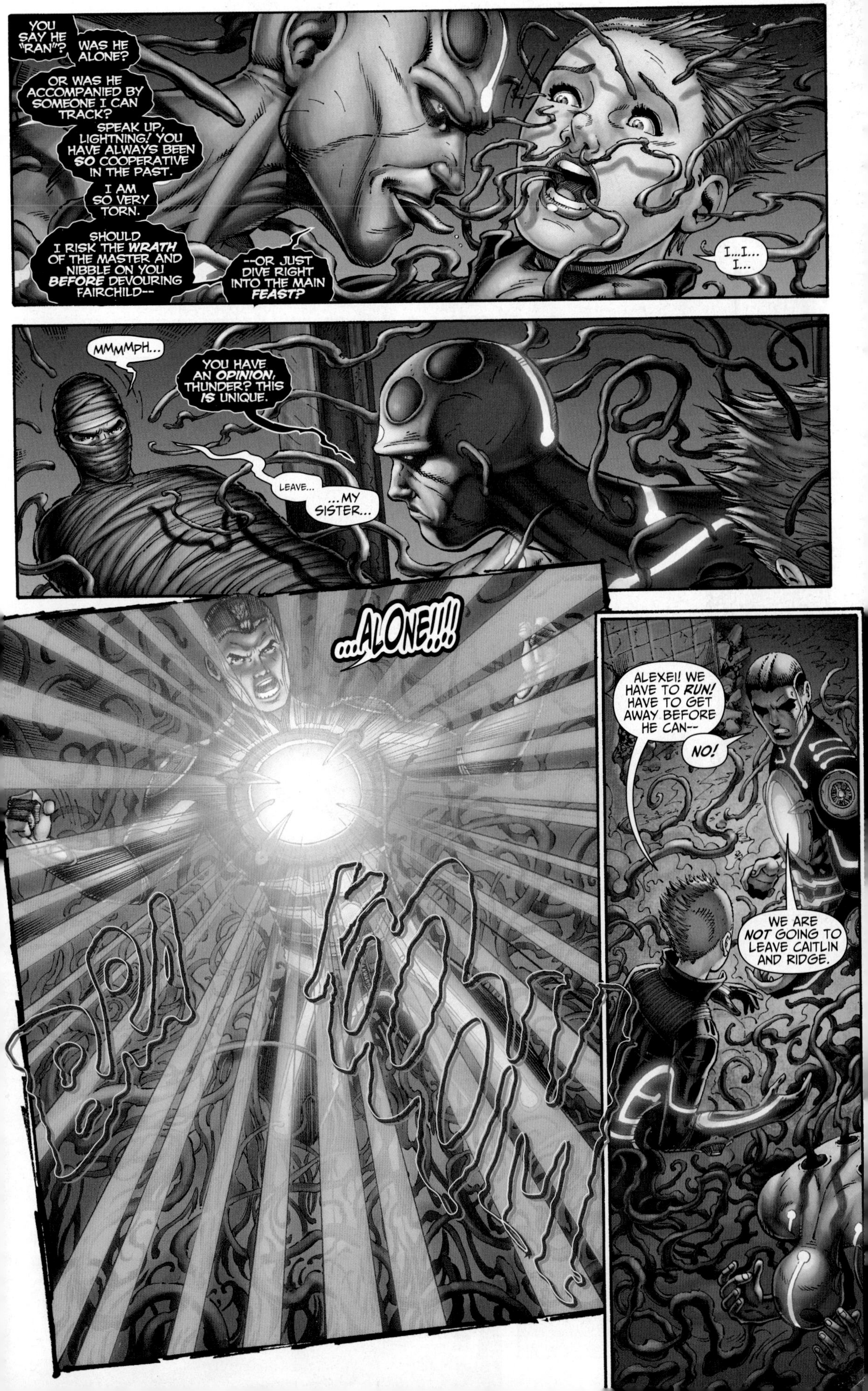

YOU SAY HE "RAN"?
WAS HE ALONE?
OR WAS HE ACCOMPANIED BY SOMEONE I CAN TRACK?
SPEAK UP, LIGHTNING! YOU HAVE ALWAYS BEEN SO COOPERATIVE IN THE PAST.
I AM SO VERY TORN.
SHOULD I RISK THE WRATH OF THE MASTER AND NIBBLE ON YOU BEFORE DEVOURING FAIRCHILD--
--OR JUST DIVE RIGHT INTO THE MAIN FEAST?
I...I... I...
MMMMPH...
YOU HAVE AN OPINION, THUNDER? THIS IS UNIQUE.
LEAVE...
...MY SISTER...
...ALONE!!!!
ALEXEI! WE HAVE TO RUN! HAVE TO GET AWAY BEFORE HE CAN--
NO!
WE ARE NOT GOING TO LEAVE CAITLIN AND RIDGE.

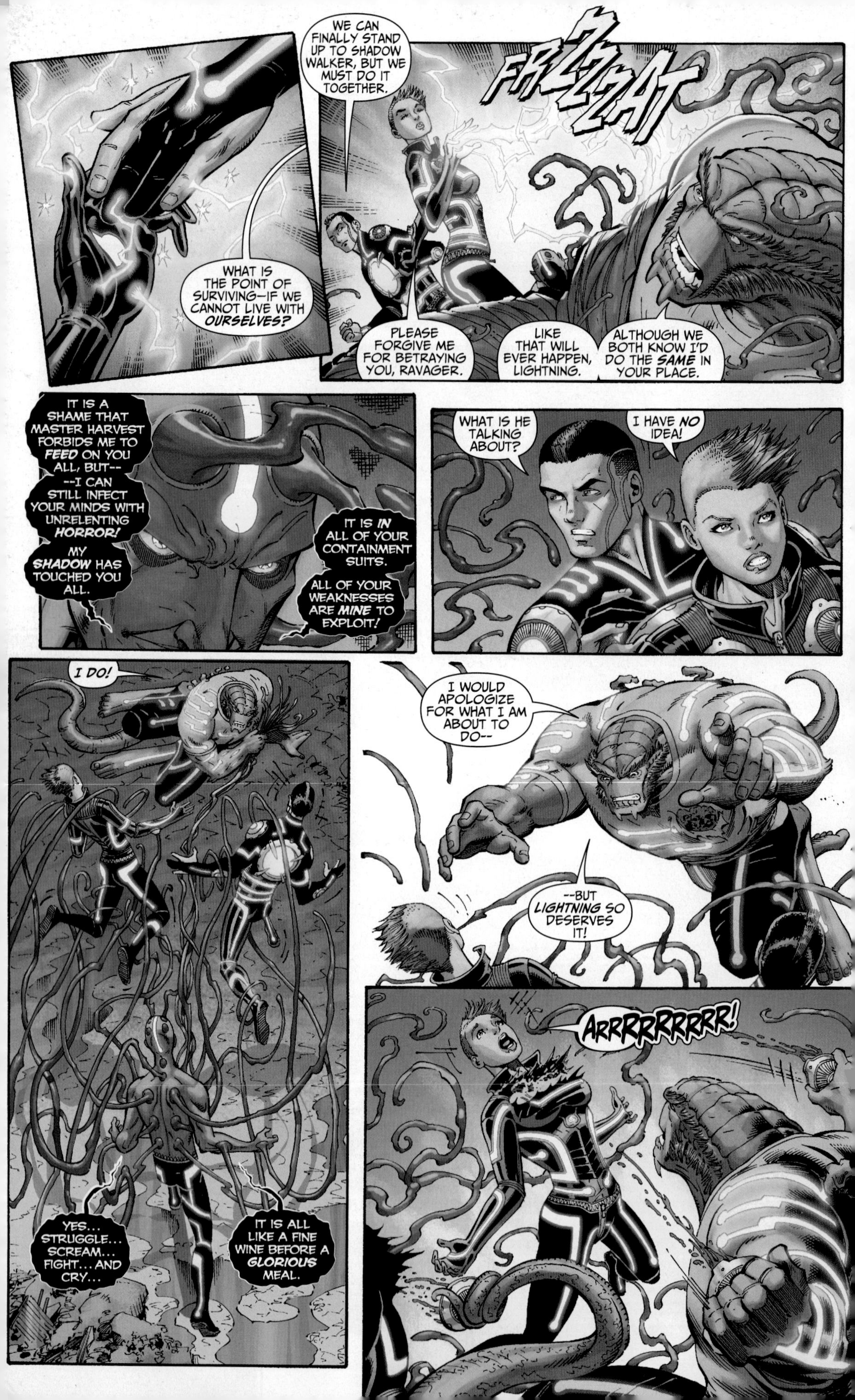
WHAT IS THE POINT OF SURVIVING—IF WE CANNOT LIVE WITH OURSELVES?
WE CAN FINALLY STAND UP TO SHADOW WALKER, BUT WE MUST DO IT TOGETHER.
FRZZZZAT
PLEASE FORGIVE ME FOR BETRAYING YOU, RAVAGER.
LIKE THAT WILL EVER HAPPEN, LIGHTNING.
ALTHOUGH WE BOTH KNOW I'D DO THE SAME IN YOUR PLACE.
IT IS A SHAME THAT MASTER HARVEST FORBIDS ME TO FEED ON YOU ALL, BUT--
--I CAN STILL INFECT YOUR MINDS WITH UNRELENTING HORROR!
MY SHADOW HAS TOUCHED YOU ALL.
IT IS IN ALL OF YOUR CONTAINMENT SUITS.
ALL OF YOUR WEAKNESSES ARE MINE TO EXPLOIT!
WHAT IS HE TALKING ABOUT?
I HAVE NO IDEA!
I DO!
YES... STRUGGLE... SCREAM... FIGHT... AND CRY...
IT IS ALL LIKE A FINE WINE BEFORE A GLORIOUS MEAL.
I WOULD APOLOGIZE FOR WHAT I AM ABOUT TO DO--
--BUT LIGHTNING SO DESERVES IT!
ARRRRRRRRR!

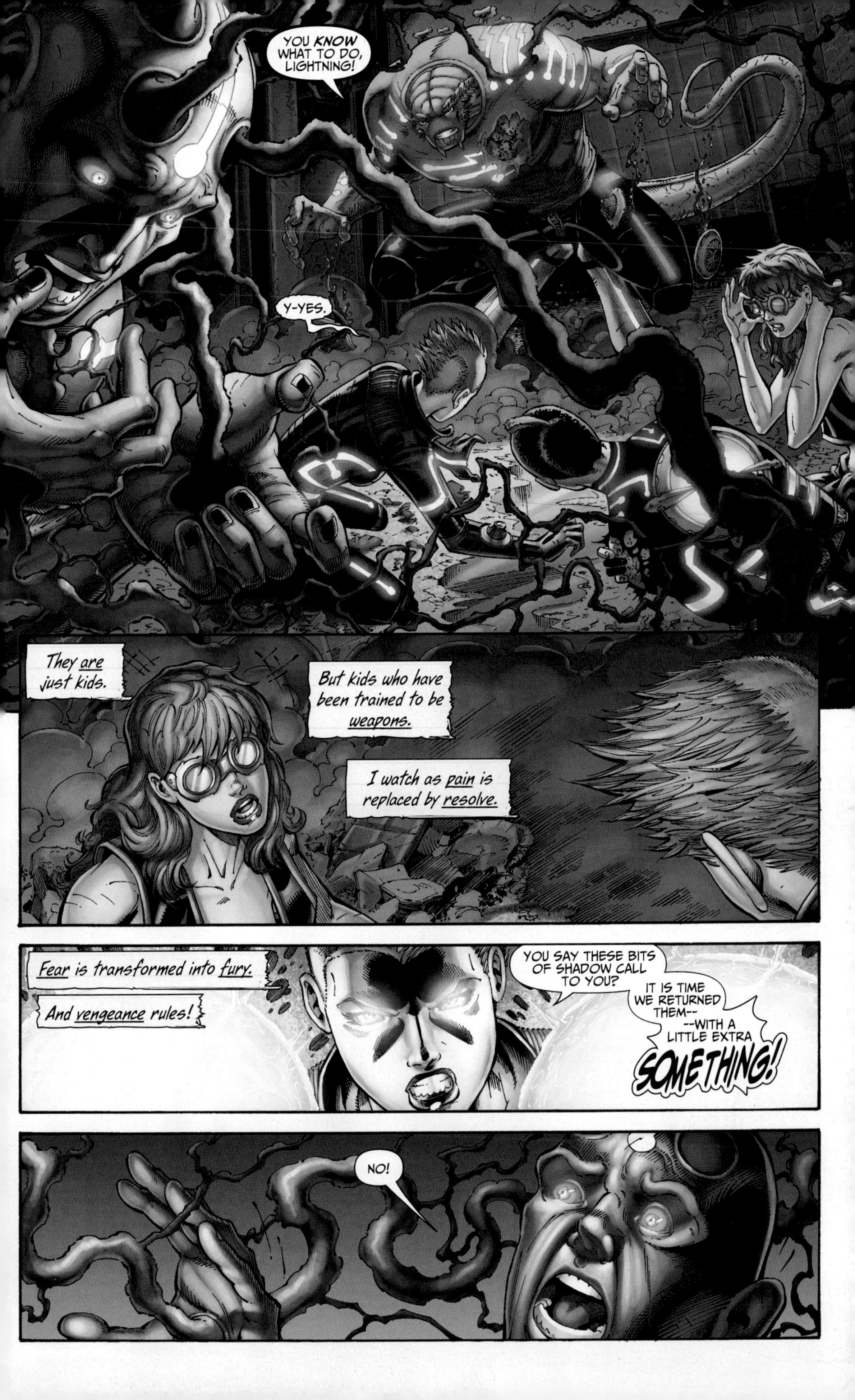

YOU KNOW WHAT TO DO, LIGHTNING!
Y-YES.
They are just kids.
But kids who have been trained to be weapons.
I watch as pain is replaced by resolve.
Fear is transformed into fury.
And vengeance rules!
YOU SAY THESE BITS OF SHADOW CALL TO YOU?
IT IS TIME WE RETURNED THEM--
--WITH A LITTLE EXTRA
SOMETHING!
NO!

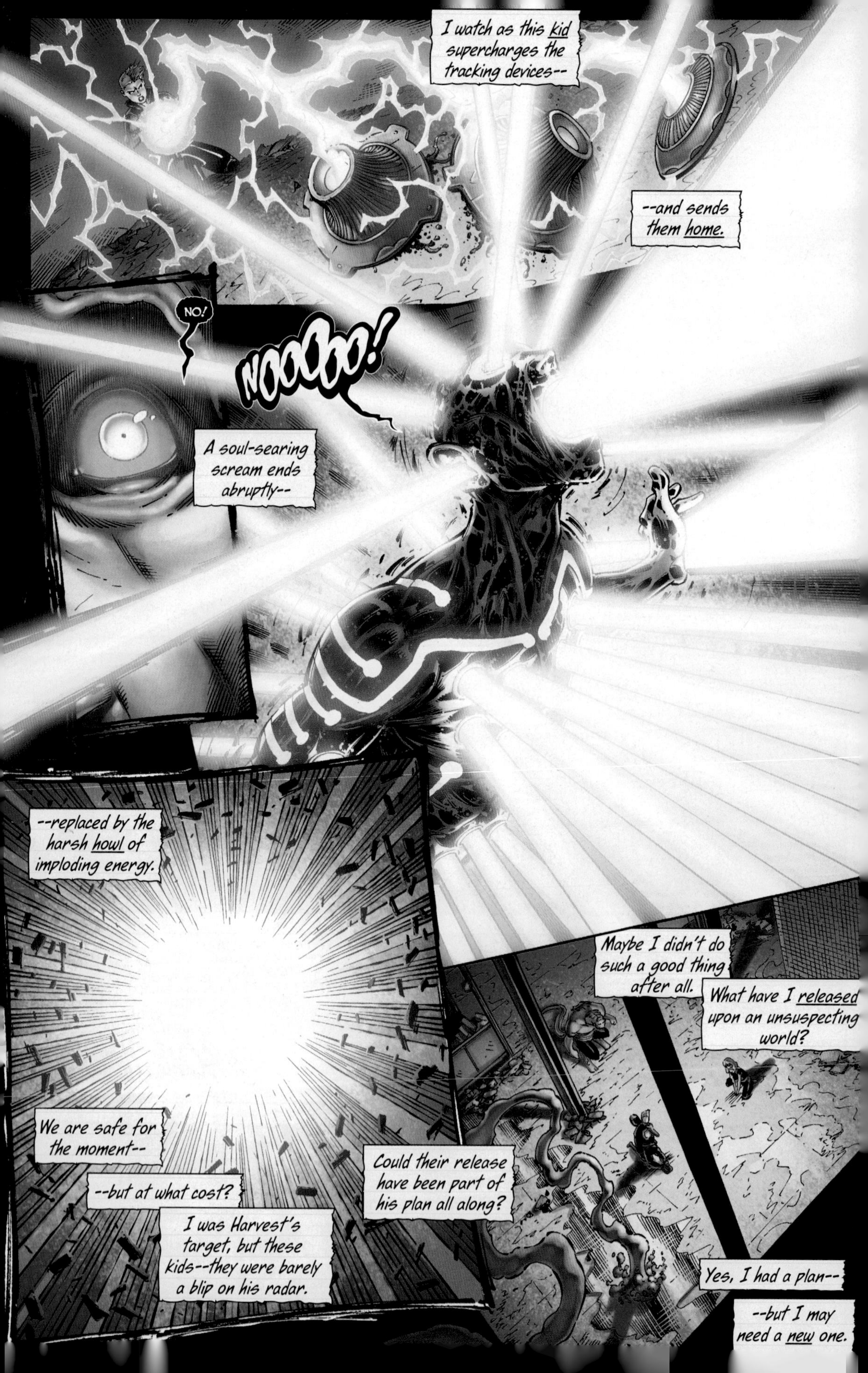

I watch as this kid supercharges the tracking devices--
--and sends them home.
NO!
NOOOOO!
A soul-searing scream ends abruptly--
--replaced by the harsh howl of imploding energy.
We are safe for the moment--
--but at what cost?
I was Harvest's target, but these kids--they were barely a blip on his radar.
Could their release have been part of his plan all along?
Maybe I didn't do such a good thing after all.
What have I released upon an unsuspecting world?
Yes, I had a plan--
--but I may need a new one.

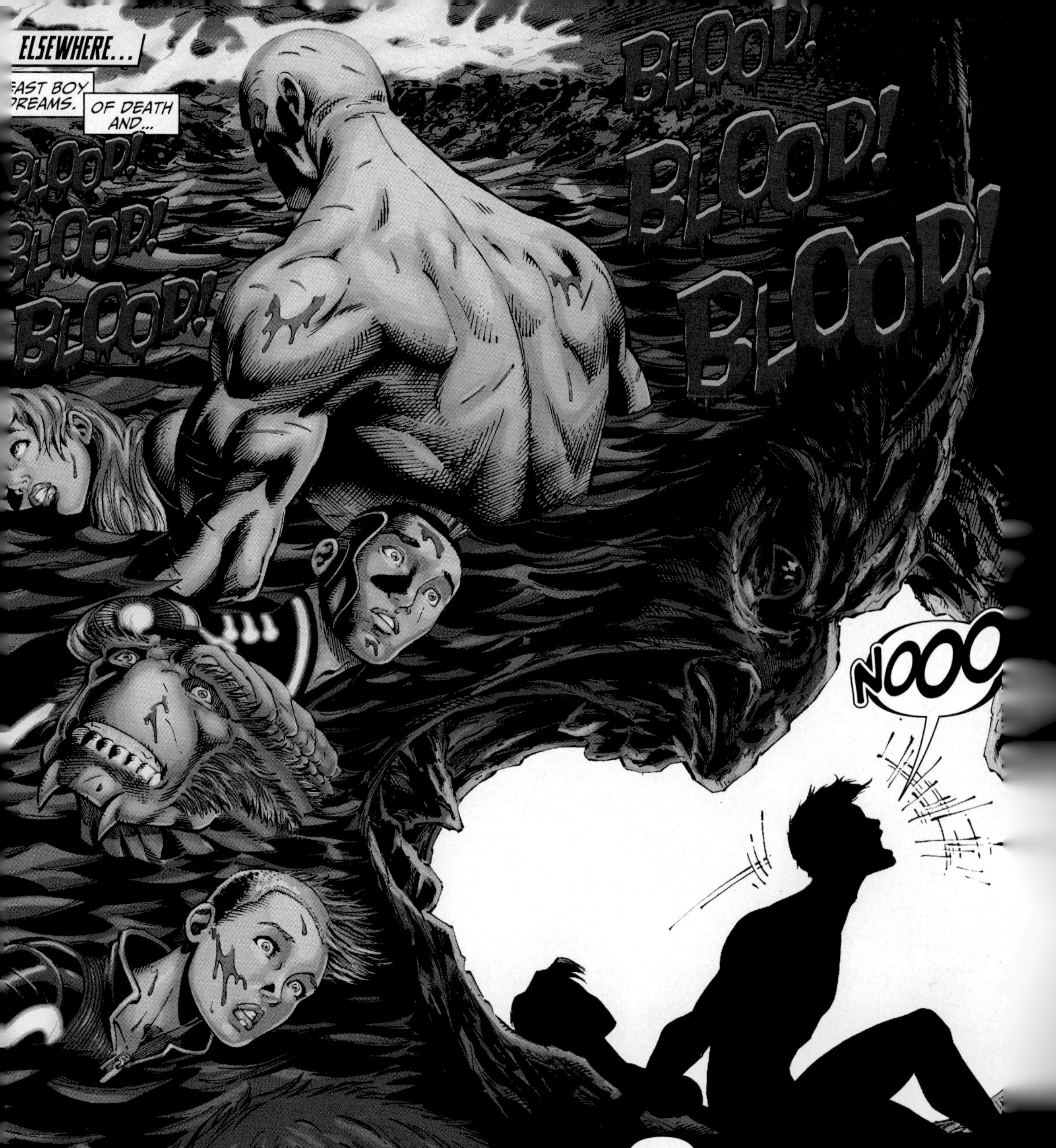
ELSEWHERE...
BEAST BOY DREAMS.
OF DEATH AND...
BLOOD!
BLOOD!
BLOOD!
BLOOD!
BLOOD!
BLOOD!
NOOO

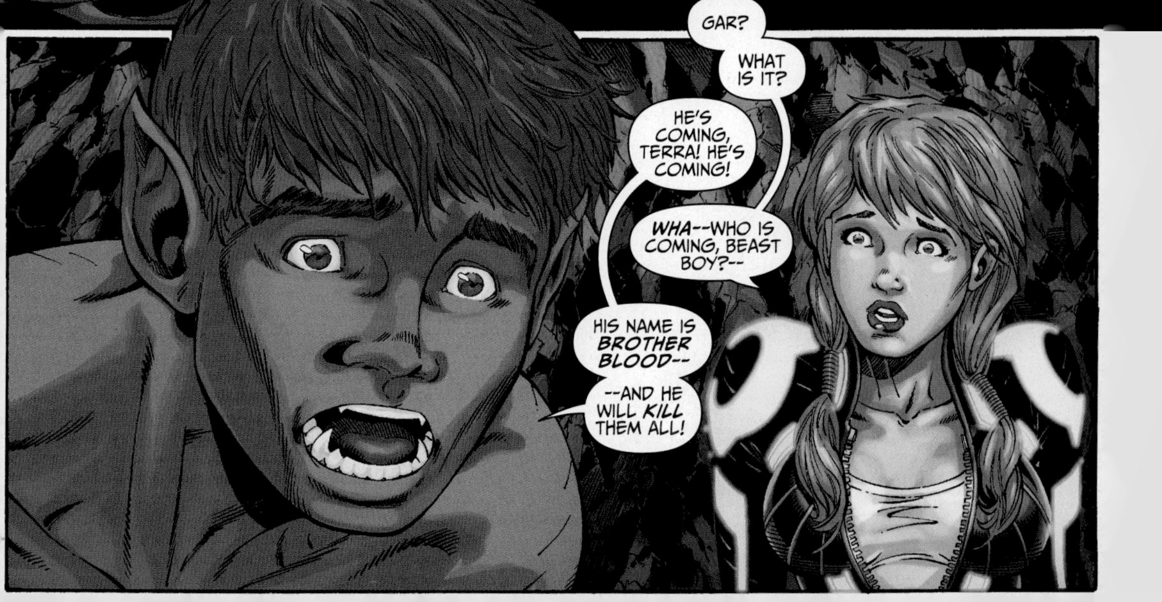
GAR?
WHAT IS IT?
HE'S COMING, TERRA! HE'S COMING!
WHA--WHO IS COMING, BEAST BOY?--
HIS NAME IS BROTHER BLOOD--
--AND HE WILL KILL THEM ALL!

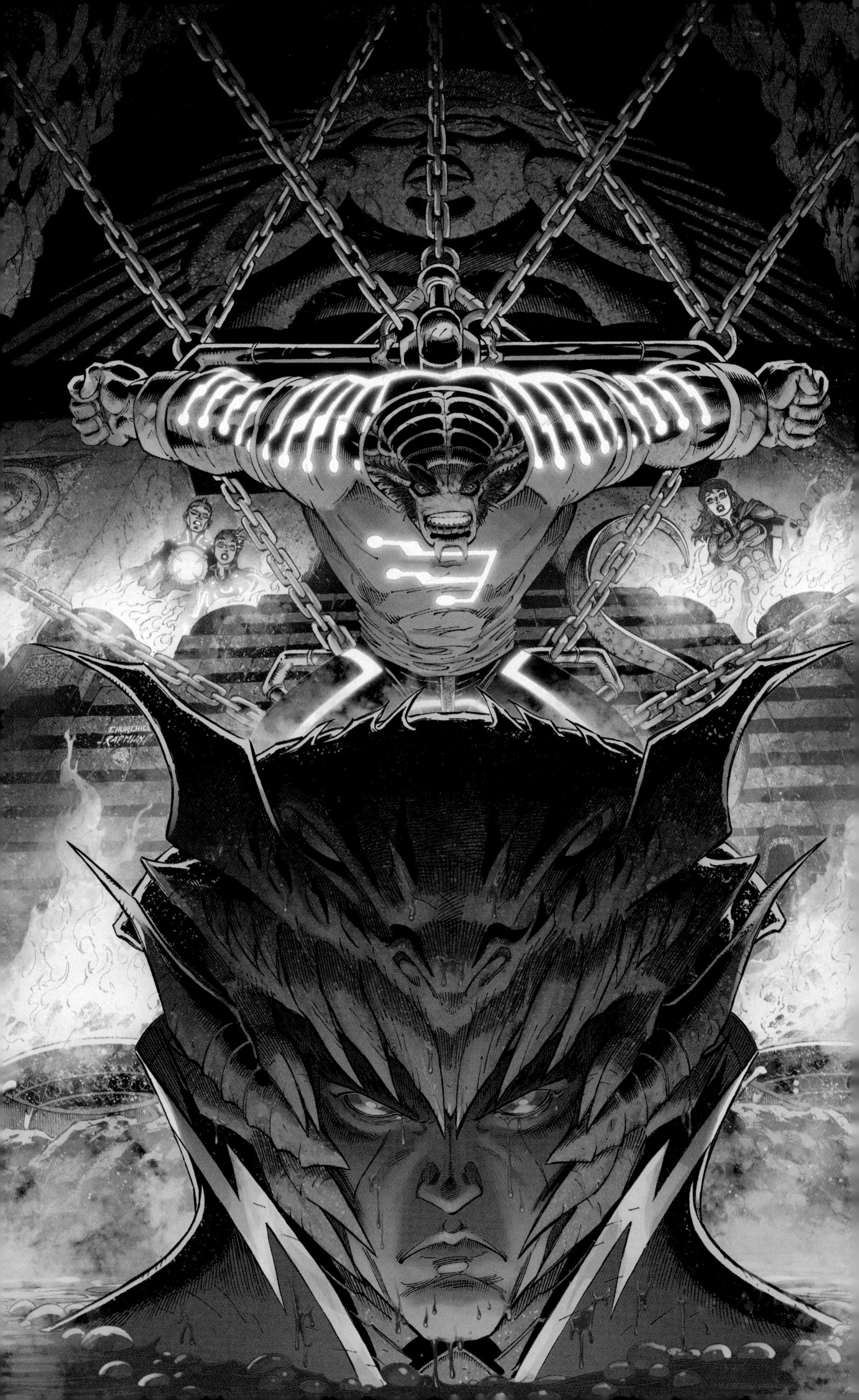
CHURCHILL

BLOOD

HOWARD MACKIE
writer

IAN CHURCHILL & TOM RANEY
pencillers

NORM RAMPUND & JON SIBAL
inkers

cover art by
IAN CHURCHILL, NORM RAMPUND & PETER STEIGERWALD

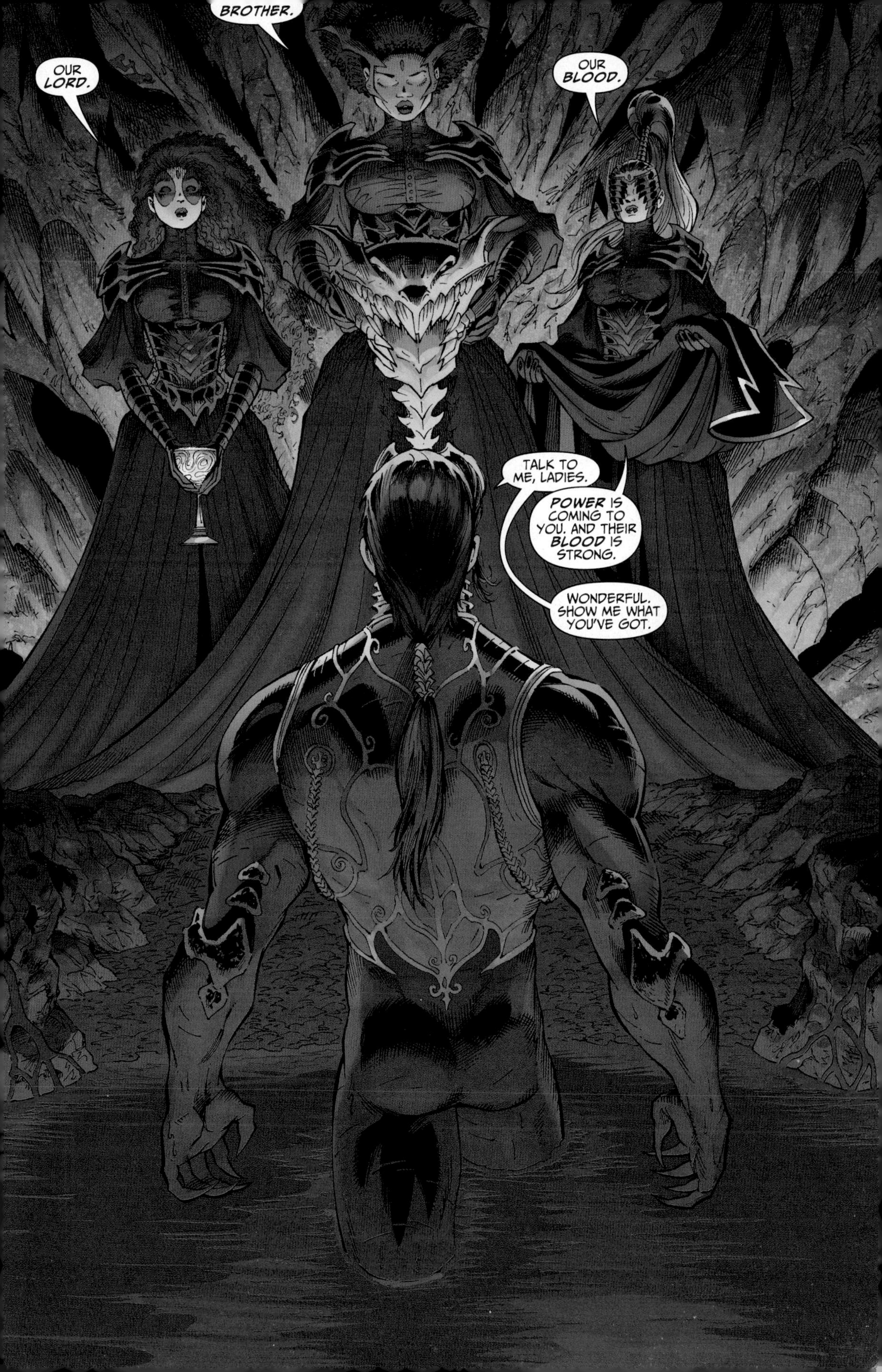

OUR LORD.
BROTHER.
OUR BLOOD.
TALK TO ME, LADIES.
POWER IS COMING TO YOU. AND THEIR BLOOD IS STRONG.
WONDERFUL. SHOW ME WHAT YOU'VE GOT.

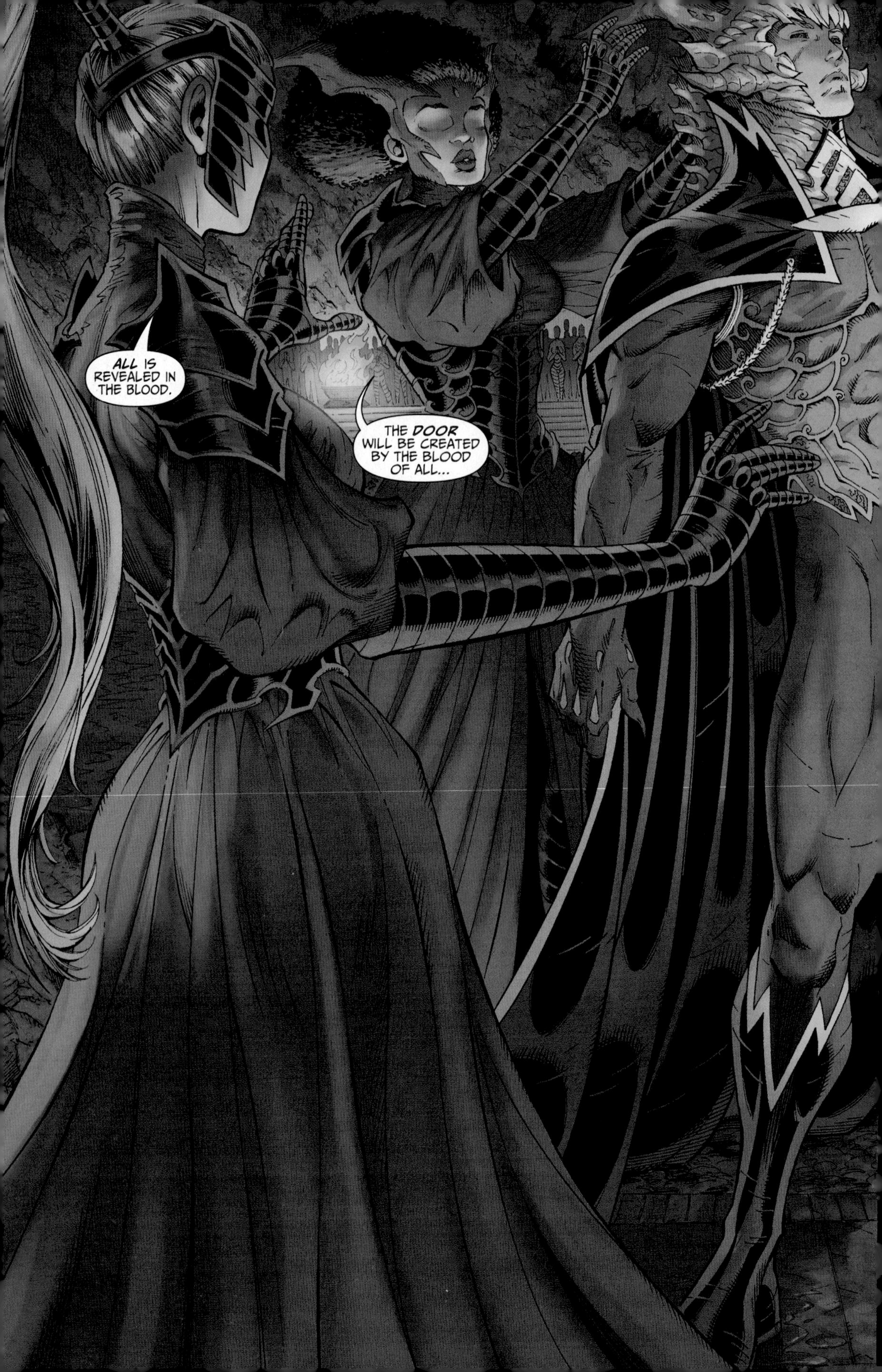
ALL IS REVEALED IN THE BLOOD.
THE DOOR WILL BE CREATED BY THE BLOOD OF ALL...

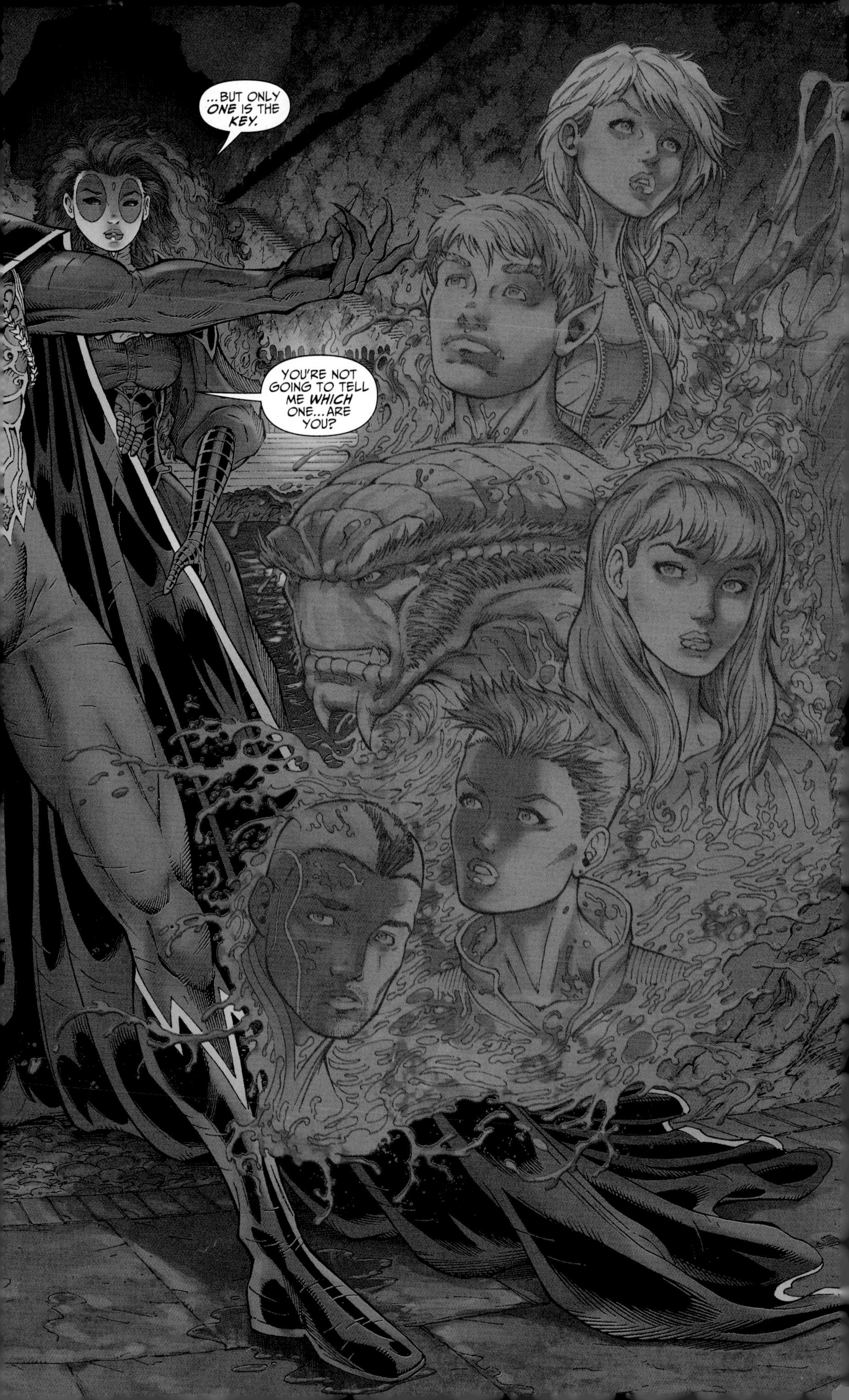
...BUT ONLY ONE IS THE KEY.
YOU'RE NOT GOING TO TELL ME WHICH ONE...ARE YOU?

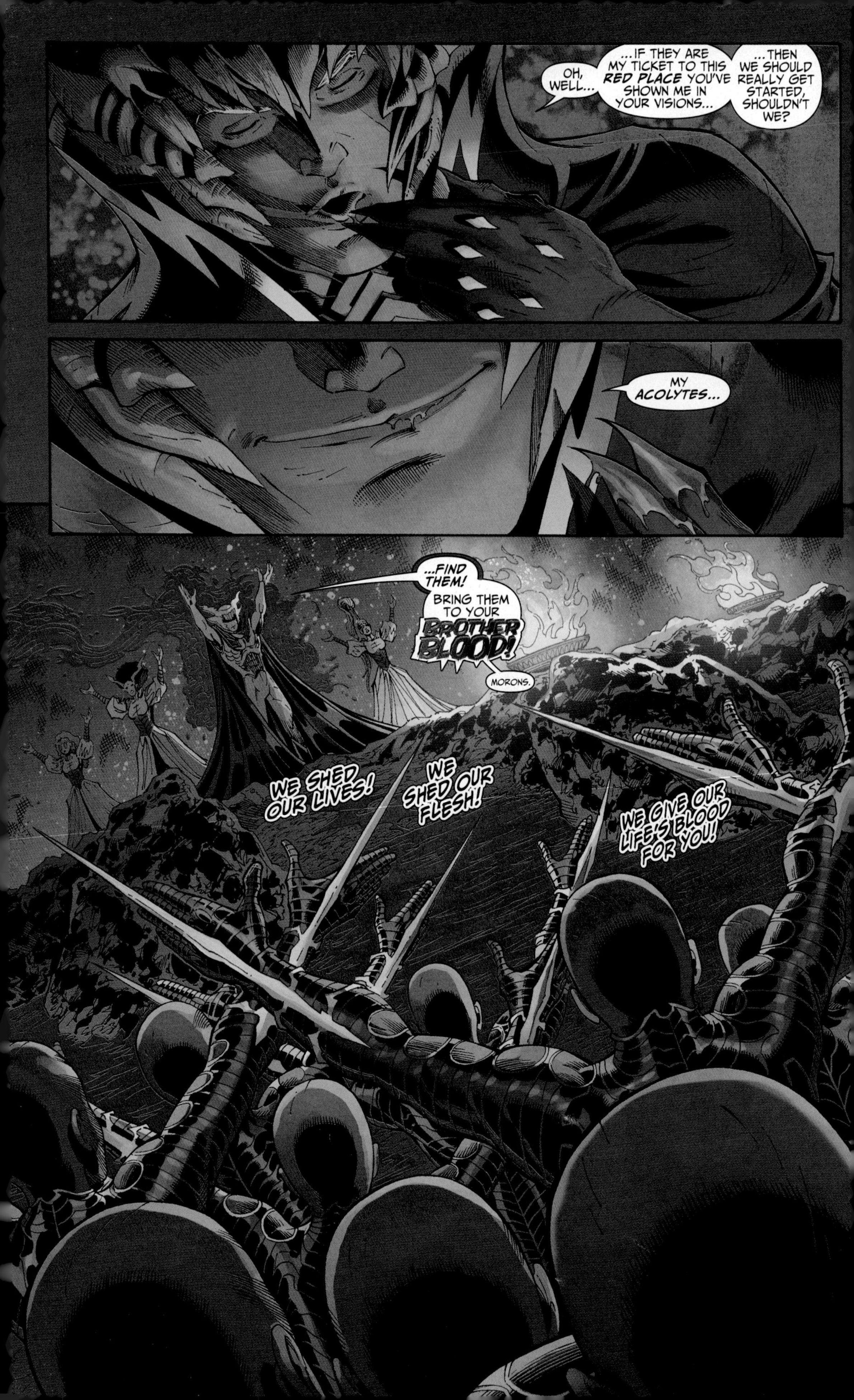
OH, WELL...
...IF THEY ARE MY TICKET TO THIS RED PLACE YOU'VE SHOWN ME IN YOUR VISIONS...
...THEN WE SHOULD REALLY GET STARTED, SHOULDN'T WE?
MY ACOLYTES...
...FIND THEM!
BRING THEM TO YOUR BROTHER BLOOD!
MORONS.
WE SHED OUR LIVES!
WE SHED OUR FLESH!
WE GIVE OUR LIFE'S BLOOD FOR YOU!

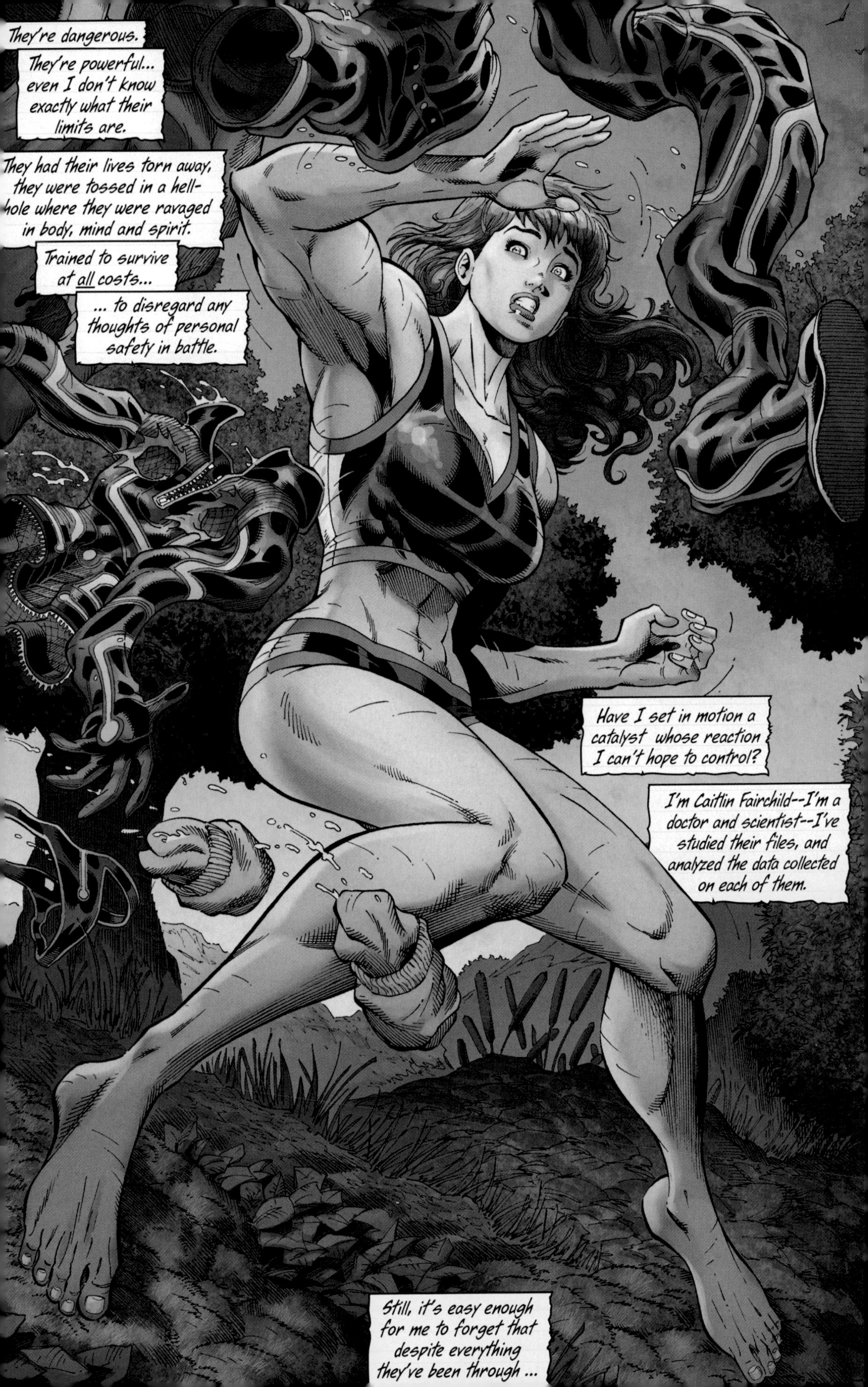
They're dangerous.
They're powerful... even I don't know exactly what their limits are.
They had their lives torn away, they were tossed in a hell-hole where they were ravaged in body, mind and spirit.
Trained to survive at all costs...
... to disregard any thoughts of personal safety in battle.
Have I set in motion a catalyst whose reaction I can't hope to control?
I'm Caitlin Fairchild--I'm a doctor and scientist--I've studied their files, and analyzed the data collected on each of them.
Still, it's easy enough for me to forget that despite everything they've been through ...

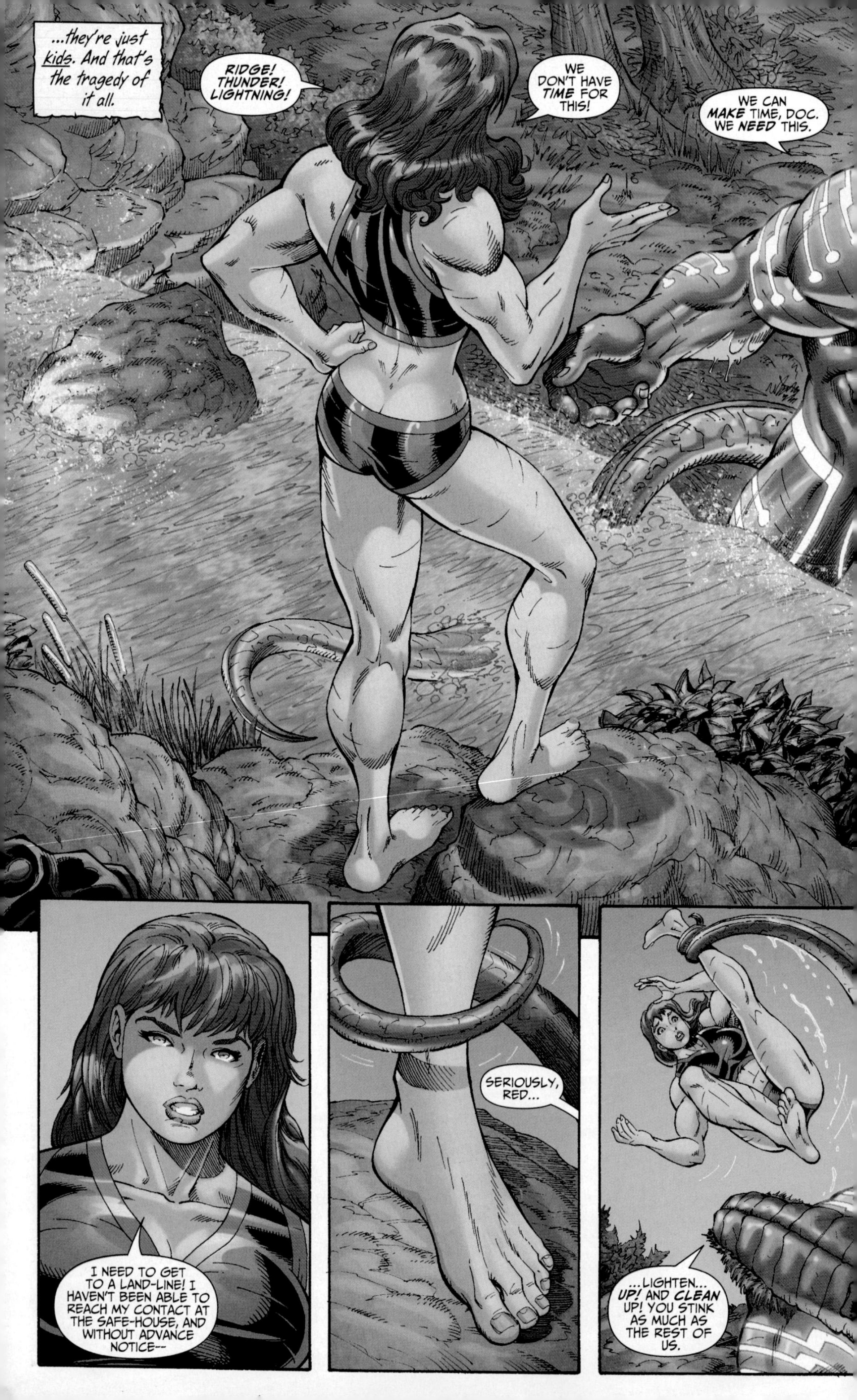
...they're just kids. And that's the tragedy of it all.
RIDGE! THUNDER! LIGHTNING!
WE DON'T HAVE TIME FOR THIS!
WE CAN MAKE TIME, DOC. WE NEED THIS.
I NEED TO GET TO A LAND-LINE! I HAVEN'T BEEN ABLE TO REACH MY CONTACT AT THE SAFE-HOUSE, AND WITHOUT ADVANCE NOTICE--
SERIOUSLY, RED...
...LIGHTEN... UP! AND CLEAN UP! YOU STINK AS MUCH AS THE REST OF US.

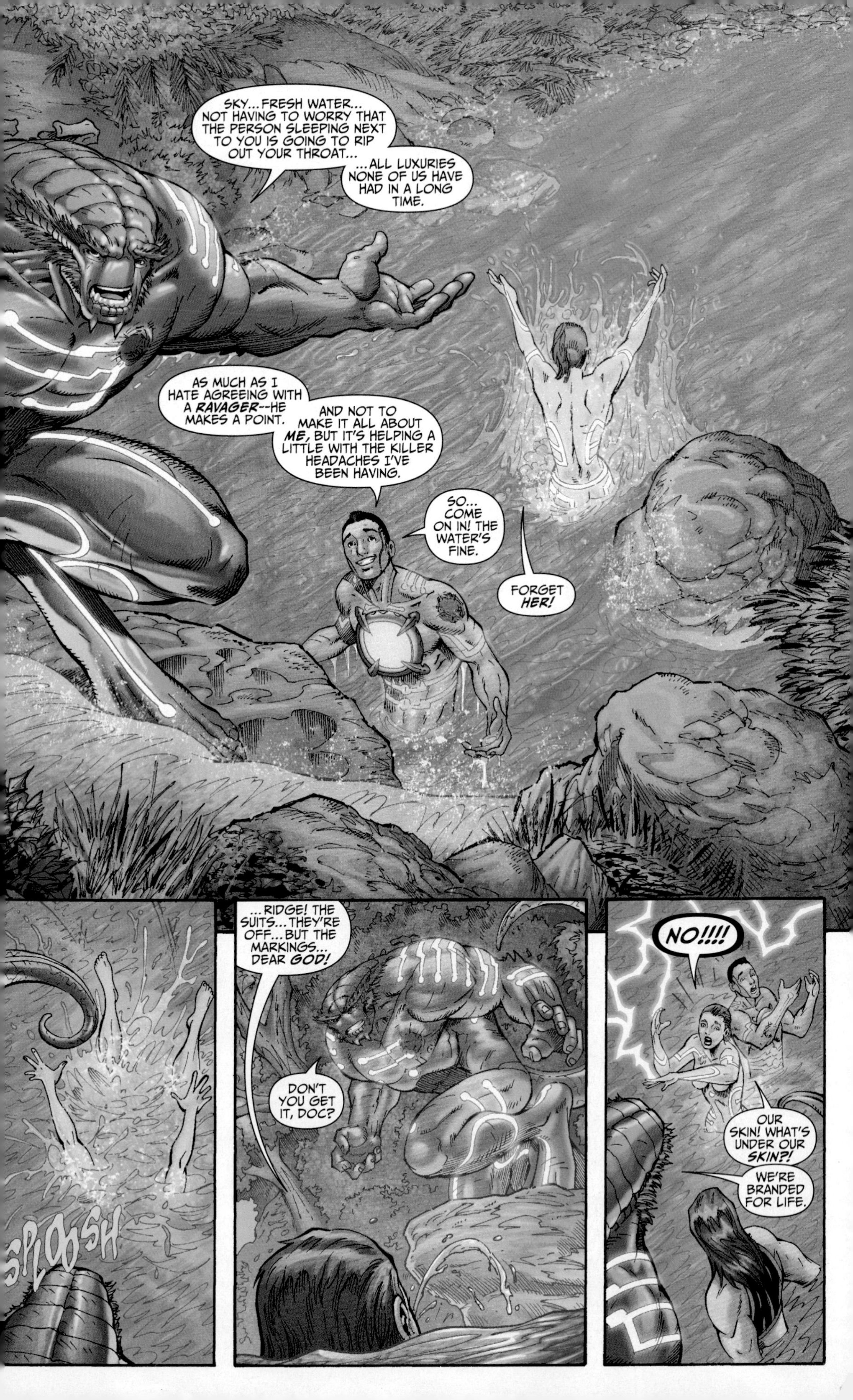
SKY...FRESH WATER... NOT HAVING TO WORRY THAT THE PERSON SLEEPING NEXT TO YOU IS GOING TO RIP OUT YOUR THROAT...
...ALL LUXURIES NONE OF US HAVE HAD IN A LONG TIME.
AS MUCH AS I HATE AGREEING WITH A RAVAGER--HE MAKES A POINT.
AND NOT TO MAKE IT ALL ABOUT ME, BUT IT'S HELPING A LITTLE WITH THE KILLER HEADACHES I'VE BEEN HAVING.
SO... COME ON IN! THE WATER'S FINE.
FORGET HER!
SPLOOSH
...RIDGE! THE SUITS...THEY'RE OFF...BUT THE MARKINGS... DEAR GOD!
DON'T YOU GET IT, DOC?
NO!!!!
OUR SKIN! WHAT'S UNDER OUR SKIN?!
WE'RE BRANDED FOR LIFE.

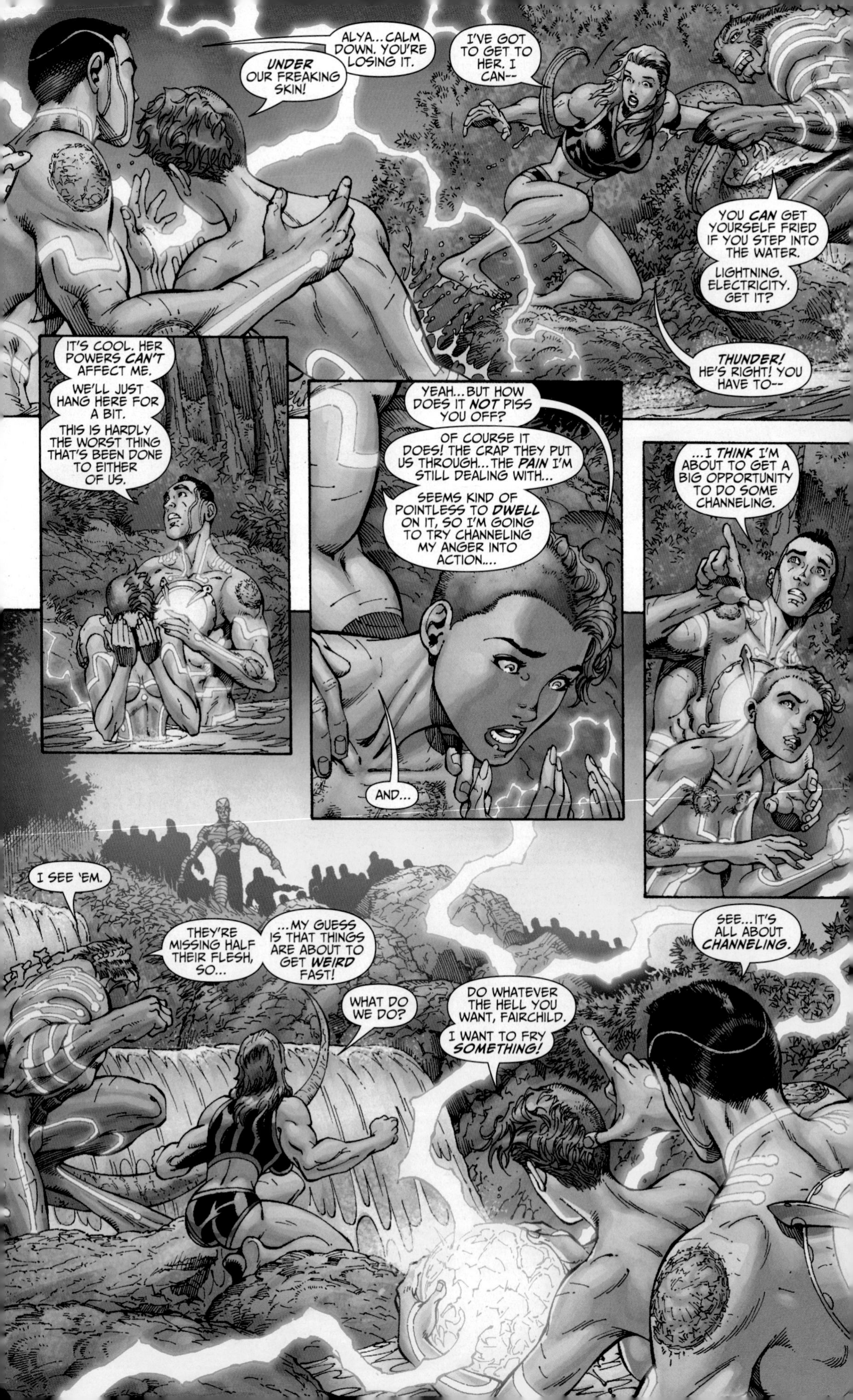
UNDER OUR FREAKING SKIN!
ALYA...CALM DOWN. YOU'RE LOSING IT.
I'VE GOT TO GET TO HER. I CAN--
YOU CAN GET YOURSELF FRIED IF YOU STEP INTO THE WATER.
LIGHTNING. ELECTRICITY. GET IT?
THUNDER! HE'S RIGHT! YOU HAVE TO--
IT'S COOL. HER POWERS CAN'T AFFECT ME.
WE'LL JUST HANG HERE FOR A BIT.
THIS IS HARDLY THE WORST THING THAT'S BEEN DONE TO EITHER OF US.
YEAH...BUT HOW DOES IT NOT PISS YOU OFF?
OF COURSE IT DOES! THE CRAP THEY PUT US THROUGH...THE PAIN I'M STILL DEALING WITH...
SEEMS KIND OF POINTLESS TO DWELL ON IT, SO I'M GOING TO TRY CHANNELING MY ANGER INTO ACTION....
AND...
...I THINK I'M ABOUT TO GET A BIG OPPORTUNITY TO DO SOME CHANNELING.
I SEE 'EM.
THEY'RE MISSING HALF THEIR FLESH, SO...
...MY GUESS IS THAT THINGS ARE ABOUT TO GET WEIRD FAST!
WHAT DO WE DO?
DO WHATEVER THE HELL YOU WANT, FAIRCHILD.
I WANT TO FRY SOMETHING!
SEE...IT'S ALL ABOUT CHANNELING.

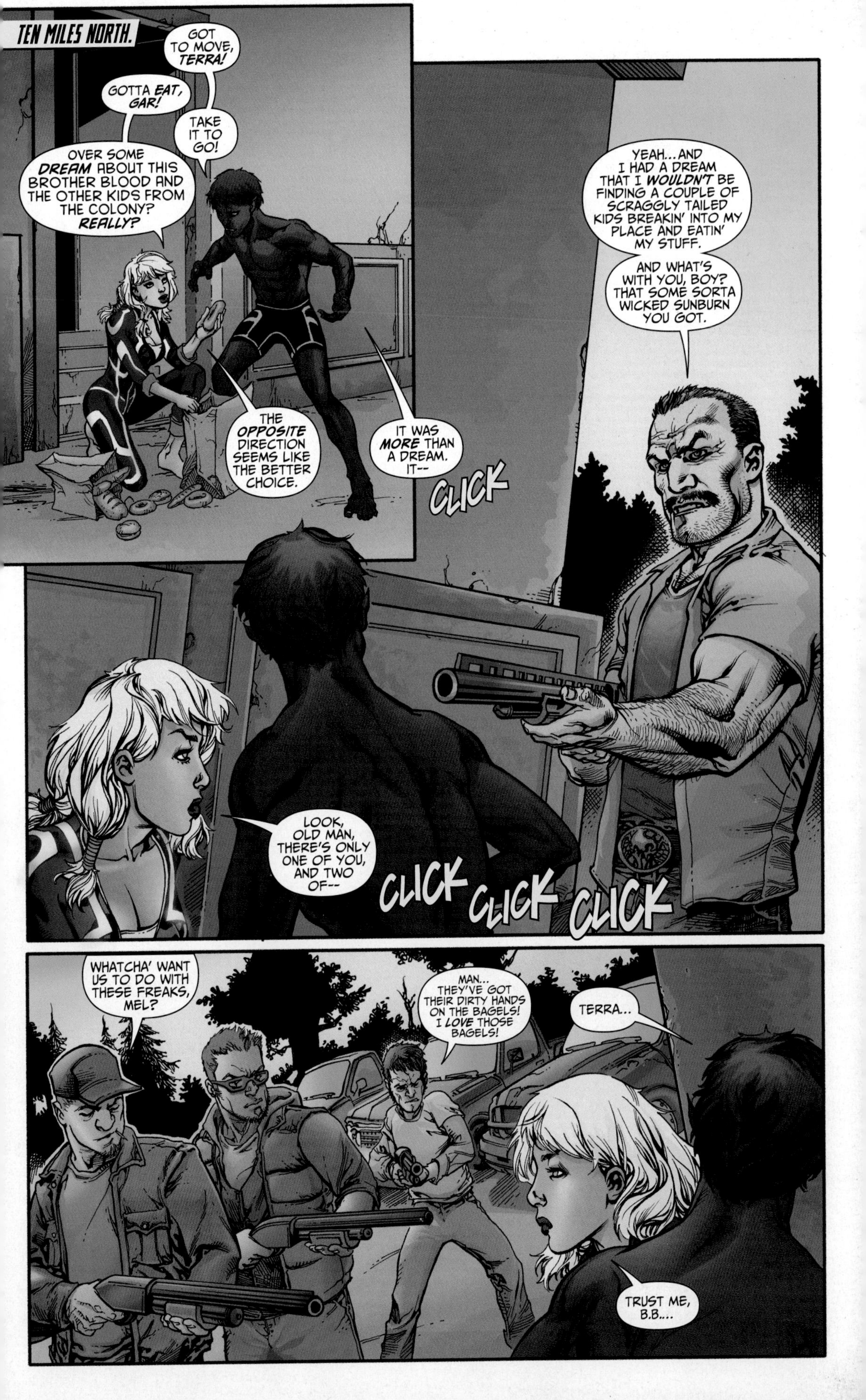

TEN MILES NORTH.
GOT TO MOVE, TERRA!
GOTTA EAT, GAR!
TAKE IT TO GO!
OVER SOME DREAM ABOUT THIS BROTHER BLOOD AND THE OTHER KIDS FROM THE COLONY? REALLY?
THE OPPOSITE DIRECTION SEEMS LIKE THE BETTER CHOICE.
IT WAS MORE THAN A DREAM. IT--
CLICK
YEAH...AND I HAD A DREAM THAT I WOULDN'T BE FINDING A COUPLE OF SCRAGGLY TAILED KIDS BREAKIN' INTO MY PLACE AND EATIN' MY STUFF.
AND WHAT'S WITH YOU, BOY? THAT SOME SORTA WICKED SUNBURN YOU GOT.
LOOK, OLD MAN, THERE'S ONLY ONE OF YOU, AND TWO OF--
CLICK CLICK CLICK
WHATCHA' WANT US TO DO WITH THESE FREAKS, MEL?
MAN... THEY'VE GOT THEIR DIRTY HANDS ON THE BAGELS! I LOVE THOSE BAGELS!
TERRA...
TRUST ME, B.B....

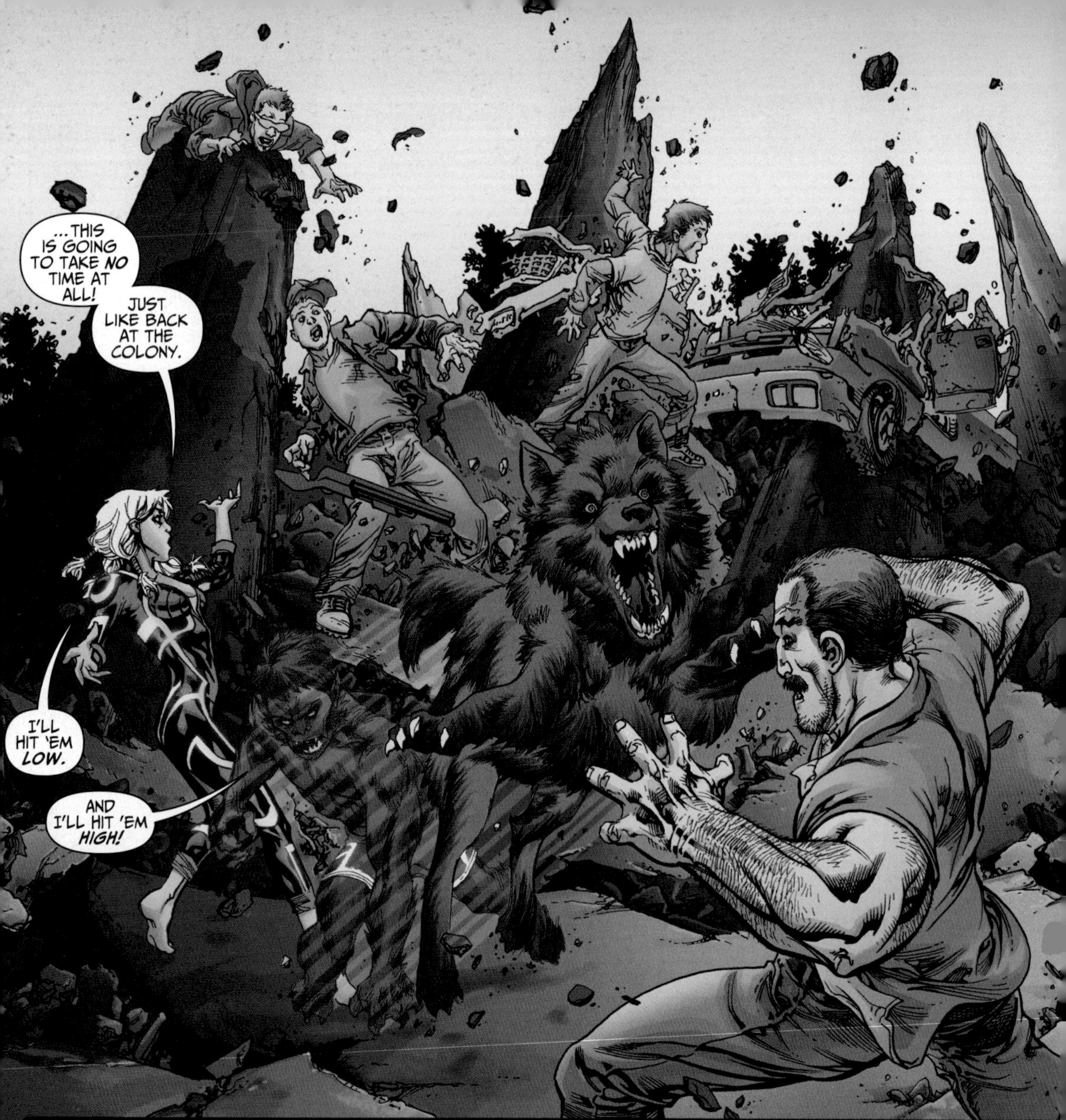
...THIS IS GOING TO TAKE *NO* TIME AT ALL!
JUST LIKE BACK AT THE COLONY.
I'LL HIT 'EM *LOW*.
AND I'LL HIT 'EM *HIGH!*

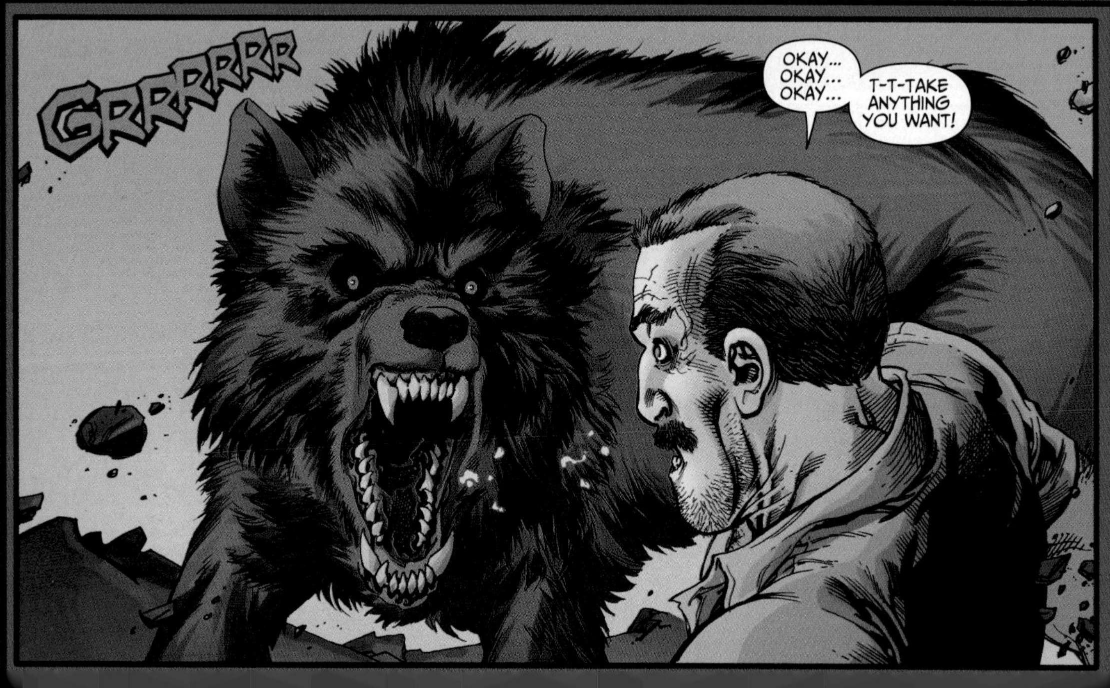
GRRRRRR
OKAY... OKAY... OKAY...
T-T-TAKE ANYTHING YOU WANT!

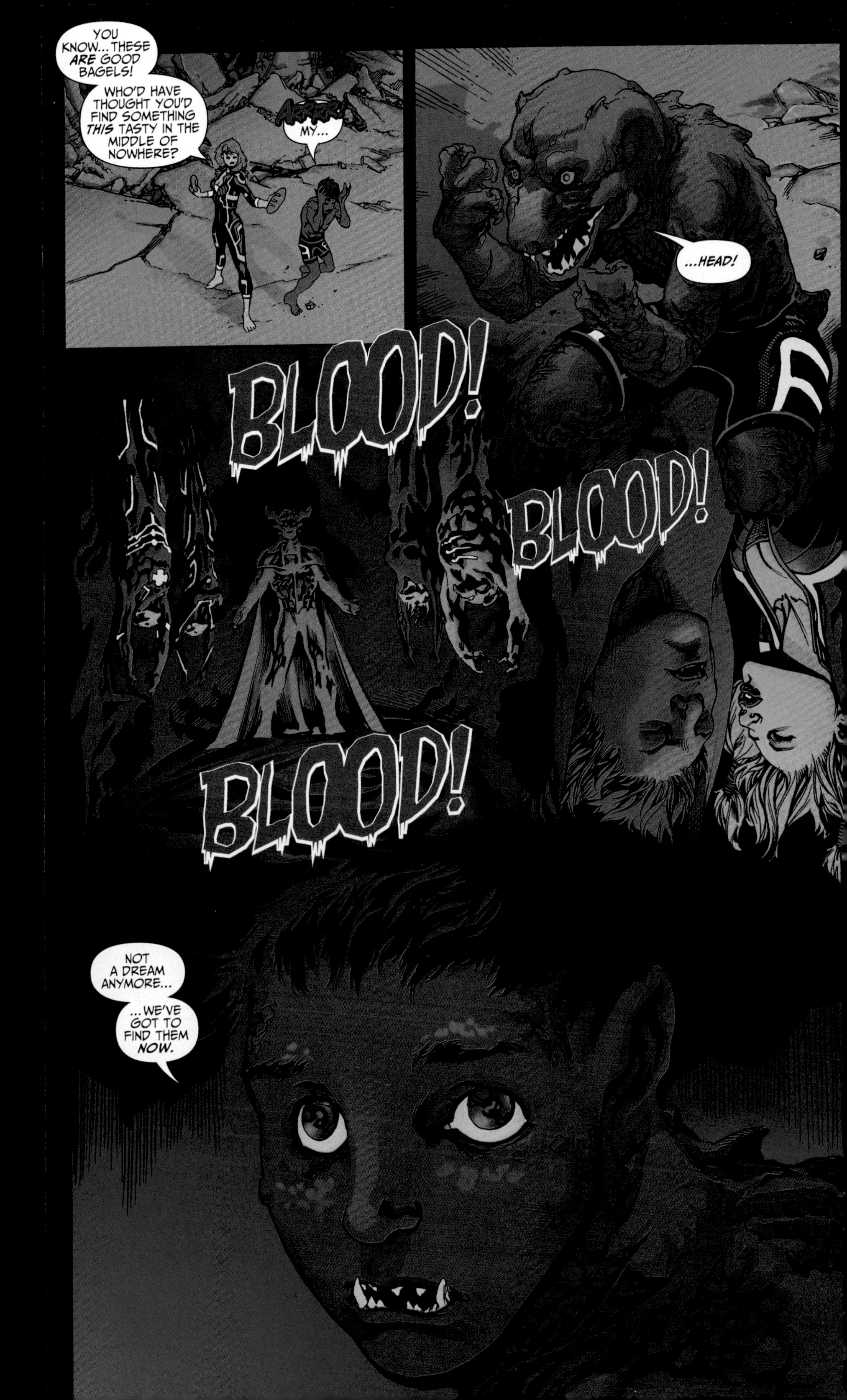
YOU KNOW... THESE *ARE* GOOD BAGELS!
WHO'D HAVE THOUGHT YOU'D FIND SOMETHING *THIS* TASTY IN THE MIDDLE OF NOWHERE?
ARRRR! MY...
...HEAD!
BLOOD!
BLOOD!
BLOOD!
NOT A DREAM ANYMORE...
...WE'VE GOT TO FIND THEM *NOW*.

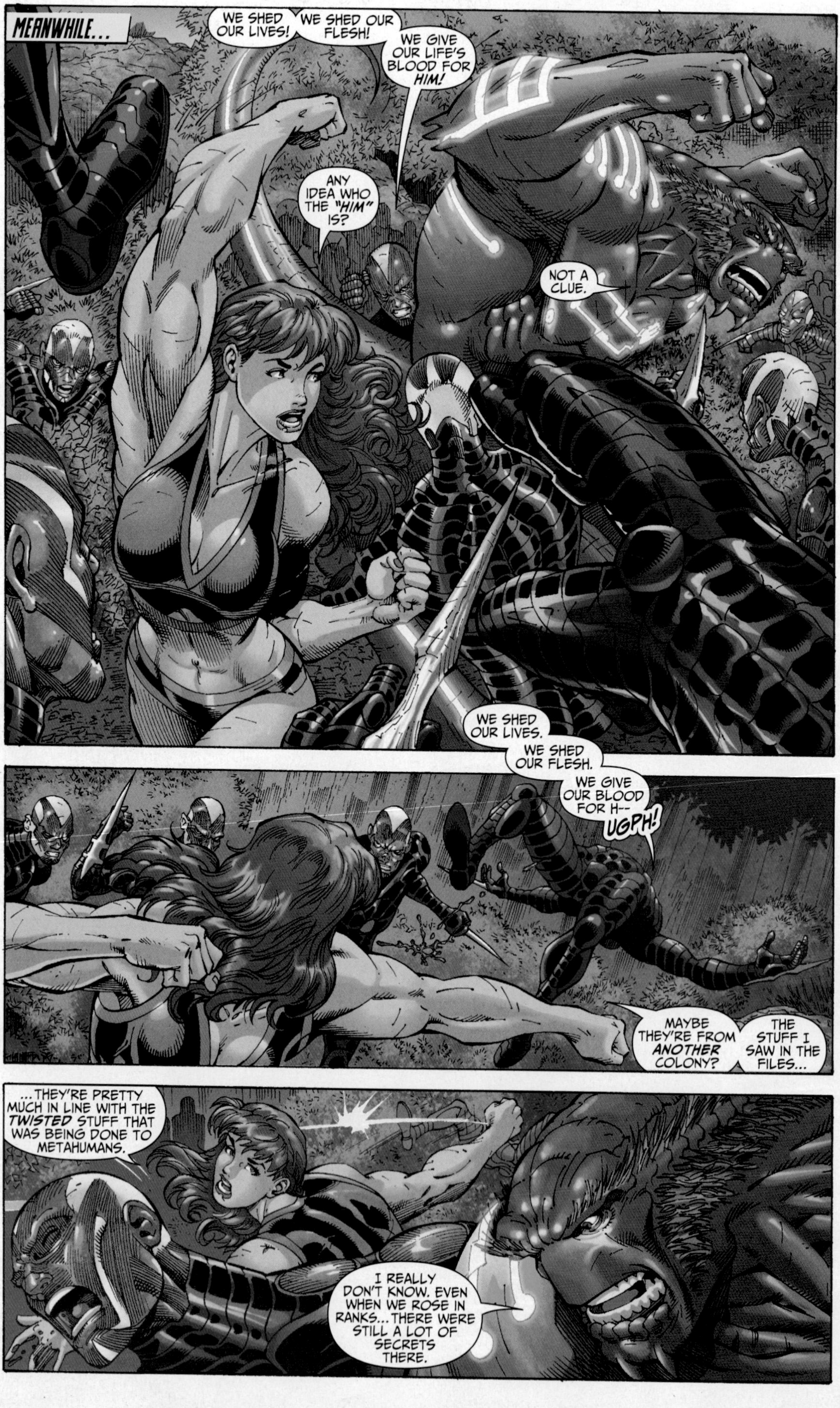
MEANWHILE...
WE SHED OUR LIVES!
WE SHED OUR FLESH!
WE GIVE OUR LIFE'S BLOOD FOR HIM!
ANY IDEA WHO THE "HIM" IS?
NOT A CLUE.
WE SHED OUR LIVES.
WE SHED OUR FLESH.
WE GIVE OUR BLOOD FOR H--
UGPH!
MAYBE THEY'RE FROM ANOTHER COLONY?
THE STUFF I SAW IN THE FILES...
...THEY'RE PRETTY MUCH IN LINE WITH THE TWISTED STUFF THAT WAS BEING DONE TO METAHUMANS.
I REALLY DON'T KNOW. EVEN WHEN WE ROSE IN RANKS...THERE WERE STILL A LOT OF SECRETS THERE.

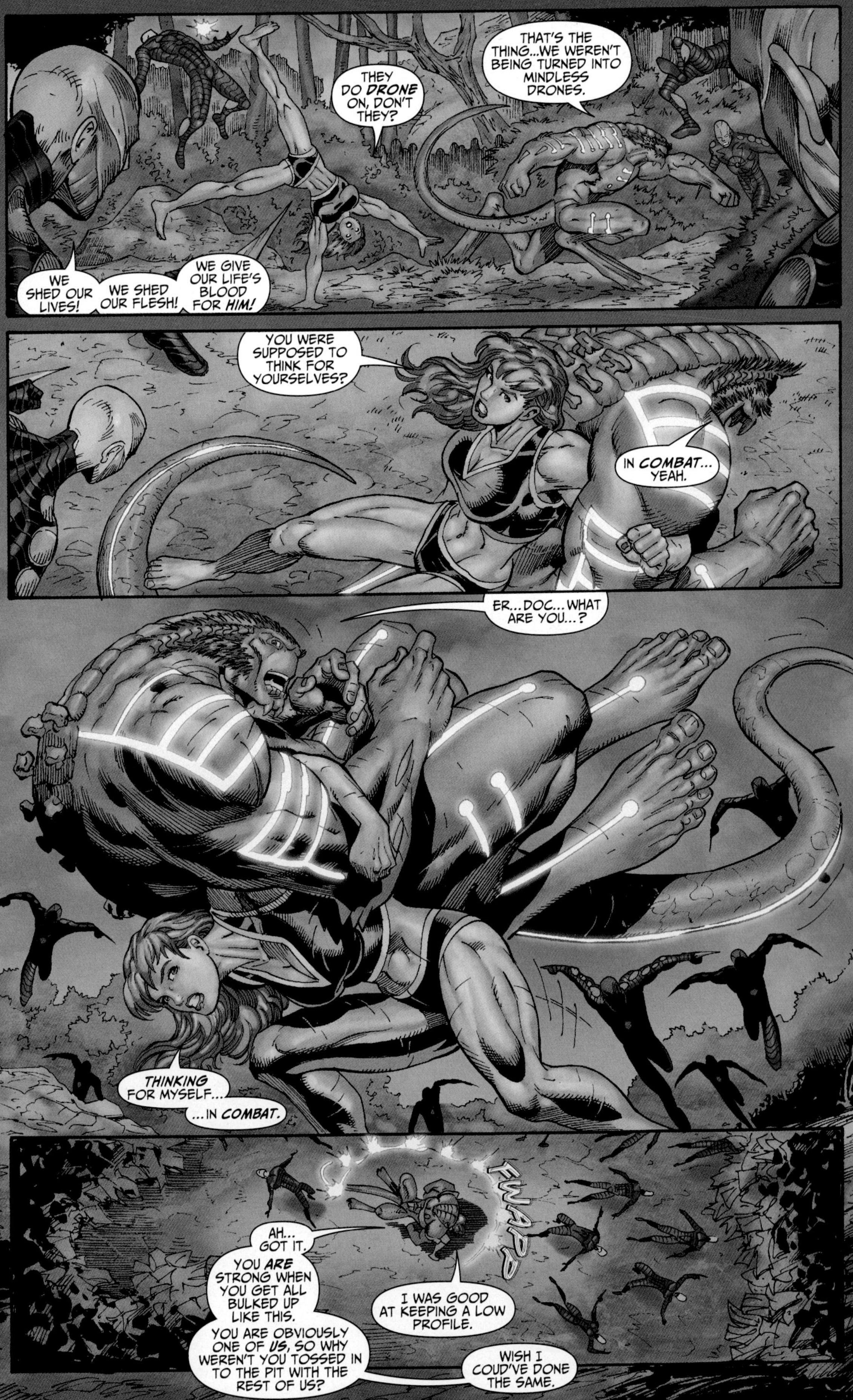
THEY DO DRONE ON, DON'T THEY?
THAT'S THE THING...WE WEREN'T BEING TURNED INTO MINDLESS DRONES.
WE SHED OUR LIVES!
WE SHED OUR FLESH!
WE GIVE OUR LIFE'S BLOOD FOR HIM!
YOU WERE SUPPOSED TO THINK FOR YOURSELVES?
IN COMBAT... YEAH.
ER...DOC...WHAT ARE YOU...?
THINKING FOR MYSELF...
...IN COMBAT.
FWAPP
AH... GOT IT.
YOU ARE STRONG WHEN YOU GET ALL BULKED UP LIKE THIS.
YOU ARE OBVIOUSLY ONE OF US, SO WHY WEREN'T YOU TOSSED IN TO THE PIT WITH THE REST OF US?
I WAS GOOD AT KEEPING A LOW PROFILE.
WISH I COUD'VE DONE THE SAME.

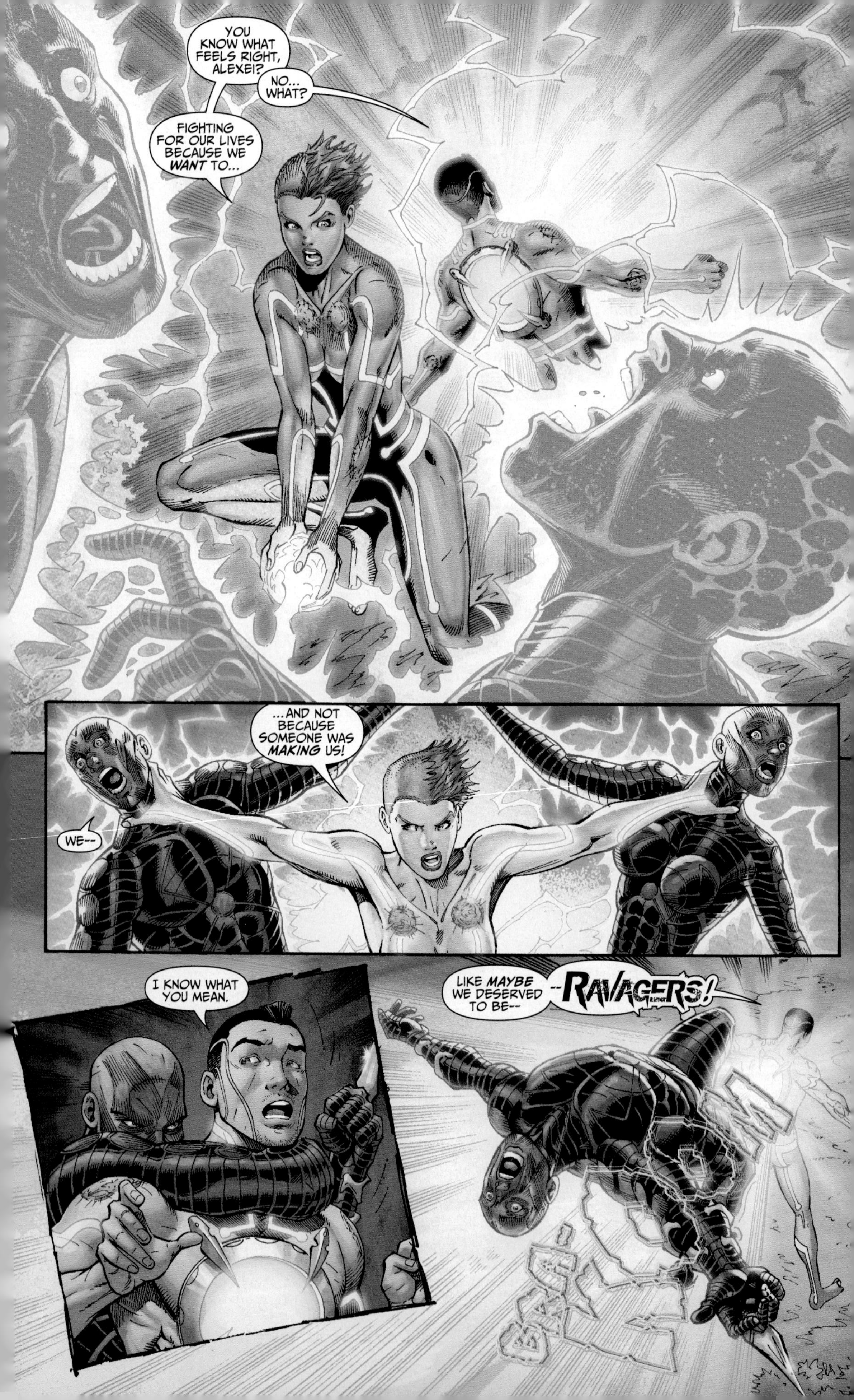
YOU KNOW WHAT FEELS RIGHT, ALEXEI?
NO... WHAT?
FIGHTING FOR OUR LIVES BECAUSE WE *WANT* TO...
...AND NOT BECAUSE SOMEONE WAS *MAKING* US!
WE--
I KNOW WHAT YOU MEAN.
LIKE *MAYBE* WE DESERVED TO BE--
--RAVAGERS!

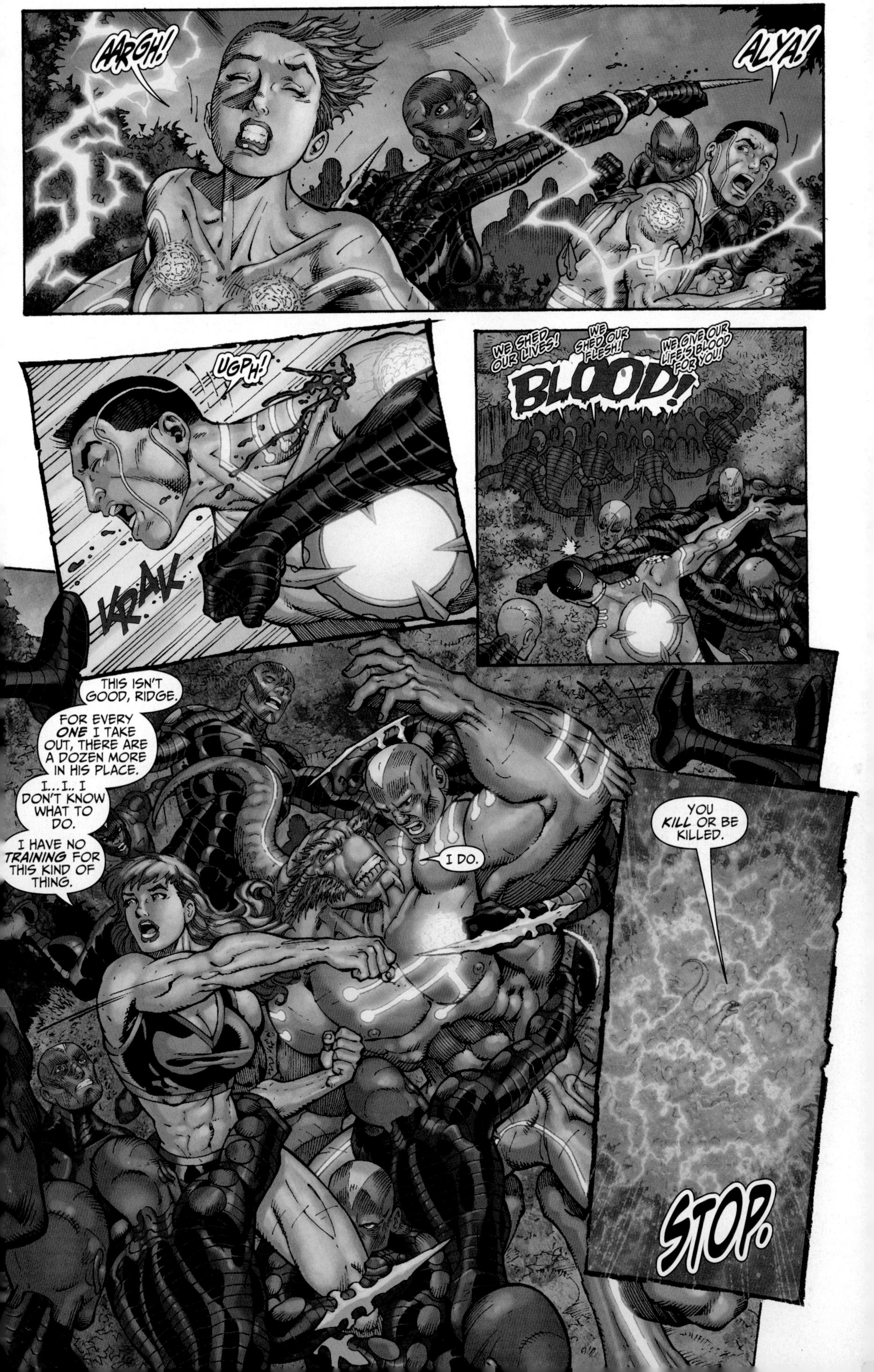
AARGH!
ALYA!
UGPH!
KRAK
WE SHED OUR LIVES!
WE SHED OUR FLESH!
WE GIVE OUR LIFE'S BLOOD FOR YOU!
BLOOD!
THIS ISN'T GOOD, RIDGE.
FOR EVERY ONE I TAKE OUT, THERE ARE A DOZEN MORE IN HIS PLACE.
I... I... I DON'T KNOW WHAT TO DO.
I HAVE NO TRAINING FOR THIS KIND OF THING.
I DO.
YOU KILL OR BE KILLED.
STOP.

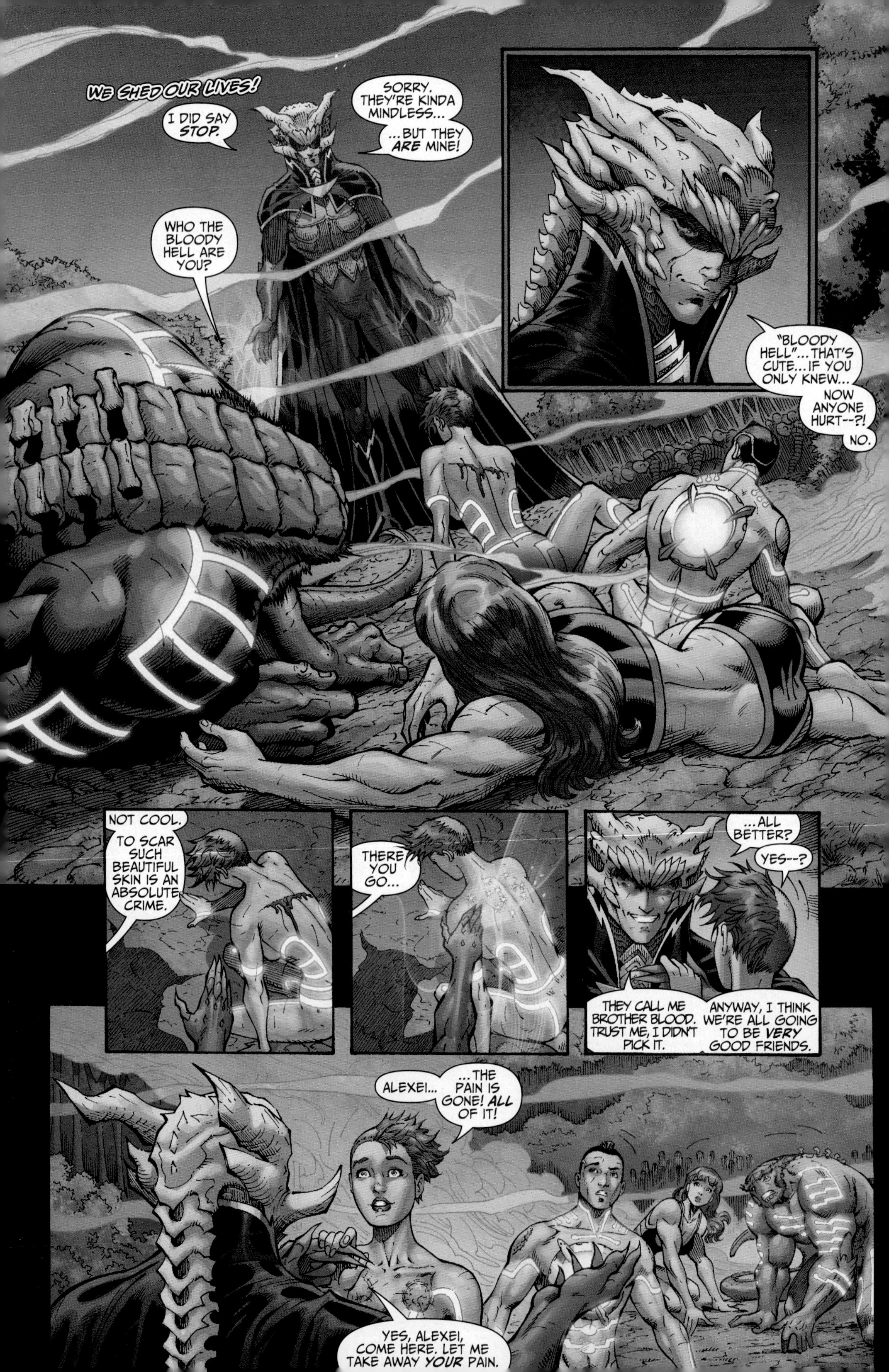
WE SHED OUR LIVES!
I DID SAY STOP.
SORRY. THEY'RE KINDA MINDLESS...
...BUT THEY ARE MINE!
WHO THE BLOODY HELL ARE YOU?
"BLOODY HELL"... THAT'S CUTE... IF YOU ONLY KNEW...
NOW ANYONE HURT--?!
NO.
NOT COOL.
TO SCAR SUCH BEAUTIFUL SKIN IS AN ABSOLUTE CRIME.
THERE YOU GO...
...ALL BETTER?
YES--?
THEY CALL ME BROTHER BLOOD. TRUST ME, I DIDN'T PICK IT.
ANYWAY, I THINK WE'RE ALL GOING TO BE VERY GOOD FRIENDS.
ALEXEI...
...THE PAIN IS GONE! ALL OF IT!
YES, ALEXEI, COME HERE. LET ME TAKE AWAY YOUR PAIN.

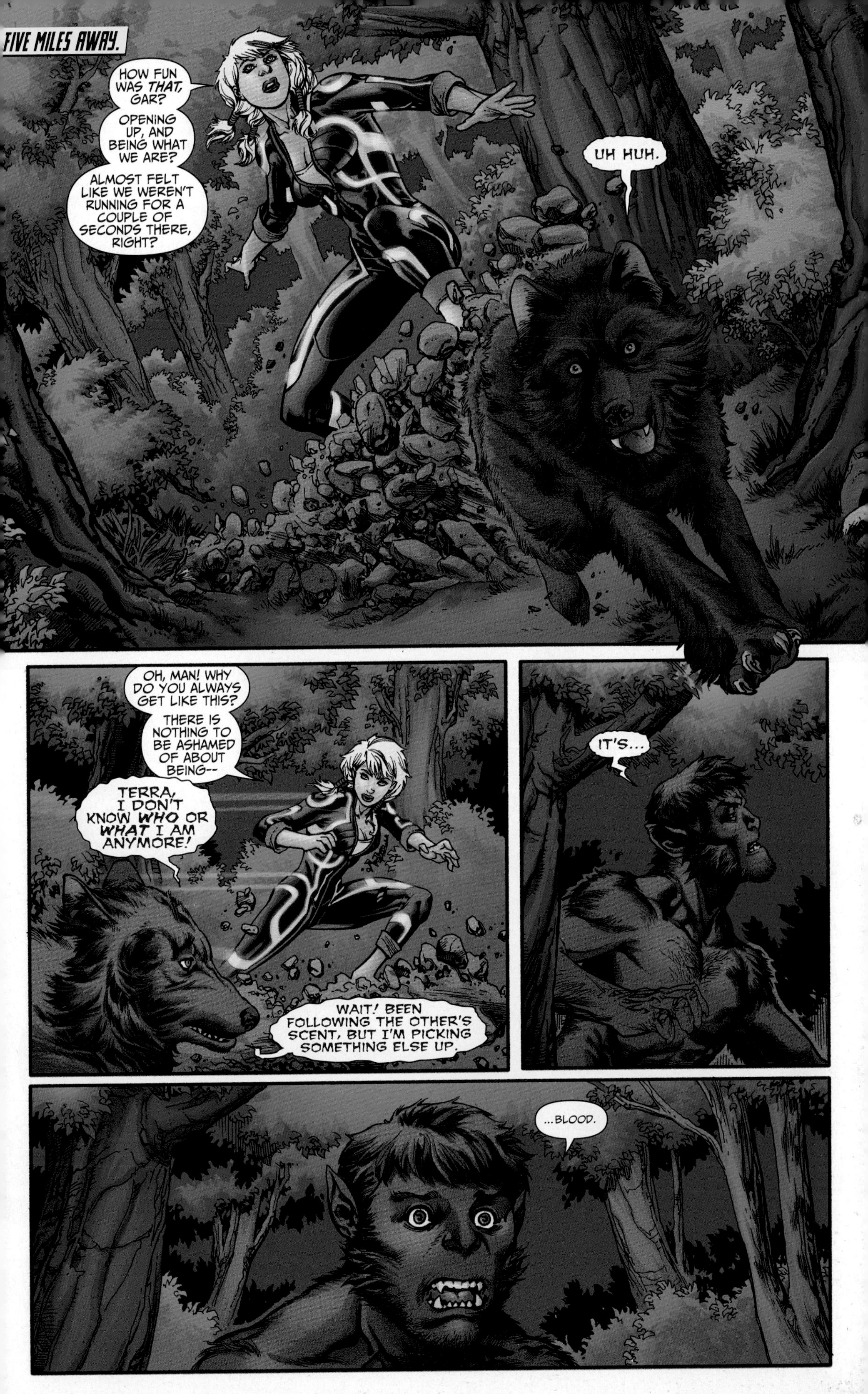
FIVE MILES AWAY.
HOW FUN WAS THAT, GAR?
OPENING UP, AND BEING WHAT WE ARE?
ALMOST FELT LIKE WE WEREN'T RUNNING FOR A COUPLE OF SECONDS THERE, RIGHT?
UH HUH.
OH, MAN! WHY DO YOU ALWAYS GET LIKE THIS?
THERE IS NOTHING TO BE ASHAMED OF ABOUT BEING--
TERRA, I DON'T KNOW WHO OR WHAT I AM ANYMORE!
WAIT! BEEN FOLLOWING THE OTHER'S SCENT, BUT I'M PICKING SOMETHING ELSE UP.
IT'S...
...BLOOD.

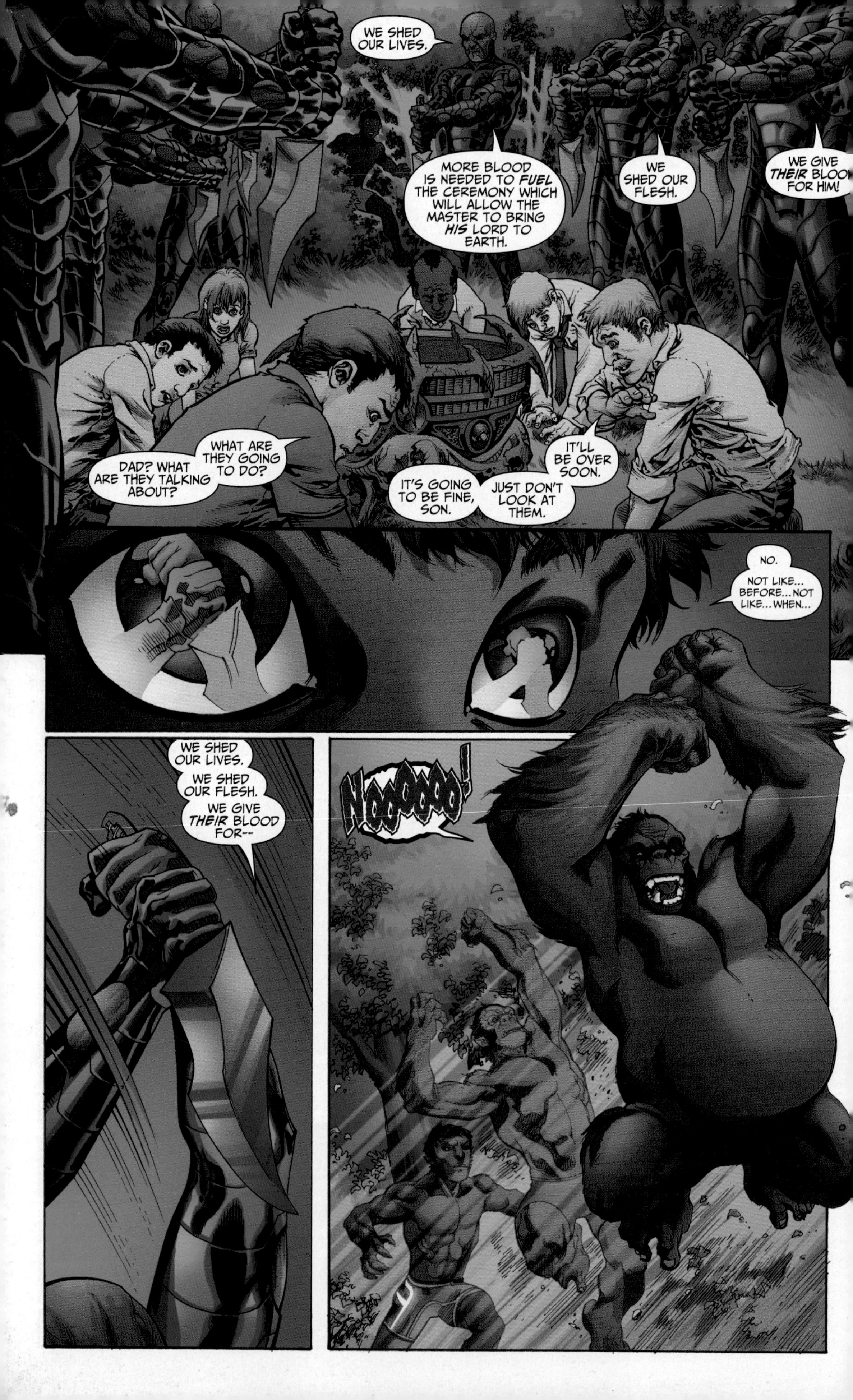
WE SHED OUR LIVES.
MORE BLOOD IS NEEDED TO *FUEL* THE CEREMONY WHICH WILL ALLOW THE MASTER TO BRING *HIS* LORD TO EARTH.
WE SHED OUR FLESH.
WE GIVE *THEIR* BLOO FOR HIM!
DAD? WHAT ARE THEY TALKING ABOUT?
WHAT ARE THEY GOING TO DO?
IT'S GOING TO BE FINE, SON.
JUST DON'T LOOK AT THEM.
IT'LL BE OVER SOON.
NO.
NOT LIKE... BEFORE...NOT LIKE...WHEN...
WE SHED OUR LIVES.
WE SHED OUR FLESH.
WE GIVE *THEIR* BLOOD FOR--
NOOOOOO!

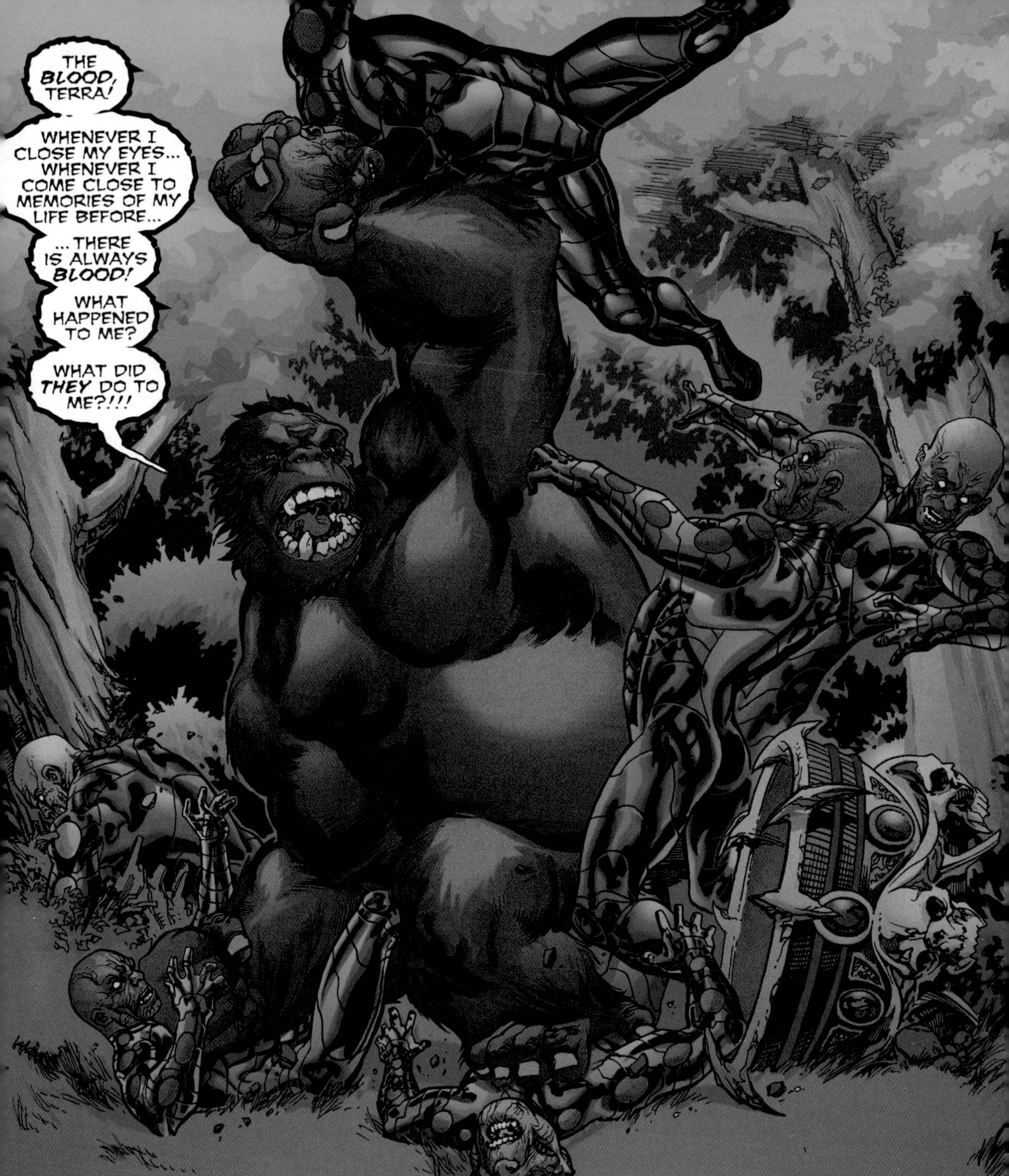
THE BLOOD, TERRA!
WHENEVER I CLOSE MY EYES... WHENEVER I COME CLOSE TO MEMORIES OF MY LIFE BEFORE...
...THERE IS ALWAYS BLOOD!
WHAT HAPPENED TO ME?
WHAT DID THEY DO TO ME?!!!

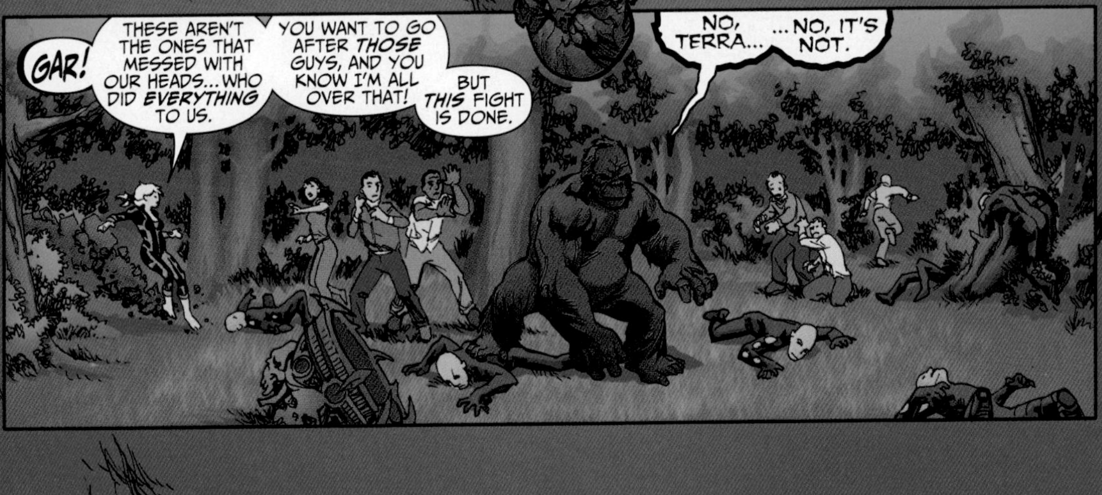
GAR!
THESE AREN'T THE ONES THAT MESSED WITH OUR HEADS...WHO DID EVERYTHING TO US.
YOU WANT TO GO AFTER THOSE GUYS, AND YOU KNOW I'M ALL OVER THAT!
BUT THIS FIGHT IS DONE.
NO, TERRA...
...NO, IT'S NOT.

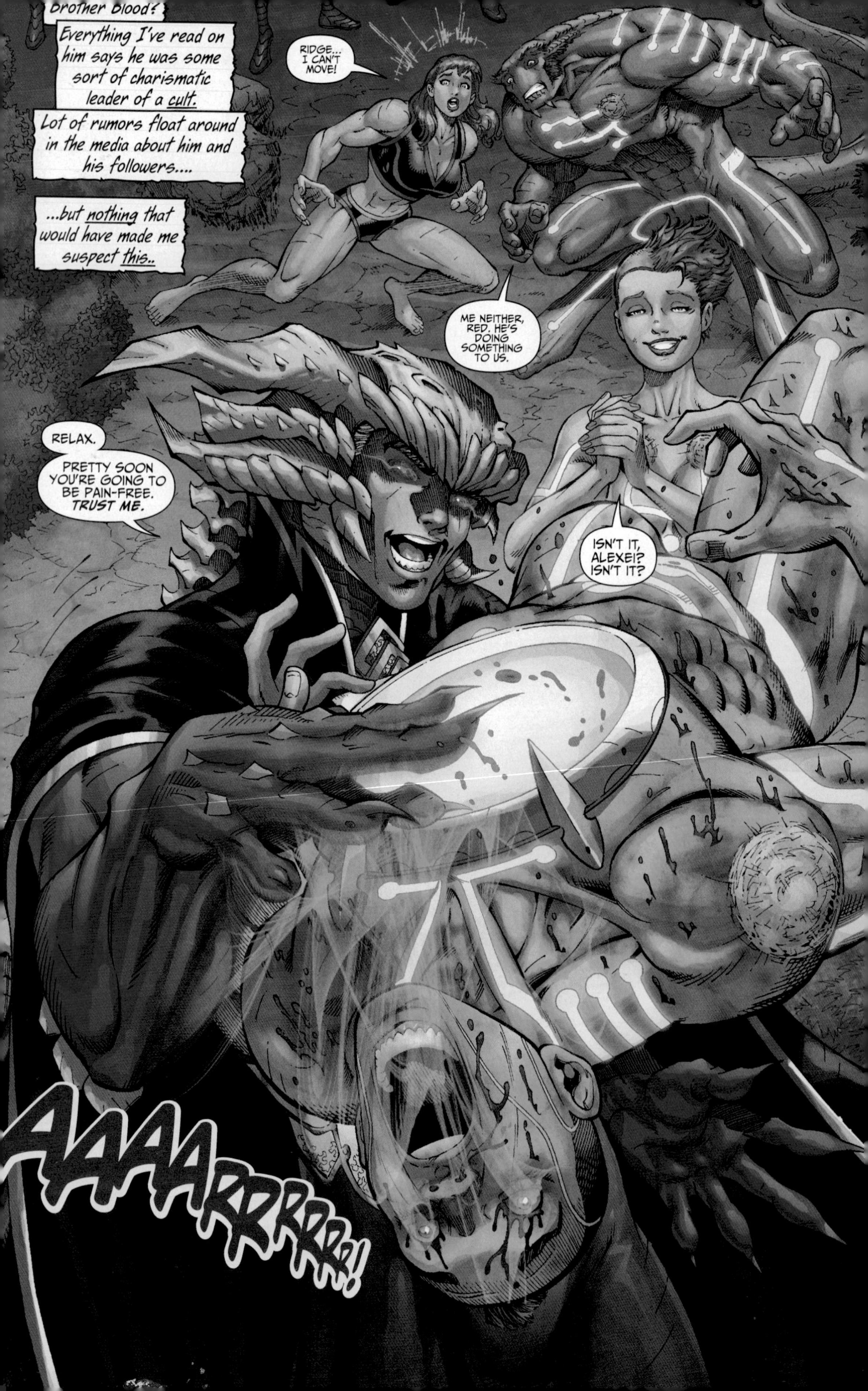
Brother Blood?
Everything I've read on him says he was some sort of charismatic leader of a cult.
Lot of rumors float around in the media about him and his followers....
...but nothing that would have made me suspect this..
RIDGE... I CAN'T MOVE!
ME NEITHER, RED. HE'S DOING SOMETHING TO US.
RELAX.
PRETTY SOON YOU'RE GOING TO BE PAIN-FREE. TRUST ME.
ISN'T IT, ALEXEI? ISN'T IT?
AAAARRRRR!!

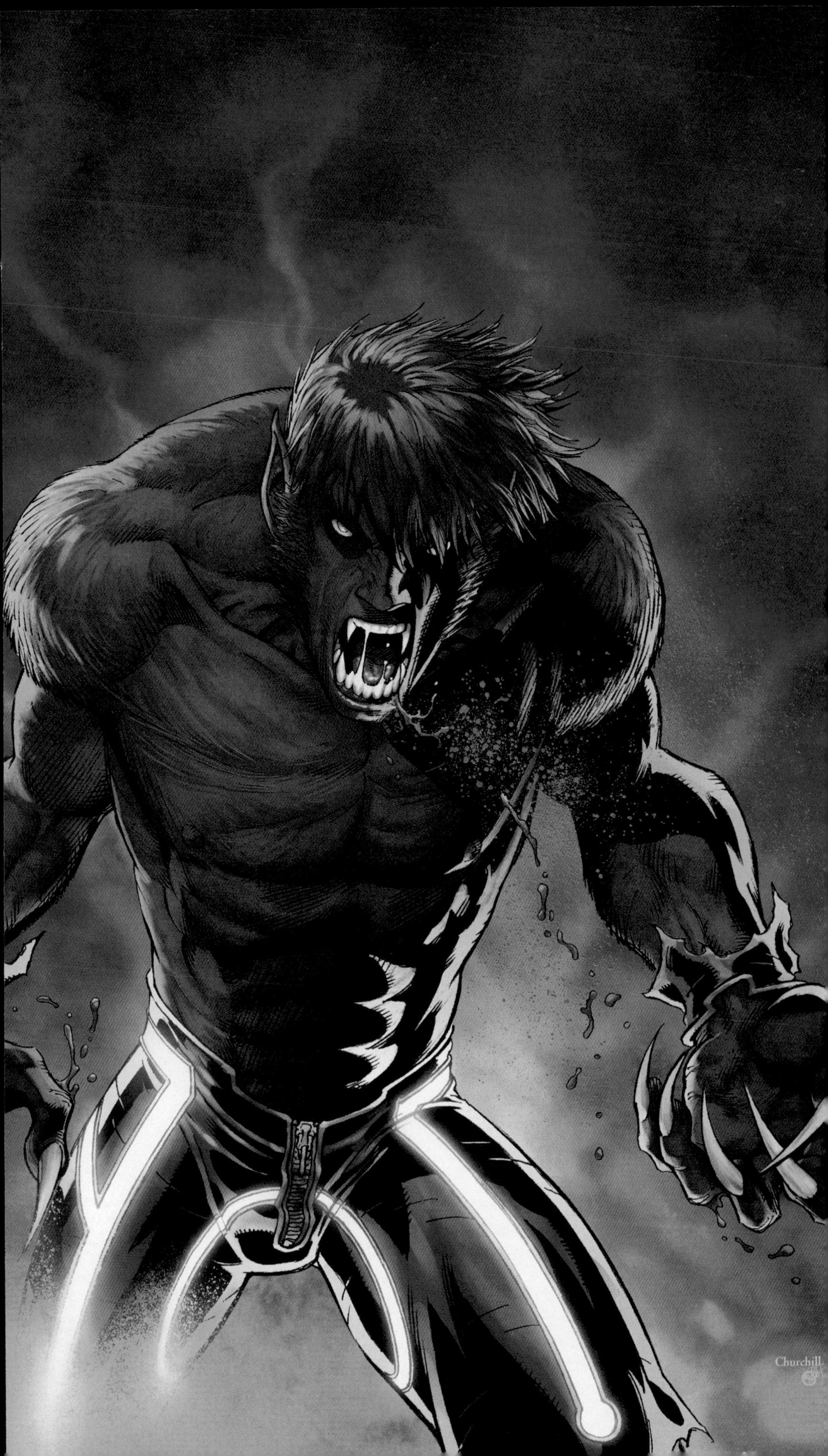
Churchill

UNCHAINED

HOWARD MACKIE
writer

DANIEL SAMPERE & STEFANO MARTINO
pencillers

NORM RAPMUND
inker

cover art by
IAN CHURCHILL & PETER STEIGERWALD

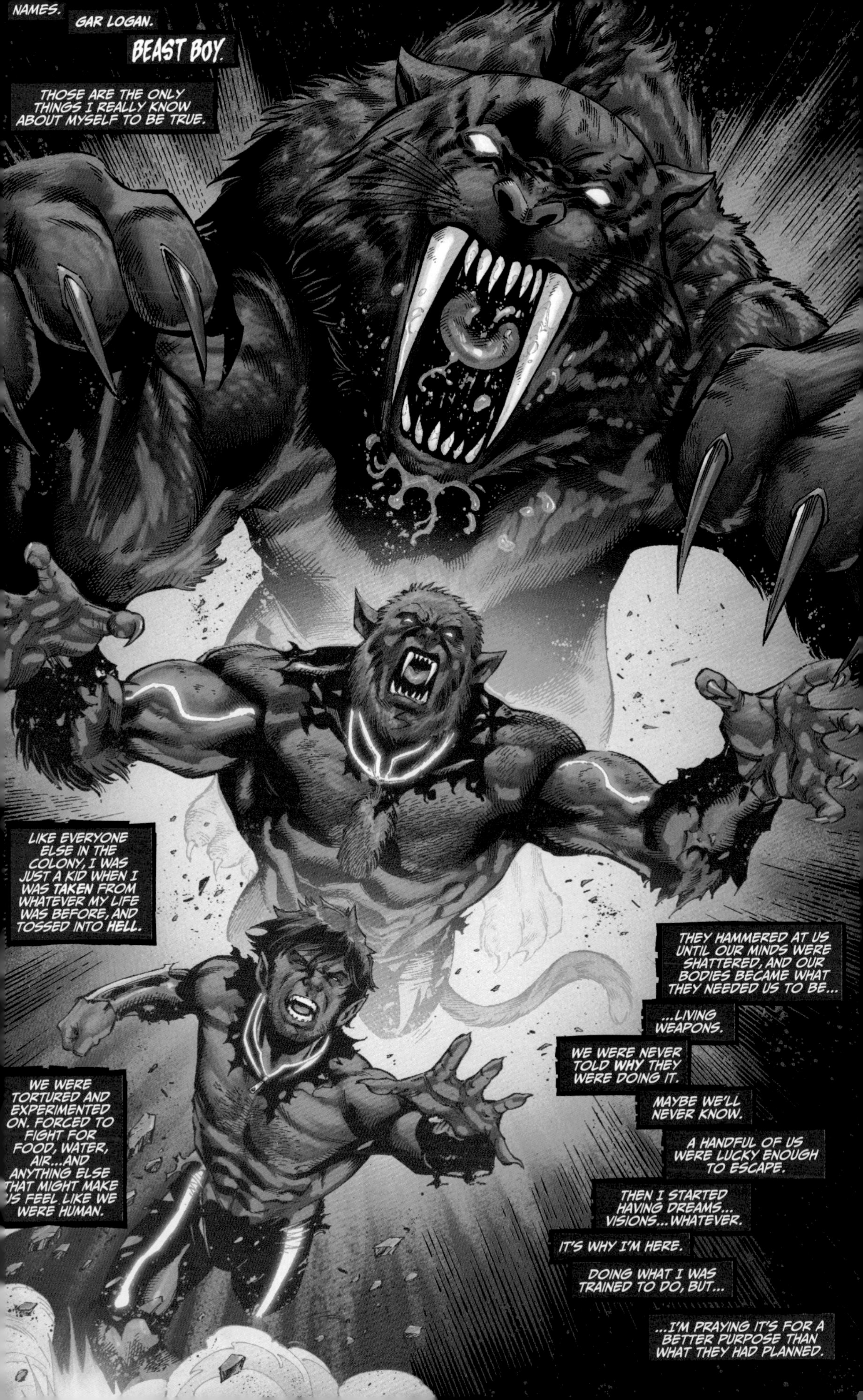
NAMES.
GAR LOGAN.
BEAST BOY.
THOSE ARE THE ONLY THINGS I REALLY KNOW ABOUT MYSELF TO BE TRUE.
LIKE EVERYONE ELSE IN THE COLONY, I WAS JUST A KID WHEN I WAS TAKEN FROM WHATEVER MY LIFE WAS BEFORE, AND TOSSED INTO HELL.
THEY HAMMERED AT US UNTIL OUR MINDS WERE SHATTERED, AND OUR BODIES BECAME WHAT THEY NEEDED US TO BE...
...LIVING WEAPONS.
WE WERE TORTURED AND EXPERIMENTED ON. FORCED TO FIGHT FOR FOOD, WATER, AIR...AND ANYTHING ELSE THAT MIGHT MAKE US FEEL LIKE WE WERE HUMAN.
WE WERE NEVER TOLD WHY THEY WERE DOING IT.
MAYBE WE'LL NEVER KNOW.
A HANDFUL OF US WERE LUCKY ENOUGH TO ESCAPE.
THEN I STARTED HAVING DREAMS... VISIONS...WHATEVER.
IT'S WHY I'M HERE.
DOING WHAT I WAS TRAINED TO DO, BUT...
...I'M PRAYING IT'S FOR A BETTER PURPOSE THAN WHAT THEY HAD PLANNED.

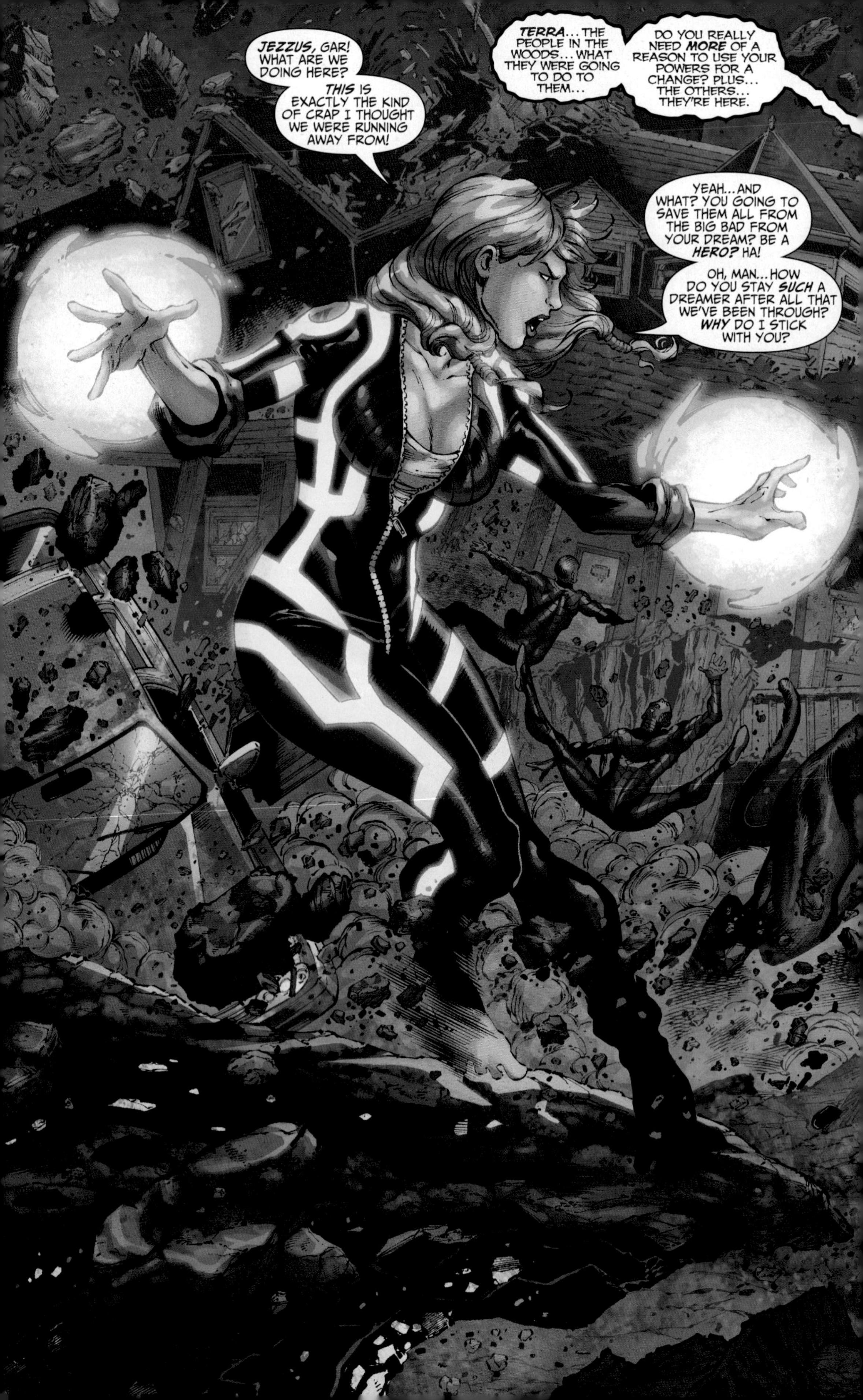
JEZZUS, GAR! WHAT ARE WE DOING HERE?
THIS IS EXACTLY THE KIND OF CRAP I THOUGHT WE WERE RUNNING AWAY FROM!
TERRA... THE PEOPLE IN THE WOODS... WHAT THEY WERE GOING TO DO TO THEM...
DO YOU REALLY NEED MORE OF A REASON TO USE YOUR POWERS FOR A CHANGE? PLUS... THE OTHERS... THEY'RE HERE.
YEAH...AND WHAT? YOU GOING TO SAVE THEM ALL FROM THE BIG BAD FROM YOUR DREAM? BE A HERO? HA!
OH, MAN...HOW DO YOU STAY SUCH A DREAMER AFTER ALL THAT WE'VE BEEN THROUGH? WHY DO I STICK WITH YOU?

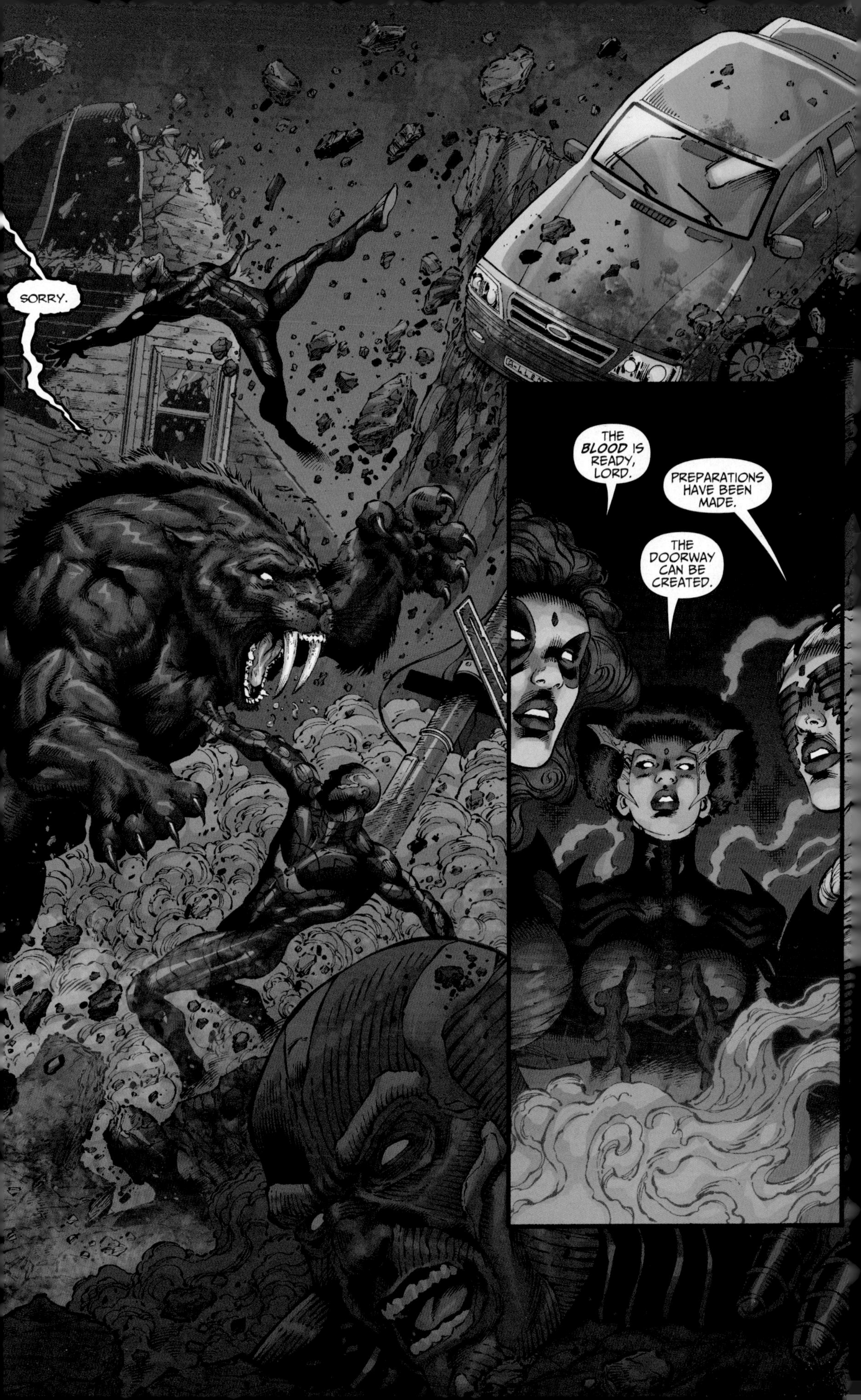
SORRY.
THE BLOOD IS READY, LORD.
PREPARATIONS HAVE BEEN MADE.
THE DOORWAY CAN BE CREATED.

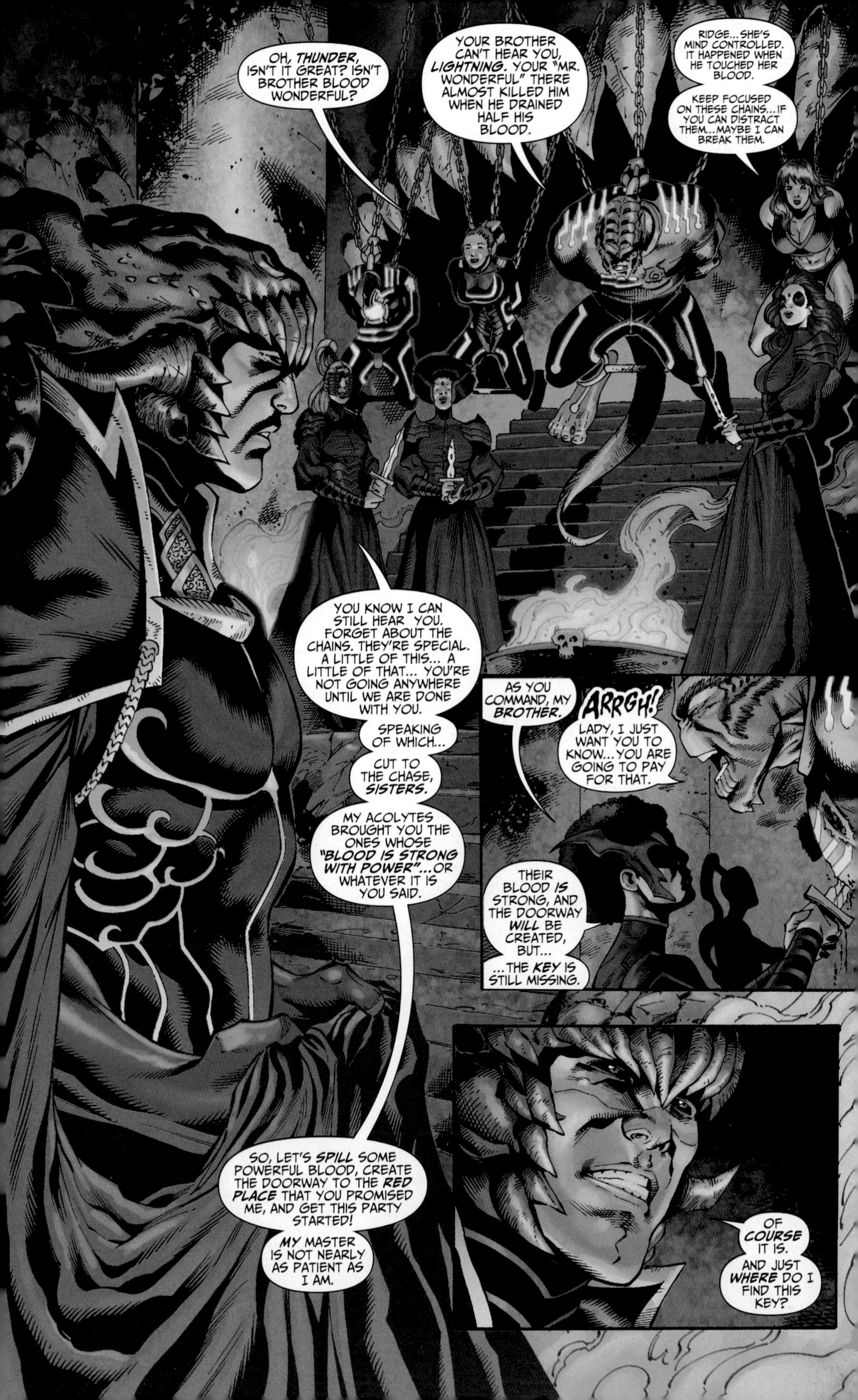
OH, THUNDER, ISN'T IT GREAT? ISN'T BROTHER BLOOD WONDERFUL?
YOUR BROTHER CAN'T HEAR YOU, LIGHTNING. YOUR "MR. WONDERFUL" THERE ALMOST KILLED HIM WHEN HE DRAINED HALF HIS BLOOD.
RIDGE...SHE'S MIND CONTROLLED. IT HAPPENED WHEN HE TOUCHED HER BLOOD.
KEEP FOCUSED ON THESE CHAINS...IF YOU CAN DISTRACT THEM...MAYBE I CAN BREAK THEM.
YOU KNOW I CAN STILL HEAR YOU. FORGET ABOUT THE CHAINS. THEY'RE SPECIAL. A LITTLE OF THIS... A LITTLE OF THAT... YOU'RE NOT GOING ANYWHERE UNTIL WE ARE DONE WITH YOU.
SPEAKING OF WHICH...
CUT TO THE CHASE, SISTERS.
MY ACOLYTES BROUGHT YOU THE ONES WHOSE "BLOOD IS STRONG WITH POWER"...OR WHATEVER IT IS YOU SAID.
SO, LET'S SPILL SOME POWERFUL BLOOD, CREATE THE DOORWAY TO THE RED PLACE THAT YOU PROMISED ME, AND GET THIS PARTY STARTED!
MY MASTER IS NOT NEARLY AS PATIENT AS I AM.
AS YOU COMMAND, MY BROTHER.
ARRGH!
LADY, I JUST WANT YOU TO KNOW...YOU ARE GOING TO PAY FOR THAT.
THEIR BLOOD IS STRONG, AND THE DOORWAY WILL BE CREATED, BUT...
...THE KEY IS STILL MISSING.
OF COURSE IT IS. AND JUST WHERE DO I FIND THIS KEY?

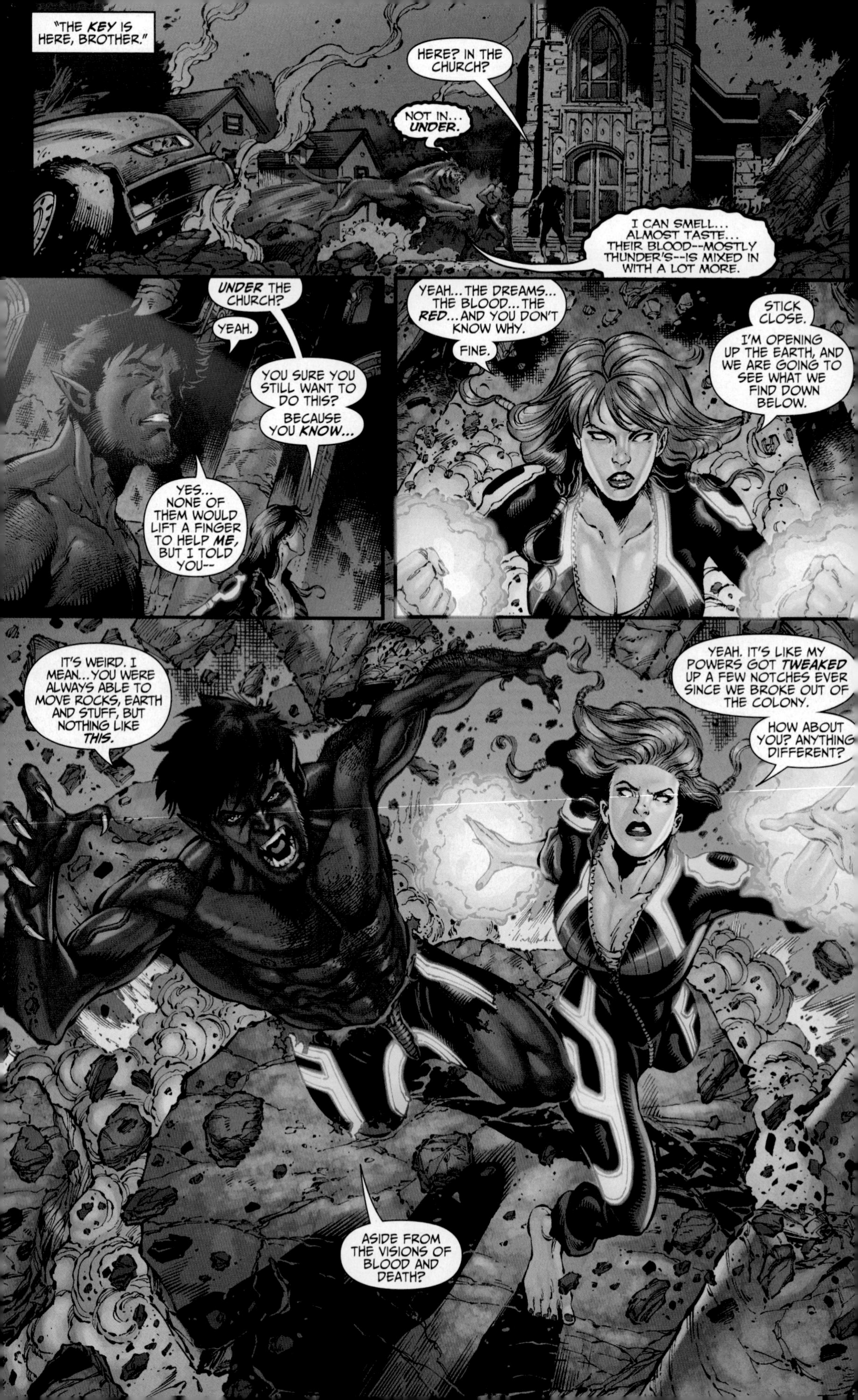
"THE KEY IS HERE, BROTHER."
HERE? IN THE CHURCH?
NOT IN... UNDER.
I CAN SMELL... ALMOST TASTE... THEIR BLOOD--MOSTLY THUNDER'S--IS MIXED IN WITH A LOT MORE.
UNDER THE CHURCH?
YEAH.
YOU SURE YOU STILL WANT TO DO THIS?
BECAUSE YOU KNOW...
YES... NONE OF THEM WOULD LIFT A FINGER TO HELP ME, BUT I TOLD YOU--
YEAH... THE DREAMS... THE BLOOD... THE RED... AND YOU DON'T KNOW WHY.
FINE.
STICK CLOSE.
I'M OPENING UP THE EARTH, AND WE ARE GOING TO SEE WHAT WE FIND DOWN BELOW.
IT'S WEIRD. I MEAN... YOU WERE ALWAYS ABLE TO MOVE ROCKS, EARTH AND STUFF, BUT NOTHING LIKE THIS.
YEAH. IT'S LIKE MY POWERS GOT TWEAKED UP A FEW NOTCHES EVER SINCE WE BROKE OUT OF THE COLONY.
HOW ABOUT YOU? ANYTHING DIFFERENT?
ASIDE FROM THE VISIONS OF BLOOD AND DEATH?

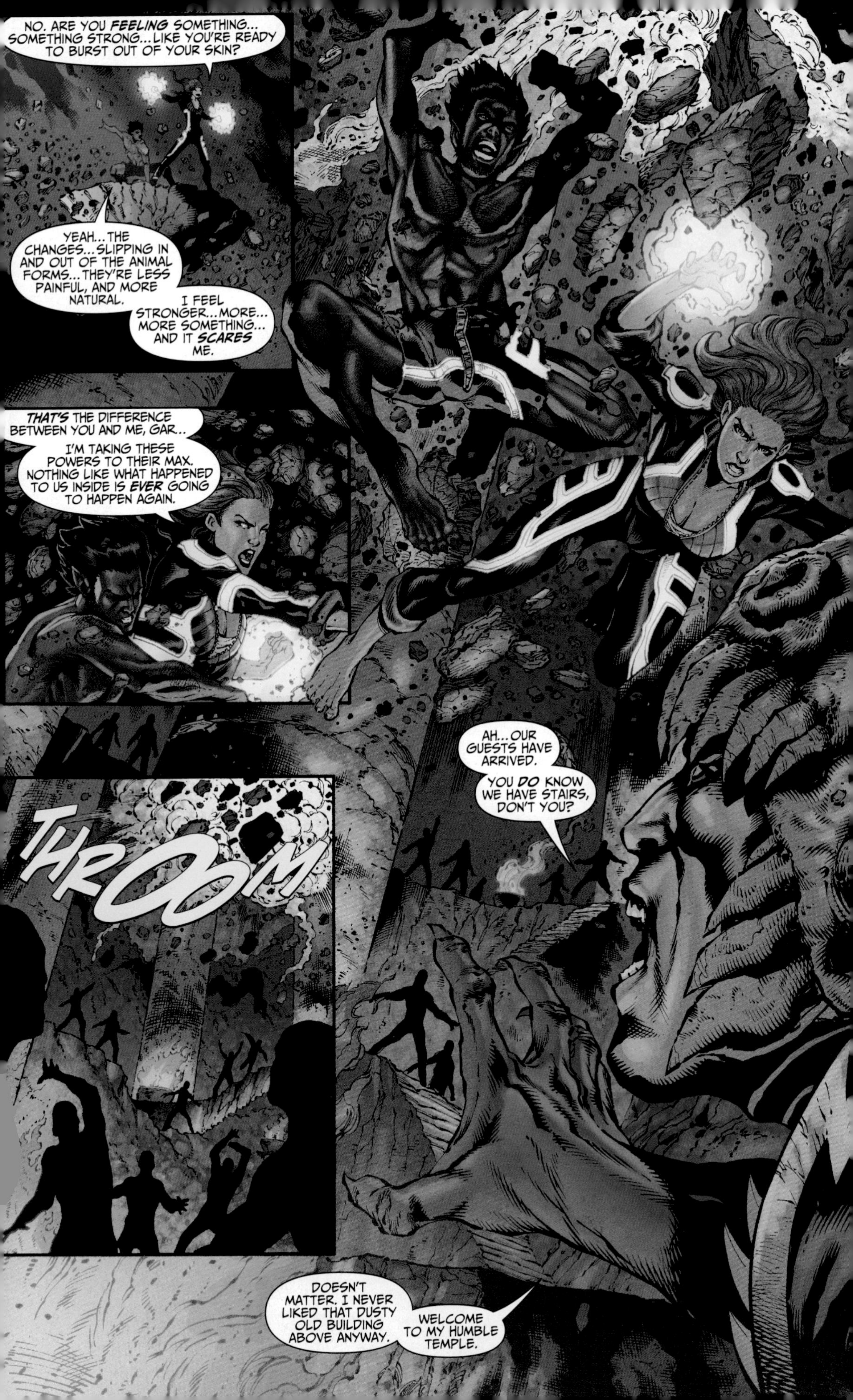
NO. ARE YOU FEELING SOMETHING... SOMETHING STRONG...LIKE YOU'RE READY TO BURST OUT OF YOUR SKIN?
YEAH...THE CHANGES...SLIPPING IN AND OUT OF THE ANIMAL FORMS...THEY'RE LESS PAINFUL, AND MORE NATURAL.
I FEEL STRONGER...MORE... MORE SOMETHING... AND IT SCARES ME.
THAT'S THE DIFFERENCE BETWEEN YOU AND ME, GAR...
I'M TAKING THESE POWERS TO THEIR MAX. NOTHING LIKE WHAT HAPPENED TO US INSIDE IS EVER GOING TO HAPPEN AGAIN.
THROOM
AH...OUR GUESTS HAVE ARRIVED.
YOU DO KNOW WE HAVE STAIRS, DON'T YOU?
DOESN'T MATTER. I NEVER LIKED THAT DUSTY OLD BUILDING ABOVE ANYWAY.
WELCOME TO MY HUMBLE TEMPLE.

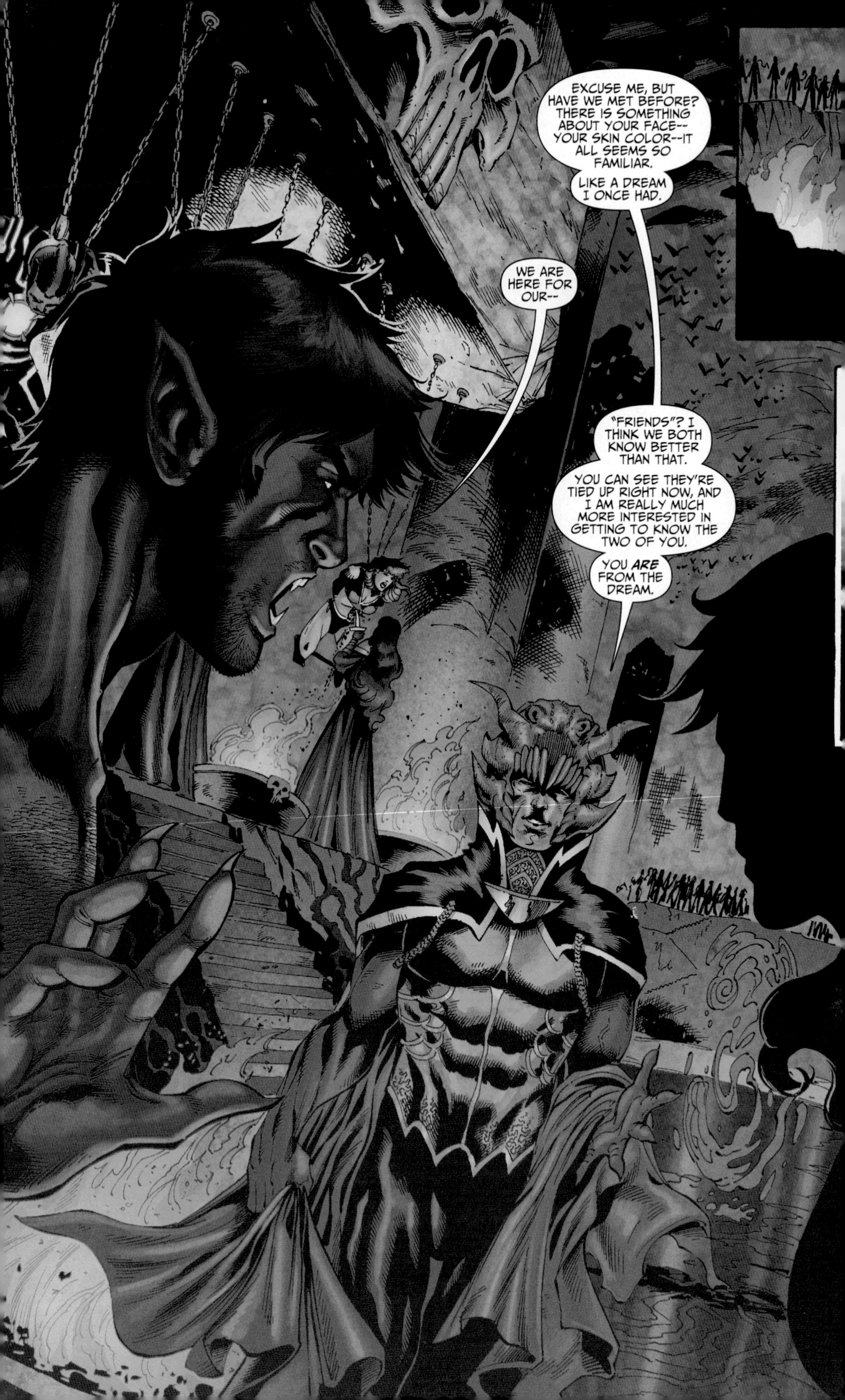
EXCUSE ME, BUT HAVE WE MET BEFORE? THERE IS SOMETHING ABOUT YOUR FACE-- YOUR SKIN COLOR--IT ALL SEEMS SO FAMILIAR.
LIKE A DREAM I ONCE HAD.
WE ARE HERE FOR OUR--
"FRIENDS"? I THINK WE BOTH KNOW BETTER THAN THAT.
YOU CAN SEE THEY'RE TIED UP RIGHT NOW, AND I AM REALLY MUCH MORE INTERESTED IN GETTING TO KNOW THE TWO OF YOU.
YOU *ARE* FROM THE DREAM.

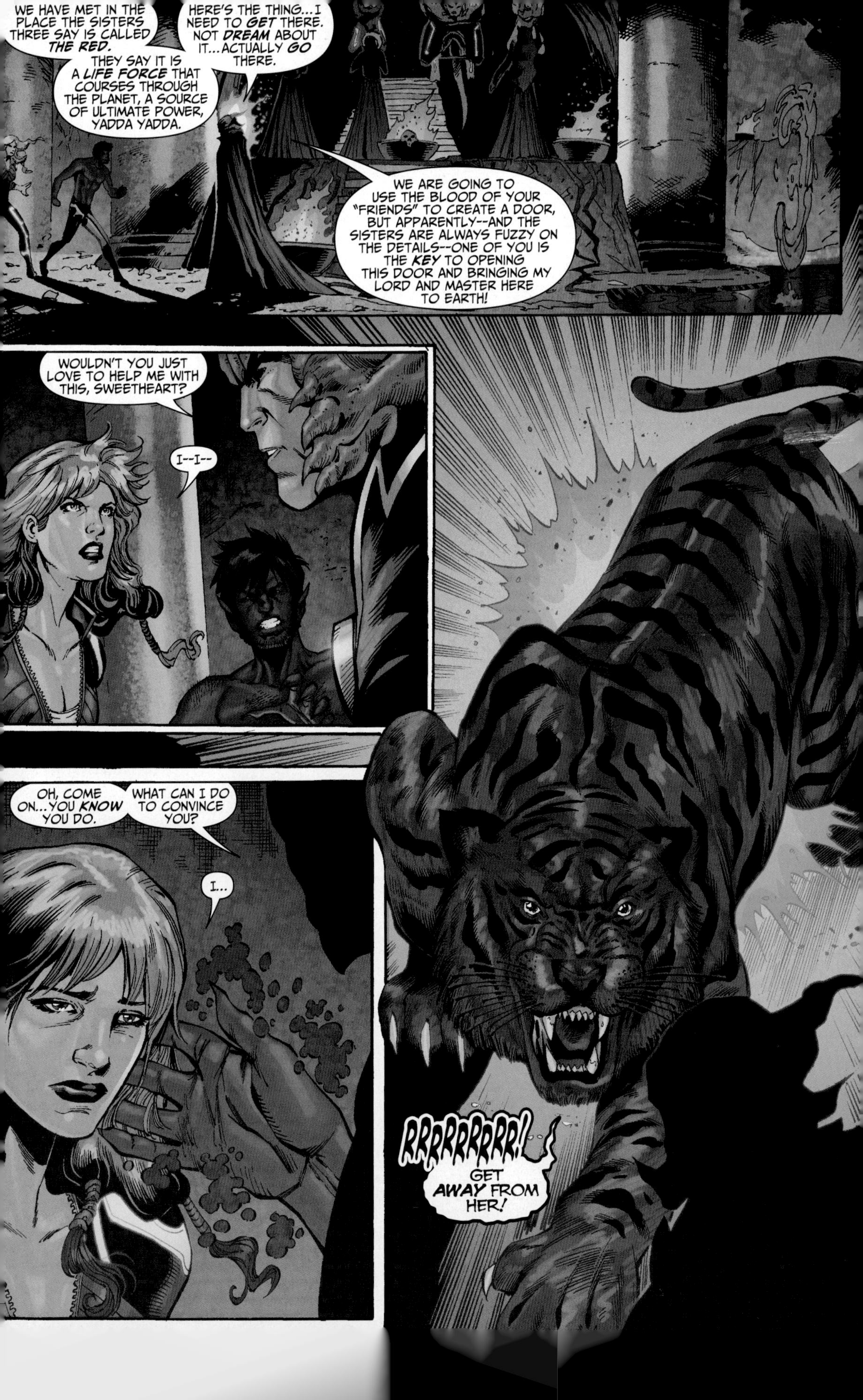
WE HAVE MET IN THE PLACE THE SISTERS THREE SAY IS CALLED THE RED.
THEY SAY IT IS A LIFE FORCE THAT COURSES THROUGH THE PLANET, A SOURCE OF ULTIMATE POWER, YADDA YADDA.
HERE'S THE THING... I NEED TO GET THERE. NOT DREAM ABOUT IT... ACTUALLY GO THERE.
WE ARE GOING TO USE THE BLOOD OF YOUR "FRIENDS" TO CREATE A DOOR, BUT APPARENTLY--AND THE SISTERS ARE ALWAYS FUZZY ON THE DETAILS--ONE OF YOU IS THE KEY TO OPENING THIS DOOR AND BRINGING MY LORD AND MASTER HERE TO EARTH!
WOULDN'T YOU JUST LOVE TO HELP ME WITH THIS, SWEETHEART?
I--I--
OH, COME ON... YOU KNOW YOU DO.
WHAT CAN I DO TO CONVINCE YOU?
I...
RRRRRRRRR!
GET AWAY FROM HER!

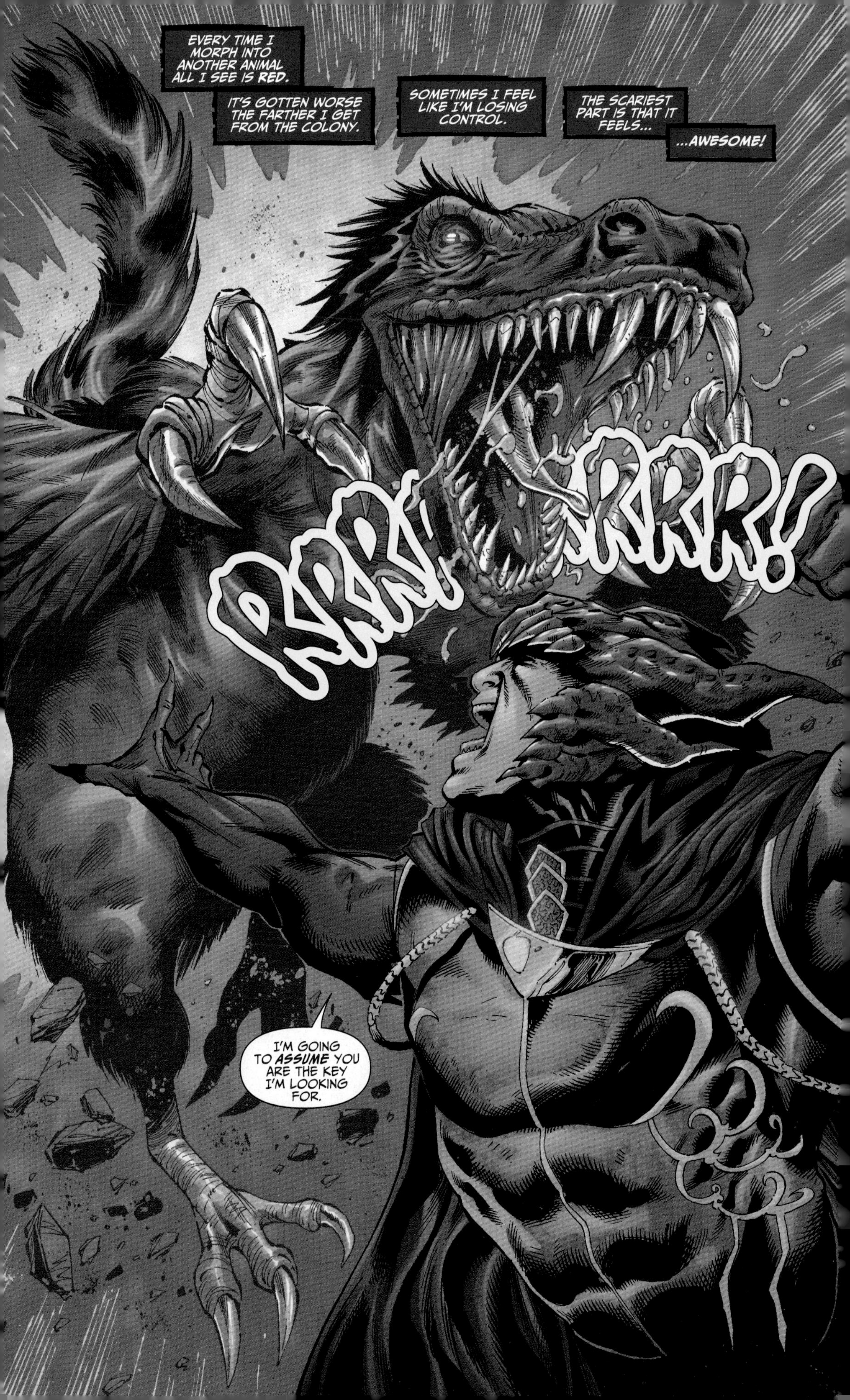
EVERY TIME I MORPH INTO ANOTHER ANIMAL ALL I SEE IS RED.
IT'S GOTTEN WORSE THE FARTHER I GET FROM THE COLONY.
SOMETIMES I FEEL LIKE I'M LOSING CONTROL.
THE SCARIEST PART IS THAT IT FEELS...
...AWESOME!
I'M GOING TO ASSUME YOU ARE THE KEY I'M LOOKING FOR.

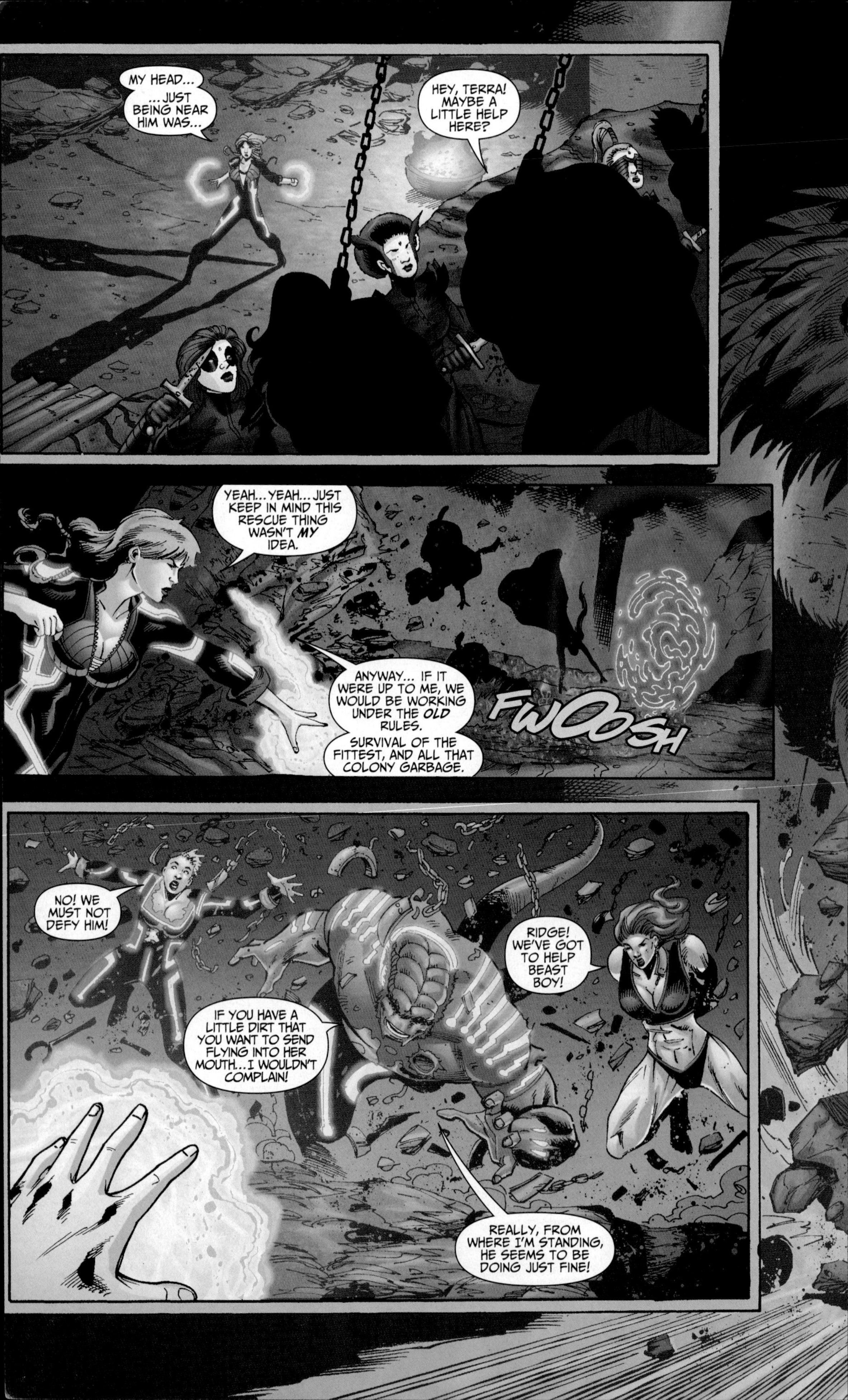

MY HEAD... ...JUST BEING NEAR HIM WAS...
HEY, TERRA! MAYBE A LITTLE HELP HERE?
YEAH...YEAH...JUST KEEP IN MIND THIS RESCUE THING WASN'T MY IDEA.
ANYWAY... IF IT WERE UP TO ME, WE WOULD BE WORKING UNDER THE OLD RULES.
SURVIVAL OF THE FITTEST, AND ALL THAT COLONY GARBAGE.
FWOOSH
NO! WE MUST NOT DEFY HIM!
RIDGE! WE'VE GOT TO HELP BEAST BOY!
IF YOU HAVE A LITTLE DIRT THAT YOU WANT TO SEND FLYING INTO HER MOUTH...I WOULDN'T COMPLAIN!
REALLY, FROM WHERE I'M STANDING, HE SEEMS TO BE DOING JUST FINE!

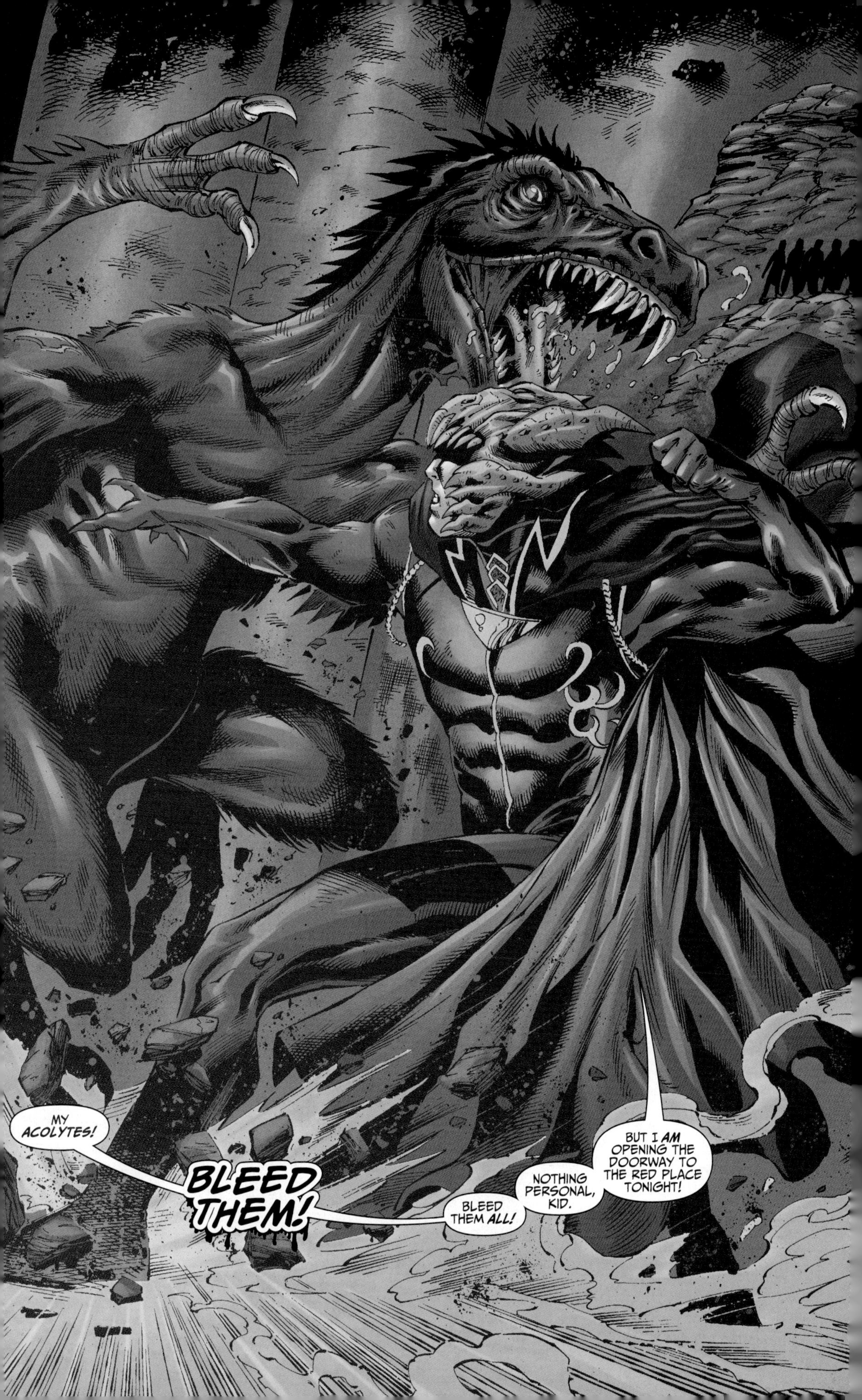
MY ACOLYTES!
BLEED THEM!
BLEED THEM ALL!
NOTHING PERSONAL, KID.
BUT I AM OPENING THE DOORWAY TO THE RED PLACE TONIGHT!

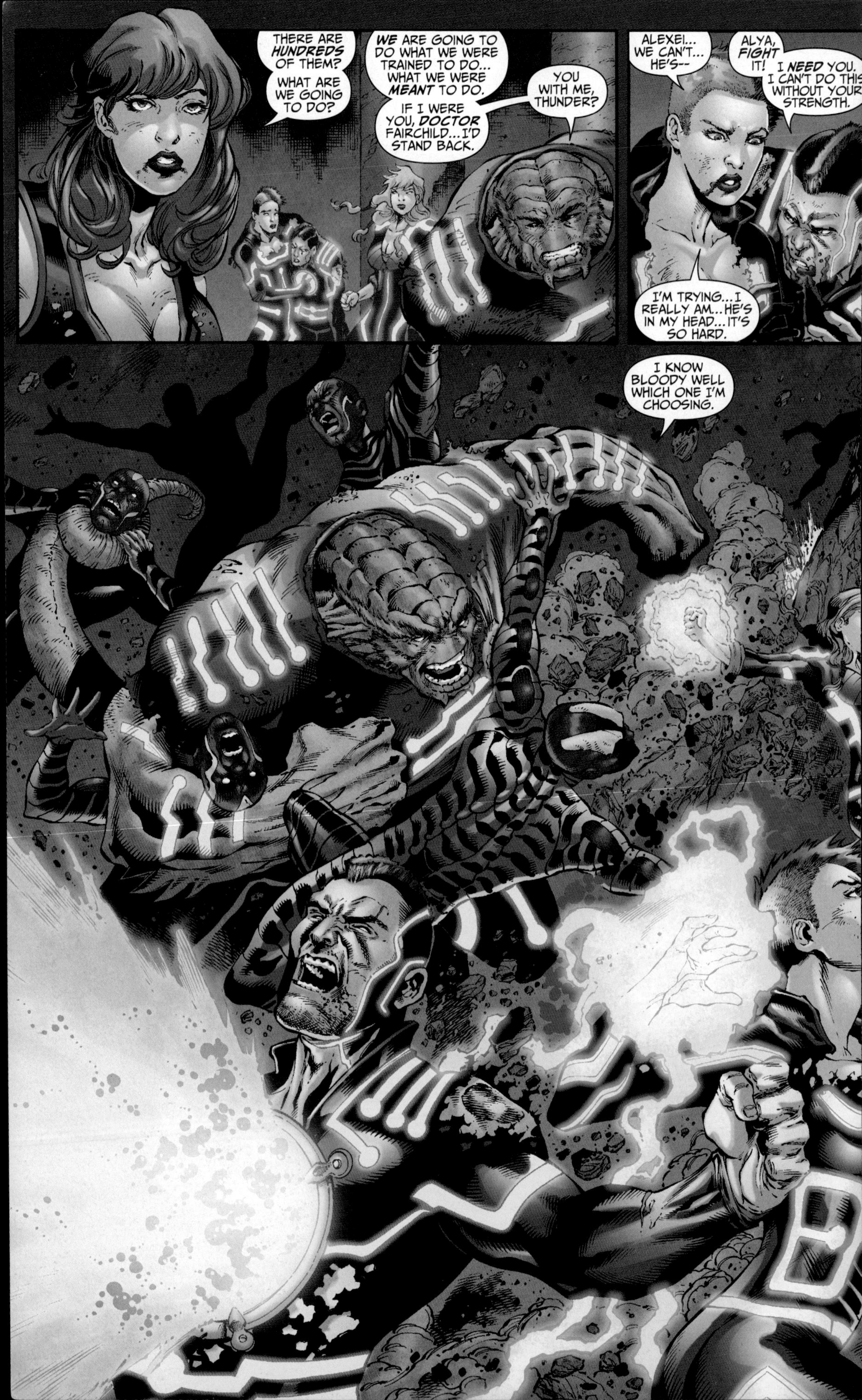
THERE ARE HUNDREDS OF THEM? WHAT ARE WE GOING TO DO?
WE ARE GOING TO DO WHAT WE WERE TRAINED TO DO... WHAT WE WERE MEANT TO DO.
IF I WERE YOU, DOCTOR FAIRCHILD...I'D STAND BACK.
YOU WITH ME, THUNDER?
ALEXEI... WE CAN'T... HE'S--
ALYA, FIGHT IT!
I NEED YOU. I CAN'T DO THIS WITHOUT YOUR STRENGTH.
I'M TRYING...I REALLY AM...HE'S IN MY HEAD...IT'S SO HARD.
I KNOW BLOODY WELL WHICH ONE I'M CHOOSING.

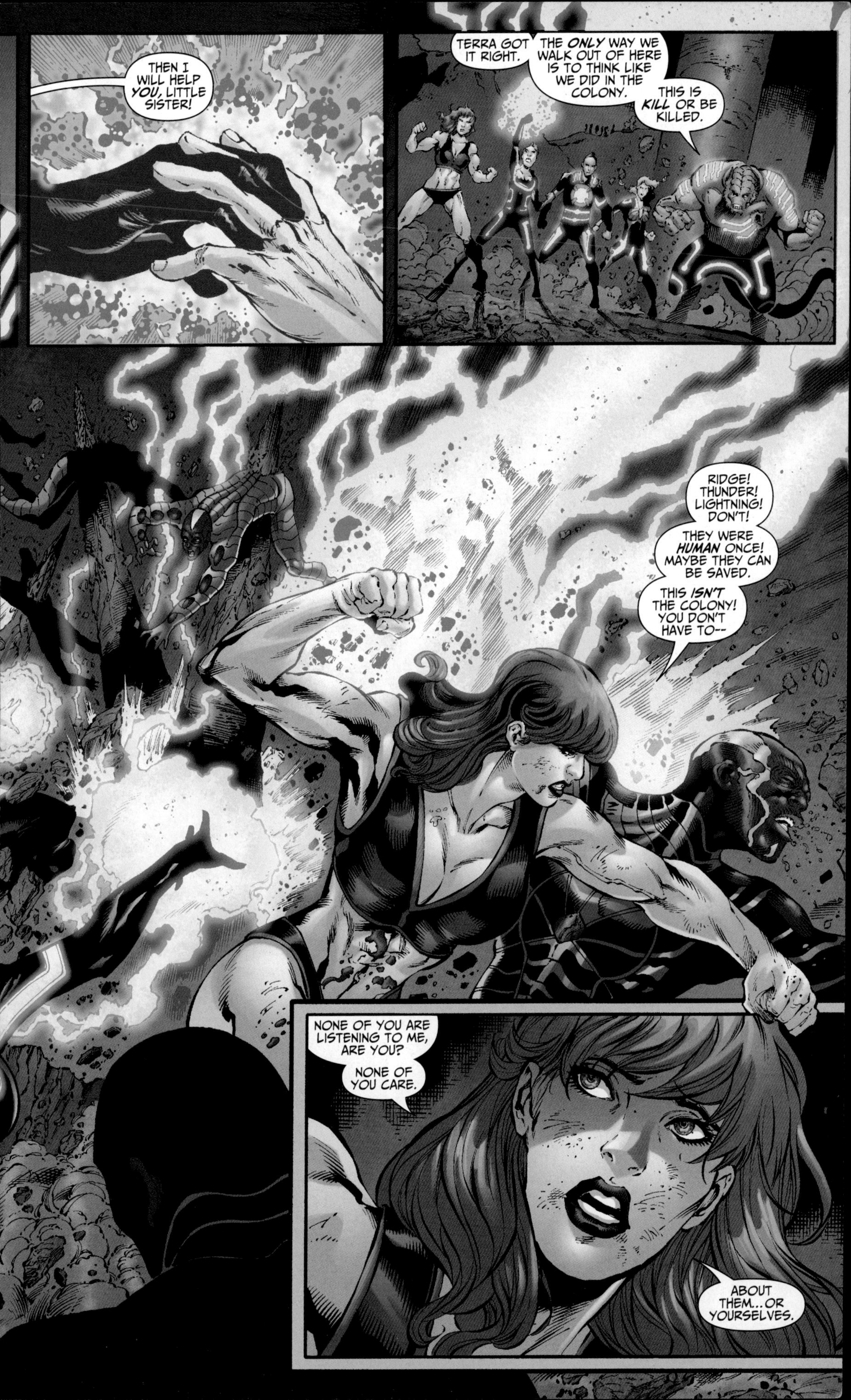
THEN I WILL HELP YOU, LITTLE SISTER!
TERRA GOT IT RIGHT.
THE ONLY WAY WE WALK OUT OF HERE IS TO THINK LIKE WE DID IN THE COLONY.
THIS IS KILL OR BE KILLED.
RIDGE! THUNDER! LIGHTNING! DON'T!
THEY WERE HUMAN ONCE! MAYBE THEY CAN BE SAVED.
THIS ISN'T THE COLONY! YOU DON'T HAVE TO--
NONE OF YOU ARE LISTENING TO ME, ARE YOU?
NONE OF YOU CARE.
ABOUT THEM...OR YOURSELVES.

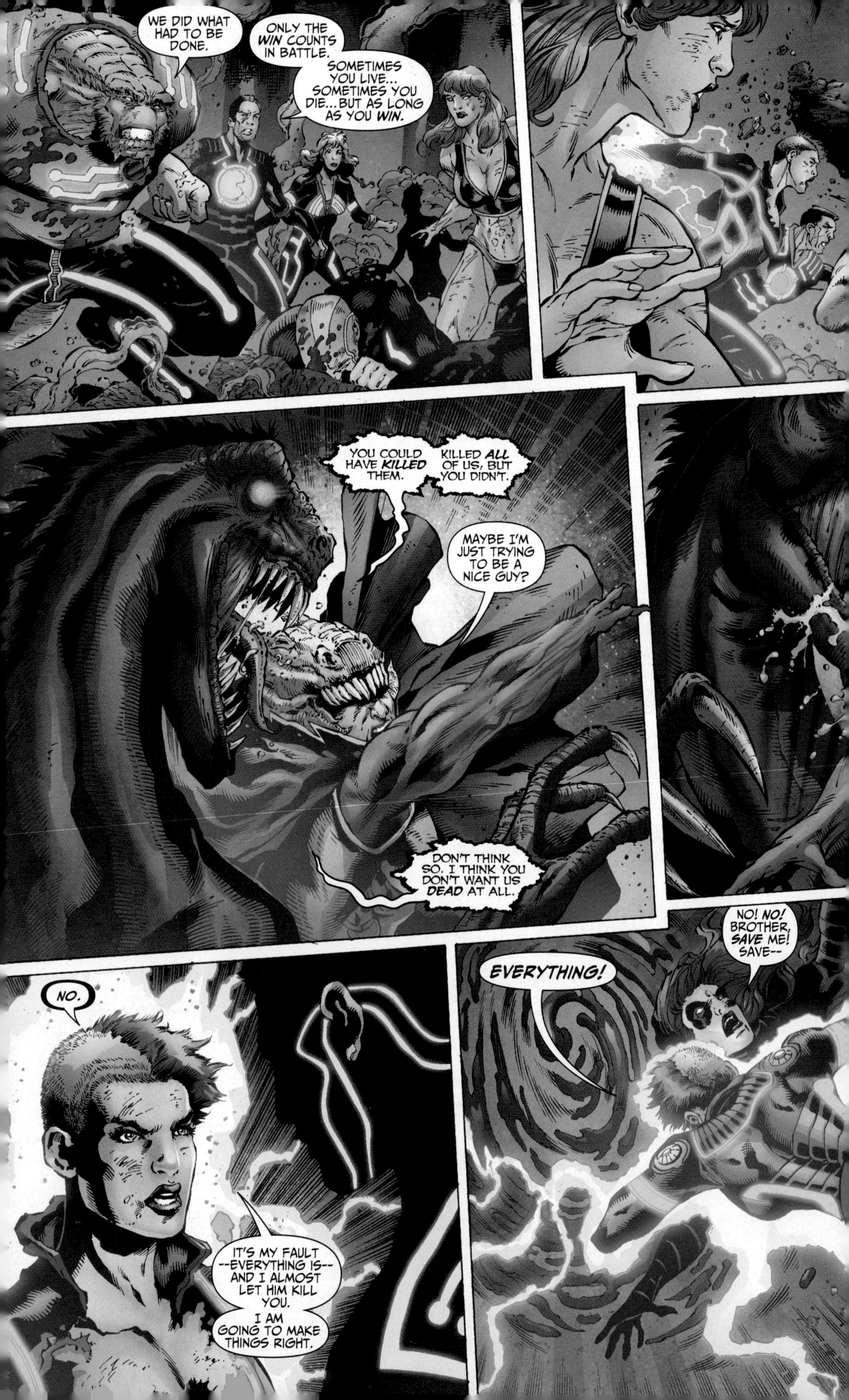
WE DID WHAT HAD TO BE DONE.
ONLY THE WIN COUNTS IN BATTLE.
SOMETIMES YOU LIVE... SOMETIMES YOU DIE...BUT AS LONG AS YOU WIN.
YOU COULD HAVE KILLED THEM.
KILLED ALL OF US, BUT YOU DIDN'T.
MAYBE I'M JUST TRYING TO BE A NICE GUY?
DON'T THINK SO. I THINK YOU DON'T WANT US DEAD AT ALL.
NO.
IT'S MY FAULT --EVERYTHING IS-- AND I ALMOST LET HIM KILL YOU.
I AM GOING TO MAKE THINGS RIGHT.
EVERYTHING!
NO! NO! BROTHER, SAVE ME! SAVE--

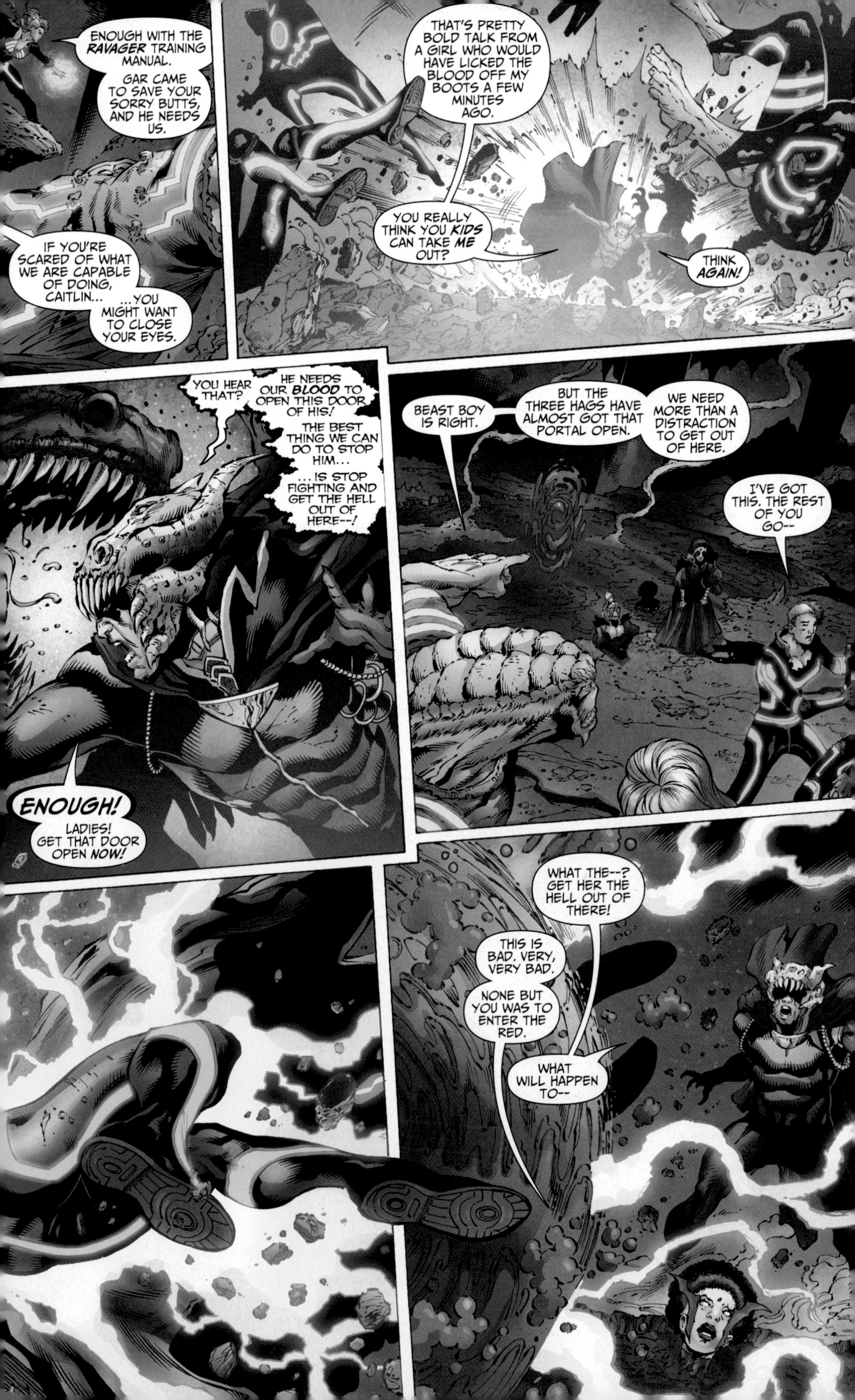
ENOUGH WITH THE RAVAGER TRAINING MANUAL.
GAR CAME TO SAVE YOUR SORRY BUTTS, AND HE NEEDS US.
IF YOU'RE SCARED OF WHAT WE ARE CAPABLE OF DOING, CAITLIN...
...YOU MIGHT WANT TO CLOSE YOUR EYES.
THAT'S PRETTY BOLD TALK FROM A GIRL WHO WOULD HAVE LICKED THE BLOOD OFF MY BOOTS A FEW MINUTES AGO.
YOU REALLY THINK YOU KIDS CAN TAKE ME OUT?
THINK AGAIN!
YOU HEAR THAT?
HE NEEDS OUR BLOOD TO OPEN THIS DOOR OF HIS!
THE BEST THING WE CAN DO TO STOP HIM...
...IS STOP FIGHTING AND GET THE HELL OUT OF HERE--!
ENOUGH!
LADIES! GET THAT DOOR OPEN NOW!
BEAST BOY IS RIGHT.
BUT THE THREE HAGS HAVE ALMOST GOT THAT PORTAL OPEN.
WE NEED MORE THAN A DISTRACTION TO GET OUT OF HERE.
I'VE GOT THIS. THE REST OF YOU GO--
WHAT THE--? GET HER THE HELL OUT OF THERE!
THIS IS BAD. VERY, VERY BAD.
NONE BUT YOU WAS TO ENTER THE RED.
WHAT WILL HAPPEN TO--

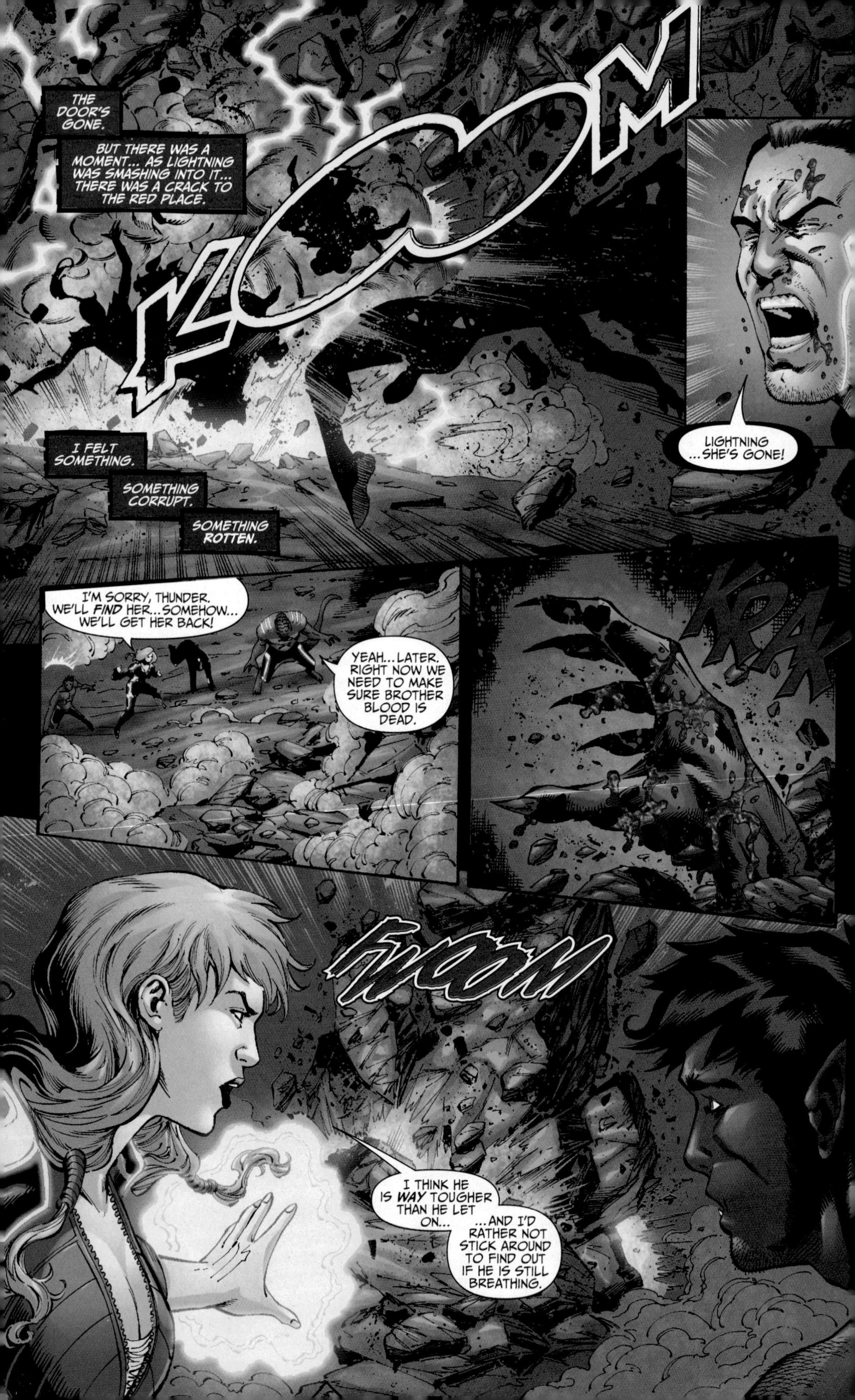
THE DOOR'S GONE.
BUT THERE WAS A MOMENT... AS LIGHTNING WAS SMASHING INTO IT... THERE WAS A CRACK TO THE RED PLACE.
KOOM
I FELT SOMETHING.
SOMETHING CORRUPT.
SOMETHING ROTTEN.
LIGHTNING ...SHE'S GONE!
I'M SORRY, THUNDER. WE'LL FIND HER...SOMEHOW... WE'LL GET HER BACK!
YEAH...LATER. RIGHT NOW WE NEED TO MAKE SURE BROTHER BLOOD IS DEAD.
KRAK
FWOOM
I THINK HE IS WAY TOUGHER THAN HE LET ON...
...AND I'D RATHER NOT STICK AROUND TO FIND OUT IF HE IS STILL BREATHING.

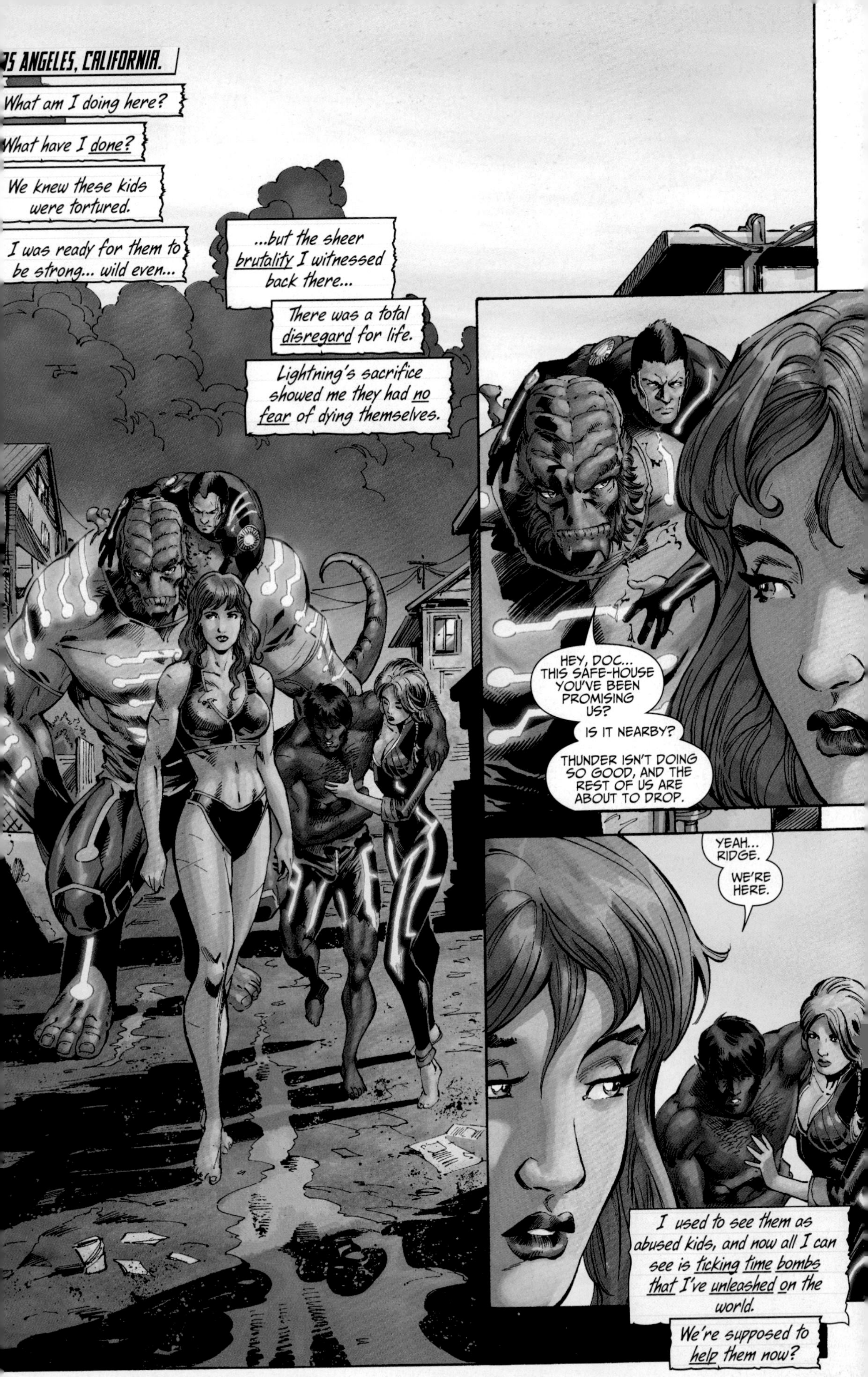

...S ANGELES, CALIFORNIA.
What am I doing here?
What have I done?
We knew these kids were tortured.
I was ready for them to be strong... wild even...
...but the sheer brutality I witnessed back there...
There was a total disregard for life.
Lightning's sacrifice showed me they had no fear of dying themselves.
HEY, DOC... THIS SAFE-HOUSE YOU'VE BEEN PROMISING US?
IS IT NEARBY?
THUNDER ISN'T DOING SO GOOD, AND THE REST OF US ARE ABOUT TO DROP.
YEAH... RIDGE.
WE'RE HERE.
I used to see them as abused kids, and now all I can see is ticking time bombs that I've unleashed on the world.
We're supposed to help them now?

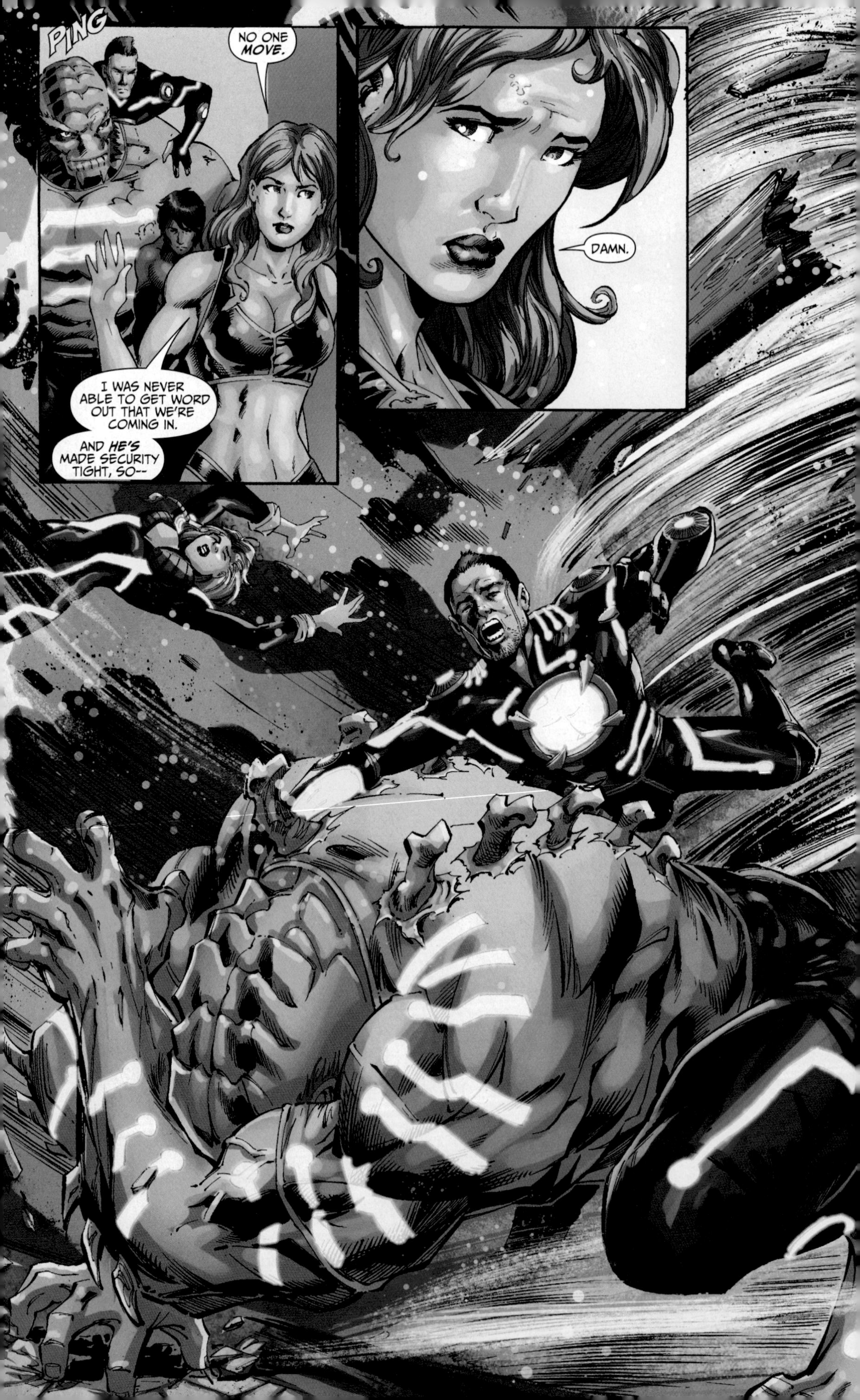
PING
NO ONE MOVE.
I WAS NEVER ABLE TO GET WORD OUT THAT WE'RE COMING IN.
AND HE'S MADE SECURITY TIGHT, SO--
DAMN.

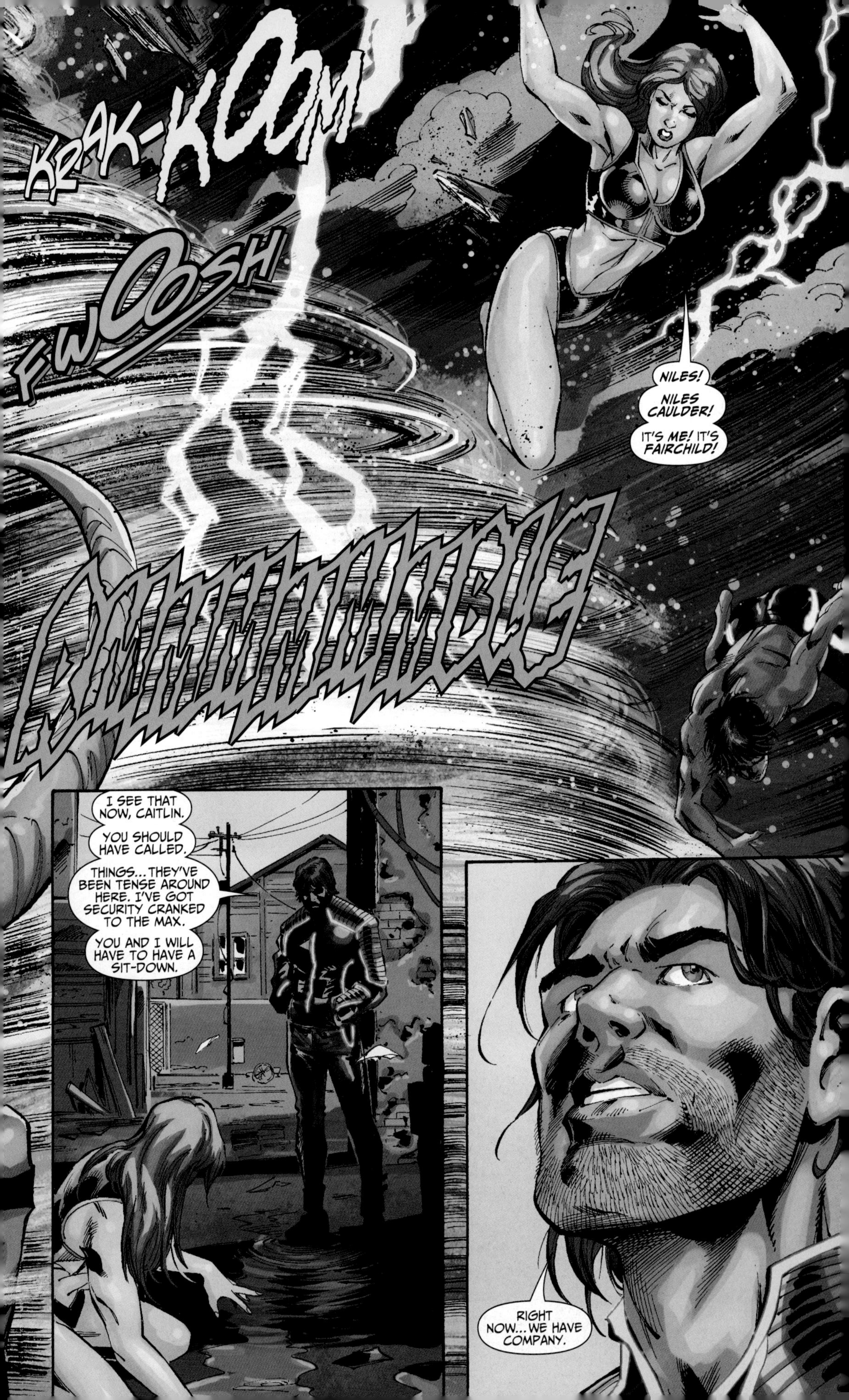
KRAK-KOOM
FWOOSH
NILES!
NILES CAULDER!
IT'S ME! IT'S FAIRCHILD!
I SEE THAT NOW, CAITLIN.
YOU SHOULD HAVE CALLED.
THINGS... THEY'VE BEEN TENSE AROUND HERE. I'VE GOT SECURITY CRANKED TO THE MAX.
YOU AND I WILL HAVE TO HAVE A SIT-DOWN.
RIGHT NOW... WE HAVE COMPANY.

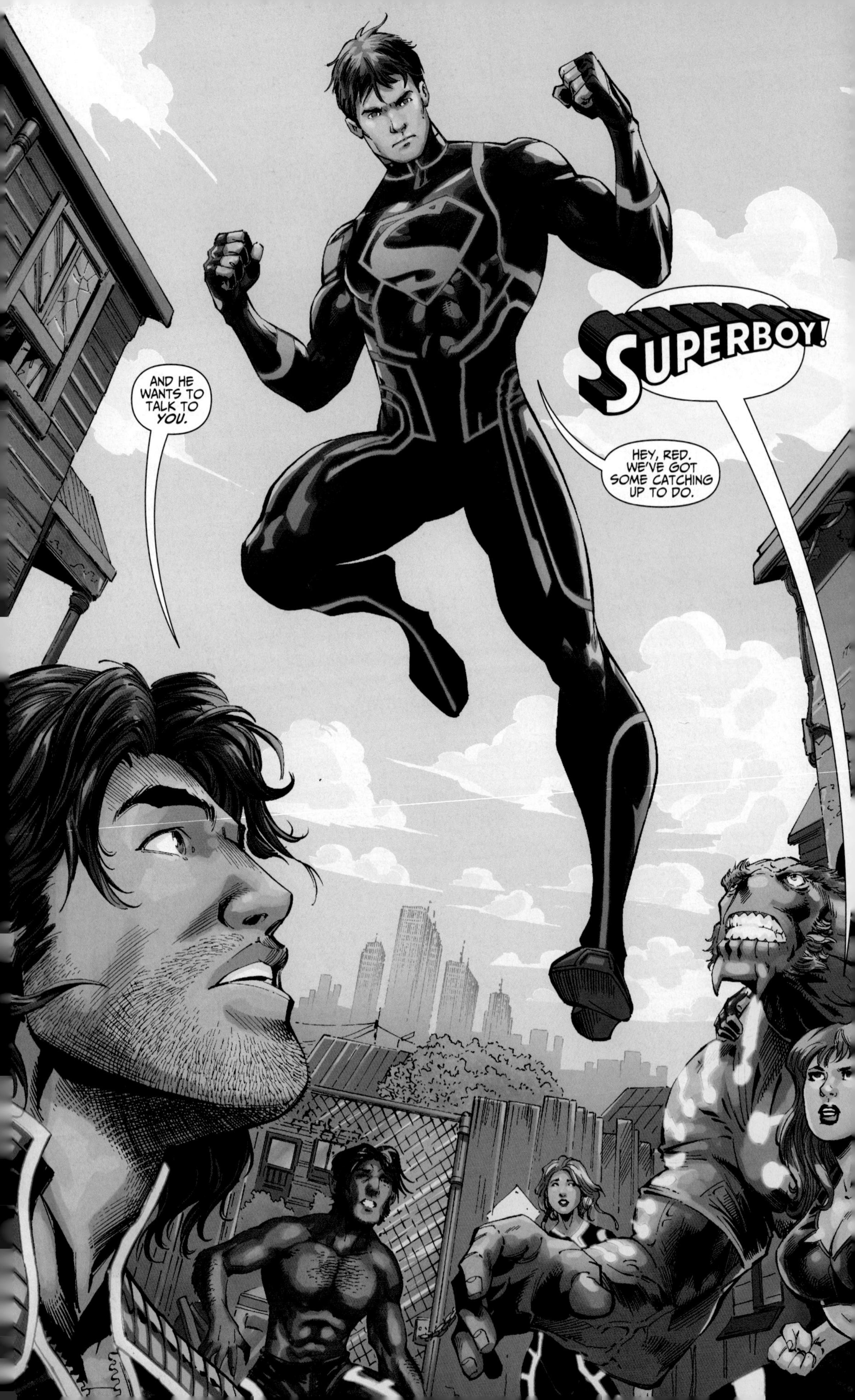
SUPERBOY!
HEY, RED. WE'VE GOT SOME CATCHING UP TO DO.
AND HE WANTS TO TALK TO YOU.

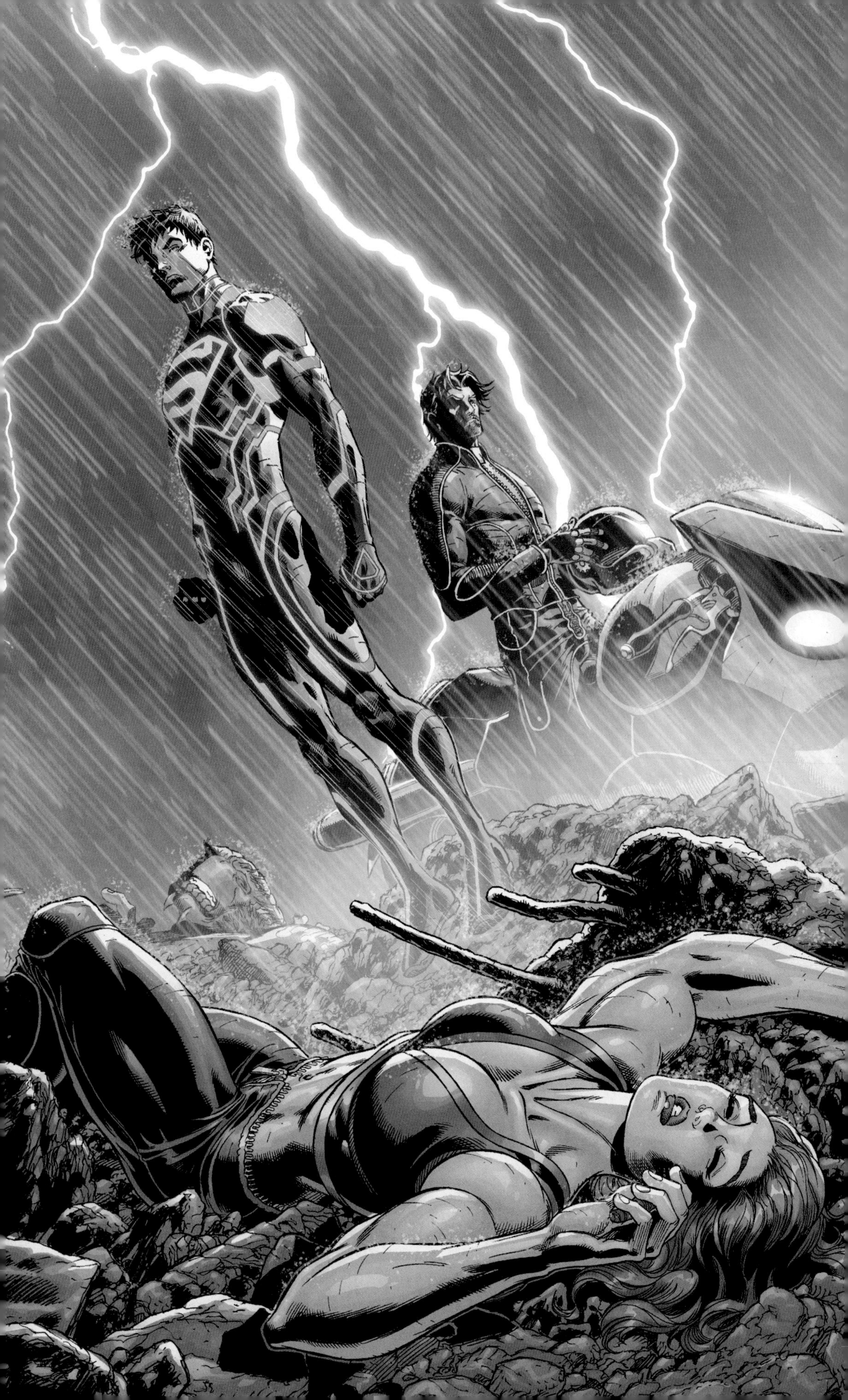

GAME CHANGER

HOWARD MACKIE
writer

IAN CHURCHILL & JULIUS GOPEZ
pencillers

NORM RAPMUND & SCOTT HANNA
inkers

cover art by
IAN CHURCHILL & HI-FI

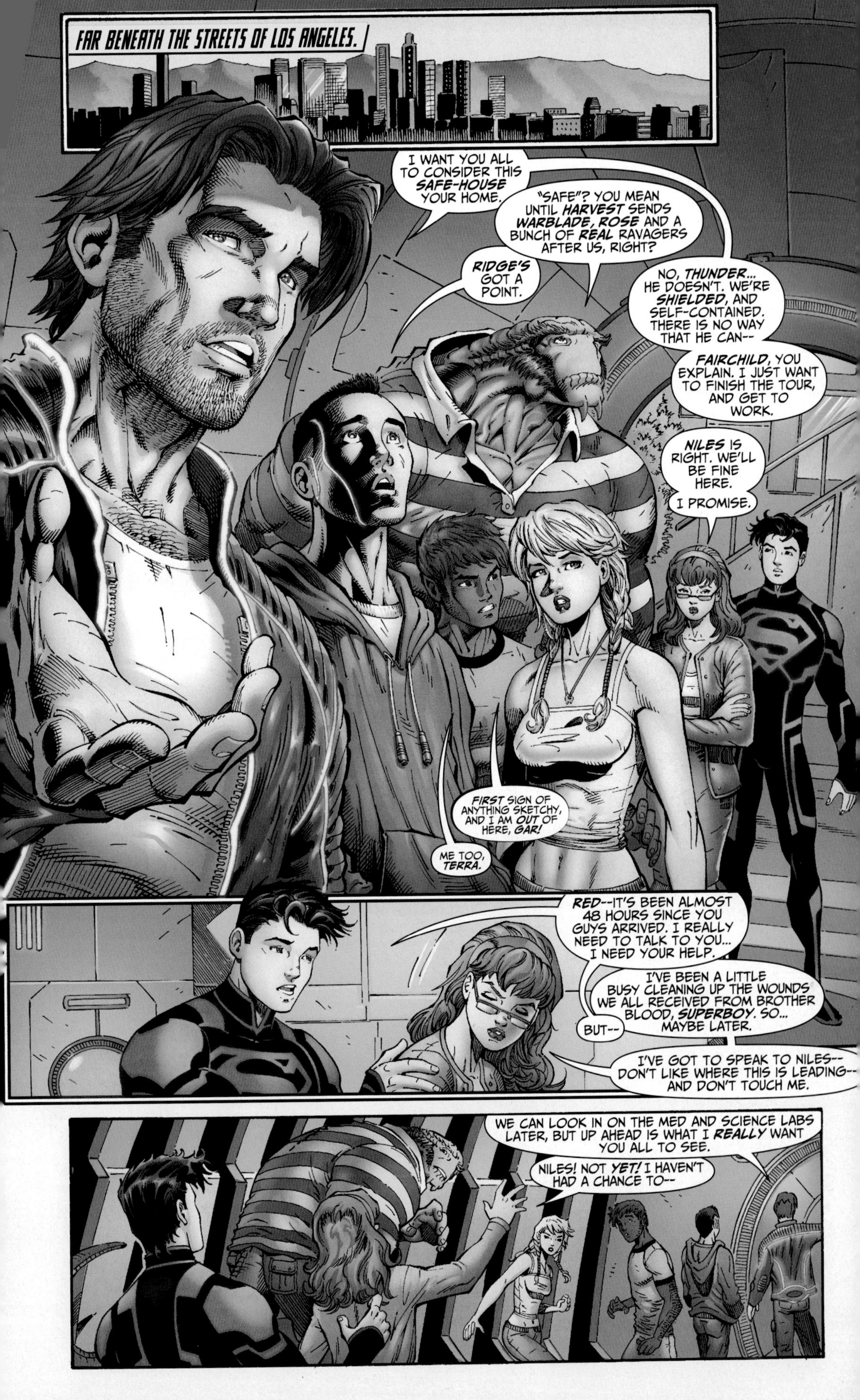
FAR BENEATH THE STREETS OF LOS ANGELES.
I WANT YOU ALL TO CONSIDER THIS SAFE-HOUSE YOUR HOME.
"SAFE"? YOU MEAN UNTIL HARVEST SENDS WARBLADE, ROSE AND A BUNCH OF REAL RAVAGERS AFTER US, RIGHT?
RIDGE'S GOT A POINT.
NO, THUNDER... HE DOESN'T. WE'RE SHIELDED, AND SELF-CONTAINED. THERE IS NO WAY THAT HE CAN--
FAIRCHILD, YOU EXPLAIN. I JUST WANT TO FINISH THE TOUR, AND GET TO WORK.
NILES IS RIGHT. WE'LL BE FINE HERE.
I PROMISE.
FIRST SIGN OF ANYTHING SKETCHY, AND I AM OUT OF HERE, GAR!
ME TOO, TERRA.
RED--IT'S BEEN ALMOST 48 HOURS SINCE YOU GUYS ARRIVED. I REALLY NEED TO TALK TO YOU... I NEED YOUR HELP.
I'VE BEEN A LITTLE BUSY CLEANING UP THE WOUNDS WE ALL RECEIVED FROM BROTHER BLOOD, SUPERBOY. SO... MAYBE LATER.
BUT--
I'VE GOT TO SPEAK TO NILES--DON'T LIKE WHERE THIS IS LEADING--AND DON'T TOUCH ME.
WE CAN LOOK IN ON THE MED AND SCIENCE LABS LATER, BUT UP AHEAD IS WHAT I REALLY WANT YOU ALL TO SEE.
NILES! NOT YET! I HAVEN'T HAD A CHANCE TO--

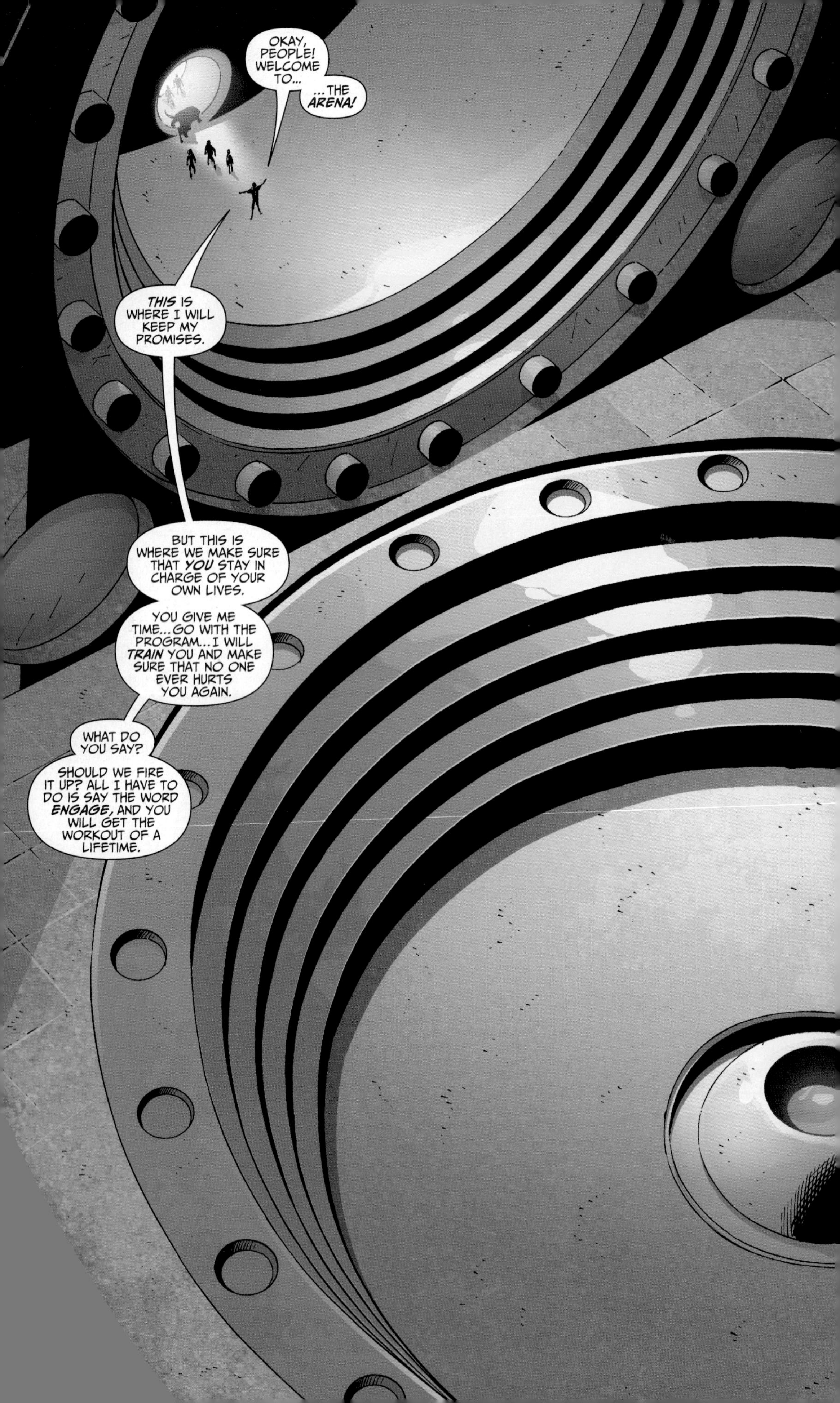
OKAY, PEOPLE! WELCOME TO...
...THE ARENA!
THIS IS WHERE I WILL KEEP MY PROMISES.
BUT THIS IS WHERE WE MAKE SURE THAT YOU STAY IN CHARGE OF YOUR OWN LIVES.
YOU GIVE ME TIME...GO WITH THE PROGRAM...I WILL TRAIN YOU AND MAKE SURE THAT NO ONE EVER HURTS YOU AGAIN.
WHAT DO YOU SAY?
SHOULD WE FIRE IT UP? ALL I HAVE TO DO IS SAY THE WORD ENGAGE, AND YOU WILL GET THE WORKOUT OF A LIFETIME.

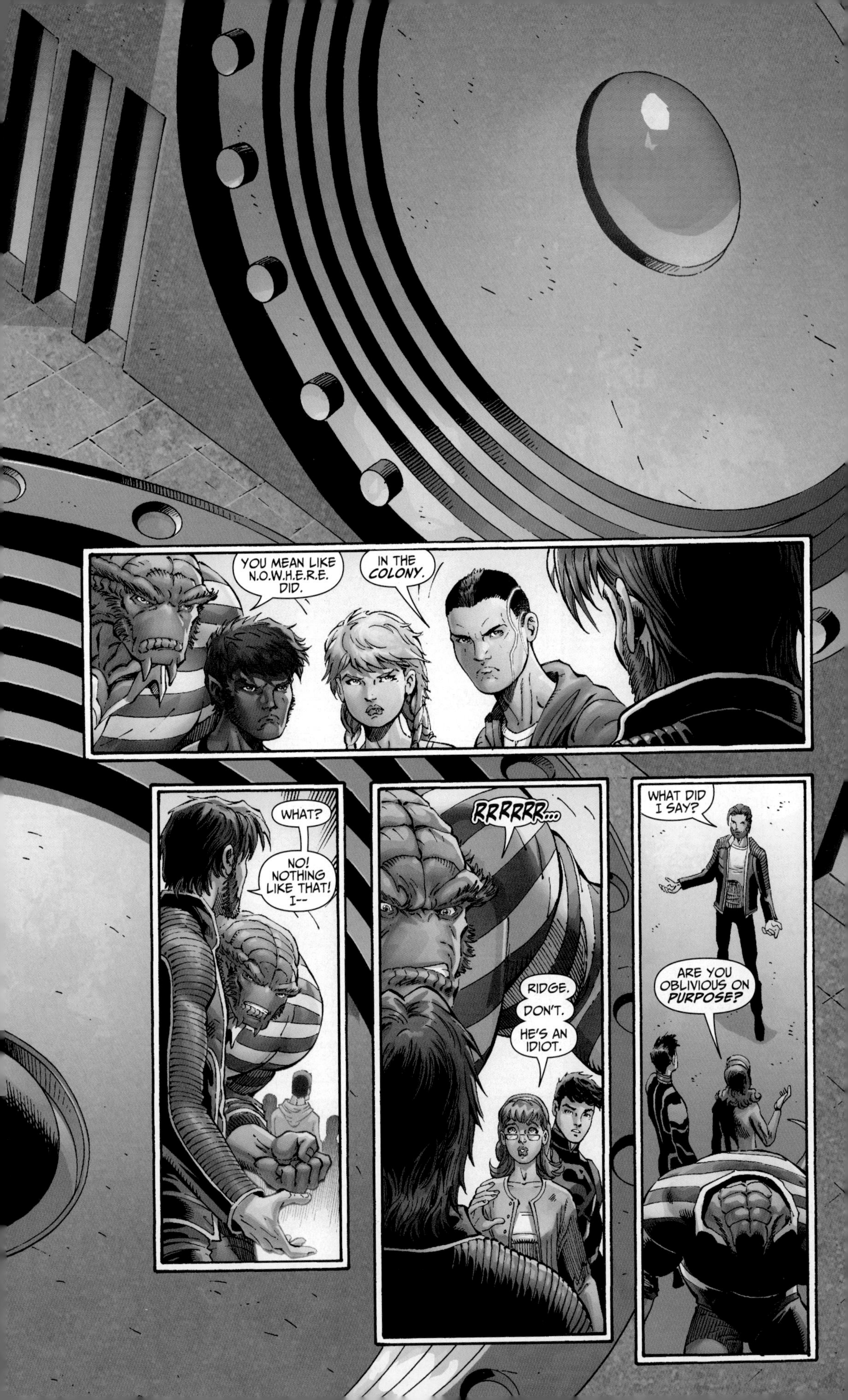
YOU MEAN LIKE N.O.W.H.E.R.E. DID.
IN THE COLONY.
WHAT?
NO! NOTHING LIKE THAT! I--
RRRRRR...
RIDGE.
DON'T.
HE'S AN IDIOT.
WHAT DID I SAY?
ARE YOU OBLIVIOUS ON PURPOSE?

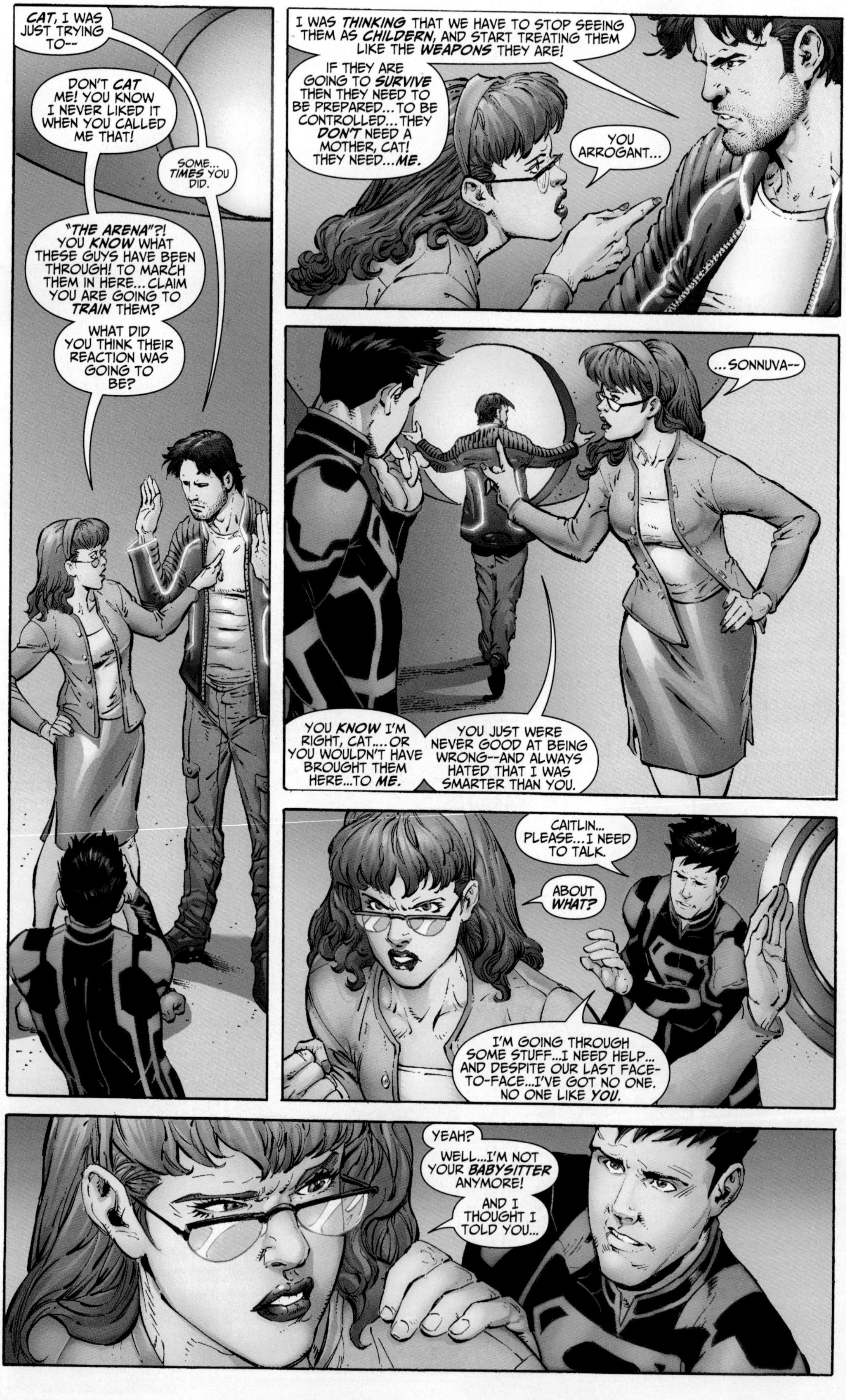
CAT, I WAS JUST TRYING TO--
DON'T CAT ME! YOU KNOW I NEVER LIKED IT WHEN YOU CALLED ME THAT!
SOME... TIMES YOU DID.
"THE ARENA"?! YOU KNOW WHAT THESE GUYS HAVE BEEN THROUGH! TO MARCH THEM IN HERE...CLAIM YOU ARE GOING TO TRAIN THEM?
WHAT DID YOU THINK THEIR REACTION WAS GOING TO BE?
I WAS THINKING THAT WE HAVE TO STOP SEEING THEM AS CHILDERN, AND START TREATING THEM LIKE THE WEAPONS THEY ARE!
IF THEY ARE GOING TO SURVIVE THEN THEY NEED TO BE PREPARED...TO BE CONTROLLED...THEY DON'T NEED A MOTHER, CAT! THEY NEED...ME.
YOU ARROGANT...
...SONNUVA--
YOU KNOW I'M RIGHT, CAT....OR YOU WOULDN'T HAVE BROUGHT THEM HERE...TO ME.
YOU JUST WERE NEVER GOOD AT BEING WRONG--AND ALWAYS HATED THAT I WAS SMARTER THAN YOU.
CAITLIN... PLEASE...I NEED TO TALK.
ABOUT WHAT?
I'M GOING THROUGH SOME STUFF...I NEED HELP... AND DESPITE OUR LAST FACE-TO-FACE...I'VE GOT NO ONE. NO ONE LIKE YOU.
YEAH?
WELL...I'M NOT YOUR BABYSITTER ANYMORE!
AND I THOUGHT I TOLD YOU...

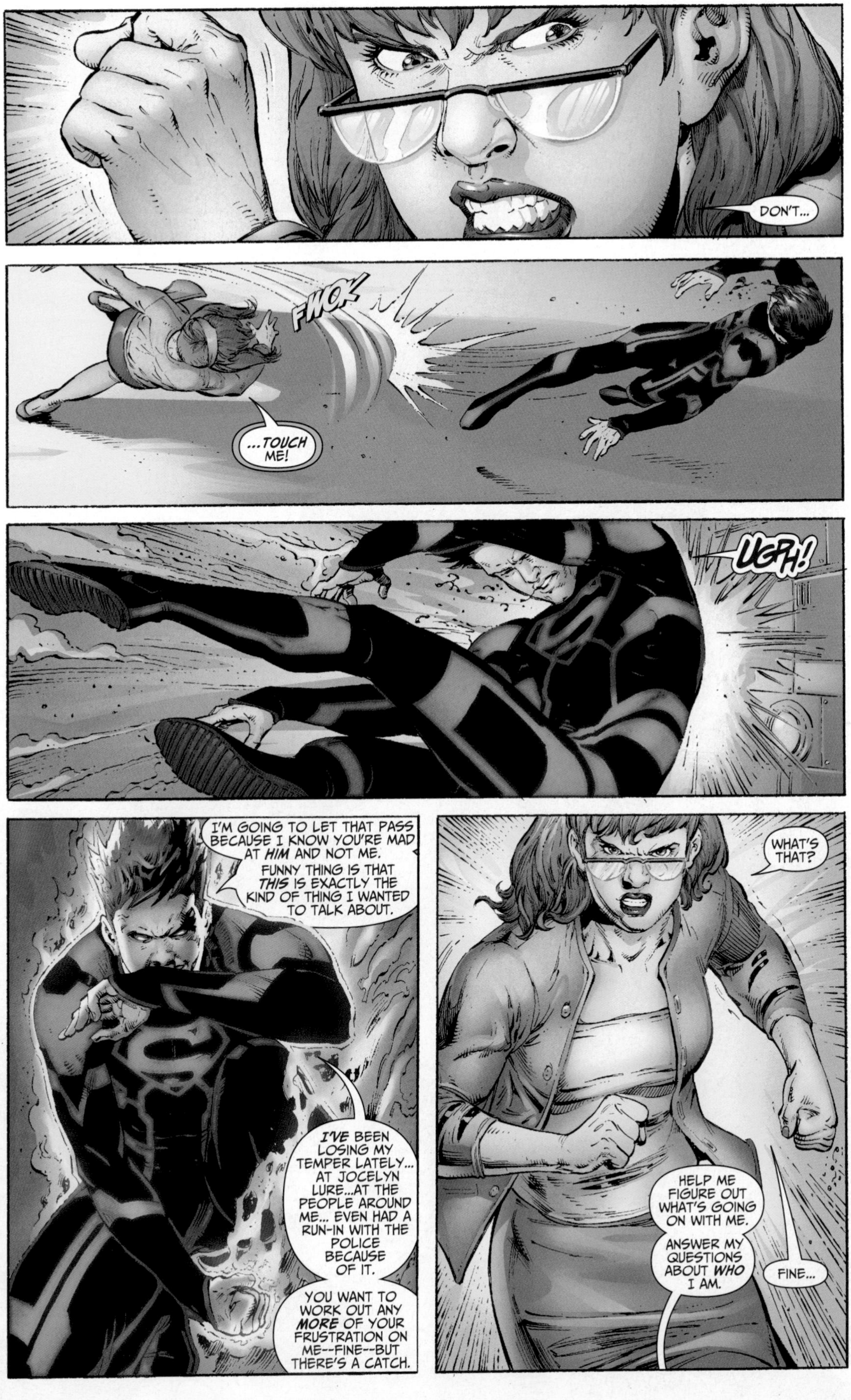

DON'T...
FWOK
...TOUCH ME!
UGPH!
I'M GOING TO LET THAT PASS BECAUSE I KNOW YOU'RE MAD AT HIM AND NOT ME.
FUNNY THING IS THAT THIS IS EXACTLY THE KIND OF THING I WANTED TO TALK ABOUT.
I'VE BEEN LOSING MY TEMPER LATELY... AT JOCELYN LURE...AT THE PEOPLE AROUND ME... EVEN HAD A RUN-IN WITH THE POLICE BECAUSE OF IT.
YOU WANT TO WORK OUT ANY MORE OF YOUR FRUSTRATION ON ME--FINE--BUT THERE'S A CATCH.
WHAT'S THAT?
HELP ME FIGURE OUT WHAT'S GOING ON WITH ME.
ANSWER MY QUESTIONS ABOUT WHO I AM.
FINE...

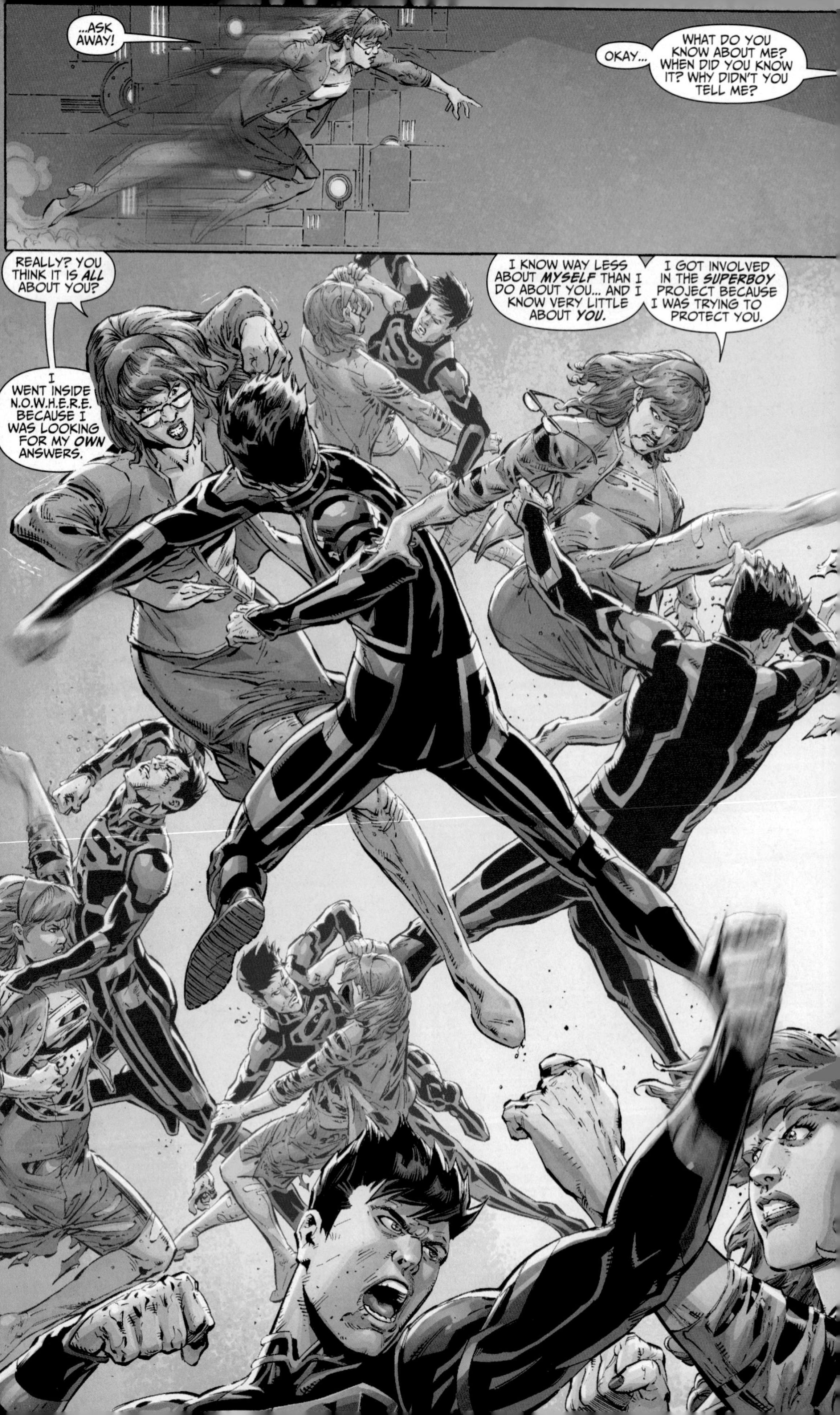
...ASK AWAY!
OKAY...
WHAT DO YOU KNOW ABOUT ME? WHEN DID YOU KNOW IT? WHY DIDN'T YOU TELL ME?
REALLY? YOU THINK IT IS ALL ABOUT YOU?
I WENT INSIDE N.O.W.H.E.R.E. BECAUSE I WAS LOOKING FOR MY OWN ANSWERS.
I KNOW WAY LESS ABOUT MYSELF THAN I DO ABOUT YOU... AND I KNOW VERY LITTLE ABOUT YOU.
I GOT INVOLVED IN THE SUPERBOY PROJECT BECAUSE I WAS TRYING TO PROTECT YOU.

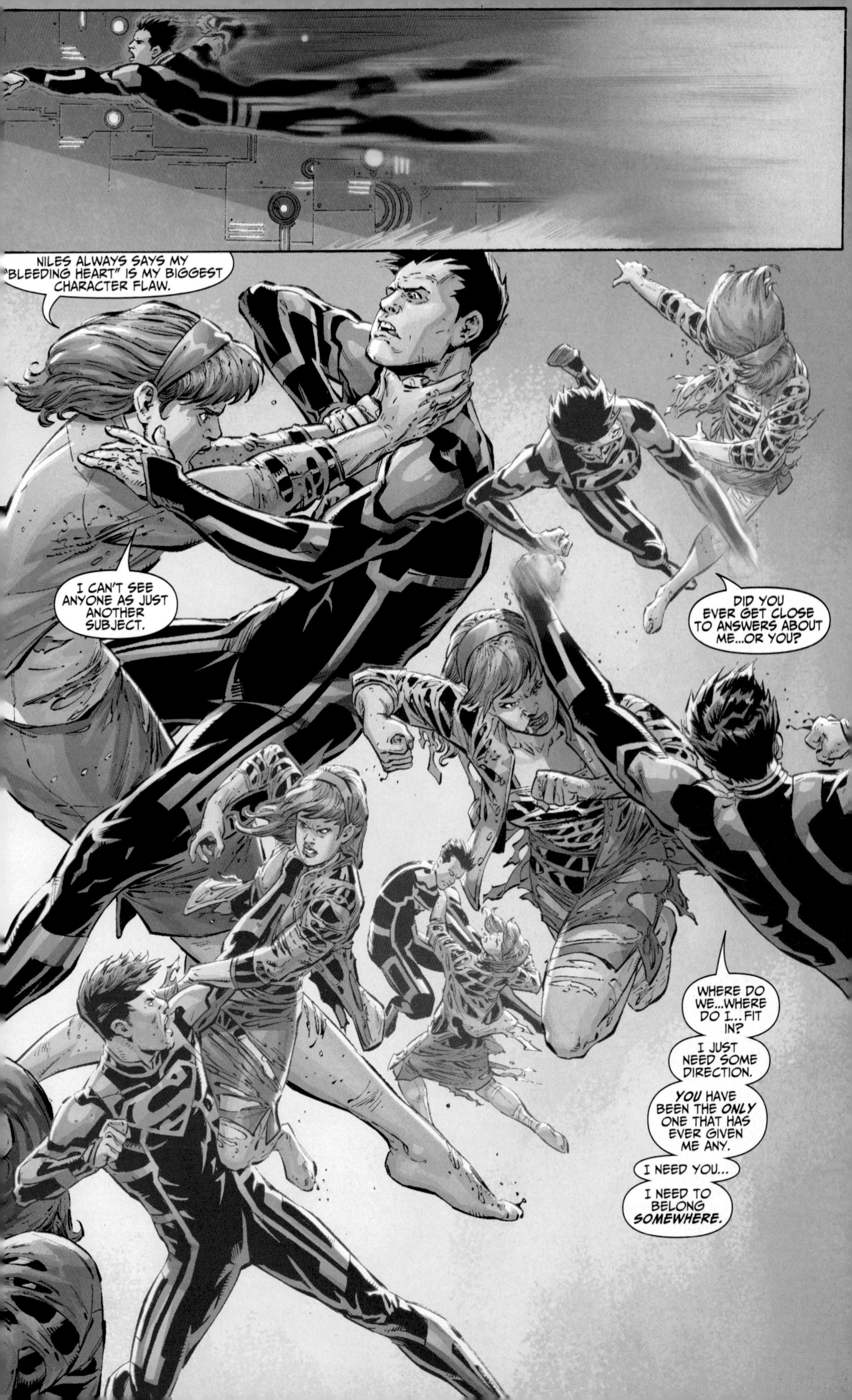
NILES ALWAYS SAYS MY "BLEEDING HEART" IS MY BIGGEST CHARACTER FLAW.
I CAN'T SEE ANYONE AS JUST ANOTHER SUBJECT.
DID YOU EVER GET CLOSE TO ANSWERS ABOUT ME...OR YOU?
WHERE DO WE...WHERE DO I...FIT IN?
I JUST NEED SOME DIRECTION.
YOU HAVE BEEN THE ONLY ONE THAT HAS EVER GIVEN ME ANY.
I NEED YOU...
I NEED TO BELONG SOMEWHERE.

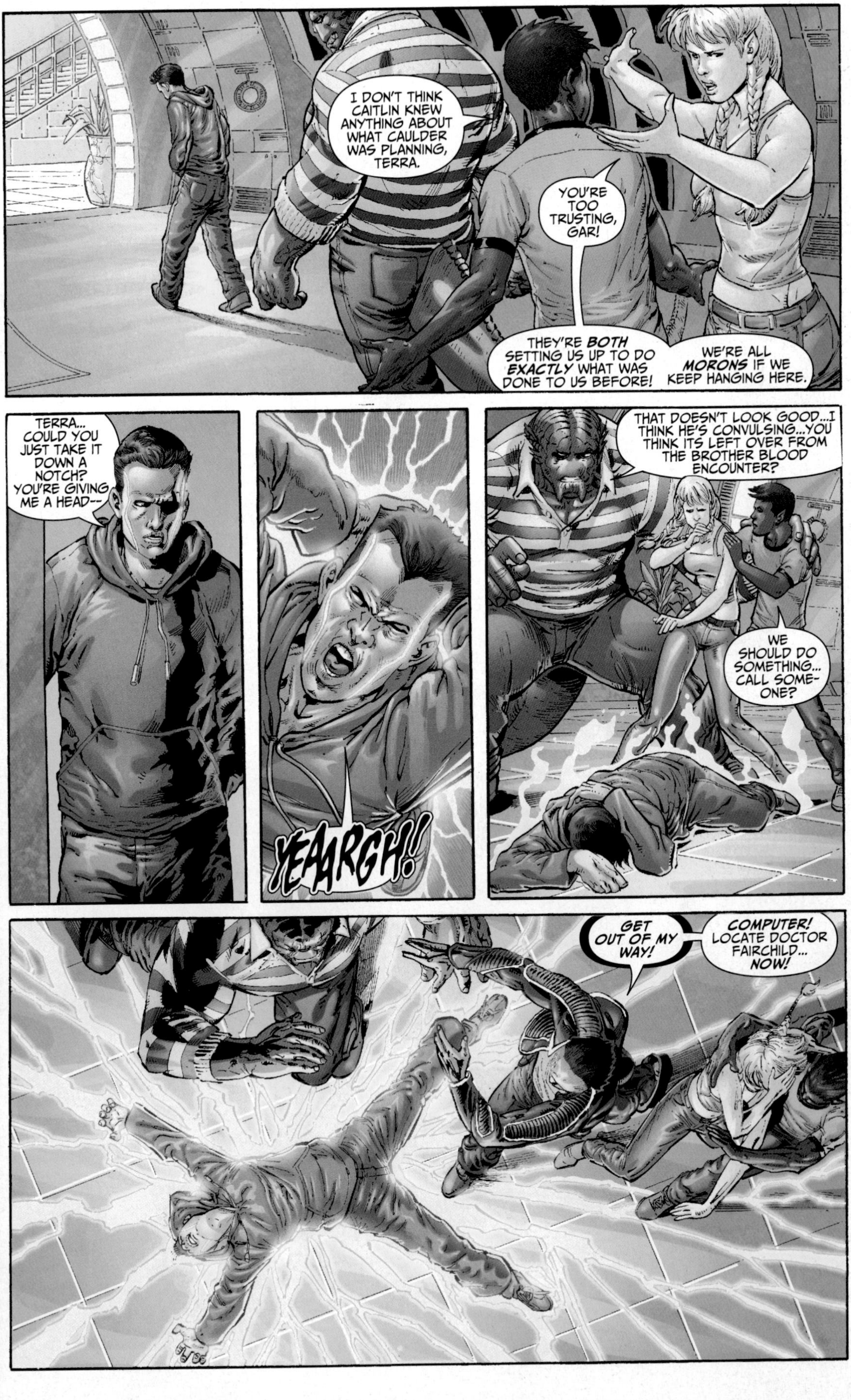
I DON'T THINK CAITLIN KNEW ANYTHING ABOUT WHAT CAULDER WAS PLANNING, TERRA.
YOU'RE TOO TRUSTING, GAR!
THEY'RE BOTH SETTING US UP TO DO EXACTLY WHAT WAS DONE TO US BEFORE!
WE'RE ALL MORONS IF WE KEEP HANGING HERE.
TERRA... COULD YOU JUST TAKE IT DOWN A NOTCH? YOU'RE GIVING ME A HEAD--
YEAARGH!
THAT DOESN'T LOOK GOOD...I THINK HE'S CONVULSING...YOU THINK ITS LEFT OVER FROM THE BROTHER BLOOD ENCOUNTER?
WE SHOULD DO SOMETHING... CALL SOME-ONE?
GET OUT OF MY WAY!
COMPUTER! LOCATE DOCTOR FAIRCHILD... NOW!

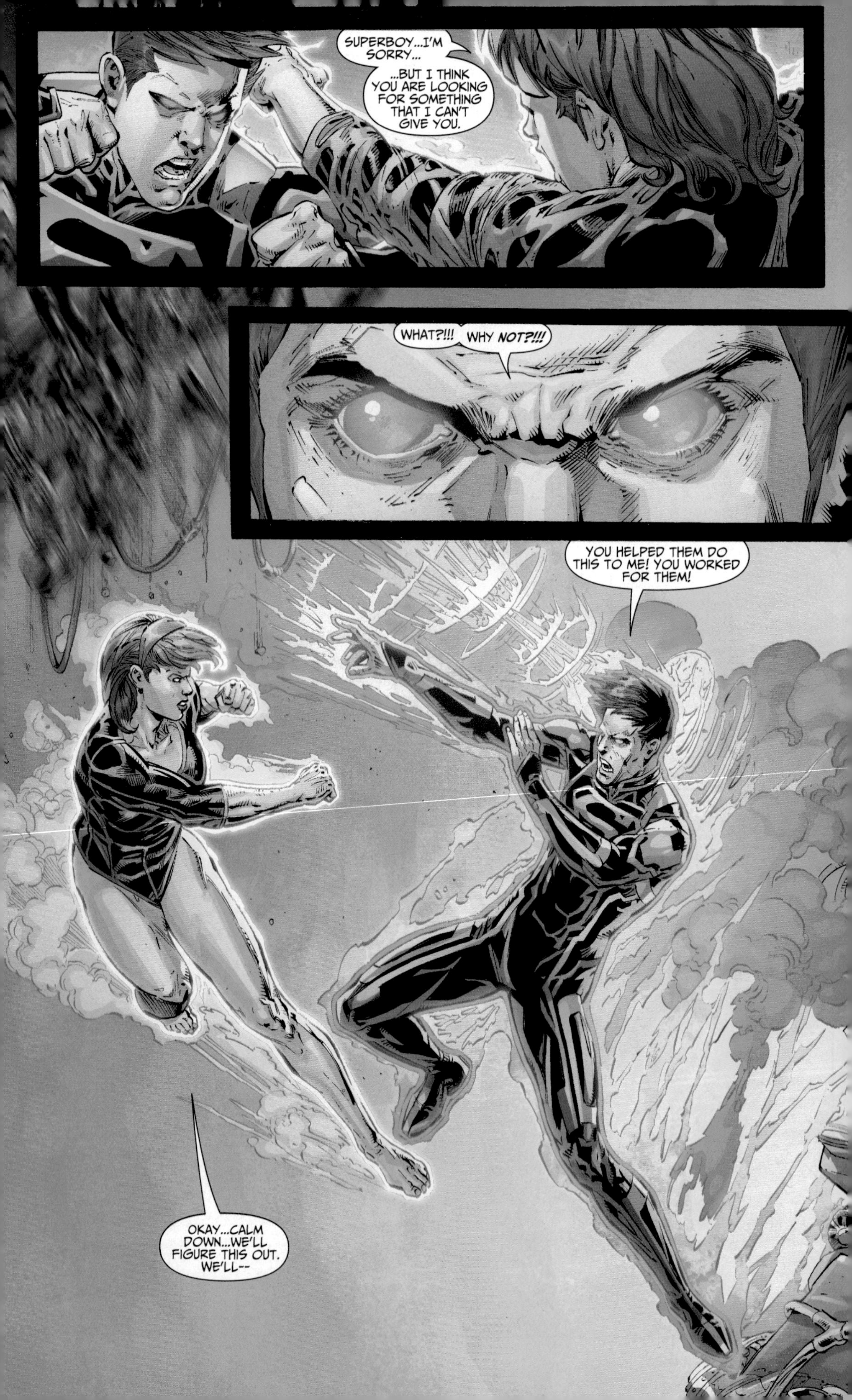
SUPERBOY...I'M SORRY...
...BUT I THINK YOU ARE LOOKING FOR SOMETHING THAT I CAN'T GIVE YOU.
WHAT?!!!
WHY NOT?!!!
YOU HELPED THEM DO THIS TO ME! YOU WORKED FOR THEM!
OKAY...CALM DOWN...WE'LL FIGURE THIS OUT. WE'LL--

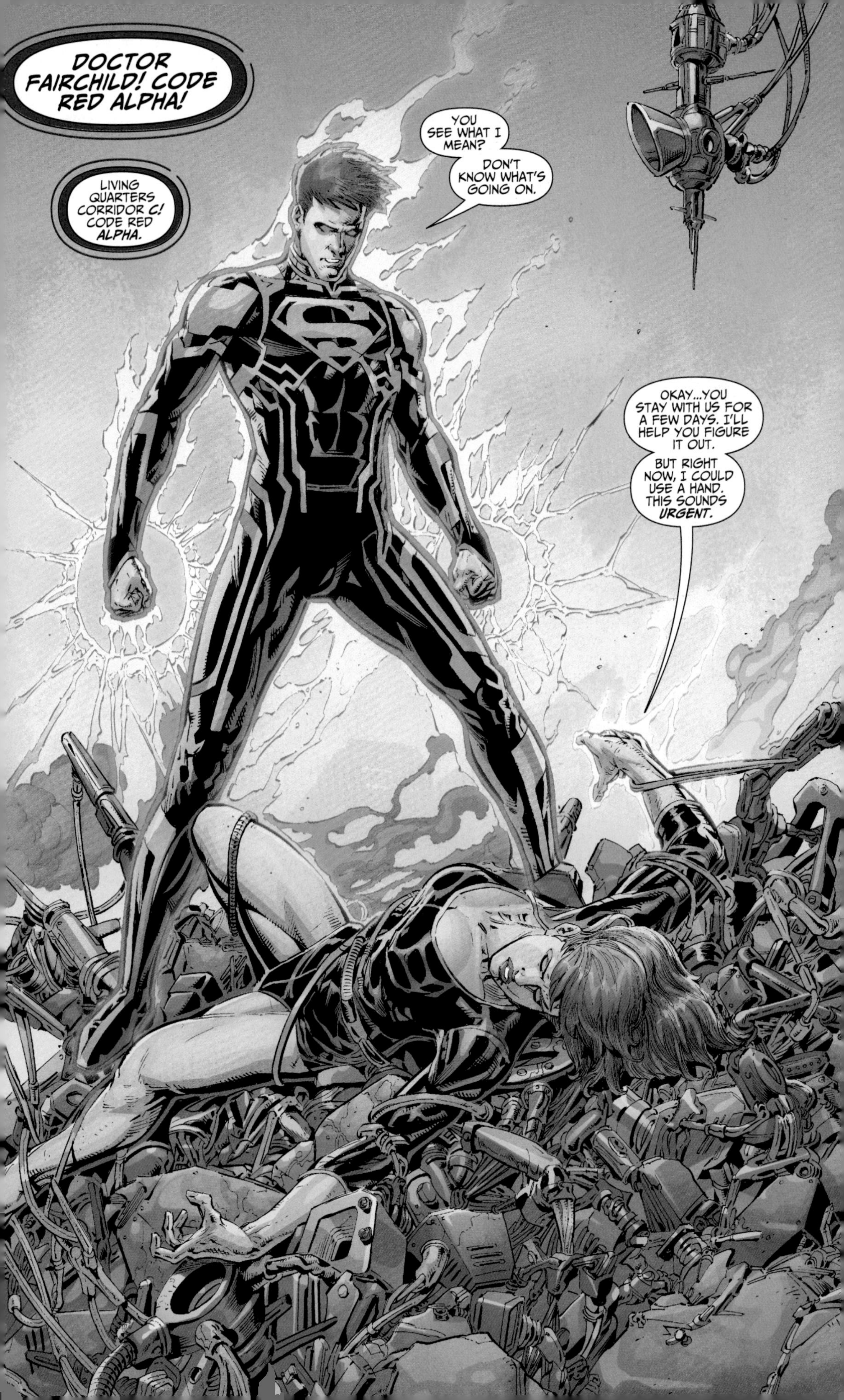
DOCTOR FAIRCHILD! CODE RED ALPHA!
LIVING QUARTERS CORRIDOR C! CODE RED ALPHA.
YOU SEE WHAT I MEAN?
DON'T KNOW WHAT'S GOING ON.
OKAY...YOU STAY WITH US FOR A FEW DAYS. I'LL HELP YOU FIGURE IT OUT.
BUT RIGHT NOW, I COULD USE A HAND. THIS SOUNDS URGENT.

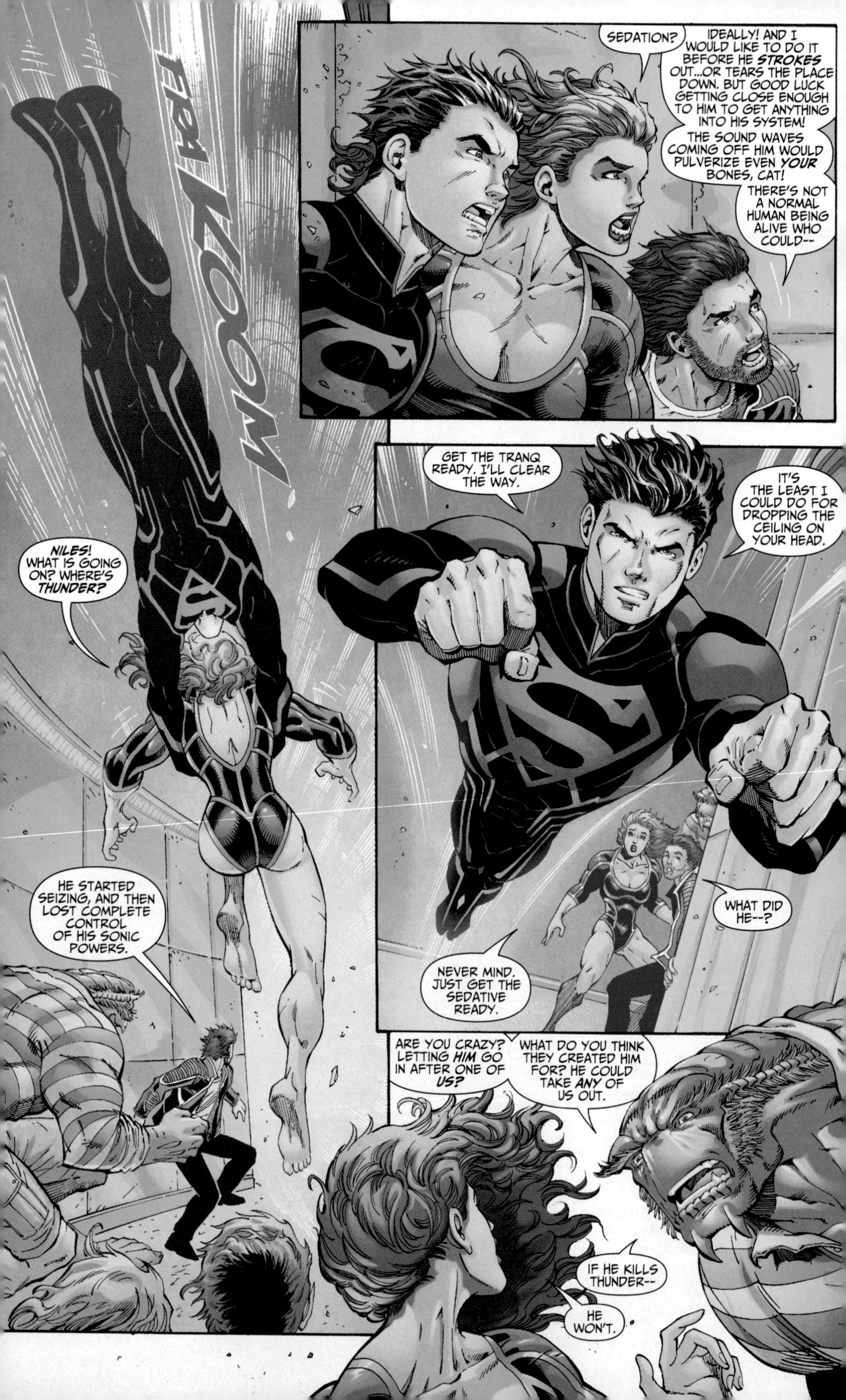
FRA KOOM
SEDATION?
IDEALLY! AND I WOULD LIKE TO DO IT BEFORE HE STROKES OUT...OR TEARS THE PLACE DOWN. BUT GOOD LUCK GETTING CLOSE ENOUGH TO HIM TO GET ANYTHING INTO HIS SYSTEM!
THE SOUND WAVES COMING OFF HIM WOULD PULVERIZE EVEN YOUR BONES, CAT!
THERE'S NOT A NORMAL HUMAN BEING ALIVE WHO COULD--
NILES! WHAT IS GOING ON? WHERE'S THUNDER?
HE STARTED SEIZING, AND THEN LOST COMPLETE CONTROL OF HIS SONIC POWERS.
GET THE TRANQ READY. I'LL CLEAR THE WAY.
IT'S THE LEAST I COULD DO FOR DROPPING THE CEILING ON YOUR HEAD.
WHAT DID HE--?
NEVER MIND. JUST GET THE SEDATIVE READY.
ARE YOU CRAZY? LETTING HIM GO IN AFTER ONE OF US?
WHAT DO YOU THINK THEY CREATED HIM FOR? HE COULD TAKE ANY OF US OUT.
IF HE KILLS THUNDER--
HE WON'T.

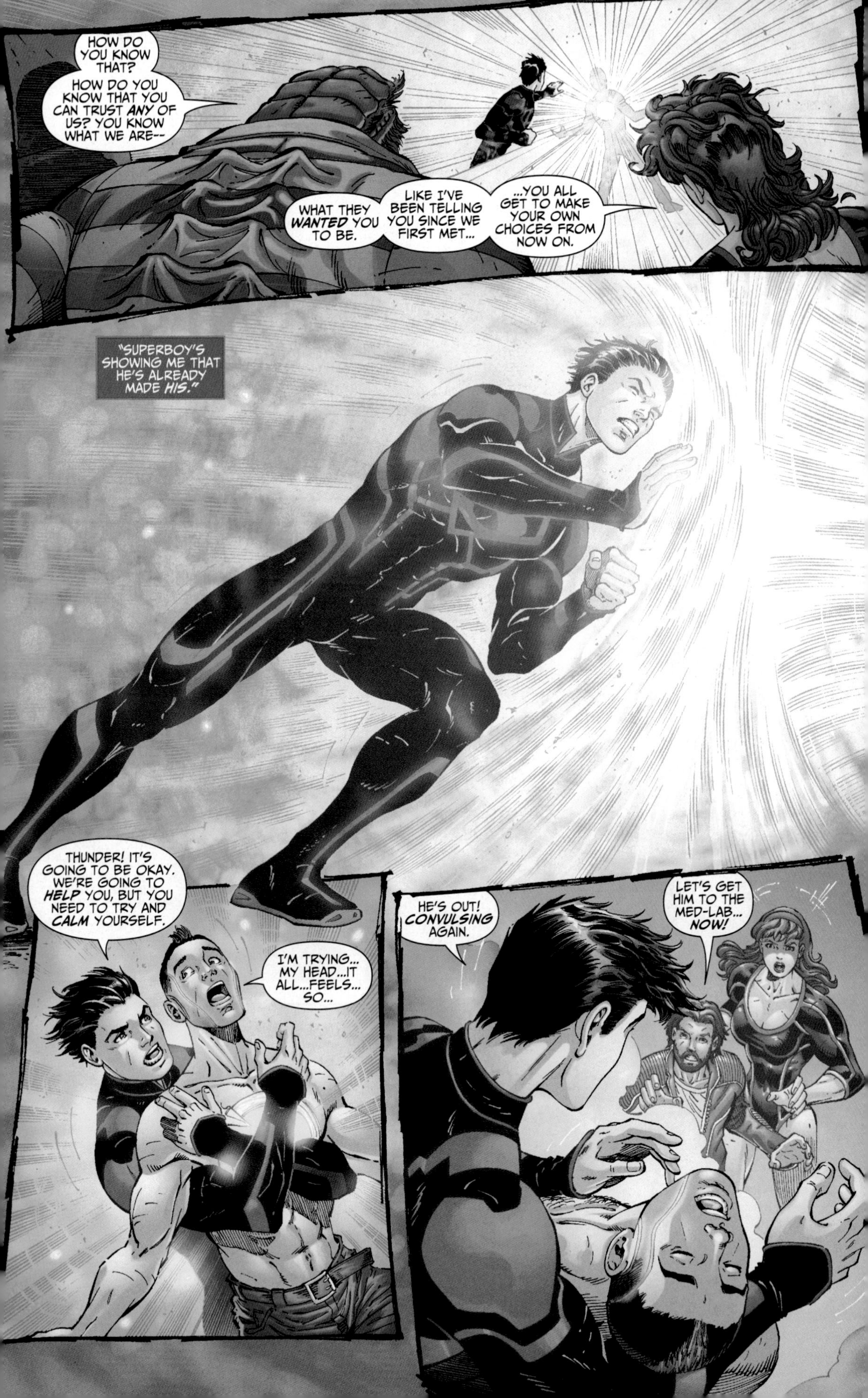
HOW DO YOU KNOW THAT?
HOW DO YOU KNOW THAT YOU CAN TRUST ANY OF US? YOU KNOW WHAT WE ARE--
WHAT THEY WANTED YOU TO BE.
LIKE I'VE BEEN TELLING YOU SINCE WE FIRST MET...
...YOU ALL GET TO MAKE YOUR OWN CHOICES FROM NOW ON.
"SUPERBOY'S SHOWING ME THAT HE'S ALREADY MADE HIS."
THUNDER! IT'S GOING TO BE OKAY. WE'RE GOING TO HELP YOU, BUT YOU NEED TO TRY AND CALM YOURSELF.
I'M TRYING... MY HEAD...IT ALL...FEELS... SO...
HE'S OUT! CONVULSING AGAIN.
LET'S GET HIM TO THE MED-LAB... NOW!

DOCTOR FAIRCHILD AND I ARE GOING TO NEED ROOM TO WORK IF WE ARE GOING TO *SAVE* YOUR FRIEND.

BUT THE REST OF YOU GET OUT OF HERE-- *NOW!*

NILES! WE'RE LOSING HIM!

I DON'T HAVE A PULSE! HIS HEART! I NEED ADRENALINE, AND--

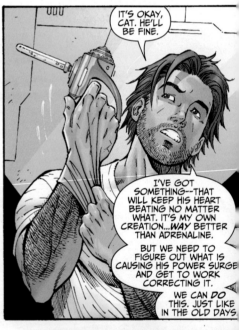

IT'S OKAY, CAT. HE'LL BE FINE.

I'VE GOT SOMETHING--THAT WILL KEEP HIS HEART BEATING NO MATTER WHAT. IT'S MY OWN CREATION...*WAY* BETTER THAN ADRENALINE.

BUT WE NEED TO FIGURE OUT WHAT IS CAUSING HIS POWER SURGE AND GET TO WORK CORRECTING IT.

WE CAN *DO* THIS. JUST LIKE IN THE OLD DAYS.

SHE'S A *DOCTOR* DOCTOR? ANYONE ELSE KNOW THAT?

WE JUST LOST HIS SISTER, *LIGHTNING!* WE CAN'T LOSE ANOTHER ONE OF US!!

JUST GET A GRIP...IT'LL BE OKAY.

IT'S NEVER GOING TO BE OKAY FOR ANY OF US AGAIN.

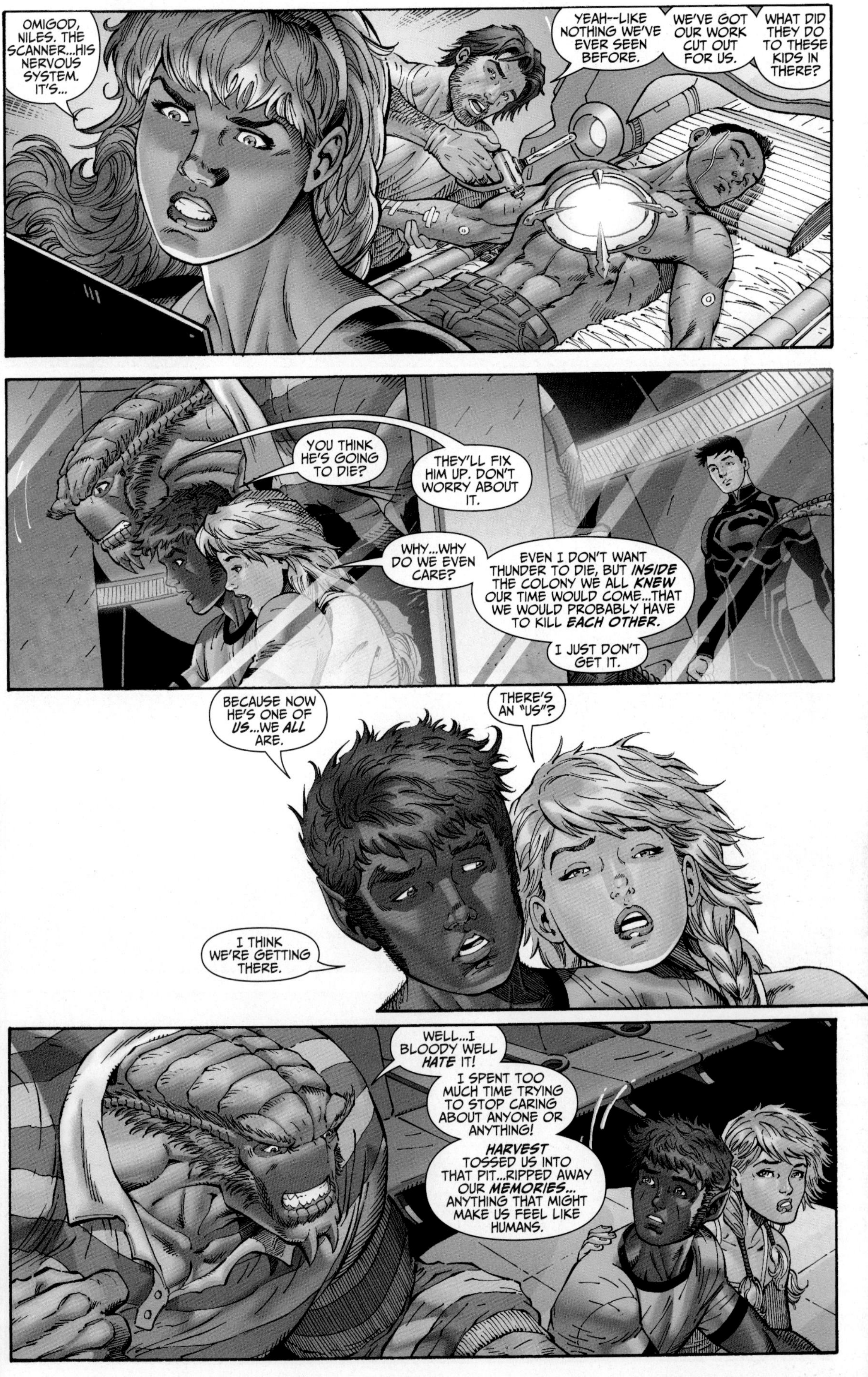
OMIGOD, NILES. THE SCANNER...HIS NERVOUS SYSTEM. IT'S...
YEAH--LIKE NOTHING WE'VE EVER SEEN BEFORE.
WE'VE GOT OUR WORK CUT OUT FOR US.
WHAT DID THEY DO TO THESE KIDS IN THERE?
YOU THINK HE'S GOING TO DIE?
THEY'LL FIX HIM UP. DON'T WORRY ABOUT IT.
WHY...WHY DO WE EVEN CARE?
EVEN I DON'T WANT THUNDER TO DIE, BUT INSIDE THE COLONY WE ALL KNEW OUR TIME WOULD COME...THAT WE WOULD PROBABLY HAVE TO KILL EACH OTHER.
I JUST DON'T GET IT.
BECAUSE NOW HE'S ONE OF US...WE ALL ARE.
THERE'S AN "US"?
I THINK WE'RE GETTING THERE.
WELL...I BLOODY WELL HATE IT!
I SPENT TOO MUCH TIME TRYING TO STOP CARING ABOUT ANYONE OR ANYTHING!
HARVEST TOSSED US INTO THAT PIT...RIPPED AWAY OUR MEMORIES... ANYTHING THAT MIGHT MAKE US FEEL LIKE HUMANS.

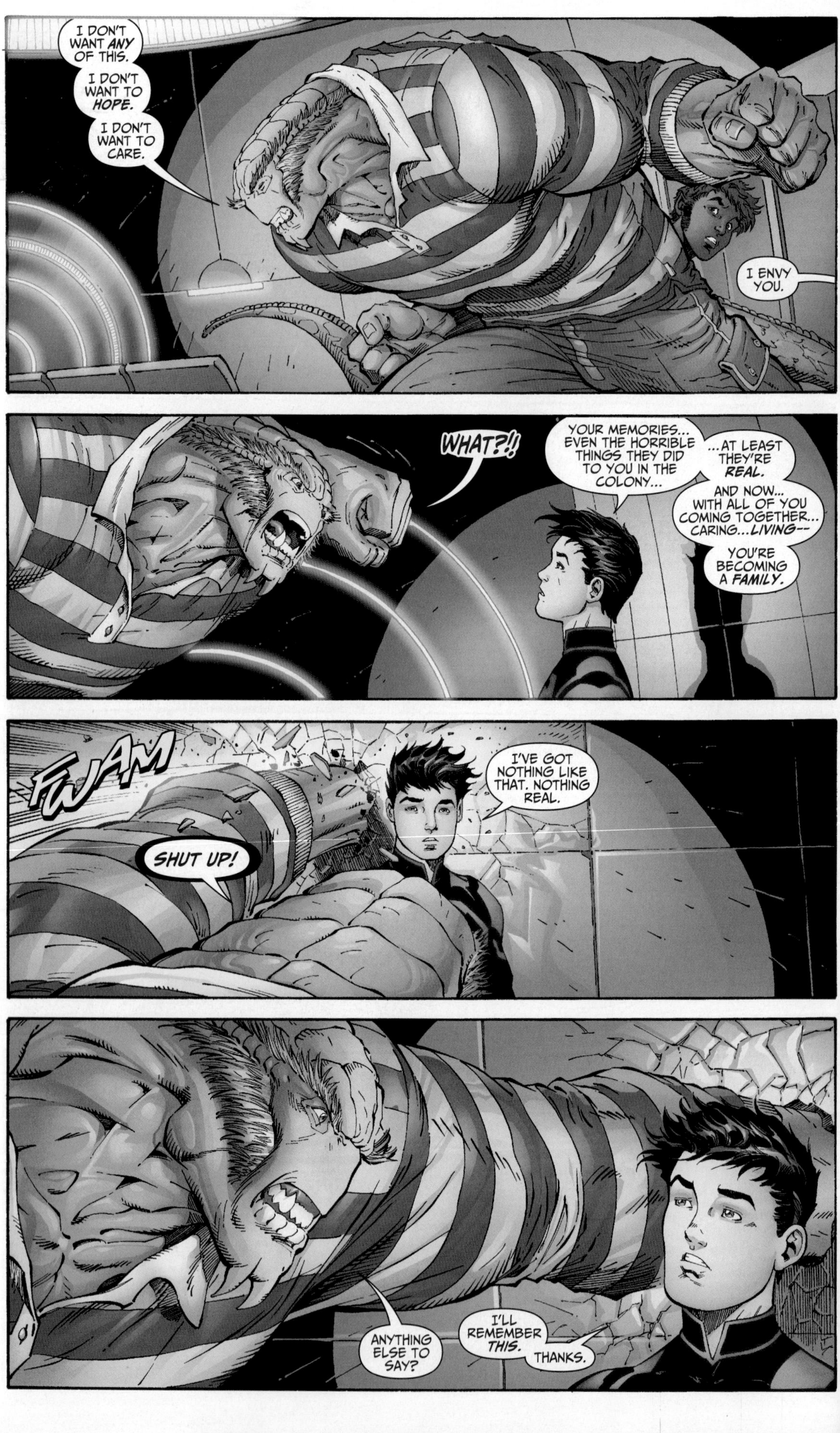
I DON'T WANT *ANY* OF THIS.
I DON'T WANT TO *HOPE.*
I DON'T WANT TO CARE.
I ENVY YOU.
WHAT?!!
YOUR MEMORIES... EVEN THE HORRIBLE THINGS THEY DID TO YOU IN THE COLONY...
...AT LEAST THEY'RE *REAL.*
AND NOW... WITH ALL OF YOU COMING TOGETHER... CARING...*LIVING*--
YOU'RE BECOMING A *FAMILY.*
FWAM
I'VE GOT NOTHING LIKE THAT. NOTHING REAL.
SHUT UP!
ANYTHING ELSE TO SAY?
I'LL REMEMBER *THIS.*
THANKS.

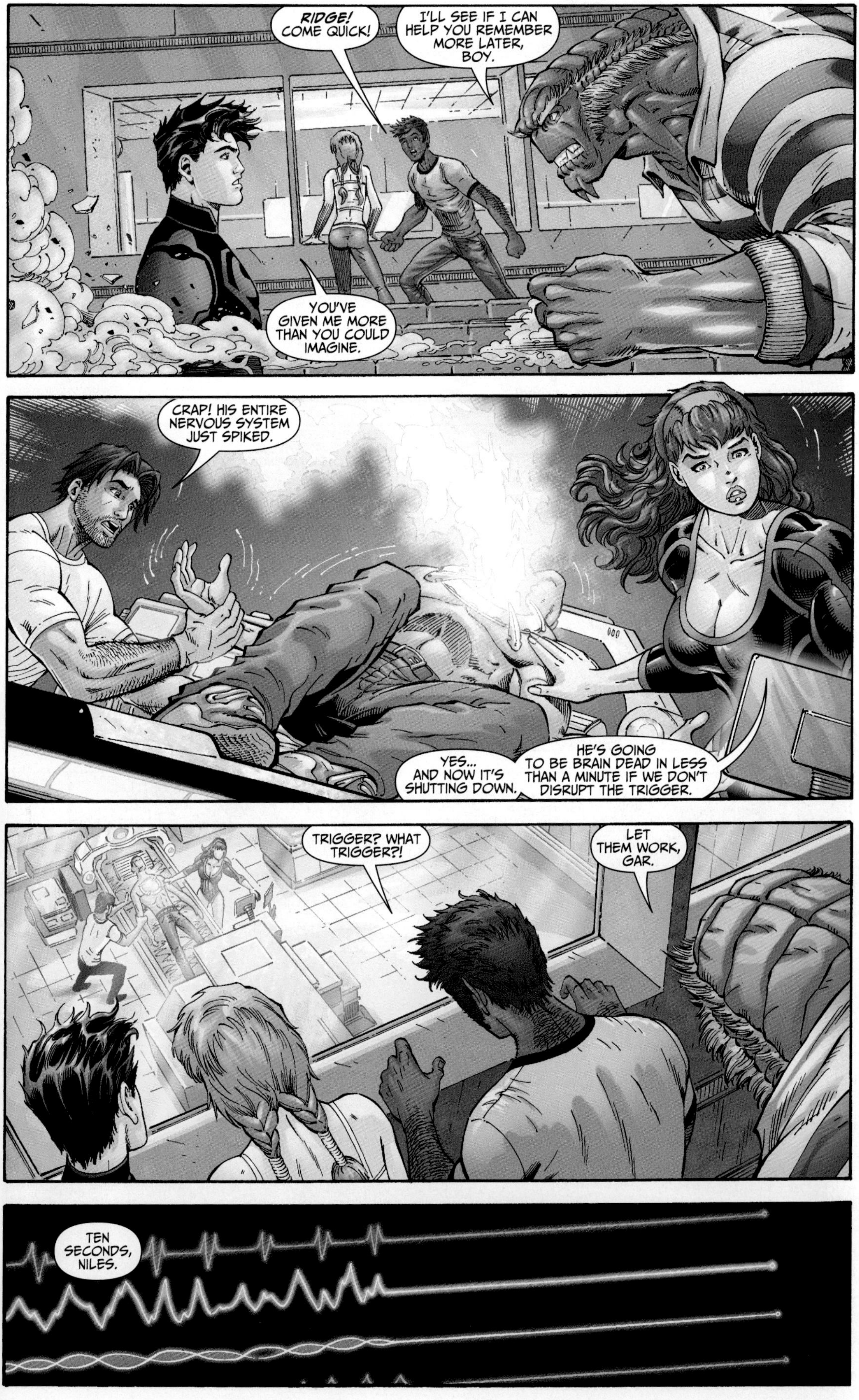
RIDGE! COME QUICK!
I'LL SEE IF I CAN HELP YOU REMEMBER MORE LATER, BOY.
YOU'VE GIVEN ME MORE THAN YOU COULD IMAGINE.
CRAP! HIS ENTIRE NERVOUS SYSTEM JUST SPIKED.
YES... AND NOW IT'S SHUTTING DOWN.
HE'S GOING TO BE BRAIN DEAD IN LESS THAN A MINUTE IF WE DON'T DISRUPT THE TRIGGER.
TRIGGER? WHAT TRIGGER?!
LET THEM WORK, GAR.
TEN SECONDS, NILES.

STAND BACK, CAT. I HAVE NO IDEA IF THIS IS GOING TO WORK, BUT--

HUUUUUUGPPHHH!

TRICKY SONS OF B--

WHAT DID YOU DO?

SOUND WAVES--SOMEONE WAS BEING CUTE--*SOUND WAVES* WERE THE KEY TO DISARMING THE TRIGGER.

DOC...YOU WANT TO LET US KNOW WHAT HAPPENED?

YEAH...WE *NEED* TO KNOW... IS THUNDER GOING TO BE OKAY?

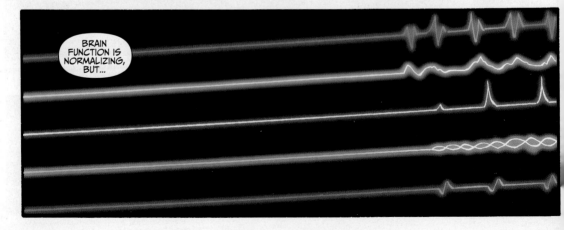

BRAIN FUNCTION IS NORMALIZING, BUT...

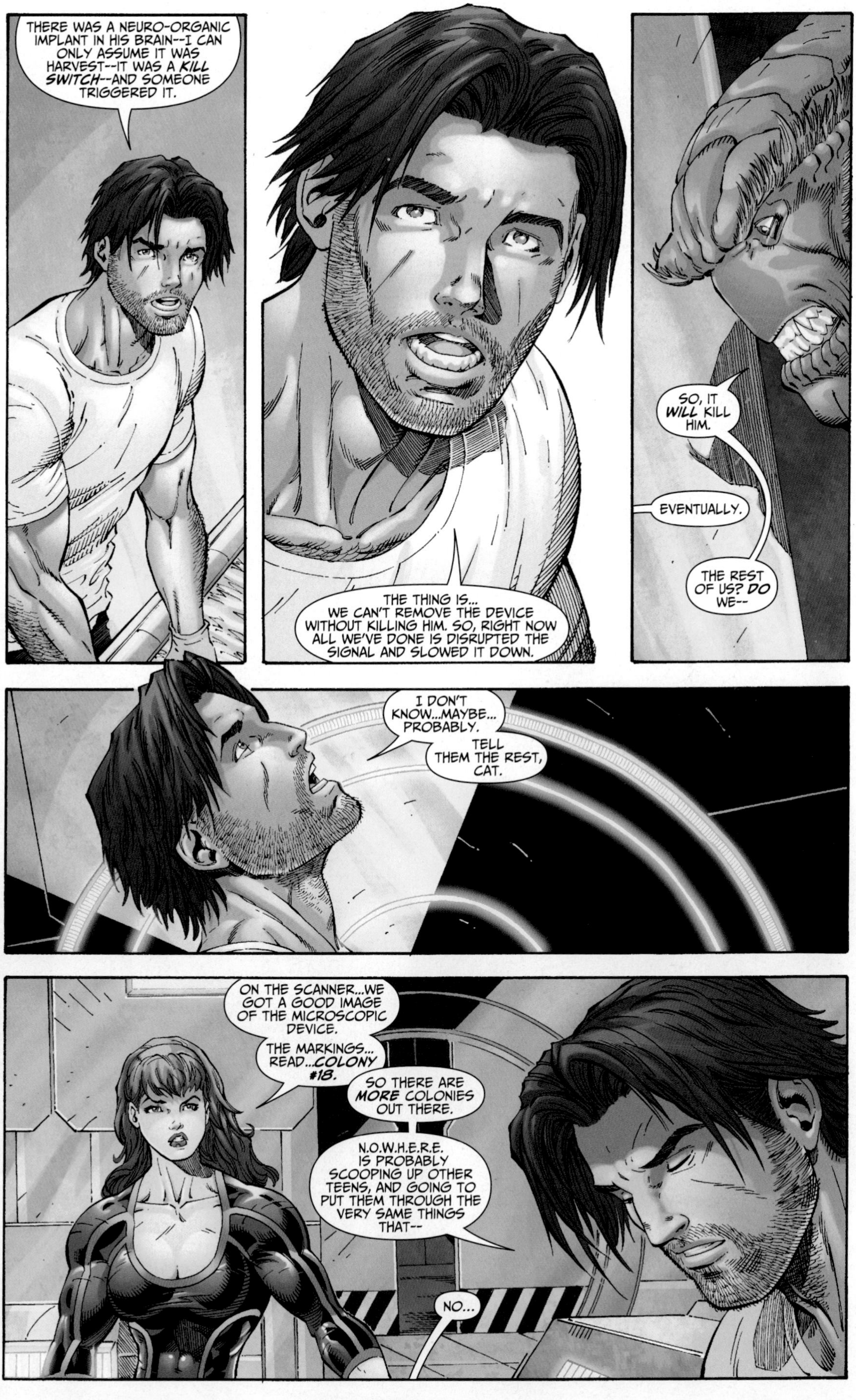
THERE WAS A NEURO-ORGANIC IMPLANT IN HIS BRAIN--I CAN ONLY ASSUME IT WAS HARVEST--IT WAS A KILL SWITCH--AND SOMEONE TRIGGERED IT.
THE THING IS... WE CAN'T REMOVE THE DEVICE WITHOUT KILLING HIM. SO, RIGHT NOW ALL WE'VE DONE IS DISRUPTED THE SIGNAL AND SLOWED IT DOWN.
SO, IT WILL KILL HIM.
EVENTUALLY.
THE REST OF US? DO WE--
I DON'T KNOW...MAYBE... PROBABLY.
TELL THEM THE REST, CAT.
ON THE SCANNER...WE GOT A GOOD IMAGE OF THE MICROSCOPIC DEVICE.
THE MARKINGS... READ...COLONY #18.
SO THERE ARE MORE COLONIES OUT THERE.
N.O.W.H.E.R.E. IS PROBABLY SCOOPING UP OTHER TEENS, AND GOING TO PUT THEM THROUGH THE VERY SAME THINGS THAT--
NO...

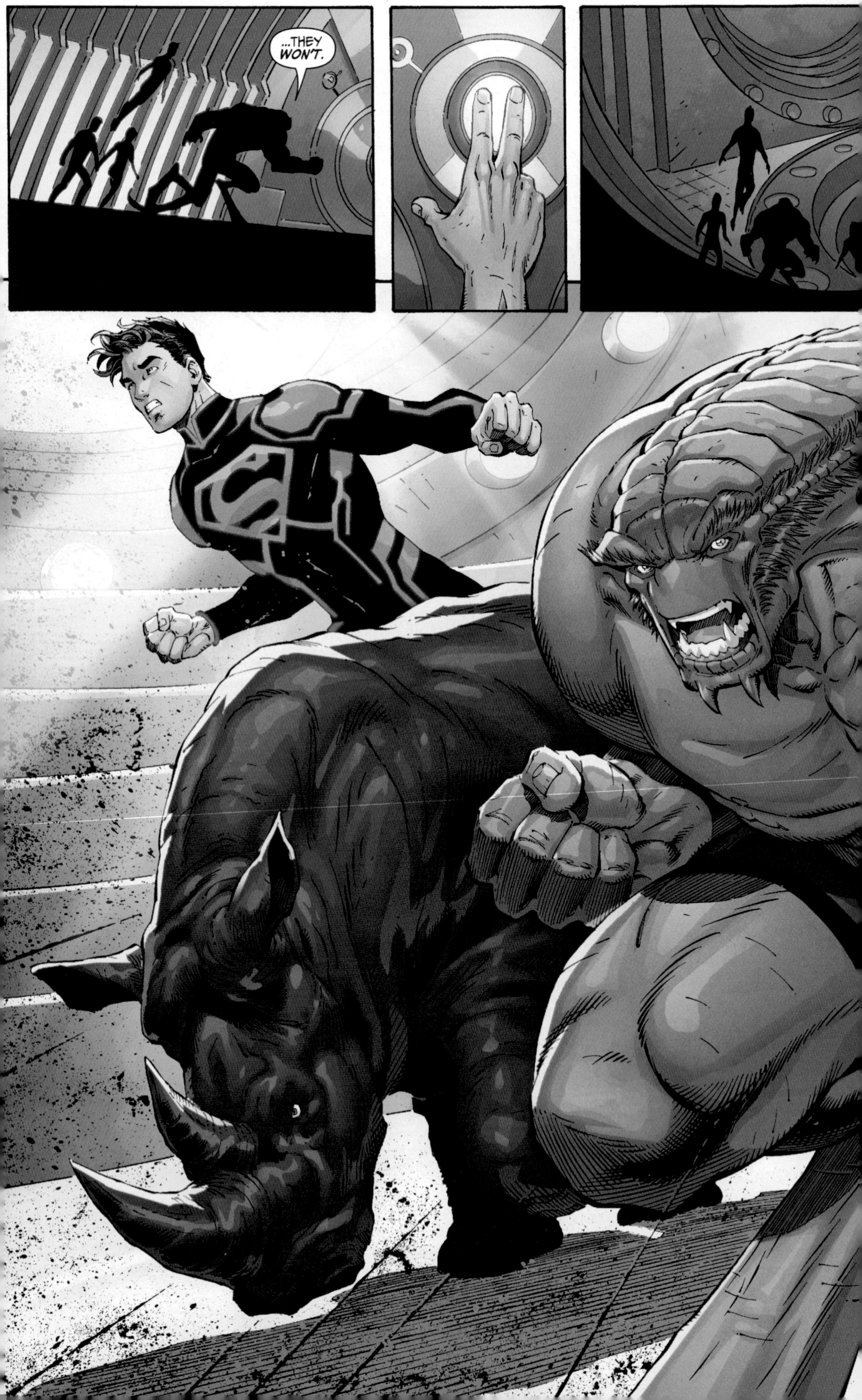
...THEY WON'T.

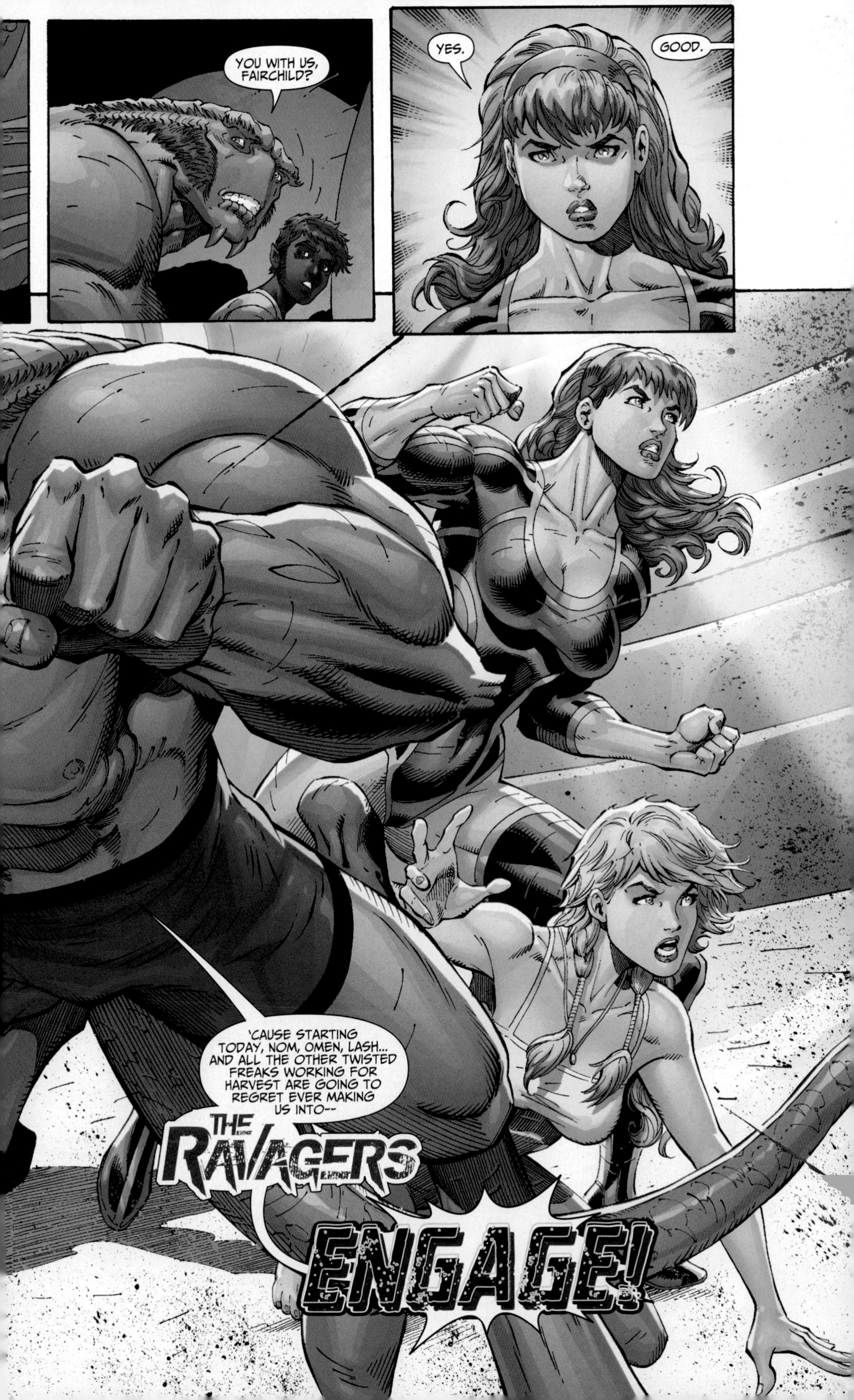
YOU WITH US, FAIRCHILD?
YES.
GOOD.
'CAUSE STARTING TODAY, NOM, OMEN, LASH... AND ALL THE OTHER TWISTED FREAKS WORKING FOR HARVEST ARE GOING TO REGRET EVER MAKING US INTO--
THE RAVAGERS
ENGAGE!

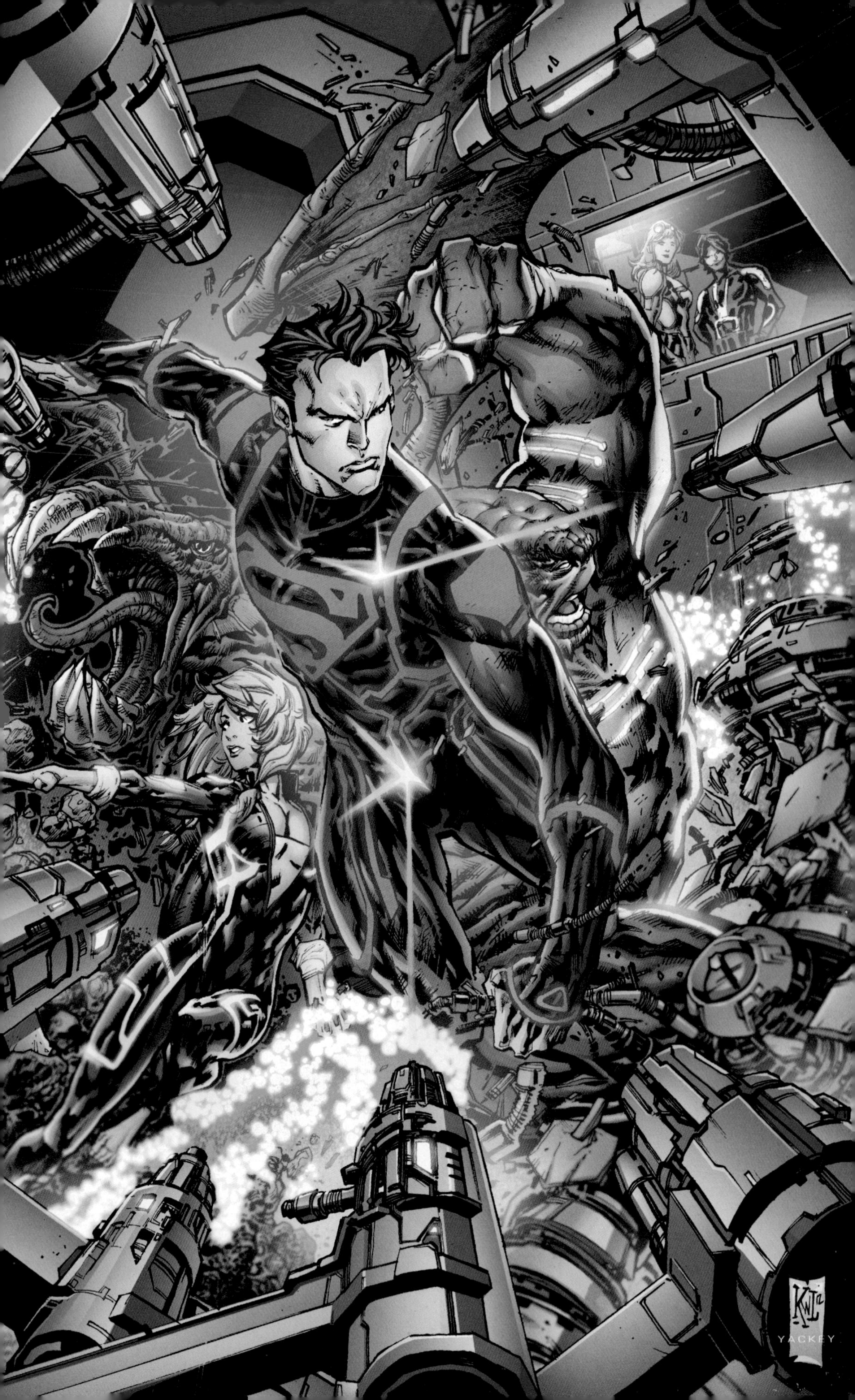
YACKEY

...ENGAGE!

HOWARD MACKIE
writer

IAN CHURCHILL & TYLER KIRKHAM
pencillers

NORM RAPMUND & MARLO ALQUIZA
inkers

cover art by
KEN LASHLEY & MATT YACKEY

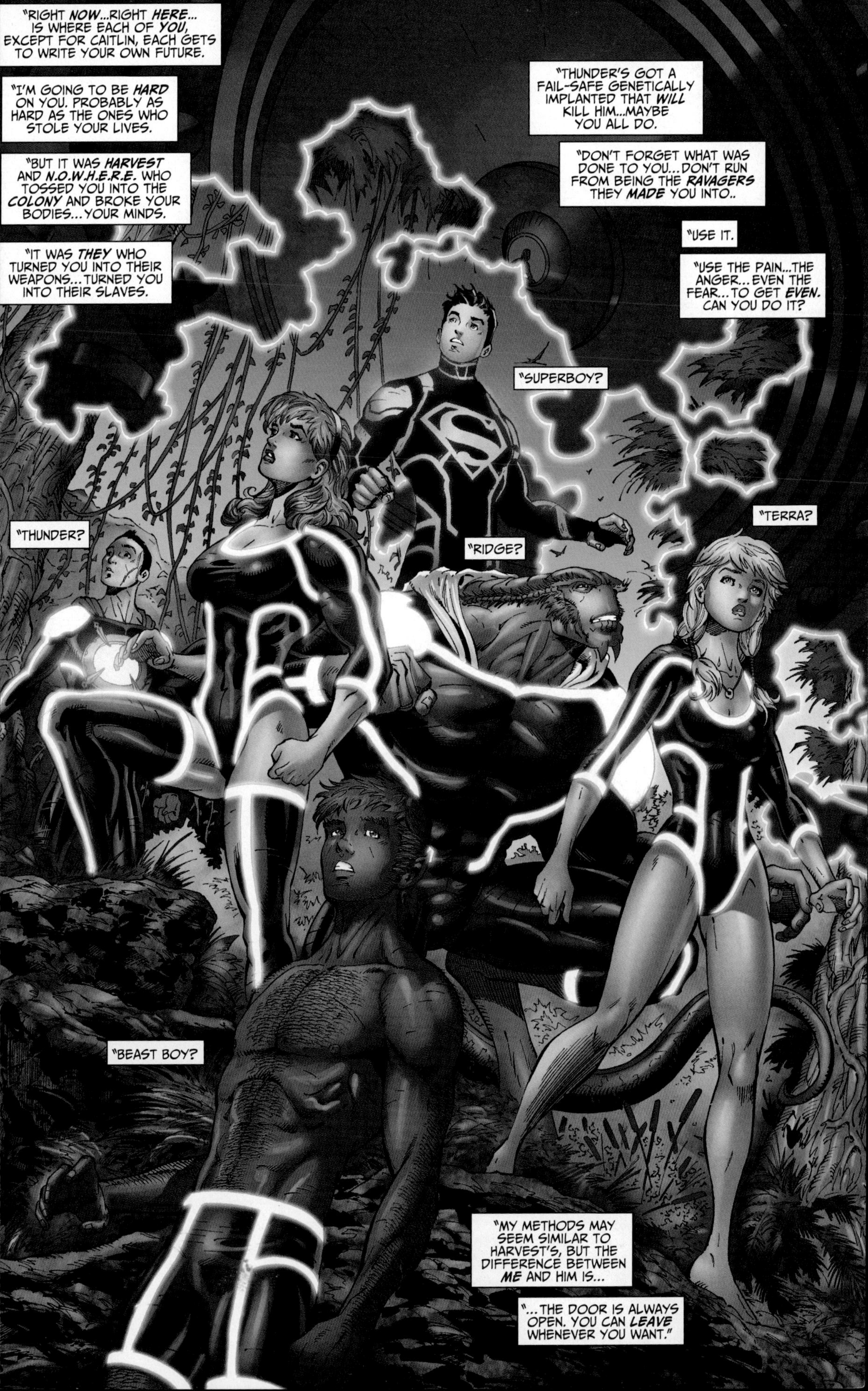
"RIGHT NOW...RIGHT HERE... IS WHERE EACH OF YOU, EXCEPT FOR CAITLIN, EACH GETS TO WRITE YOUR OWN FUTURE.
"I'M GOING TO BE HARD ON YOU. PROBABLY AS HARD AS THE ONES WHO STOLE YOUR LIVES.
"BUT IT WAS HARVEST AND N.O.W.H.E.R.E. WHO TOSSED YOU INTO THE COLONY AND BROKE YOUR BODIES... YOUR MINDS.
"IT WAS THEY WHO TURNED YOU INTO THEIR WEAPONS... TURNED YOU INTO THEIR SLAVES.
"THUNDER'S GOT A FAIL-SAFE GENETICALLY IMPLANTED THAT WILL KILL HIM...MAYBE YOU ALL DO.
"DON'T FORGET WHAT WAS DONE TO YOU...DON'T RUN FROM BEING THE RAVAGERS THEY MADE YOU INTO..
"USE IT.
"USE THE PAIN...THE ANGER... EVEN THE FEAR... TO GET EVEN. CAN YOU DO IT?
"SUPERBOY?
"THUNDER?
"RIDGE?
"TERRA?
"BEAST BOY?
"MY METHODS MAY SEEM SIMILAR TO HARVEST'S, BUT THE DIFFERENCE BETWEEN ME AND HIM IS...
"...THE DOOR IS ALWAYS OPEN. YOU CAN LEAVE WHENEVER YOU WANT."

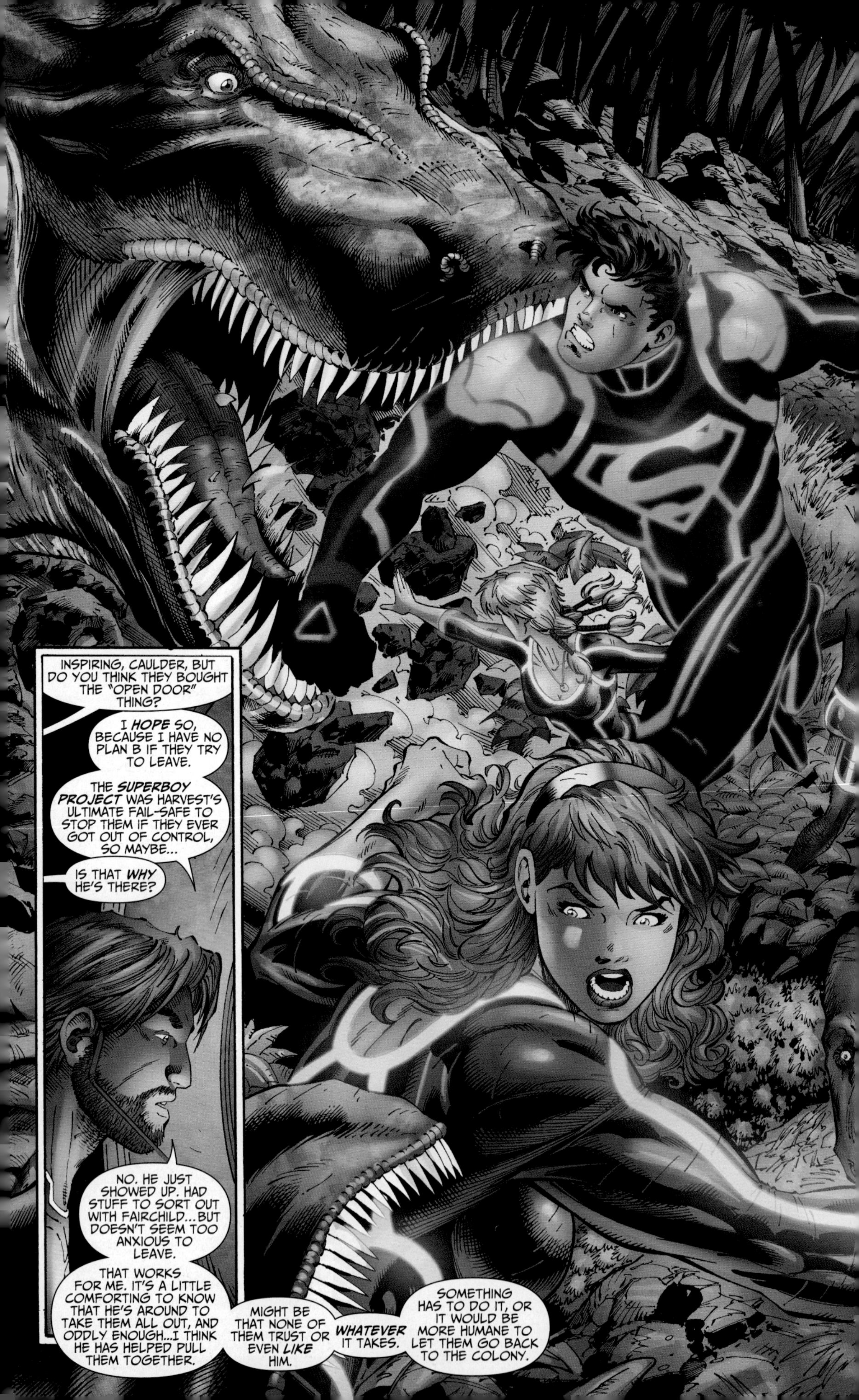
INSPIRING, CAULDER, BUT DO YOU THINK THEY BOUGHT THE "OPEN DOOR" THING?
I HOPE SO, BECAUSE I HAVE NO PLAN B IF THEY TRY TO LEAVE.
THE SUPERBOY PROJECT WAS HARVEST'S ULTIMATE FAIL-SAFE TO STOP THEM IF THEY EVER GOT OUT OF CONTROL, SO MAYBE...
IS THAT WHY HE'S THERE?
NO. HE JUST SHOWED UP. HAD STUFF TO SORT OUT WITH FAIRCHILD...BUT DOESN'T SEEM TOO ANXIOUS TO LEAVE.
THAT WORKS FOR ME. IT'S A LITTLE COMFORTING TO KNOW THAT HE'S AROUND TO TAKE THEM ALL OUT, AND ODDLY ENOUGH...I THINK HE HAS HELPED PULL THEM TOGETHER.
MIGHT BE THAT NONE OF THEM TRUST OR EVEN LIKE HIM.
WHATEVER IT TAKES.
SOMETHING HAS TO DO IT, OR IT WOULD BE MORE HUMANE TO LET THEM GO BACK TO THE COLONY.

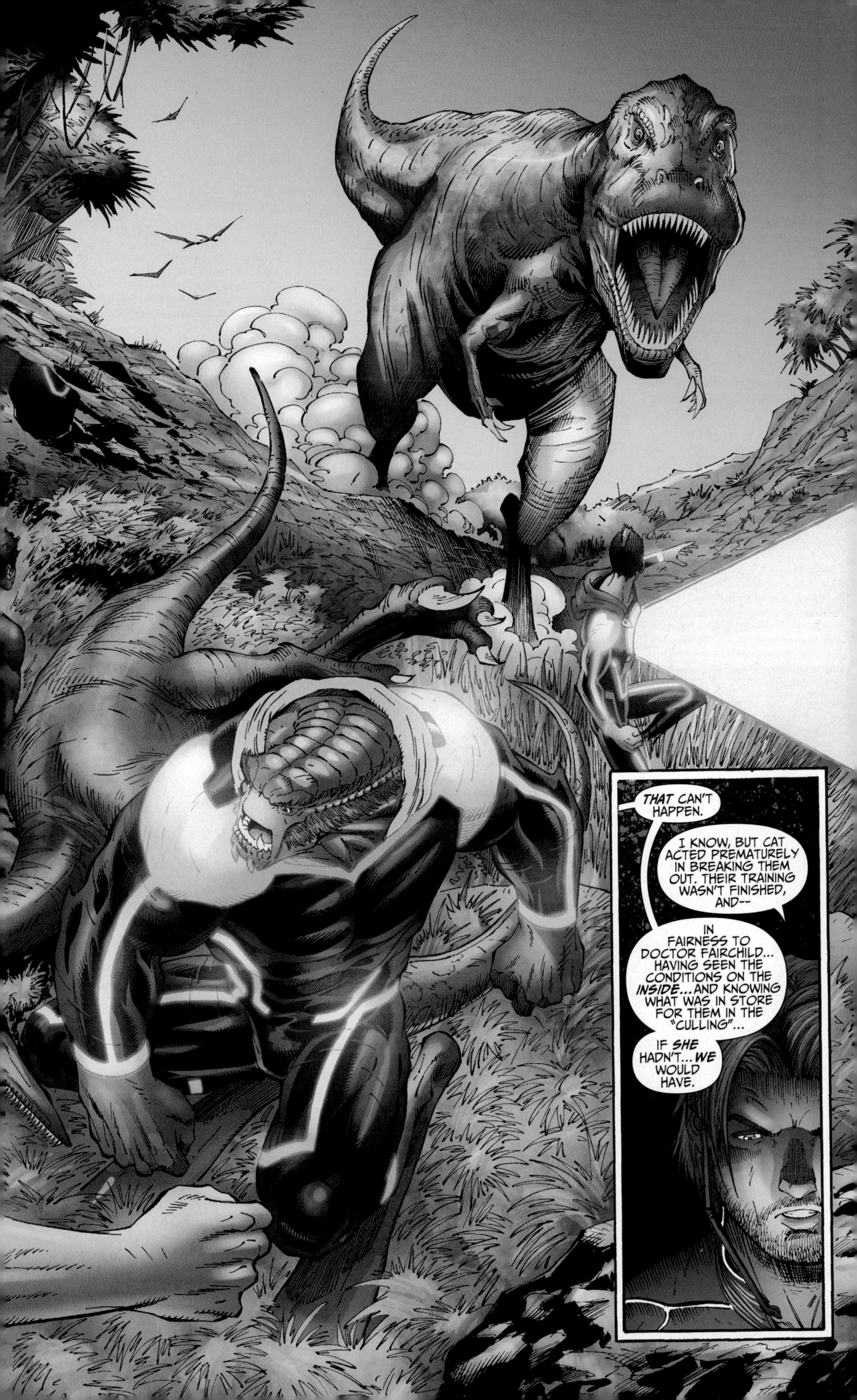

THAT CAN'T HAPPEN.
I KNOW, BUT CAT ACTED PREMATURELY IN BREAKING THEM OUT. THEIR TRAINING WASN'T FINISHED, AND--
IN FAIRNESS TO DOCTOR FAIRCHILD... HAVING SEEN THE CONDITIONS ON THE INSIDE... AND KNOWING WHAT WAS IN STORE FOR THEM IN THE "CULLING"...
IF SHE HADN'T... WE WOULD HAVE.

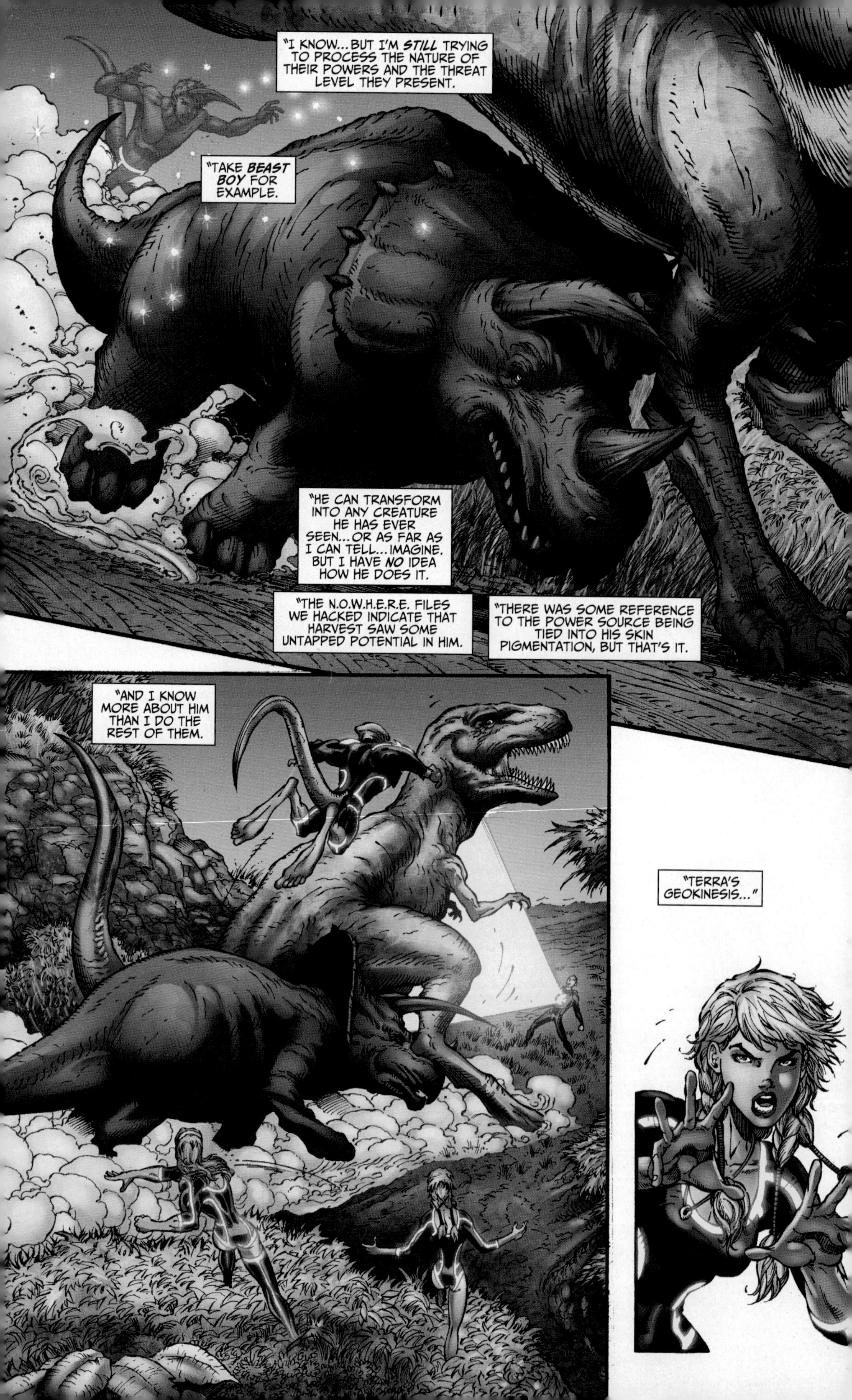
"I KNOW...BUT I'M STILL TRYING TO PROCESS THE NATURE OF THEIR POWERS AND THE THREAT LEVEL THEY PRESENT.
"TAKE BEAST BOY FOR EXAMPLE.
"HE CAN TRANSFORM INTO ANY CREATURE HE HAS EVER SEEN...OR AS FAR AS I CAN TELL...IMAGINE. BUT I HAVE NO IDEA HOW HE DOES IT.
"THE N.O.W.H.E.R.E. FILES WE HACKED INDICATE THAT HARVEST SAW SOME UNTAPPED POTENTIAL IN HIM.
"THERE WAS SOME REFERENCE TO THE POWER SOURCE BEING TIED INTO HIS SKIN PIGMENTATION, BUT THAT'S IT.
"AND I KNOW MORE ABOUT HIM THAN I DO THE REST OF THEM.
"TERRA'S GEOKINESIS..."

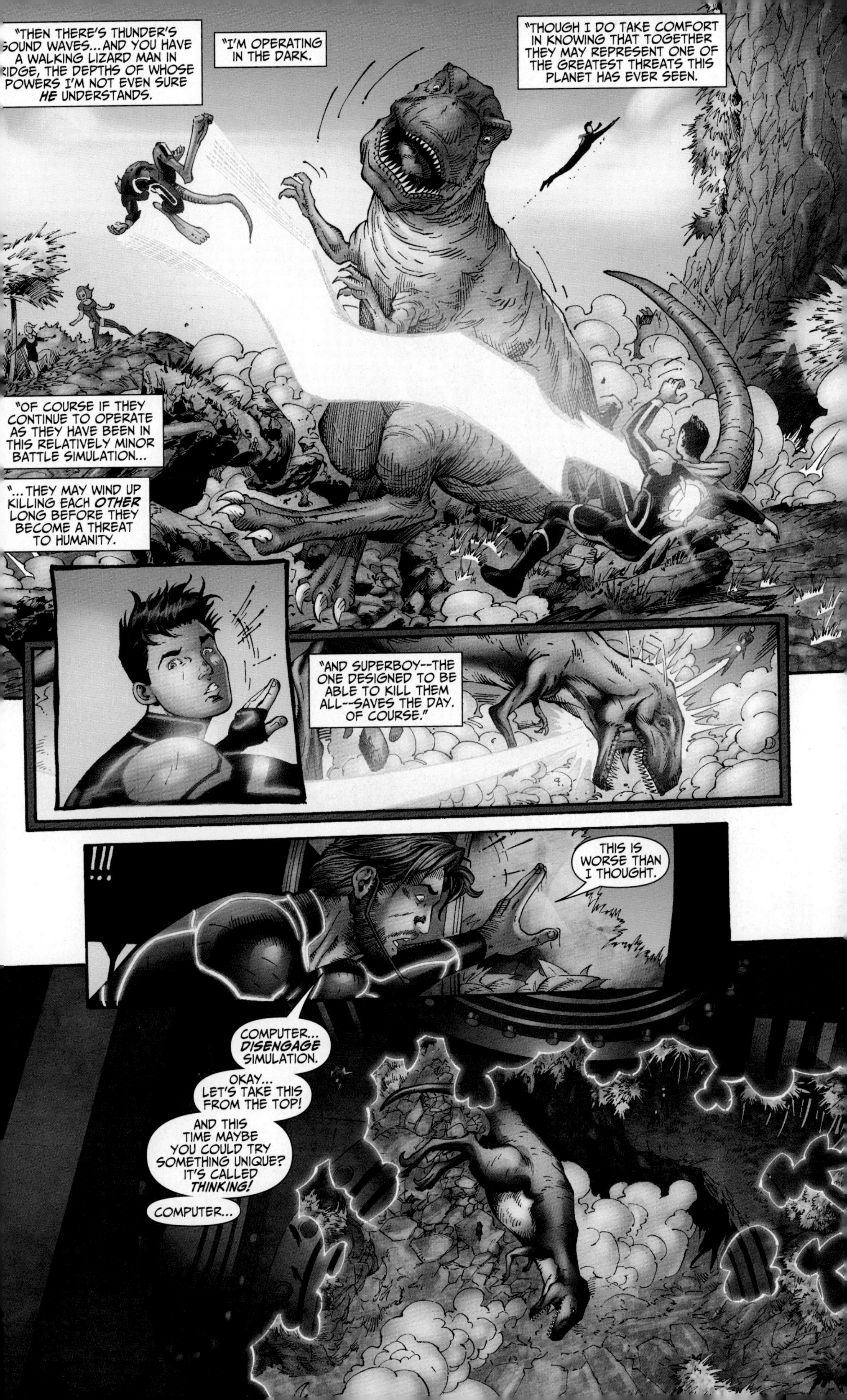

"THEN THERE'S THUNDER'S SOUND WAVES...AND YOU HAVE A WALKING LIZARD MAN IN RIDGE, THE DEPTHS OF WHOSE POWERS I'M NOT EVEN SURE HE UNDERSTANDS.
"I'M OPERATING IN THE DARK.
"THOUGH I DO TAKE COMFORT IN KNOWING THAT TOGETHER THEY MAY REPRESENT ONE OF THE GREATEST THREATS THIS PLANET HAS EVER SEEN.
"OF COURSE IF THEY CONTINUE TO OPERATE AS THEY HAVE BEEN IN THIS RELATIVELY MINOR BATTLE SIMULATION...
"...THEY MAY WIND UP KILLING EACH OTHER LONG BEFORE THEY BECOME A THREAT TO HUMANITY.
"AND SUPERBOY--THE ONE DESIGNED TO BE ABLE TO KILL THEM ALL--SAVES THE DAY. OF COURSE."
!!!
THIS IS WORSE THAN I THOUGHT.
COMPUTER... DISENGAGE SIMULATION.
OKAY... LET'S TAKE THIS FROM THE TOP!
AND THIS TIME MAYBE YOU COULD TRY SOMETHING UNIQUE? IT'S CALLED THINKING!
COMPUTER...

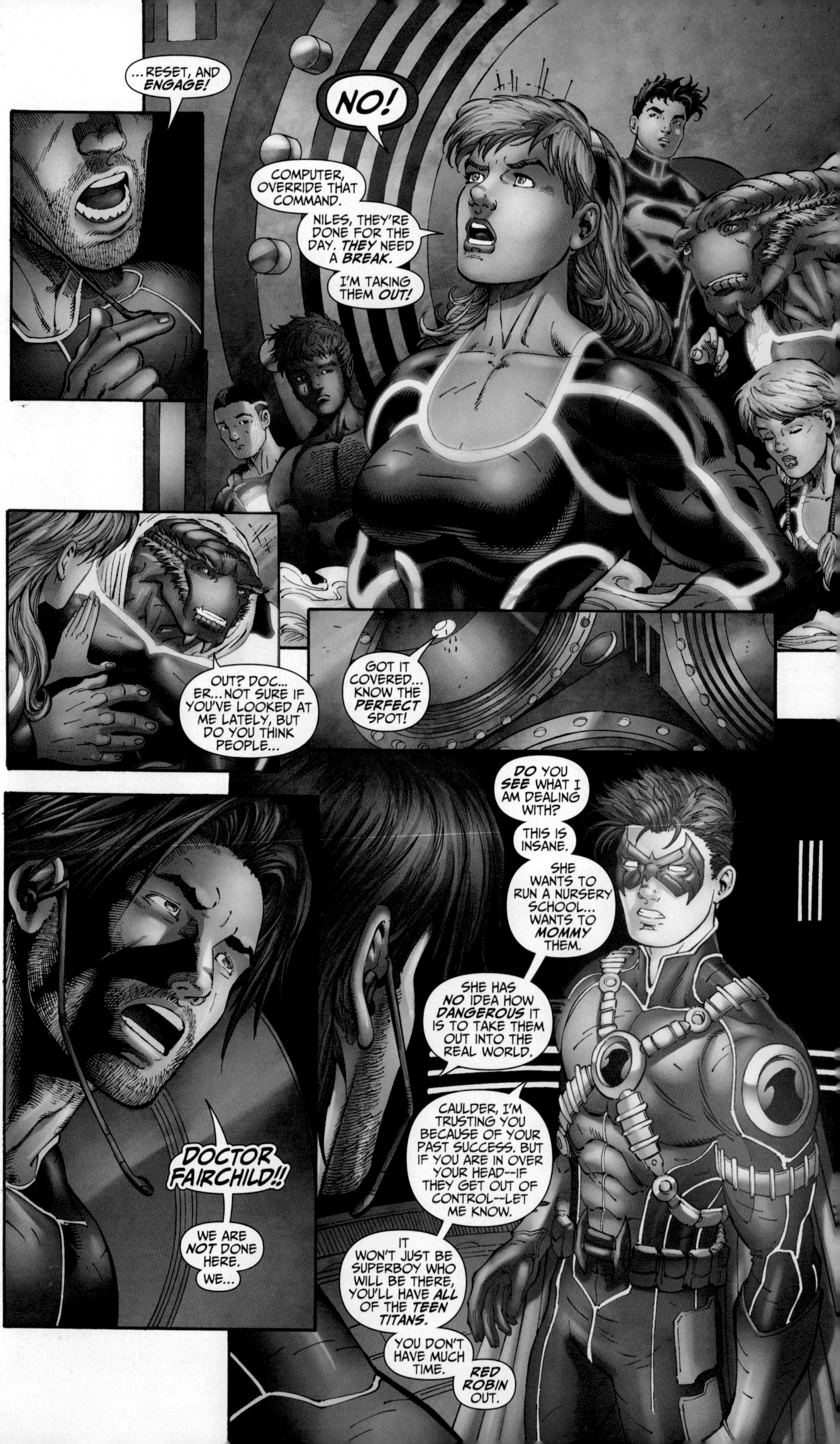

...RESET, AND ENGAGE!
NO!
COMPUTER, OVERRIDE THAT COMMAND.
NILES, THEY'RE DONE FOR THE DAY. THEY NEED A BREAK.
I'M TAKING THEM OUT!
OUT? DOC... ER...NOT SURE IF YOU'VE LOOKED AT ME LATELY, BUT DO YOU THINK PEOPLE...
GOT IT COVERED... KNOW THE PERFECT SPOT!
DOCTOR FAIRCHILD!!
WE ARE NOT DONE HERE.
WE...
DO YOU SEE WHAT I AM DEALING WITH?
THIS IS INSANE.
SHE WANTS TO RUN A NURSERY SCHOOL... WANTS TO MOMMY THEM.
SHE HAS NO IDEA HOW DANGEROUS IT IS TO TAKE THEM OUT INTO THE REAL WORLD.
CAULDER, I'M TRUSTING YOU BECAUSE OF YOUR PAST SUCCESS. BUT IF YOU ARE IN OVER YOUR HEAD--IF THEY GET OUT OF CONTROL--LET ME KNOW.
IT WON'T JUST BE SUPERBOY WHO WILL BE THERE, YOU'LL HAVE ALL OF THE TEEN TITANS.
YOU DON'T HAVE MUCH TIME.
RED ROBIN OUT.

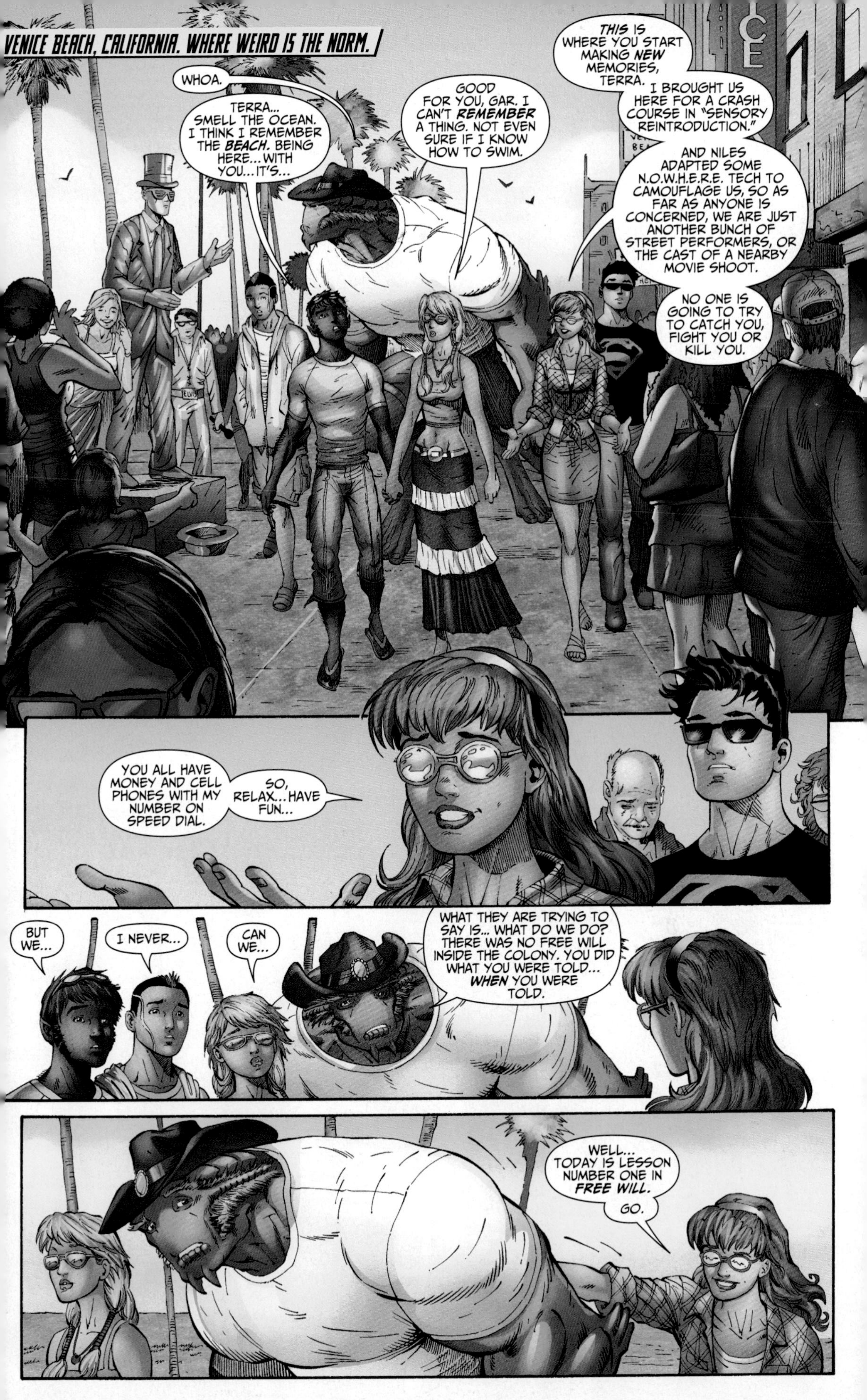
VENICE BEACH, CALIFORNIA. WHERE WEIRD IS THE NORM.
WHOA.
TERRA... SMELL THE OCEAN. I THINK I REMEMBER THE BEACH. BEING HERE...WITH YOU...IT'S...
GOOD FOR YOU, GAR. I CAN'T REMEMBER A THING. NOT EVEN SURE IF I KNOW HOW TO SWIM.
THIS IS WHERE YOU START MAKING NEW MEMORIES, TERRA.
I BROUGHT US HERE FOR A CRASH COURSE IN "SENSORY REINTRODUCTION."
AND NILES ADAPTED SOME N.O.W.H.E.R.E. TECH TO CAMOUFLAGE US, SO AS FAR AS ANYONE IS CONCERNED, WE ARE JUST ANOTHER BUNCH OF STREET PERFORMERS, OR THE CAST OF A NEARBY MOVIE SHOOT.
NO ONE IS GOING TO TRY TO CATCH YOU, FIGHT YOU OR KILL YOU.
YOU ALL HAVE MONEY AND CELL PHONES WITH MY NUMBER ON SPEED DIAL.
SO, RELAX...HAVE FUN...
BUT WE...
I NEVER...
CAN WE...
WHAT THEY ARE TRYING TO SAY IS... WHAT DO WE DO? THERE WAS NO FREE WILL INSIDE THE COLONY. YOU DID WHAT YOU WERE TOLD... WHEN YOU WERE TOLD.
WELL... TODAY IS LESSON NUMBER ONE IN FREE WILL.
GO.

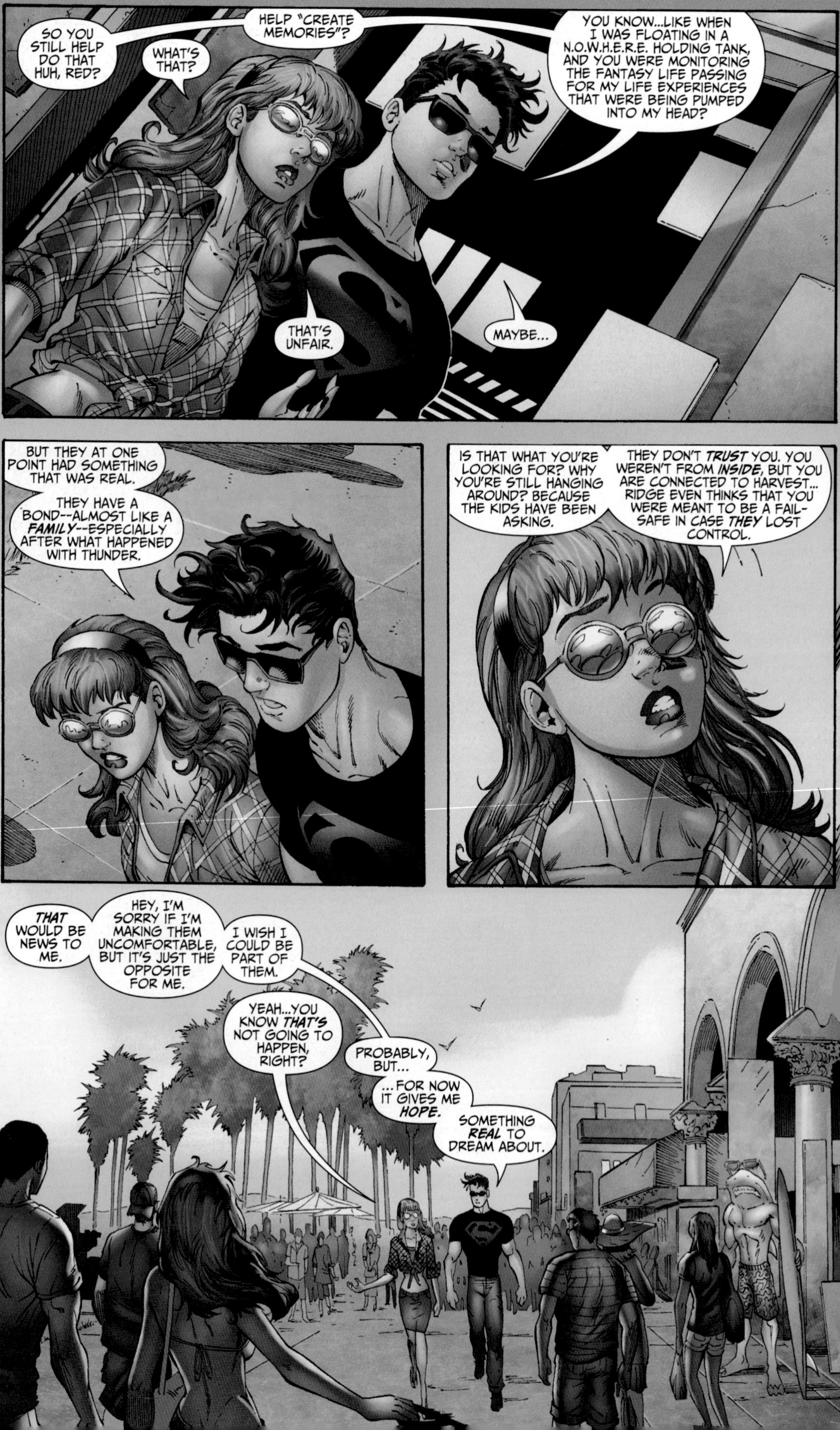
SO YOU STILL HELP DO THAT HUH, RED?
WHAT'S THAT?
HELP "CREATE MEMORIES"?
YOU KNOW...LIKE WHEN I WAS FLOATING IN A N.O.W.H.E.R.E. HOLDING TANK, AND YOU WERE MONITORING THE FANTASY LIFE PASSING FOR MY LIFE EXPERIENCES THAT WERE BEING PUMPED INTO MY HEAD?
THAT'S UNFAIR.
MAYBE...
BUT THEY AT ONE POINT HAD SOMETHING THAT WAS REAL.
THEY HAVE A BOND--ALMOST LIKE A *FAMILY*--ESPECIALLY AFTER WHAT HAPPENED WITH THUNDER.
IS THAT WHAT YOU'RE LOOKING FOR? WHY YOU'RE STILL HANGING AROUND? BECAUSE THE KIDS HAVE BEEN ASKING.
THEY DON'T *TRUST* YOU. YOU WEREN'T FROM *INSIDE*, BUT YOU ARE CONNECTED TO HARVEST... RIDGE EVEN THINKS THAT YOU WERE MEANT TO BE A FAIL-SAFE IN CASE *THEY* LOST CONTROL.
THAT WOULD BE NEWS TO ME.
HEY, I'M SORRY IF I'M MAKING THEM UNCOMFORTABLE, BUT IT'S JUST THE OPPOSITE FOR ME.
I WISH I COULD BE PART OF THEM.
YEAH...YOU KNOW *THAT'S* NOT GOING TO HAPPEN, RIGHT?
PROBABLY, BUT...
...FOR NOW IT GIVES ME *HOPE.*
SOMETHING *REAL* TO DREAM ABOUT.

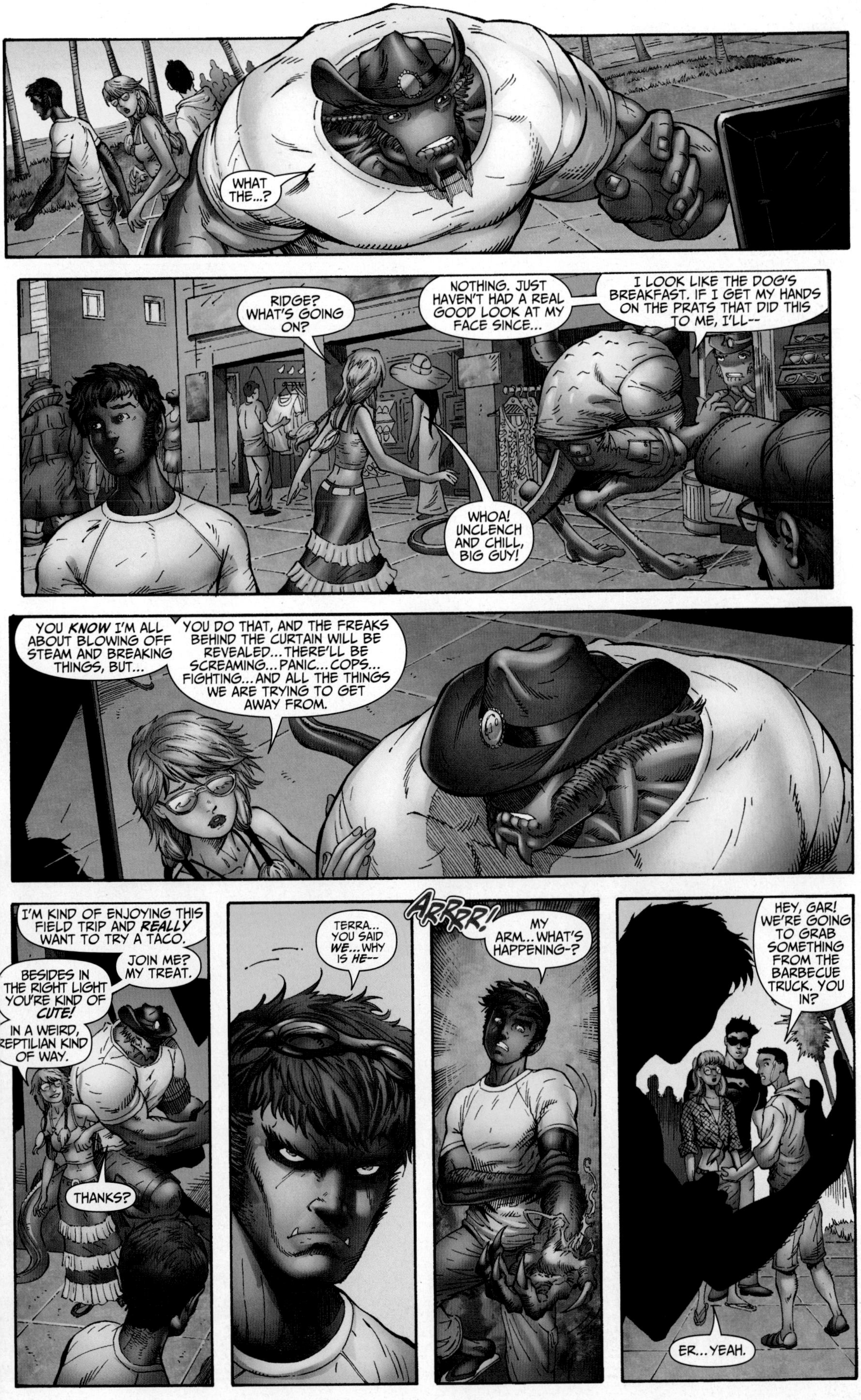
WHAT THE...?
RIDGE? WHAT'S GOING ON?
NOTHING. JUST HAVEN'T HAD A REAL GOOD LOOK AT MY FACE SINCE...
I LOOK LIKE THE DOG'S BREAKFAST. IF I GET MY HANDS ON THE PRATS THAT DID THIS TO ME, I'LL--
WHOA! UNCLENCH AND CHILL, BIG GUY!
YOU KNOW I'M ALL ABOUT BLOWING OFF STEAM AND BREAKING THINGS, BUT...
YOU DO THAT, AND THE FREAKS BEHIND THE CURTAIN WILL BE REVEALED...THERE'LL BE SCREAMING...PANIC...COPS... FIGHTING...AND ALL THE THINGS WE ARE TRYING TO GET AWAY FROM.
I'M KIND OF ENJOYING THIS FIELD TRIP AND REALLY WANT TO TRY A TACO.
JOIN ME? MY TREAT.
BESIDES IN THE RIGHT LIGHT YOU'RE KIND OF CUTE!
IN A WEIRD, REPTILIAN KIND OF WAY.
THANKS?
TERRA... YOU SAID WE...WHY IS HE--
ARRRR!
MY ARM...WHAT'S HAPPENING-?
HEY, GAR! WE'RE GOING TO GRAB SOMETHING FROM THE BARBECUE TRUCK. YOU IN?
ER...YEAH.

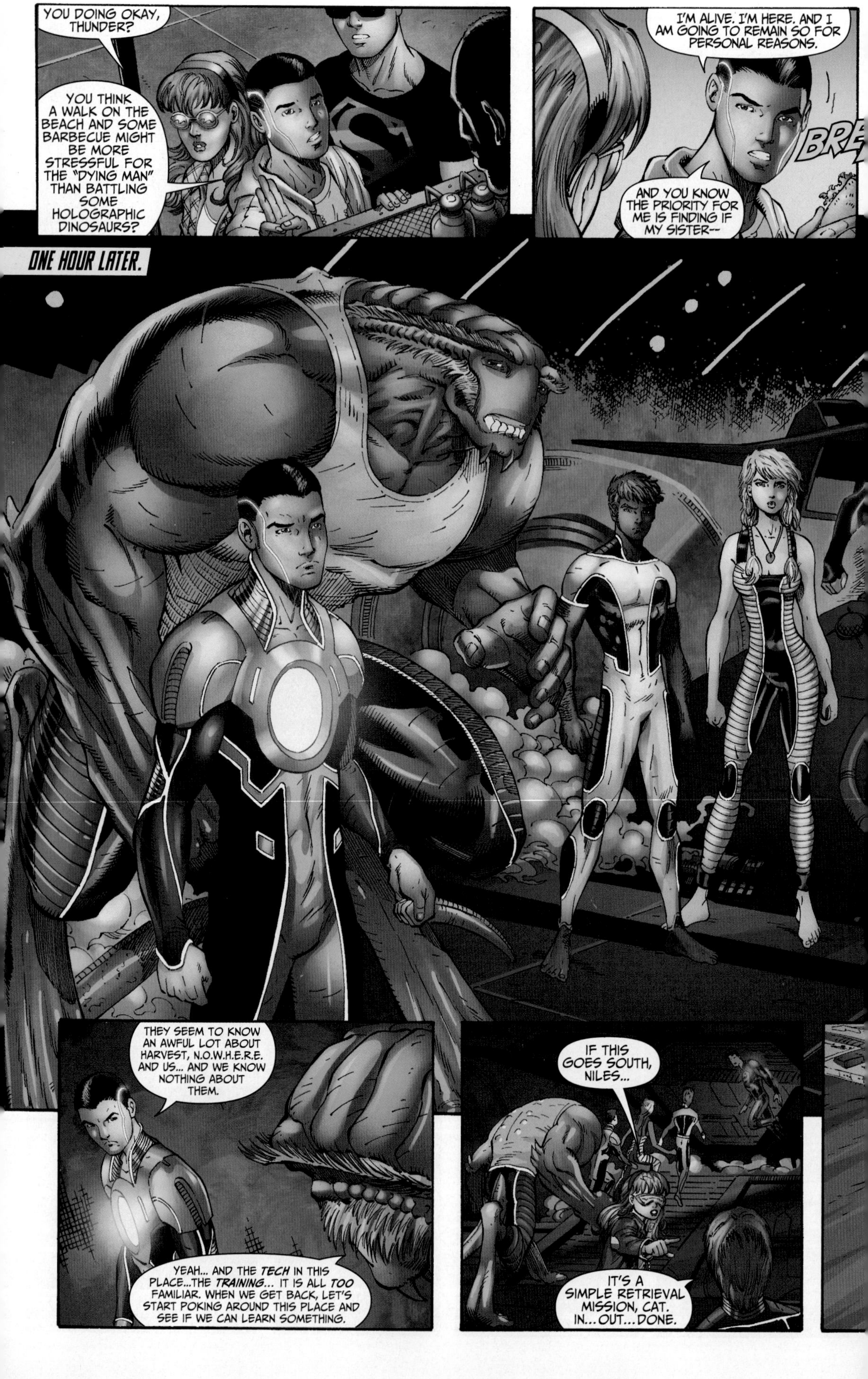

YOU DOING OKAY, THUNDER?
YOU THINK A WALK ON THE BEACH AND SOME BARBECUE MIGHT BE MORE STRESSFUL FOR THE "DYING MAN" THAN BATTLING SOME HOLOGRAPHIC DINOSAURS?
I'M ALIVE. I'M HERE. AND I AM GOING TO REMAIN SO FOR PERSONAL REASONS.
AND YOU KNOW THE PRIORITY FOR ME IS FINDING IF MY SISTER--
BRE
ONE HOUR LATER.
THEY SEEM TO KNOW AN AWFUL LOT ABOUT HARVEST, N.O.W.H.E.R.E. AND US... AND WE KNOW NOTHING ABOUT THEM.
YEAH... AND THE TECH IN THIS PLACE...THE TRAINING... IT IS ALL TOO FAMILIAR. WHEN WE GET BACK, LET'S START POKING AROUND THIS PLACE AND SEE IF WE CAN LEARN SOMETHING.
IF THIS GOES SOUTH, NILES...
IT'S A SIMPLE RETRIEVAL MISSION, CAT. IN...OUT...DONE.

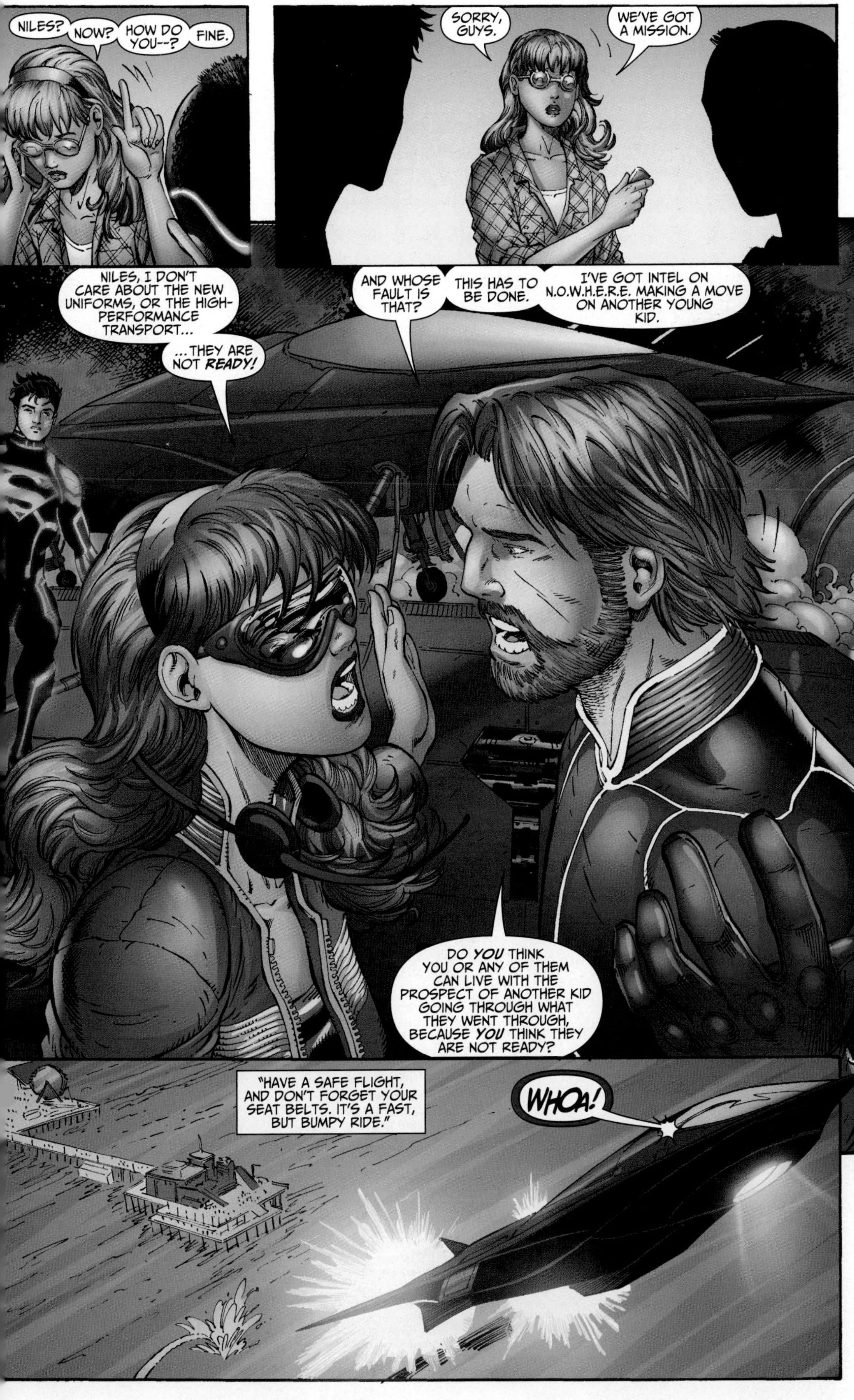
NILES?
NOW?
HOW DO YOU--?
FINE.
SORRY, GUYS.
WE'VE GOT A MISSION.
NILES, I DON'T CARE ABOUT THE NEW UNIFORMS, OR THE HIGH-PERFORMANCE TRANSPORT...
...THEY ARE NOT *READY!*
AND WHOSE FAULT IS THAT?
THIS HAS TO BE DONE.
I'VE GOT INTEL ON N.O.W.H.E.R.E. MAKING A MOVE ON ANOTHER YOUNG KID.
DO *YOU* THINK YOU OR ANY OF THEM CAN LIVE WITH THE PROSPECT OF ANOTHER KID GOING THROUGH WHAT THEY WENT THROUGH, BECAUSE *YOU* THINK THEY ARE NOT READY?
"HAVE A SAFE FLIGHT, AND DON'T FORGET YOUR SEAT BELTS. IT'S A FAST, BUT BUMPY RIDE."
WHOA!

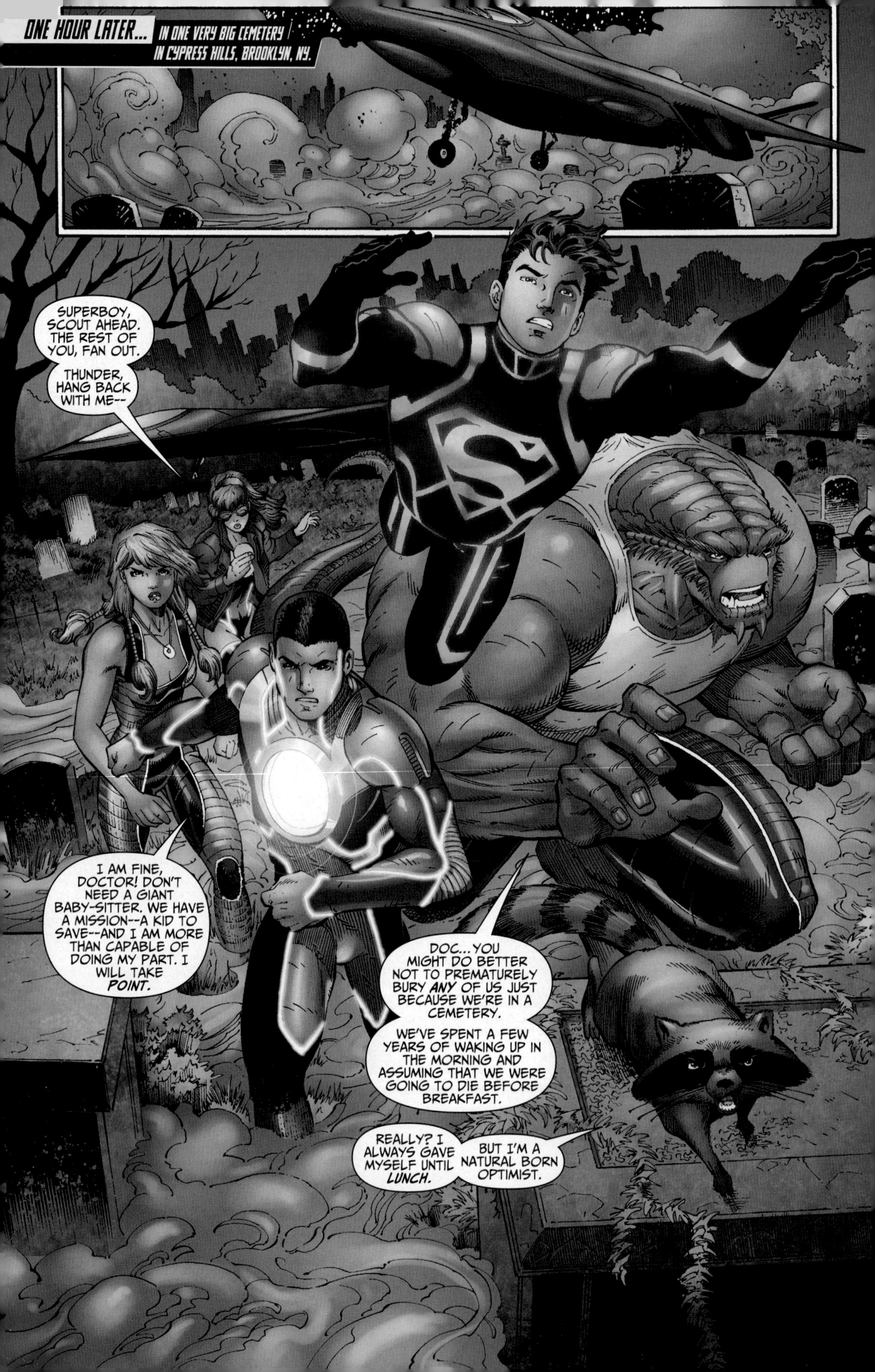
ONE HOUR LATER...
IN ONE VERY BIG CEMETERY IN CYPRESS HILLS, BROOKLYN, NY.
SUPERBOY, SCOUT AHEAD. THE REST OF YOU, FAN OUT.
THUNDER, HANG BACK WITH ME--
I AM FINE, DOCTOR! DON'T NEED A GIANT BABY-SITTER. WE HAVE A MISSION--A KID TO SAVE--AND I AM MORE THAN CAPABLE OF DOING MY PART. I WILL TAKE *POINT.*
DOC...YOU MIGHT DO BETTER NOT TO PREMATURELY BURY *ANY* OF US JUST BECAUSE WE'RE IN A CEMETERY.
WE'VE SPENT A FEW YEARS OF WAKING UP IN THE MORNING AND ASSUMING THAT WE WERE GOING TO DIE BEFORE BREAKFAST.
REALLY? I ALWAYS GAVE MYSELF UNTIL *LUNCH.*
BUT I'M A NATURAL BORN OPTIMIST.

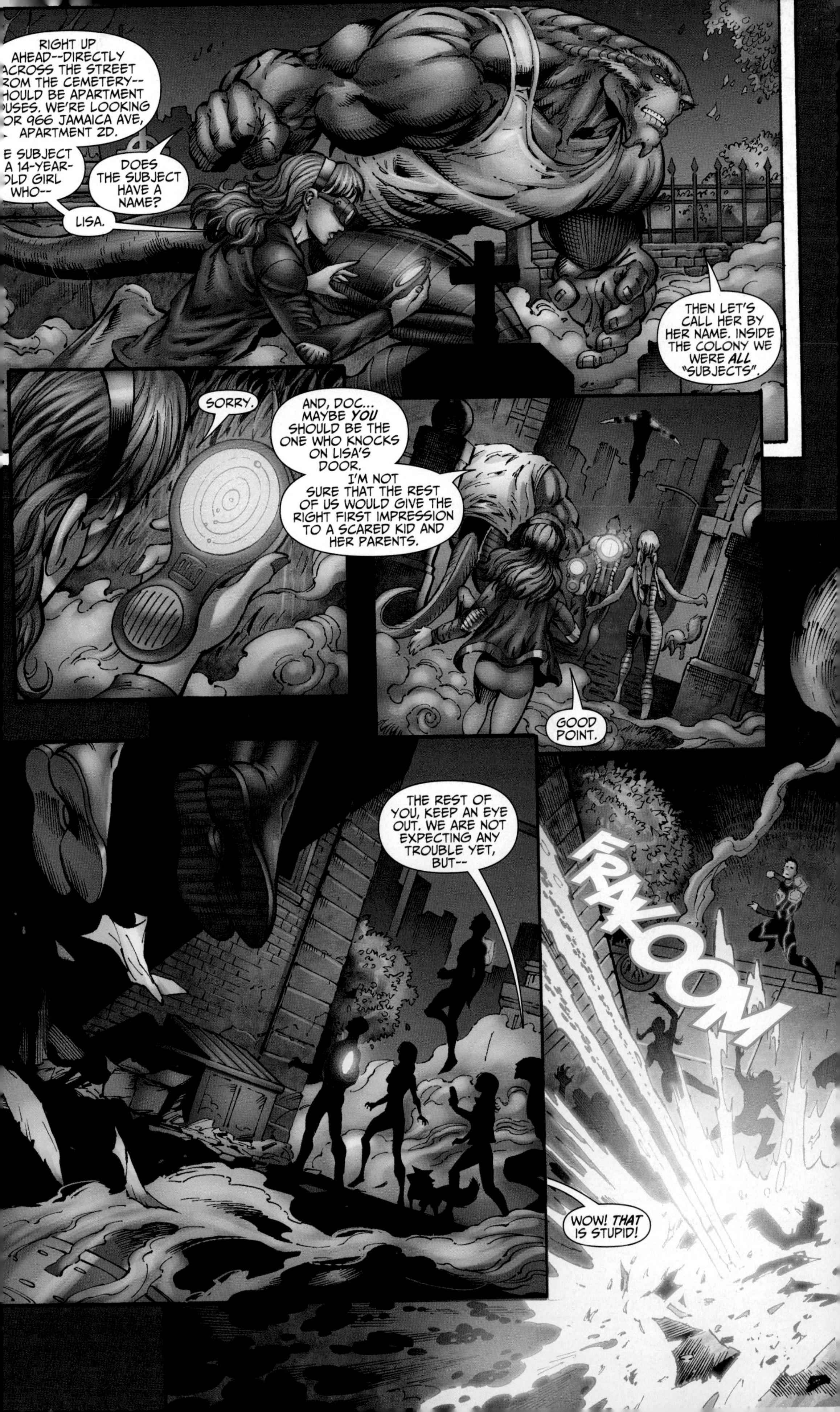

RIGHT UP AHEAD--DIRECTLY ACROSS THE STREET FROM THE CEMETERY--SHOULD BE APARTMENT HOUSES. WE'RE LOOKING FOR 966 JAMAICA AVE, APARTMENT 2D.
E SUBJECT A 14-YEAR-OLD GIRL WHO--
DOES THE SUBJECT HAVE A NAME?
LISA.
THEN LET'S CALL HER BY HER NAME. INSIDE THE COLONY WE WERE *ALL* "SUBJECTS".
SORRY.
AND, DOC... MAYBE *YOU* SHOULD BE THE ONE WHO KNOCKS ON LISA'S DOOR.
I'M NOT SURE THAT THE REST OF US WOULD GIVE THE RIGHT FIRST IMPRESSION TO A SCARED KID AND HER PARENTS.
GOOD POINT.
THE REST OF YOU, KEEP AN EYE OUT. WE ARE NOT EXPECTING ANY TROUBLE YET, BUT--
FRAKOOM
WOW! *THAT* IS STUPID!

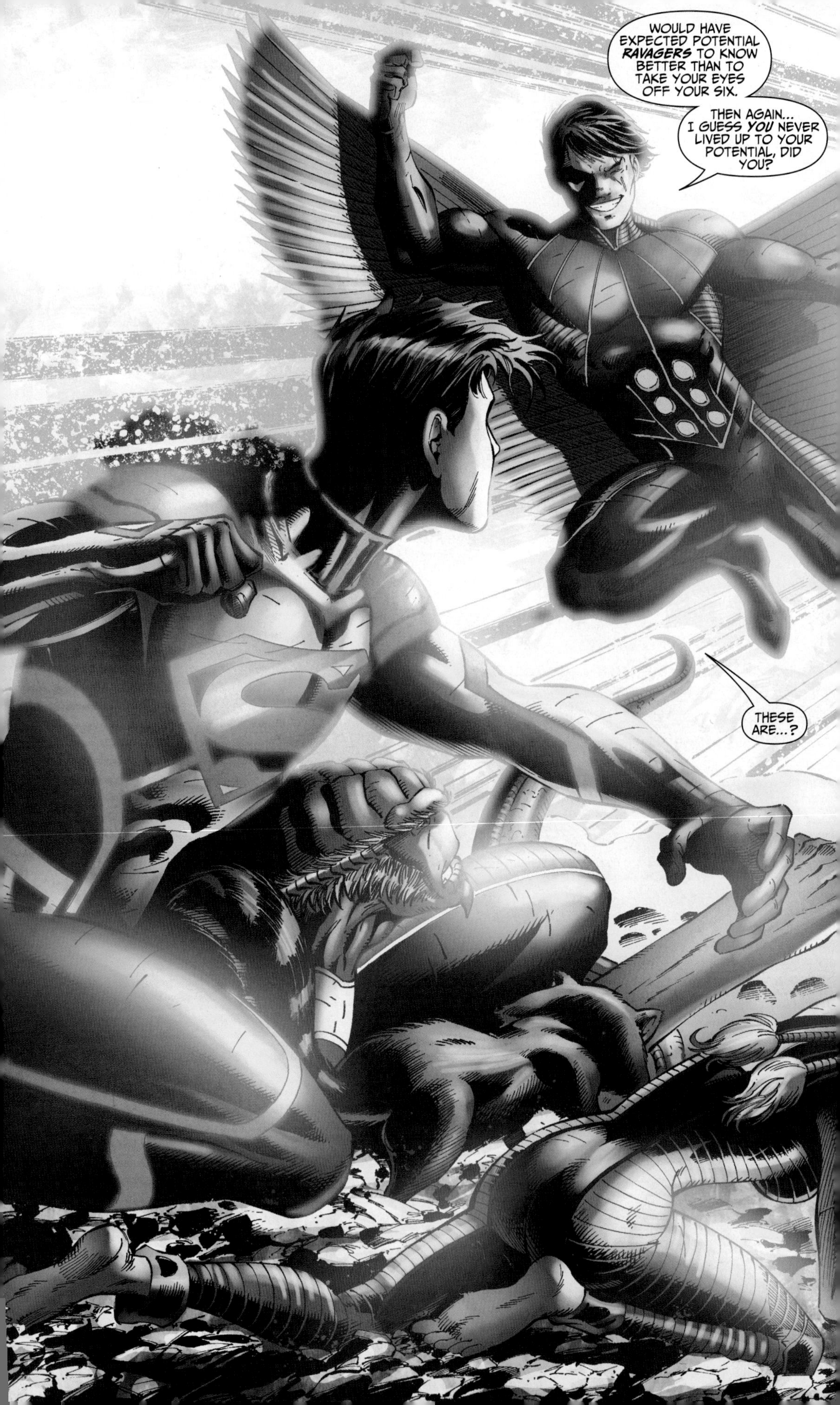
WOULD HAVE EXPECTED POTENTIAL RAVAGERS TO KNOW BETTER THAN TO TAKE YOUR EYES OFF YOUR SIX.
THEN AGAIN... I GUESS YOU NEVER LIVED UP TO YOUR POTENTIAL, DID YOU?
THESE ARE...?

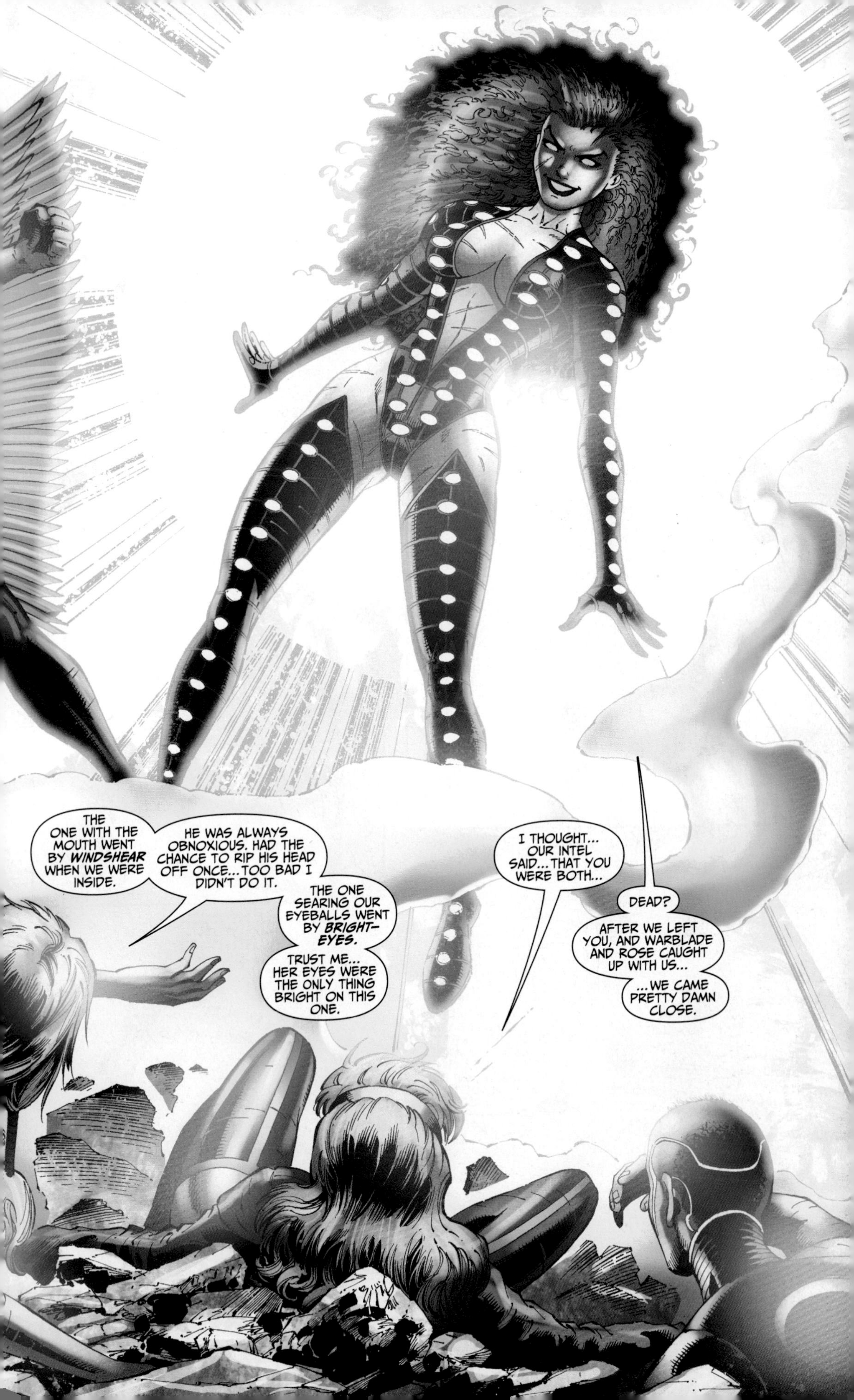

THE ONE WITH THE MOUTH WENT BY WINDSHEAR WHEN WE WERE INSIDE.
HE WAS ALWAYS OBNOXIOUS. HAD THE CHANCE TO RIP HIS HEAD OFF ONCE...TOO BAD I DIDN'T DO IT.
THE ONE SEARING OUR EYEBALLS WENT BY BRIGHT-EYES.
TRUST ME... HER EYES WERE THE ONLY THING BRIGHT ON THIS ONE.
I THOUGHT... OUR INTEL SAID...THAT YOU WERE BOTH...
DEAD?
AFTER WE LEFT YOU, AND WARBLADE AND ROSE CAUGHT UP WITH US...
...WE CAME PRETTY DAMN CLOSE.

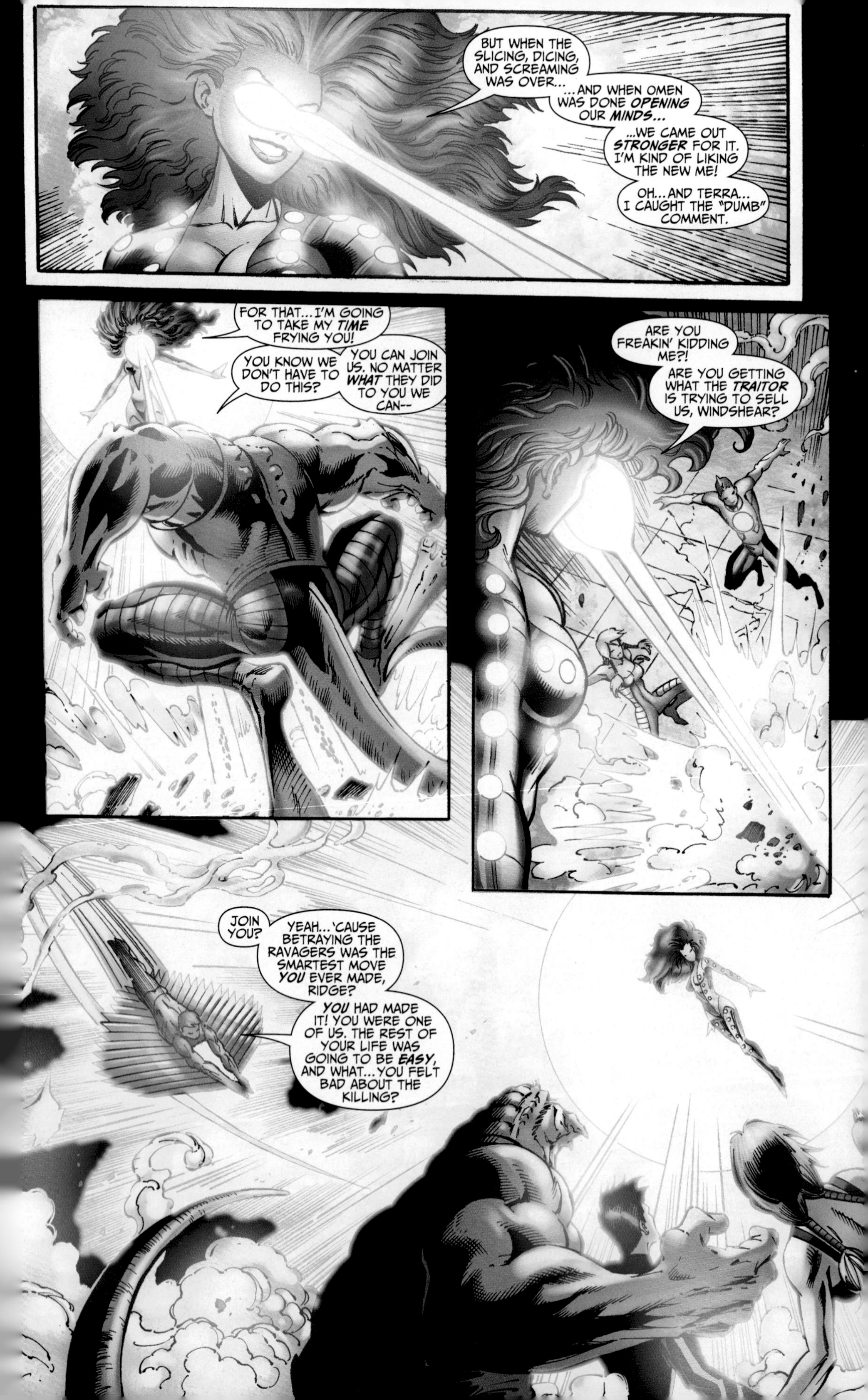
BUT WHEN THE SLICING, DICING, AND SCREAMING WAS OVER...
...AND WHEN OMEN WAS DONE OPENING OUR MINDS...
...WE CAME OUT STRONGER FOR IT. I'M KIND OF LIKING THE NEW ME!
OH...AND TERRA... I CAUGHT THE "DUMB" COMMENT.
FOR THAT...I'M GOING TO TAKE MY TIME FRYING YOU!
YOU KNOW WE DON'T HAVE TO DO THIS?
YOU CAN JOIN US. NO MATTER WHAT THEY DID TO YOU WE CAN--
ARE YOU FREAKIN' KIDDING ME?!
ARE YOU GETTING WHAT THE TRAITOR IS TRYING TO SELL US, WINDSHEAR?
JOIN YOU?
YEAH...'CAUSE BETRAYING THE RAVAGERS WAS THE SMARTEST MOVE YOU EVER MADE, RIDGE?
YOU HAD MADE IT! YOU WERE ONE OF US. THE REST OF YOUR LIFE WAS GOING TO BE EASY, AND WHAT...YOU FELT BAD ABOUT THE KILLING?

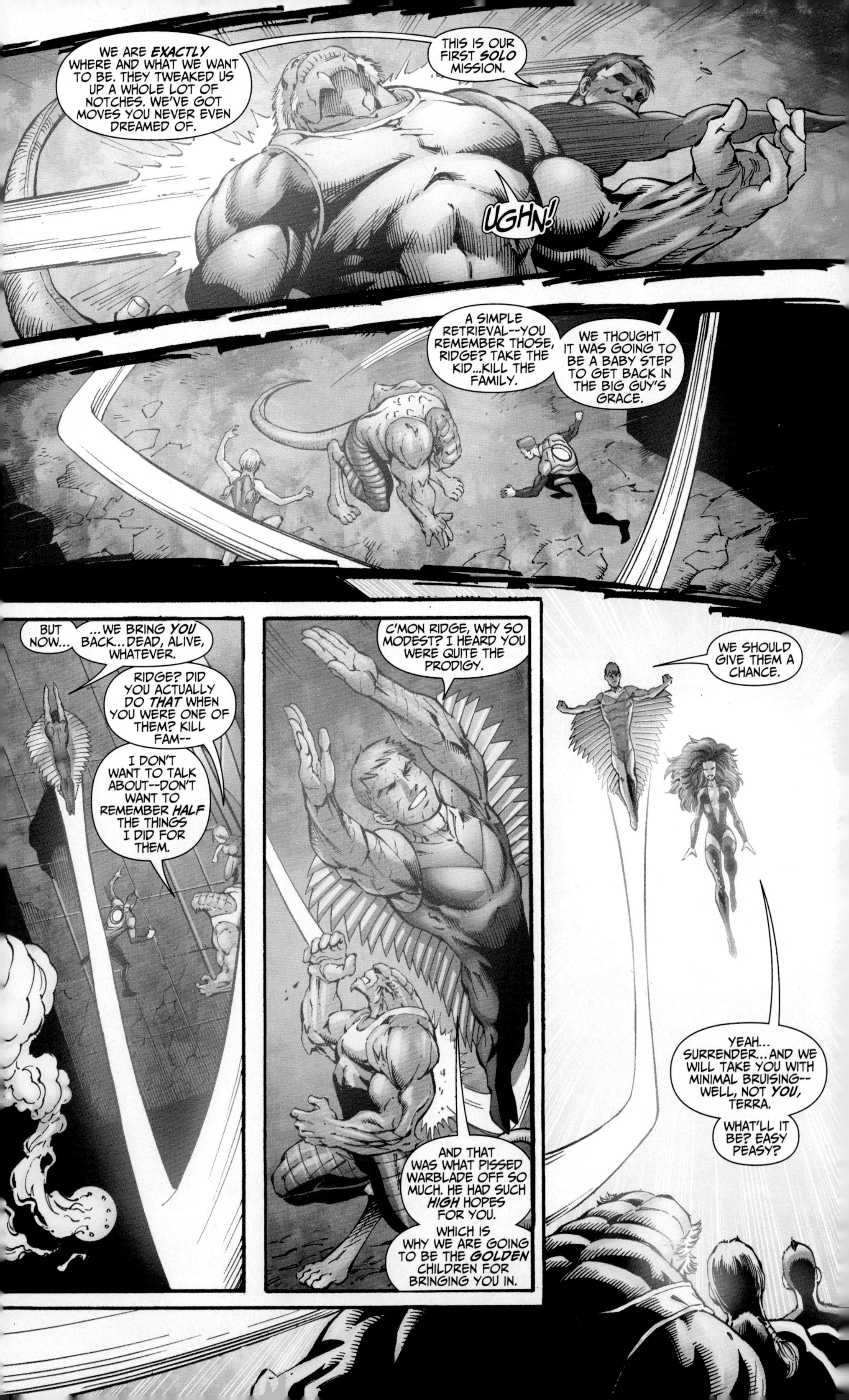
WE ARE EXACTLY WHERE AND WHAT WE WANT TO BE. THEY TWEAKED US UP A WHOLE LOT OF NOTCHES. WE'VE GOT MOVES YOU NEVER EVEN DREAMED OF.
THIS IS OUR FIRST SOLO MISSION.
UGHN!
A SIMPLE RETRIEVAL--YOU REMEMBER THOSE, RIDGE? TAKE THE KID...KILL THE FAMILY.
WE THOUGHT IT WAS GOING TO BE A BABY STEP TO GET BACK IN THE BIG GUY'S GRACE.
BUT NOW...
...WE BRING YOU BACK...DEAD, ALIVE, WHATEVER.
RIDGE? DID YOU ACTUALLY DO THAT WHEN YOU WERE ONE OF THEM? KILL FAM--
I DON'T WANT TO TALK ABOUT--DON'T WANT TO REMEMBER HALF THE THINGS I DID FOR THEM.
C'MON RIDGE, WHY SO MODEST? I HEARD YOU WERE QUITE THE PRODIGY.
AND THAT WAS WHAT PISSED WARBLADE OFF SO MUCH. HE HAD SUCH HIGH HOPES FOR YOU.
WHICH IS WHY WE ARE GOING TO BE THE GOLDEN CHILDREN FOR BRINGING YOU IN.
WE SHOULD GIVE THEM A CHANCE.
YEAH... SURRENDER...AND WE WILL TAKE YOU WITH MINIMAL BRUISING--WELL, NOT YOU, TERRA.
WHAT'LL IT BE? EASY PEASY?

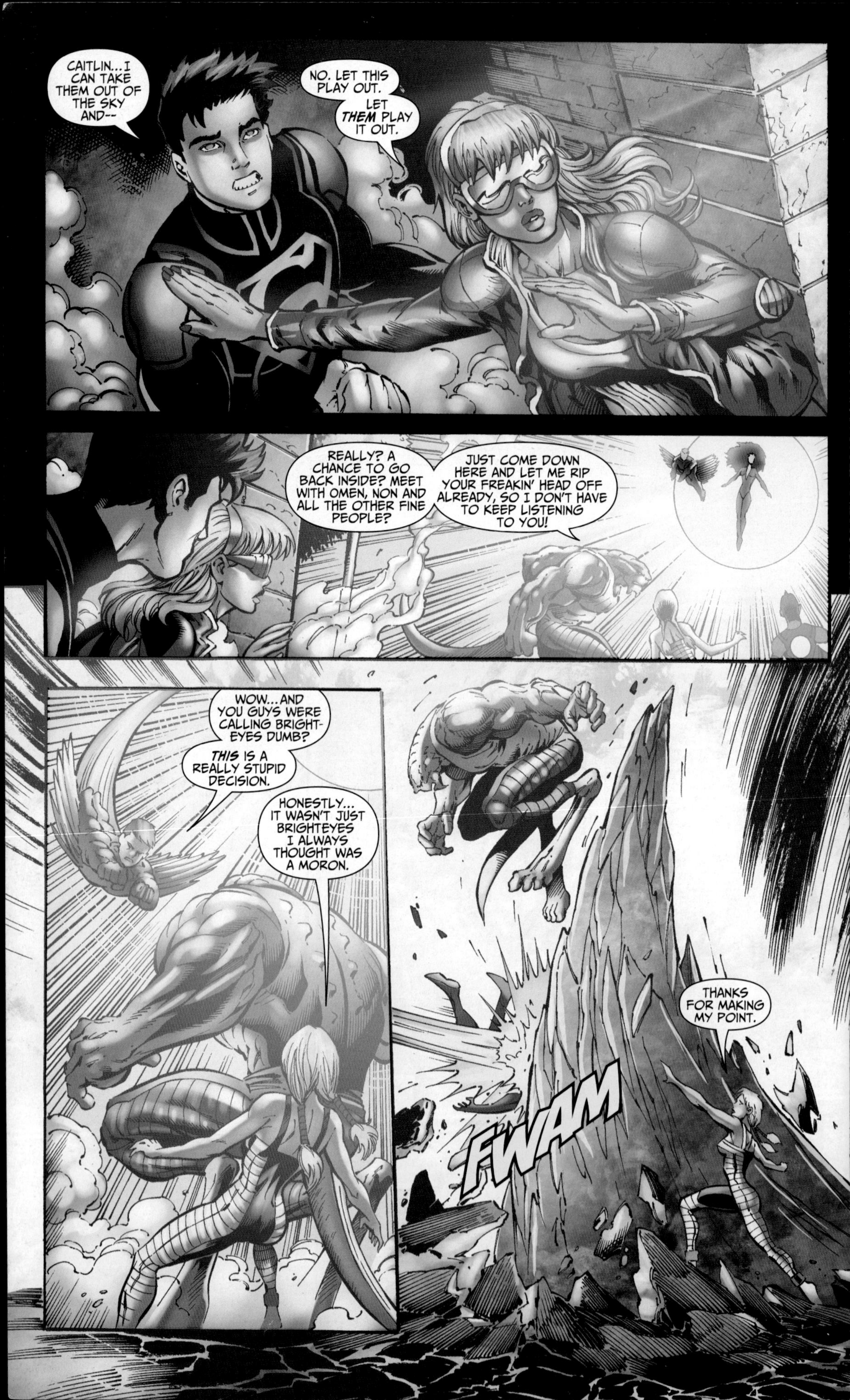
CAITLIN...I CAN TAKE THEM OUT OF THE SKY AND--
NO. LET THIS PLAY OUT.
LET *THEM* PLAY IT OUT.
REALLY? A CHANCE TO GO BACK INSIDE? MEET WITH OMEN, NON AND ALL THE OTHER FINE PEOPLE?
JUST COME DOWN HERE AND LET ME RIP YOUR FREAKIN' HEAD OFF ALREADY, SO I DON'T HAVE TO KEEP LISTENING TO YOU!
WOW...AND YOU GUYS WERE CALLING BRIGHT-EYES DUMB?
THIS IS A REALLY STUPID DECISION.
HONESTLY... IT WASN'T JUST BRIGHTEYES I ALWAYS THOUGHT WAS A MORON.
FWAM
THANKS FOR MAKING MY POINT.

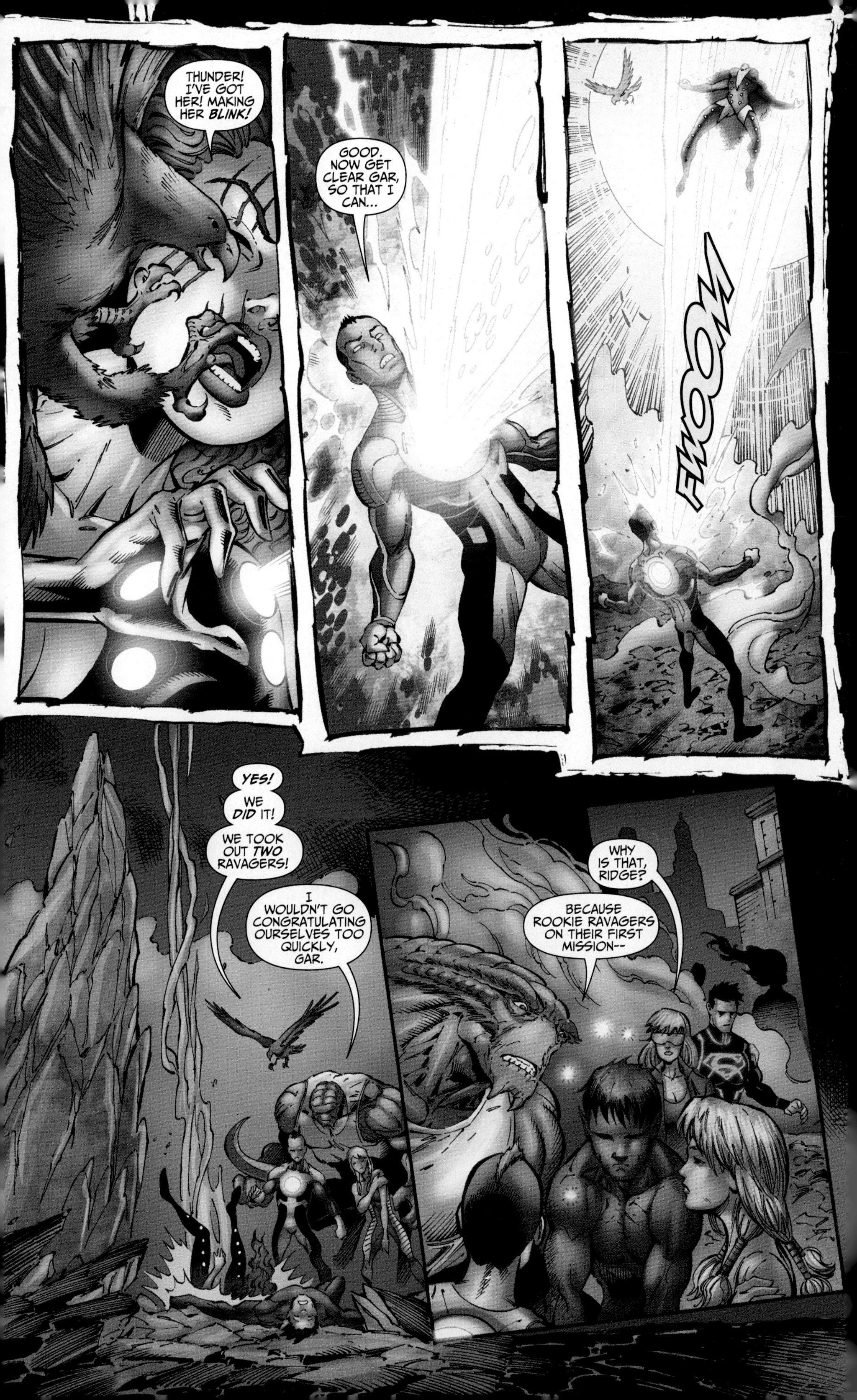
THUNDER! I'VE GOT HER! MAKING HER *BLINK!*
GOOD. NOW GET CLEAR GAR, SO THAT I CAN...
FWOOM
YES!
WE *DID* IT!
WE TOOK OUT *TWO* RAVAGERS!
I WOULDN'T GO CONGRATULATING OURSELVES TOO QUICKLY, GAR.
WHY IS THAT, RIDGE?
BECAUSE ROOKIE RAVAGERS ON THEIR FIRST MISSION--

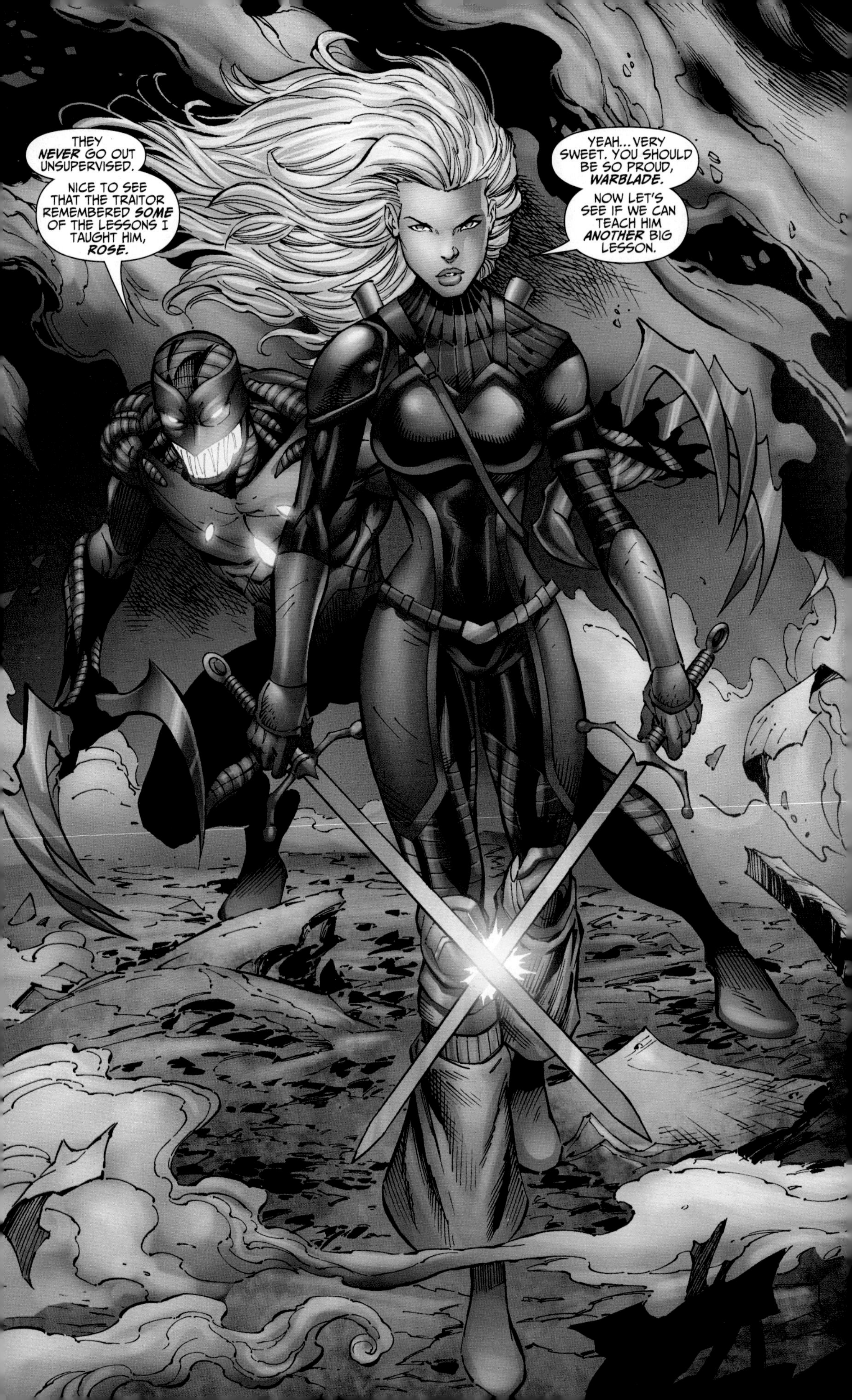

THEY NEVER GO OUT UNSUPERVISED.
NICE TO SEE THAT THE TRAITOR REMEMBERED SOME OF THE LESSONS I TAUGHT HIM, ROSE.
YEAH... VERY SWEET. YOU SHOULD BE SO PROUD, WARBLADE.
NOW LET'S SEE IF WE CAN TEACH HIM ANOTHER BIG LESSON.

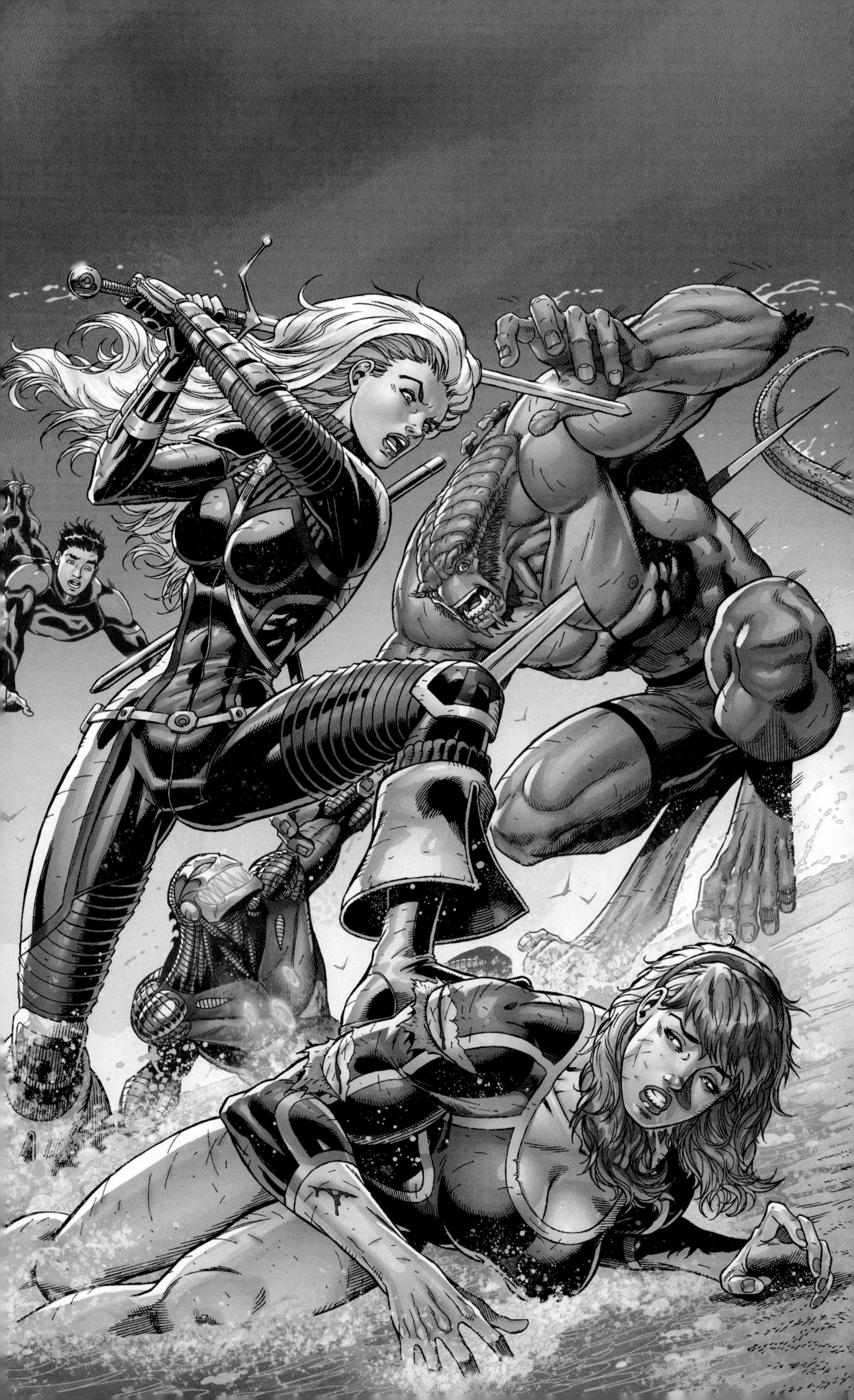

GHOSTS OF FUTURE PRESENT

HOWARD MACKIE
writer

EDUARDO PANSICA, DANIEL HDR & GERALDO BORGES
artists

IAN CHURCHILL
layouts

cover art by
IAN CHURCHILL & HI-FI

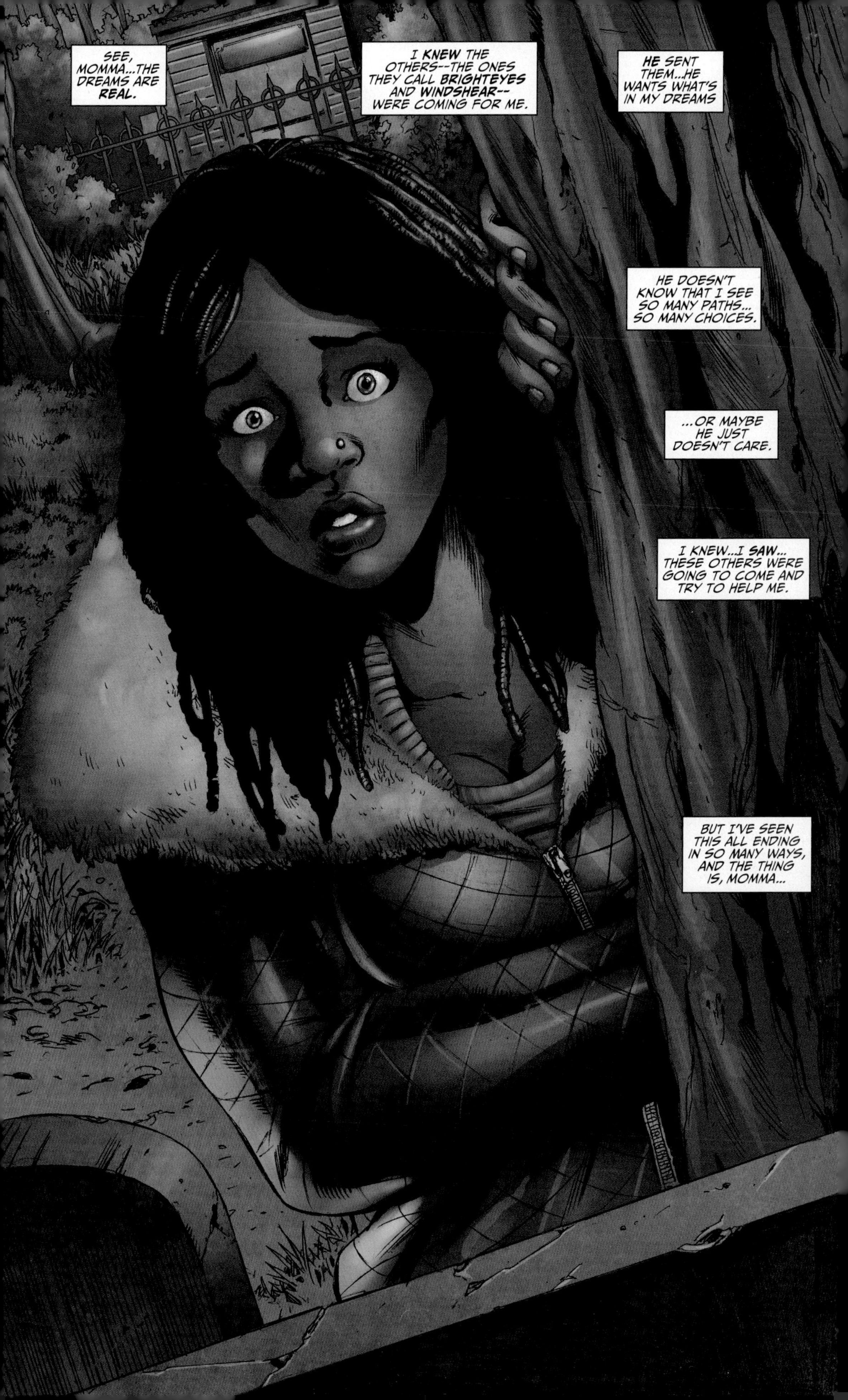

SEE, MOMMA...THE DREAMS ARE REAL.
I KNEW THE OTHERS--THE ONES THEY CALL BRIGHTEYES AND WINDSHEAR--WERE COMING FOR ME.
HE SENT THEM...HE WANTS WHAT'S IN MY DREAMS
HE DOESN'T KNOW THAT I SEE SO MANY PATHS... SO MANY CHOICES.
...OR MAYBE HE JUST DOESN'T CARE.
I KNEW...I SAW... THESE OTHERS WERE GOING TO COME AND TRY TO HELP ME.
BUT I'VE SEEN THIS ALL ENDING IN SO MANY WAYS, AND THE THING IS, MOMMA...

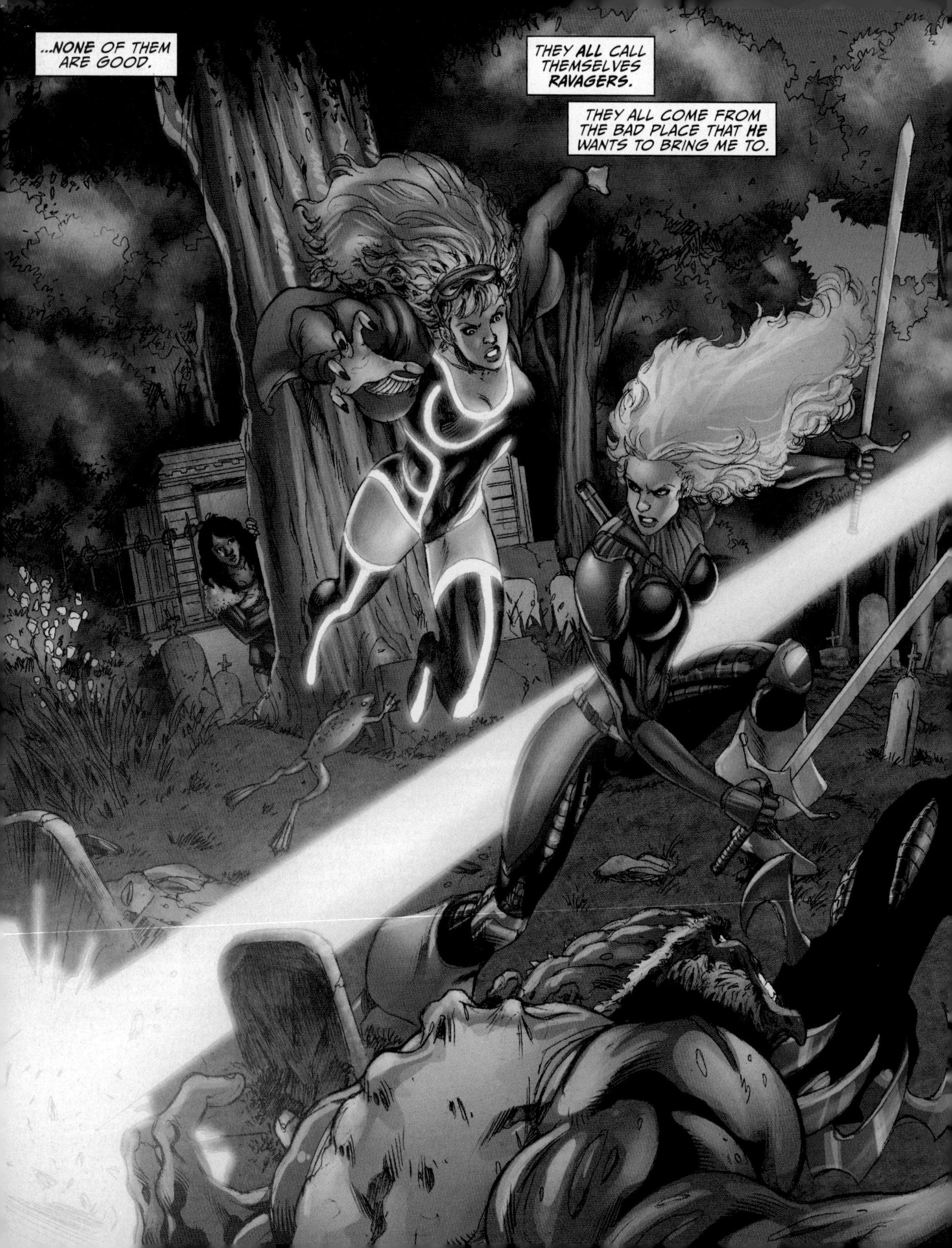
...NONE OF THEM ARE GOOD.
THEY ALL CALL THEMSELVES RAVAGERS.
THEY ALL COME FROM THE BAD PLACE THAT HE WANTS TO BRING ME TO.

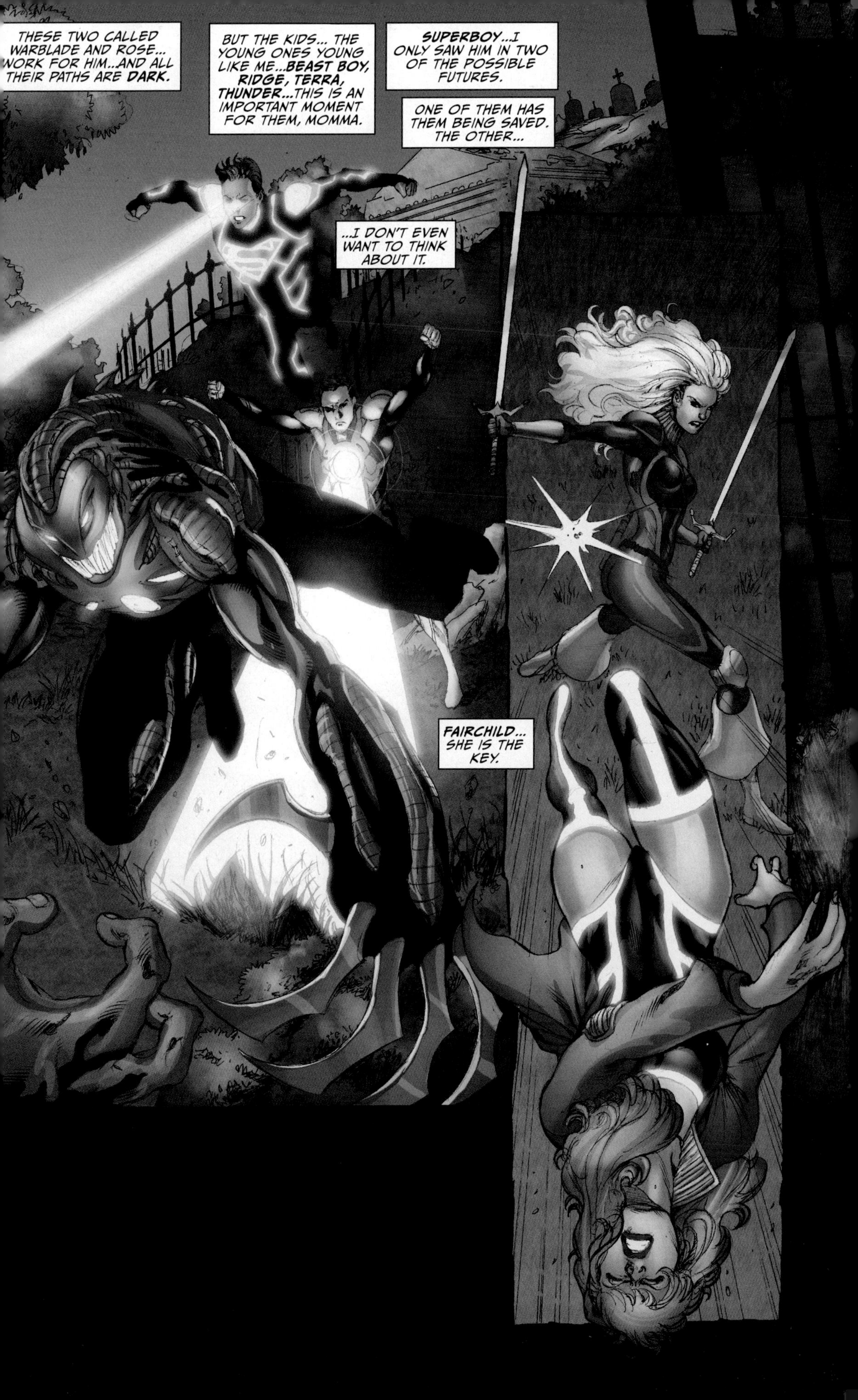
THESE TWO CALLED WARBLADE AND ROSE... WORK FOR HIM...AND ALL THEIR PATHS ARE **DARK.**
BUT THE KIDS... THE YOUNG ONES YOUNG LIKE ME...**BEAST BOY, RIDGE, TERRA, THUNDER...**THIS IS AN IMPORTANT MOMENT FOR THEM, MOMMA.
SUPERBOY...I ONLY SAW HIM IN TWO OF THE POSSIBLE FUTURES.
ONE OF THEM HAS THEM BEING SAVED. THE OTHER...
...I DON'T EVEN WANT TO THINK ABOUT IT.
FAIRCHILD... SHE IS THE KEY.

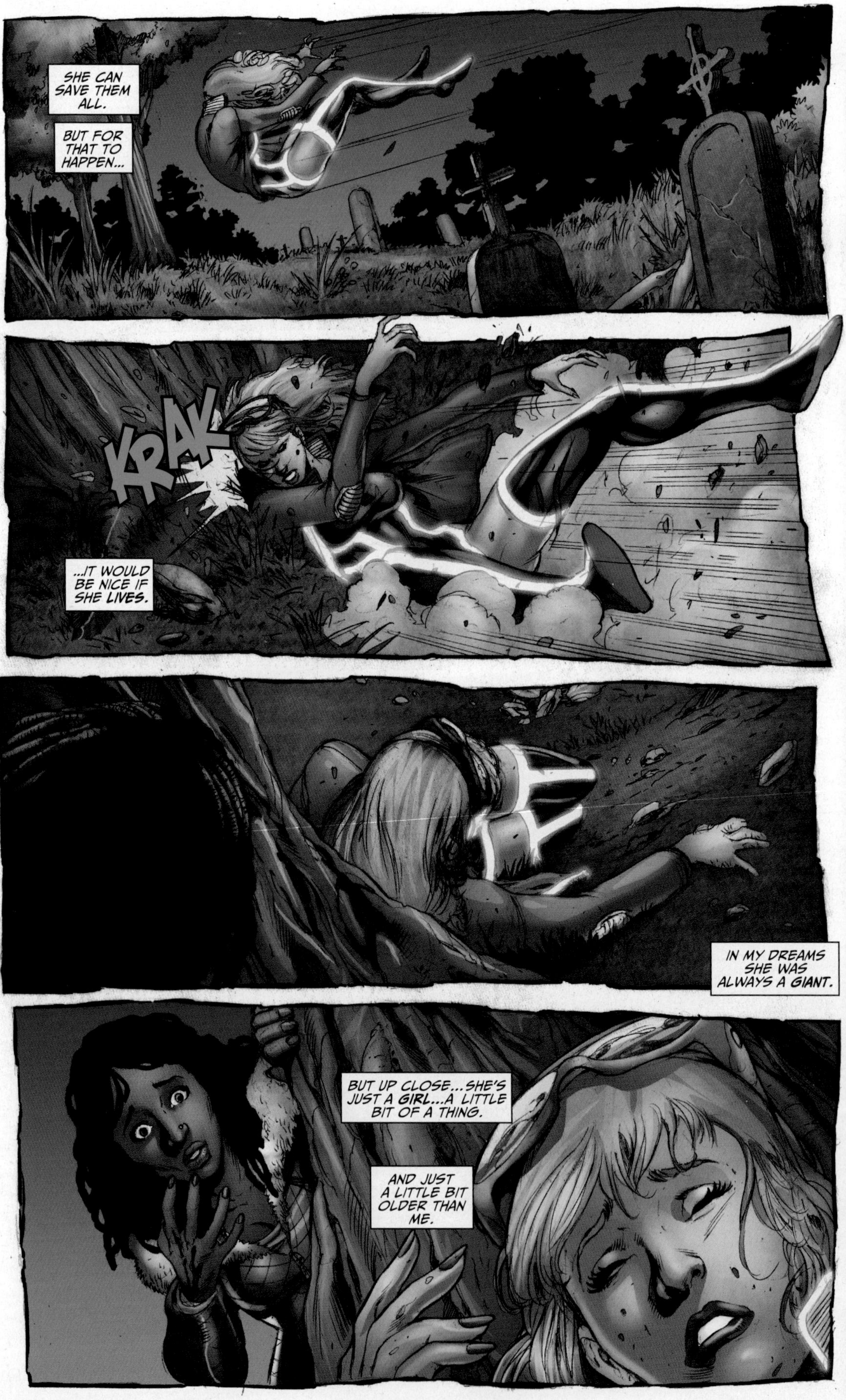
SHE CAN SAVE THEM ALL.
BUT FOR THAT TO HAPPEN...
KRAK
...IT WOULD BE NICE IF SHE LIVES.
IN MY DREAMS SHE WAS ALWAYS A GIANT.
BUT UP CLOSE... SHE'S JUST A GIRL... A LITTLE BIT OF A THING.
AND JUST A LITTLE BIT OLDER THAN ME.

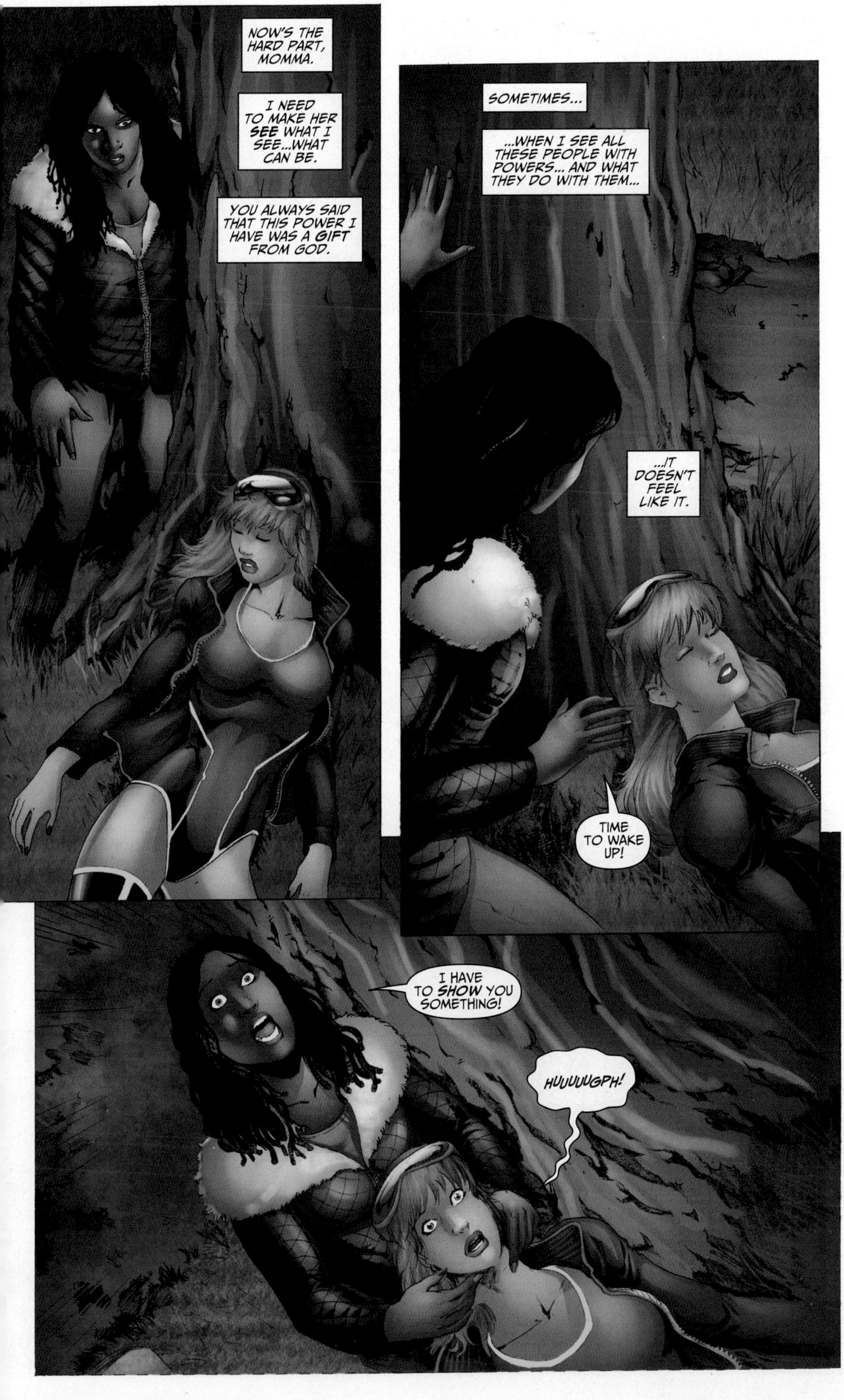
NOW'S THE HARD PART, MOMMA.
I NEED TO MAKE HER SEE WHAT I SEE...WHAT CAN BE.
YOU ALWAYS SAID THAT THIS POWER I HAVE WAS A GIFT FROM GOD.
SOMETIMES...
...WHEN I SEE ALL THESE PEOPLE WITH POWERS... AND WHAT THEY DO WITH THEM...
...IT DOESN'T FEEL LIKE IT.
TIME TO WAKE UP!
I HAVE TO SHOW YOU SOMETHING!
HUUUUUGPH!

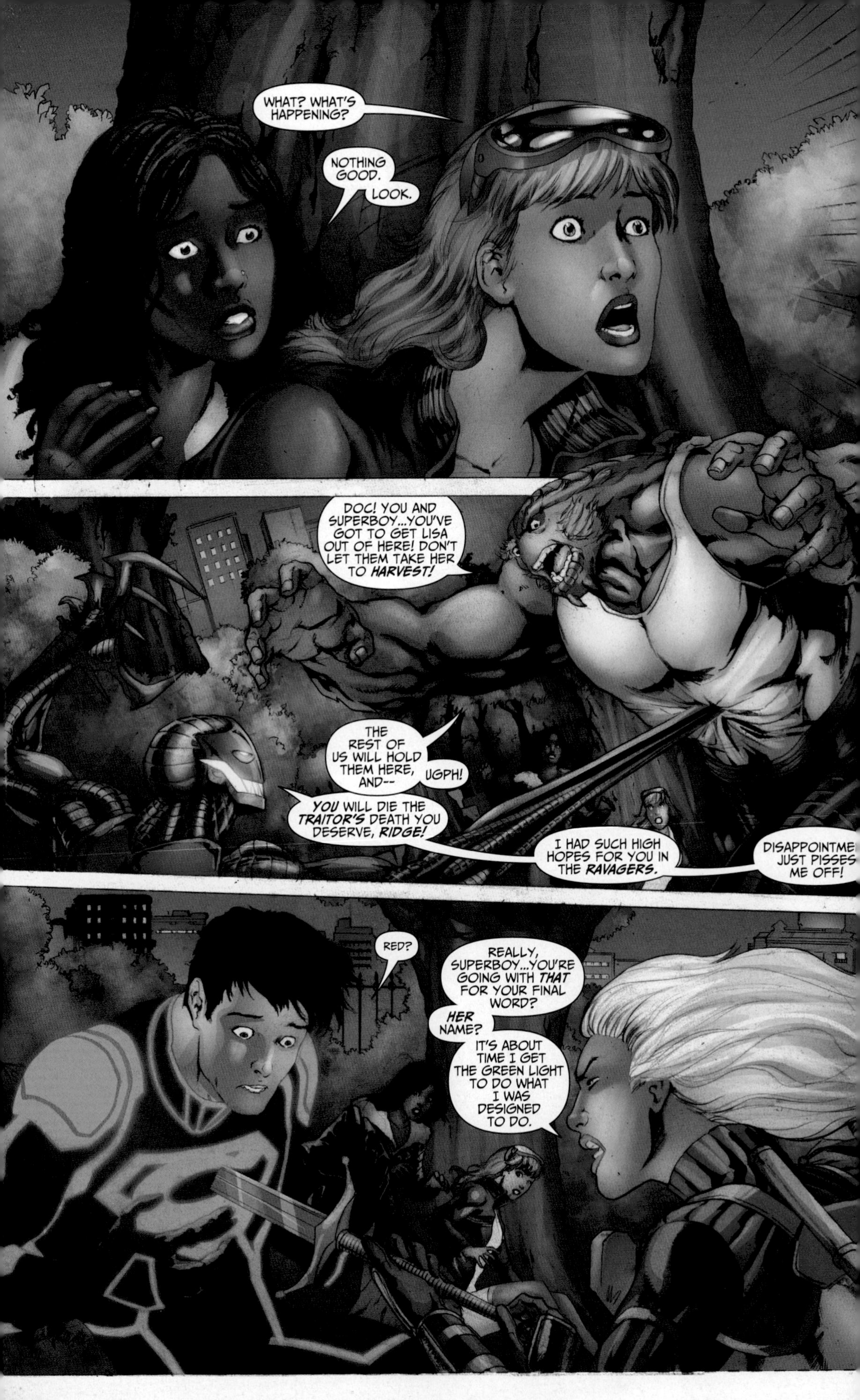

WHAT? WHAT'S HAPPENING?
NOTHING GOOD.
LOOK.
DOC! YOU AND SUPERBOY...YOU'VE GOT TO GET LISA OUT OF HERE! DON'T LET THEM TAKE HER TO *HARVEST!*
THE REST OF US WILL HOLD THEM HERE, AND--
UGPH!
YOU WILL DIE THE ***TRAITOR'S*** DEATH YOU DESERVE, ***RIDGE!***
I HAD SUCH HIGH HOPES FOR YOU IN THE ***RAVAGERS.***
DISAPPOINTME JUST PISSES ME OFF!
RED?
REALLY, SUPERBOY...YOU'RE GOING WITH ***THAT*** FOR YOUR FINAL WORD?
HER NAME?
IT'S ABOUT TIME I GET THE GREEN LIGHT TO DO WHAT I WAS DESIGNED TO DO.

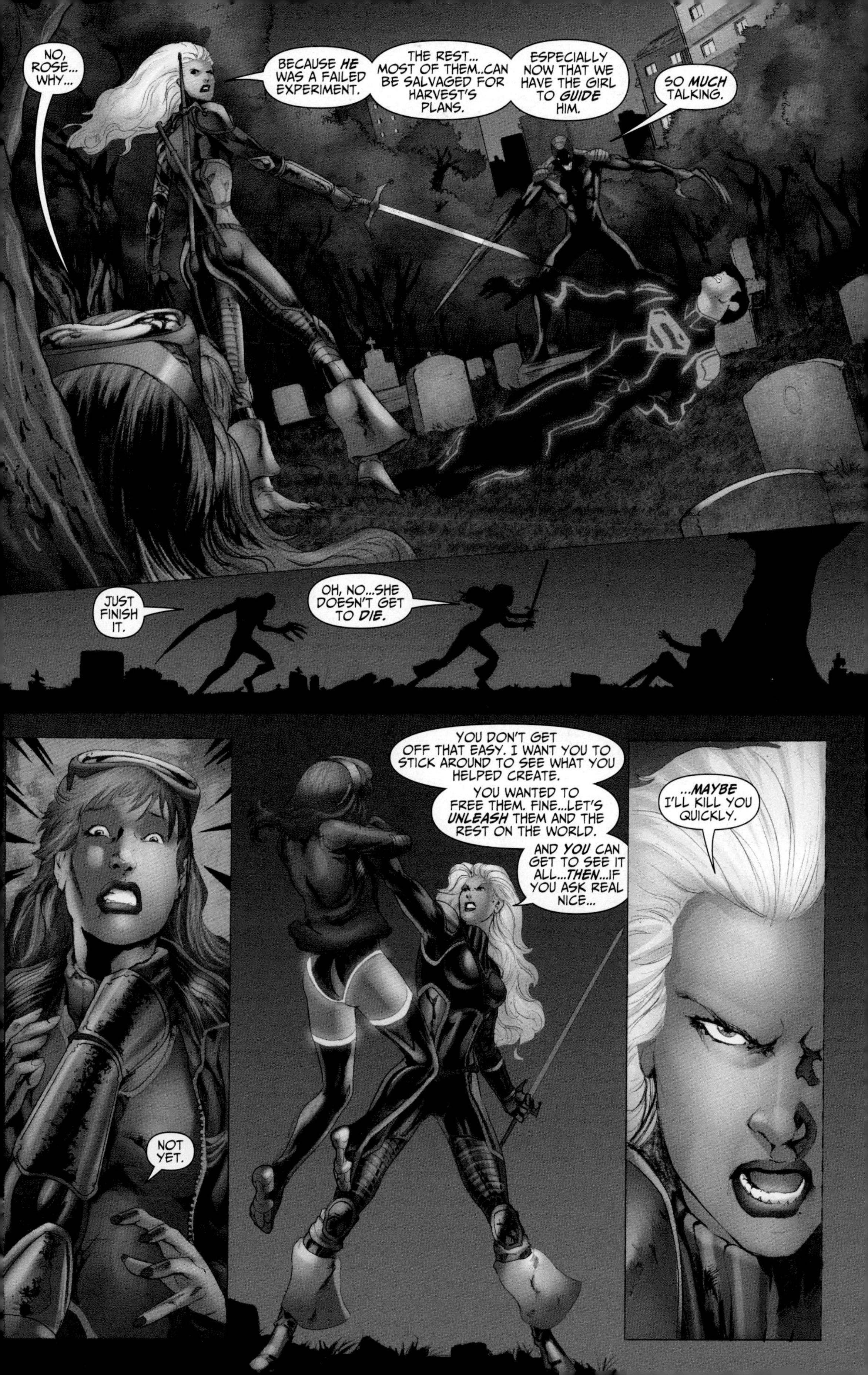
NO, ROSE... WHY...
BECAUSE HE WAS A FAILED EXPERIMENT.
THE REST... MOST OF THEM..CAN BE SALVAGED FOR HARVEST'S PLANS.
ESPECIALLY NOW THAT WE HAVE THE GIRL TO GUIDE HIM.
SO MUCH TALKING.
JUST FINISH IT.
OH, NO...SHE DOESN'T GET TO DIE.
NOT YET.
YOU DON'T GET OFF THAT EASY. I WANT YOU TO STICK AROUND TO SEE WHAT YOU HELPED CREATE.
YOU WANTED TO FREE THEM. FINE...LET'S UNLEASH THEM AND THE REST ON THE WORLD.
AND YOU CAN GET TO SEE IT ALL...THEN...IF YOU ASK REAL NICE...
...MAYBE I'LL KILL YOU QUICKLY.

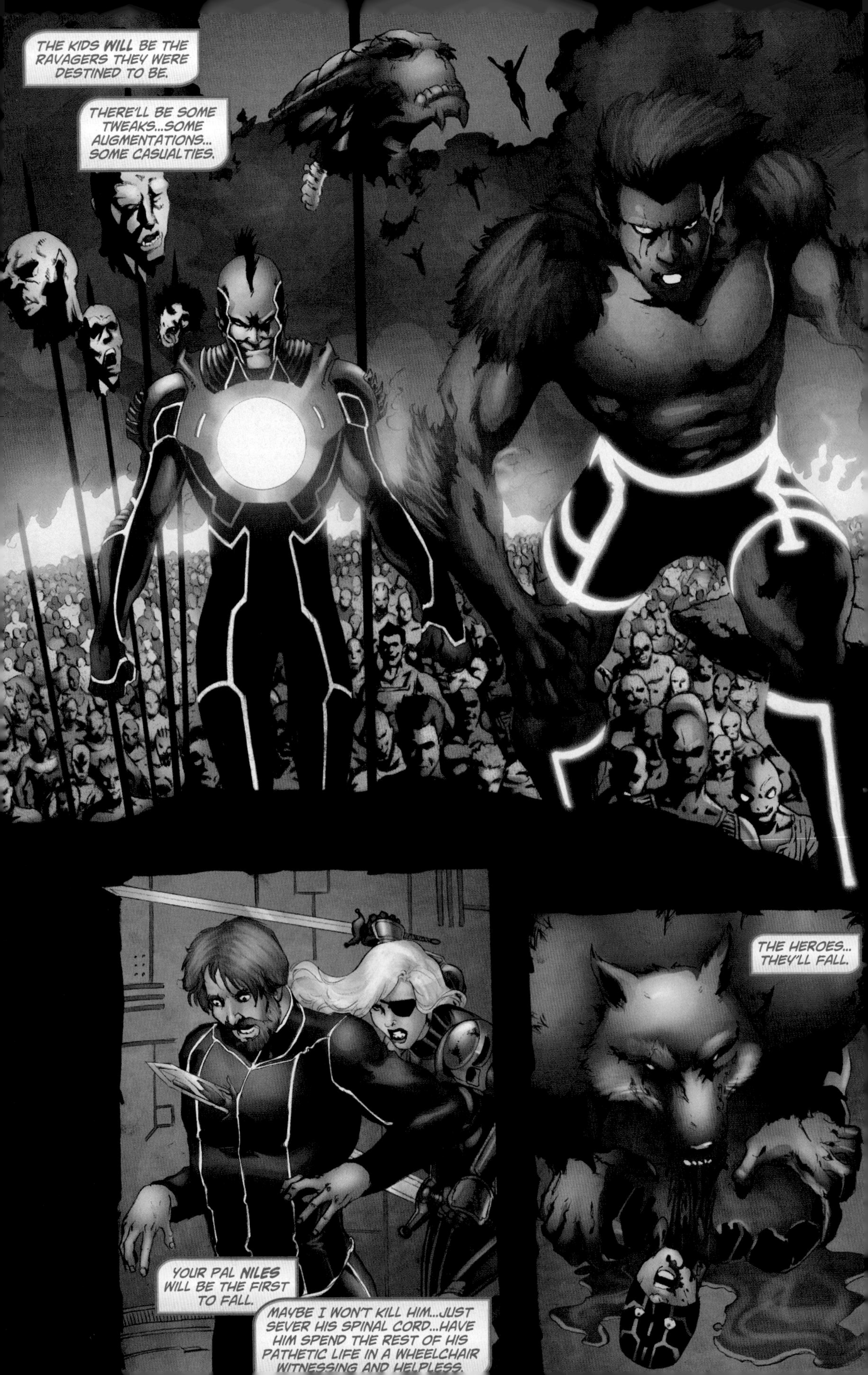
THE KIDS WILL BE THE RAVAGERS THEY WERE DESTINED TO BE.
THERE'LL BE SOME TWEAKS...SOME AUGMENTATIONS... SOME CASUALTIES.
YOUR PAL NILES WILL BE THE FIRST TO FALL.
MAYBE I WON'T KILL HIM...JUST SEVER HIS SPINAL CORD...HAVE HIM SPEND THE REST OF HIS PATHETIC LIFE IN A WHEELCHAIR WITNESSING AND HELPLESS.
THE HEROES... THEY'LL FALL.

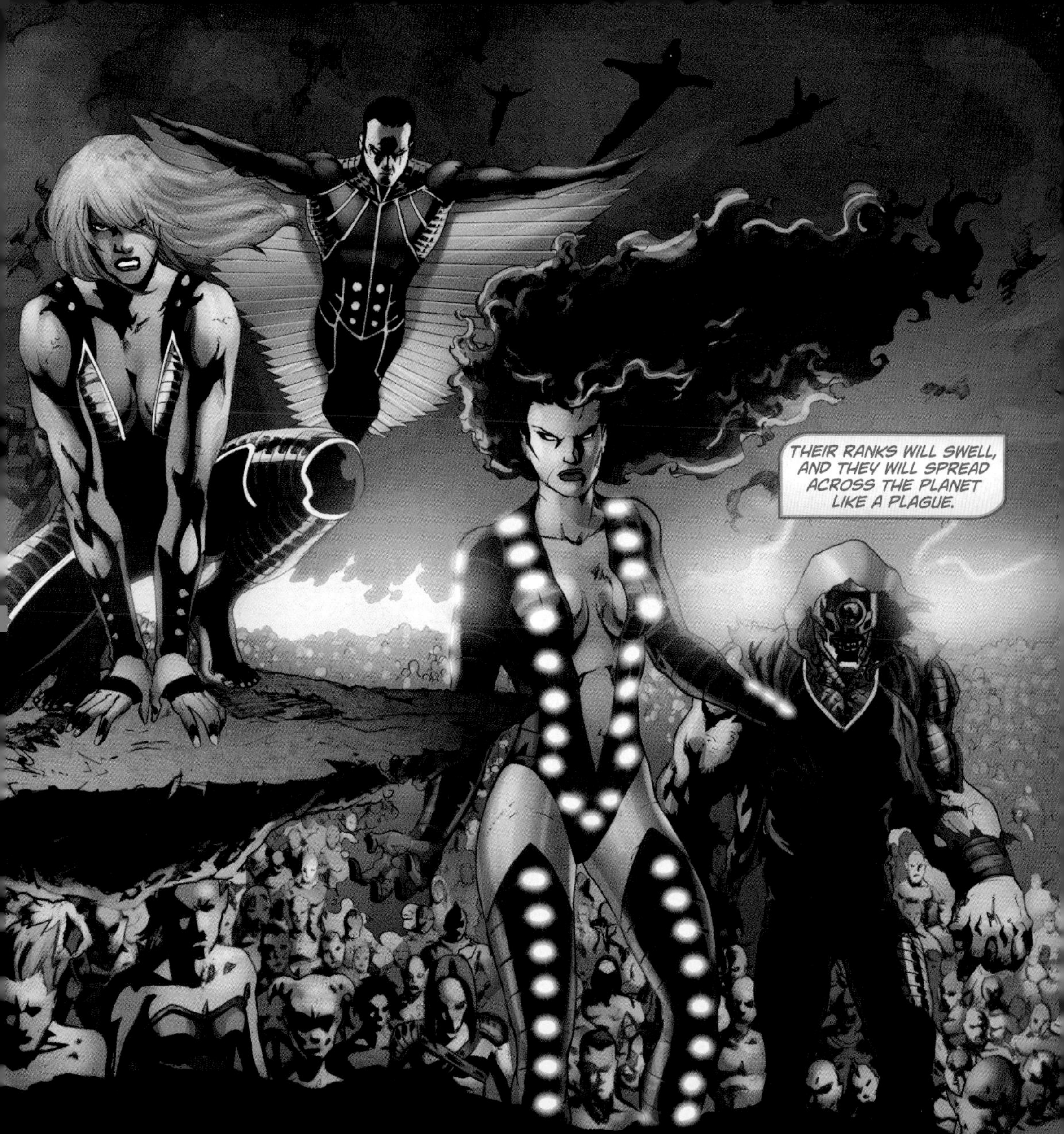
THEIR RANKS WILL SWELL, AND THEY WILL SPREAD ACROSS THE PLANET LIKE A PLAGUE.

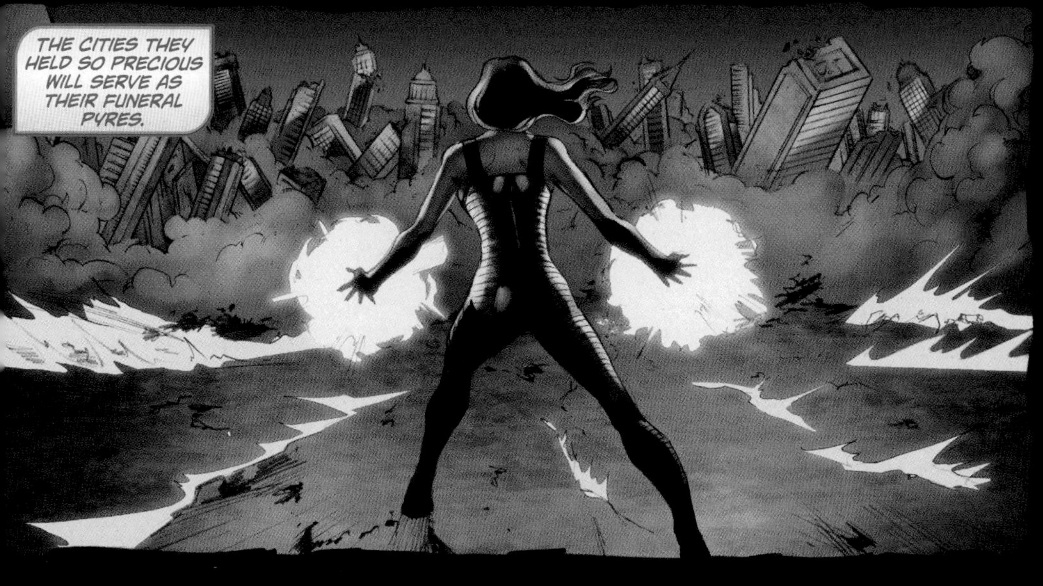
THE CITIES THEY HELD SO PRECIOUS WILL SERVE AS THEIR FUNERAL PYRES.

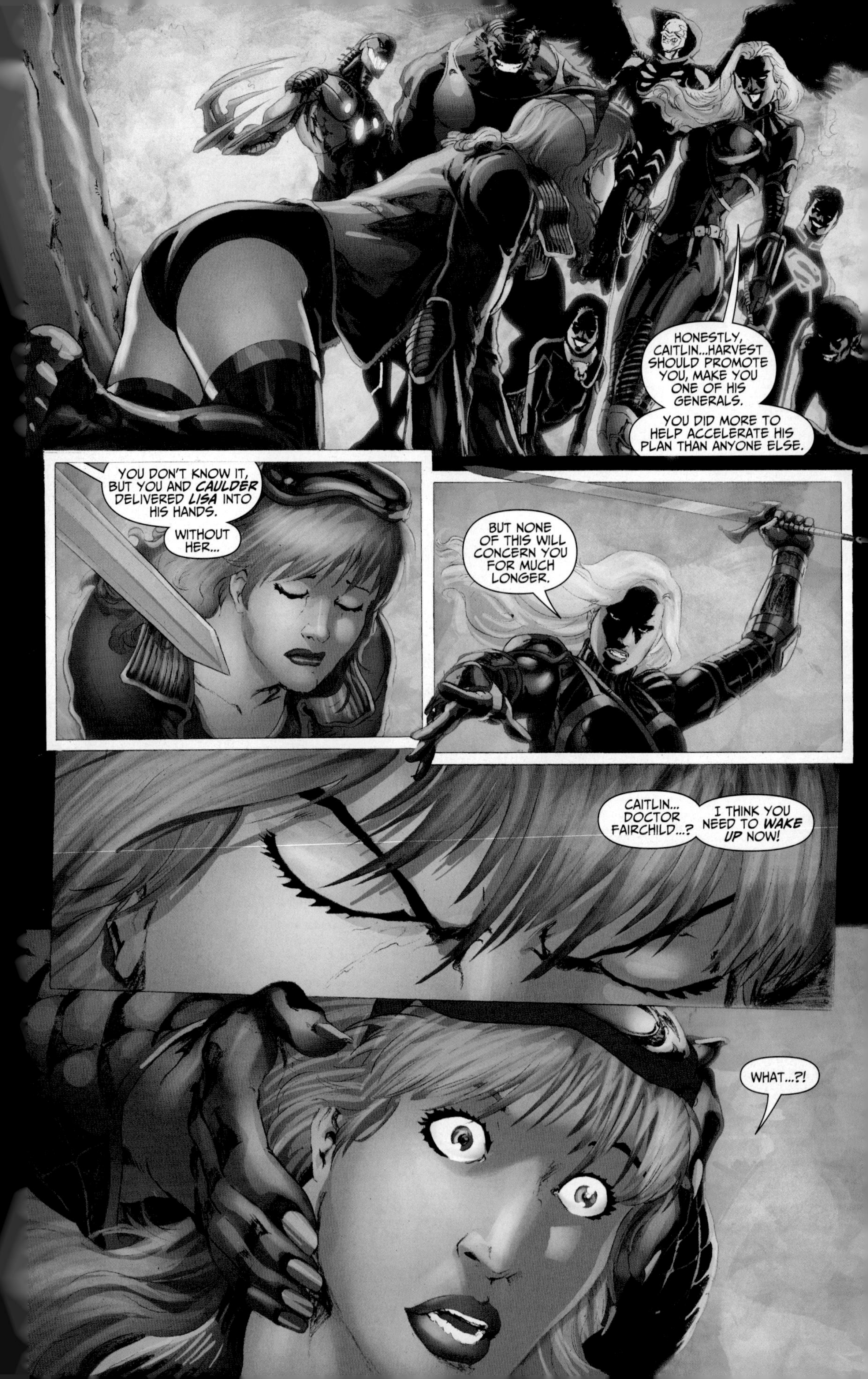
HONESTLY, CAITLIN...HARVEST SHOULD PROMOTE YOU, MAKE YOU ONE OF HIS GENERALS.
YOU DID MORE TO HELP ACCELERATE HIS PLAN THAN ANYONE ELSE.
YOU DON'T KNOW IT, BUT YOU AND **CAULDER** DELIVERED **LISA** INTO HIS HANDS.
WITHOUT HER...
BUT NONE OF THIS WILL CONCERN YOU FOR MUCH LONGER.
CAITLIN... DOCTOR FAIRCHILD...?
I THINK YOU NEED TO **WAKE UP** NOW!
WHAT...?!

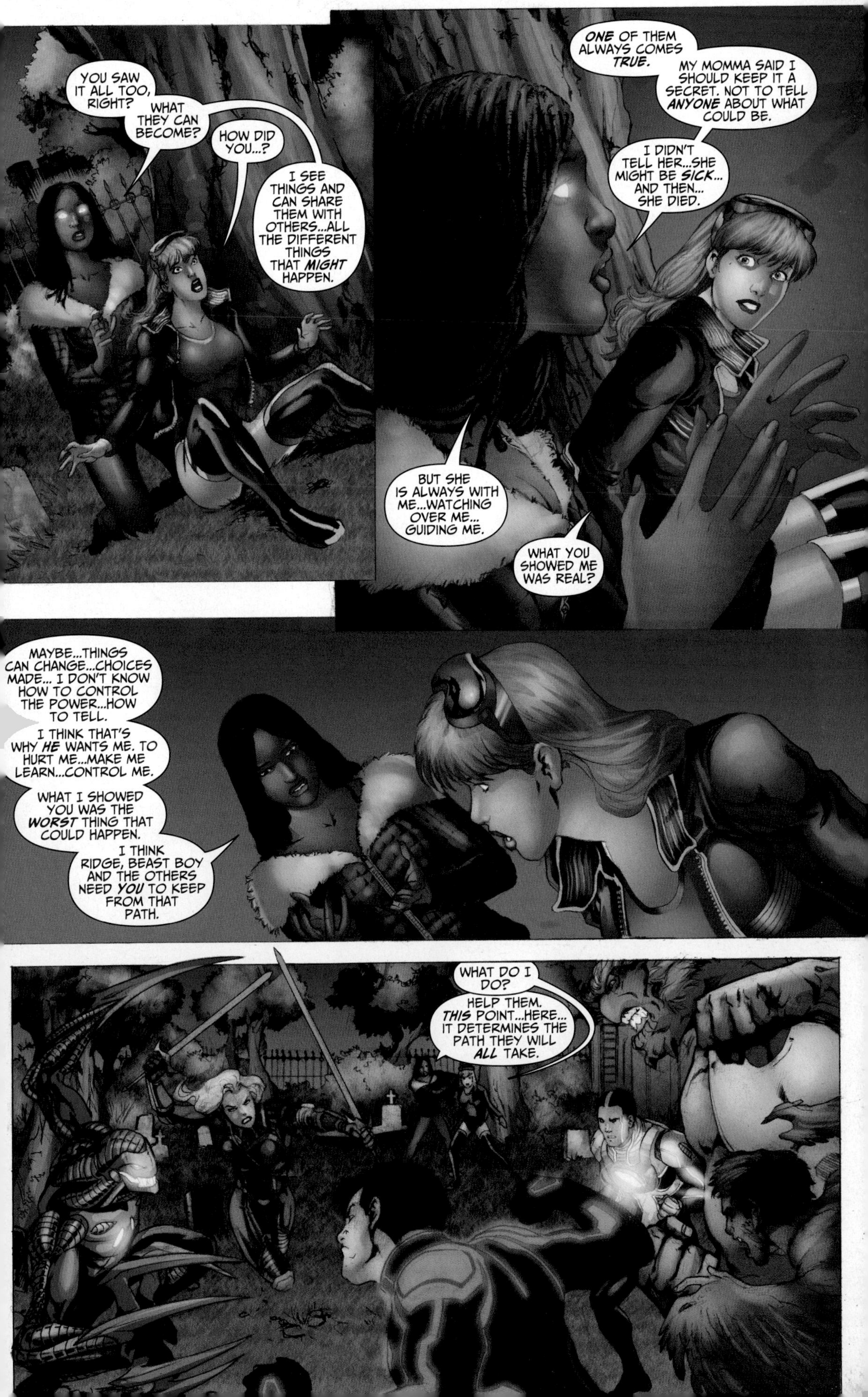
YOU SAW IT ALL TOO, RIGHT?
WHAT THEY CAN BECOME?
HOW DID YOU...?
I SEE THINGS AND CAN SHARE THEM WITH OTHERS...ALL THE DIFFERENT THINGS THAT MIGHT HAPPEN.
ONE OF THEM ALWAYS COMES TRUE.
MY MOMMA SAID I SHOULD KEEP IT A SECRET. NOT TO TELL ANYONE ABOUT WHAT COULD BE.
I DIDN'T TELL HER...SHE MIGHT BE SICK... AND THEN... SHE DIED.
BUT SHE IS ALWAYS WITH ME...WATCHING OVER ME... GUIDING ME.
WHAT YOU SHOWED ME WAS REAL?
MAYBE...THINGS CAN CHANGE...CHOICES MADE... I DON'T KNOW HOW TO CONTROL THE POWER...HOW TO TELL.
I THINK THAT'S WHY HE WANTS ME. TO HURT ME...MAKE ME LEARN...CONTROL ME.
WHAT I SHOWED YOU WAS THE WORST THING THAT COULD HAPPEN.
I THINK RIDGE, BEAST BOY AND THE OTHERS NEED YOU TO KEEP FROM THAT PATH.
WHAT DO I DO?
HELP THEM. THIS POINT...HERE... IT DETERMINES THE PATH THEY WILL ALL TAKE.

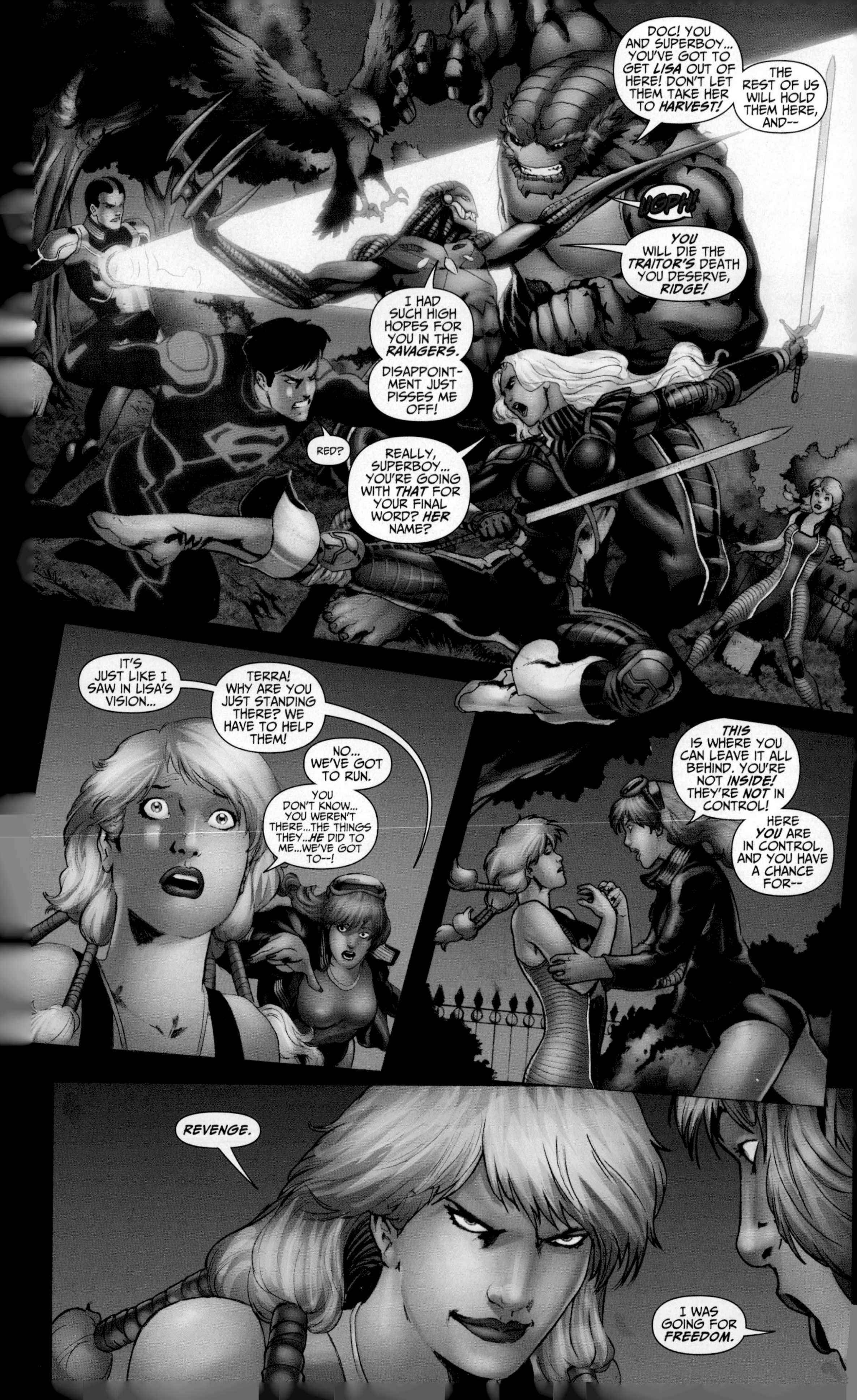
DOC! YOU AND SUPERBOY... YOU'VE GOT TO GET LISA OUT OF HERE! DON'T LET THEM TAKE HER TO HARVEST!
THE REST OF US WILL HOLD THEM HERE, AND--
UOPH!
YOU WILL DIE THE TRAITOR'S DEATH YOU DESERVE, RIDGE!
I HAD SUCH HIGH HOPES FOR YOU IN THE RAVAGERS.
DISAPPOINTMENT JUST PISSES ME OFF!
RED?
REALLY, SUPERBOY... YOU'RE GOING WITH THAT FOR YOUR FINAL WORD? HER NAME?
IT'S JUST LIKE I SAW IN LISA'S VISION...
TERRA! WHY ARE YOU JUST STANDING THERE? WE HAVE TO HELP THEM!
NO... WE'VE GOT TO RUN.
YOU DON'T KNOW... YOU WEREN'T THERE...THE THINGS THEY...HE DID TO ME...WE'VE GOT TO--!
THIS IS WHERE YOU CAN LEAVE IT ALL BEHIND. YOU'RE NOT INSIDE! THEY'RE NOT IN CONTROL!
HERE YOU ARE IN CONTROL, AND YOU HAVE A CHANCE FOR--
REVENGE.
I WAS GOING FOR FREEDOM.

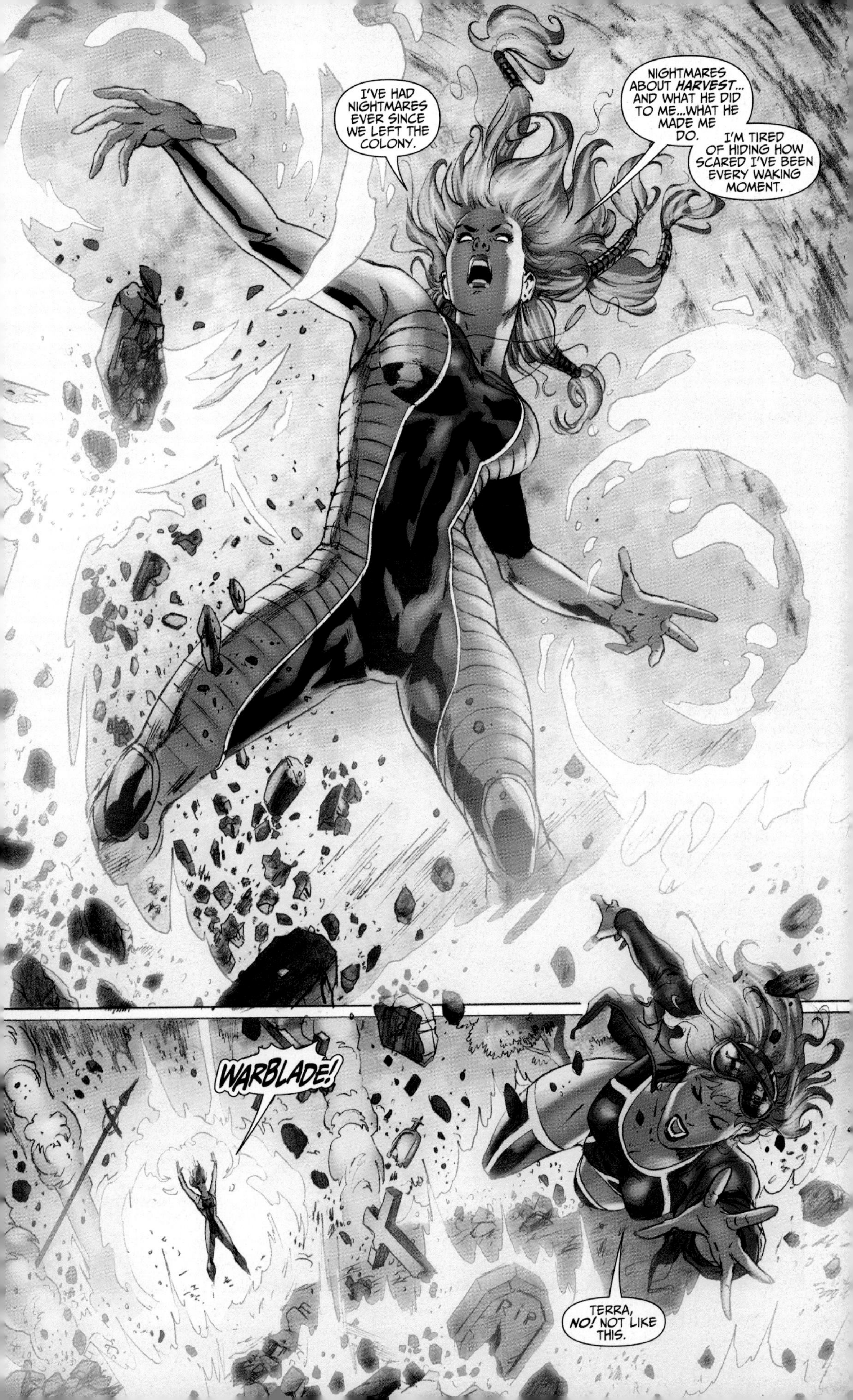
I'VE HAD NIGHTMARES EVER SINCE WE LEFT THE COLONY.
NIGHTMARES ABOUT HARVEST... AND WHAT HE DID TO ME...WHAT HE MADE ME DO.
I'M TIRED OF HIDING HOW SCARED I'VE BEEN EVERY WAKING MOMENT.
WARBLADE!
TERRA, NO! NOT LIKE THIS.
RIP

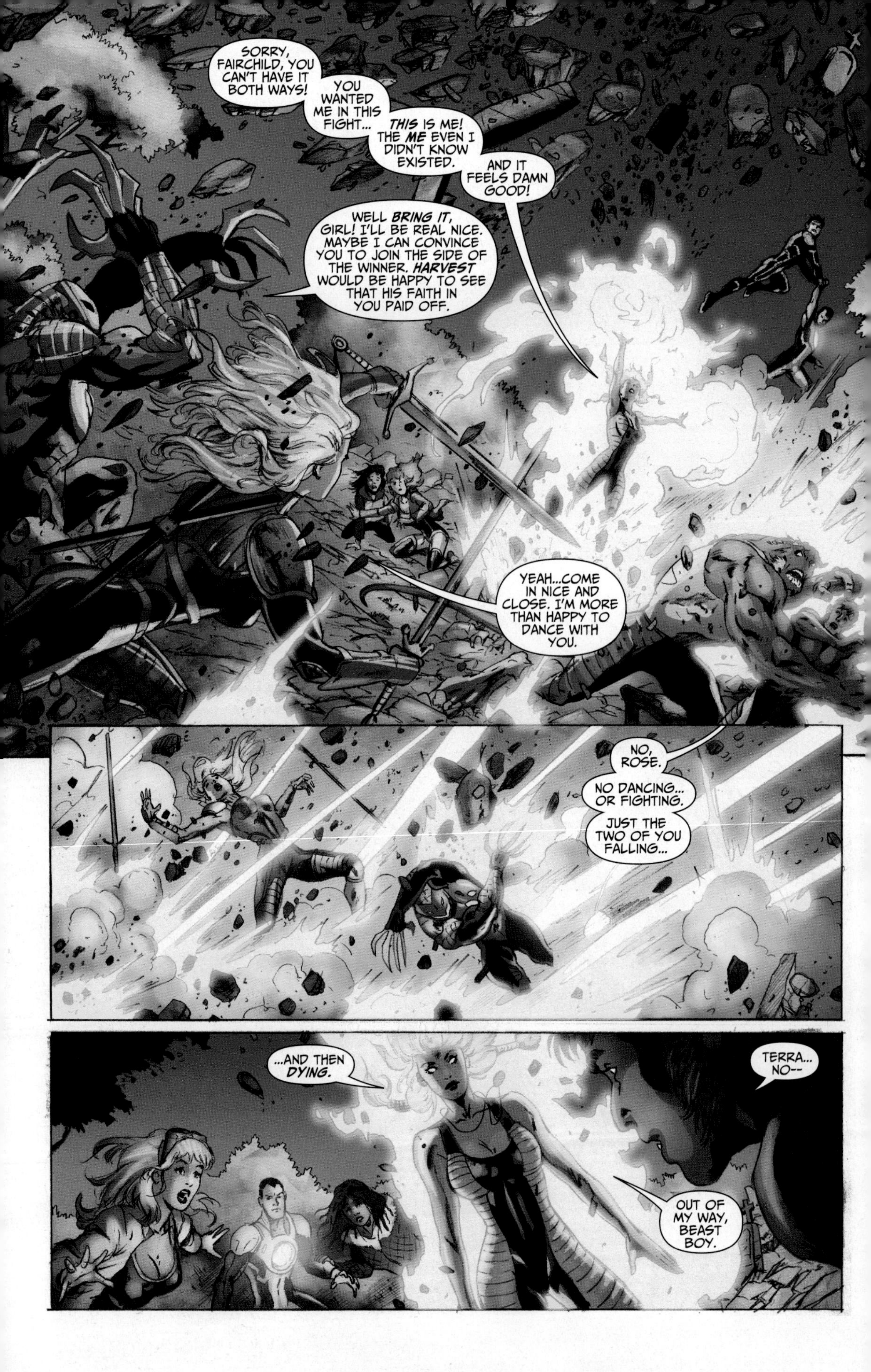
SORRY, FAIRCHILD, YOU CAN'T HAVE IT BOTH WAYS!
YOU WANTED ME IN THIS FIGHT...
THIS IS ME! THE ME EVEN I DIDN'T KNOW EXISTED.
AND IT FEELS DAMN GOOD!
WELL BRING IT, GIRL! I'LL BE REAL NICE. MAYBE I CAN CONVINCE YOU TO JOIN THE SIDE OF THE WINNER. HARVEST WOULD BE HAPPY TO SEE THAT HIS FAITH IN YOU PAID OFF.
YEAH...COME IN NICE AND CLOSE. I'M MORE THAN HAPPY TO DANCE WITH YOU.
NO, ROSE.
NO DANCING... OR FIGHTING.
JUST THE TWO OF YOU FALLING...
...AND THEN DYING.
TERRA... NO--
OUT OF MY WAY, BEAST BOY.

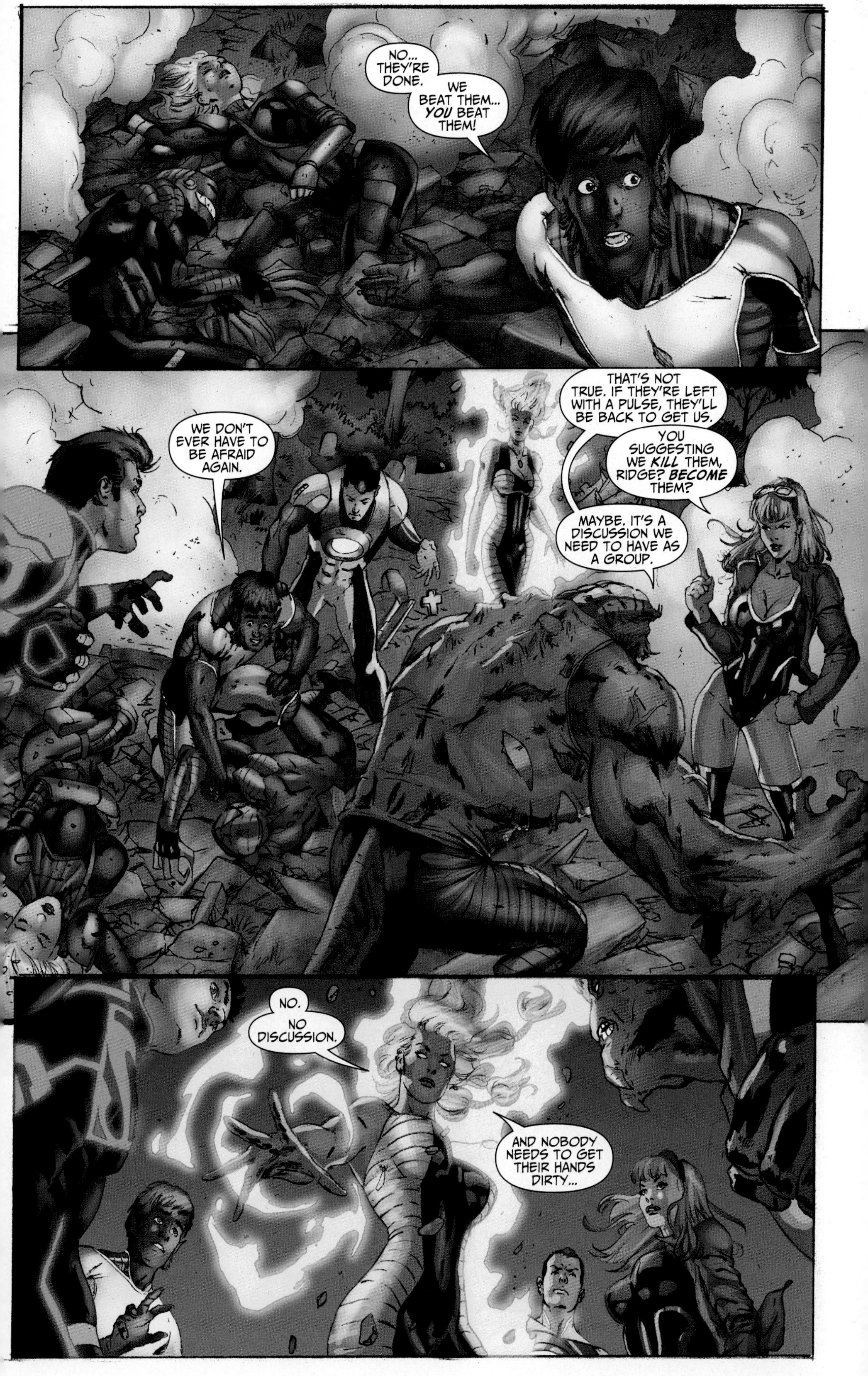
NO... THEY'RE DONE.
WE BEAT THEM... YOU BEAT THEM!
WE DON'T EVER HAVE TO BE AFRAID AGAIN.
THAT'S NOT TRUE. IF THEY'RE LEFT WITH A PULSE, THEY'LL BE BACK TO GET US.
YOU SUGGESTING WE KILL THEM, RIDGE? BECOME THEM?
MAYBE. IT'S A DISCUSSION WE NEED TO HAVE AS A GROUP.
NO.
NO DISCUSSION.
AND NOBODY NEEDS TO GET THEIR HANDS DIRTY...

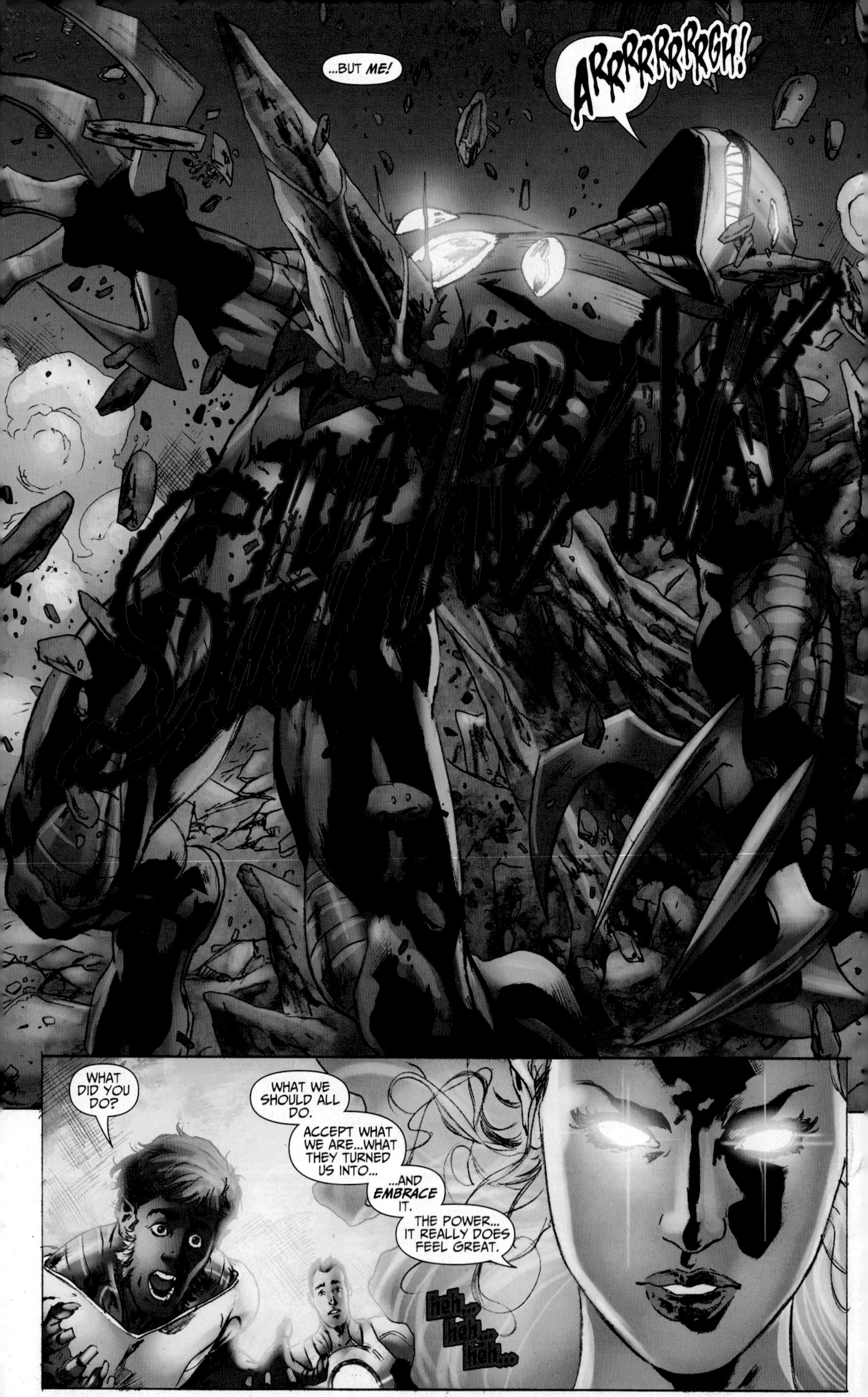

...BUT ME!
ARRRRRRRGH!
WHAT DID YOU DO?
WHAT WE SHOULD ALL DO.
ACCEPT WHAT WE ARE...WHAT THEY TURNED US INTO...
...AND EMBRACE IT.
THE POWER... IT REALLY DOES FEEL GREAT.
heh... heh... heh...

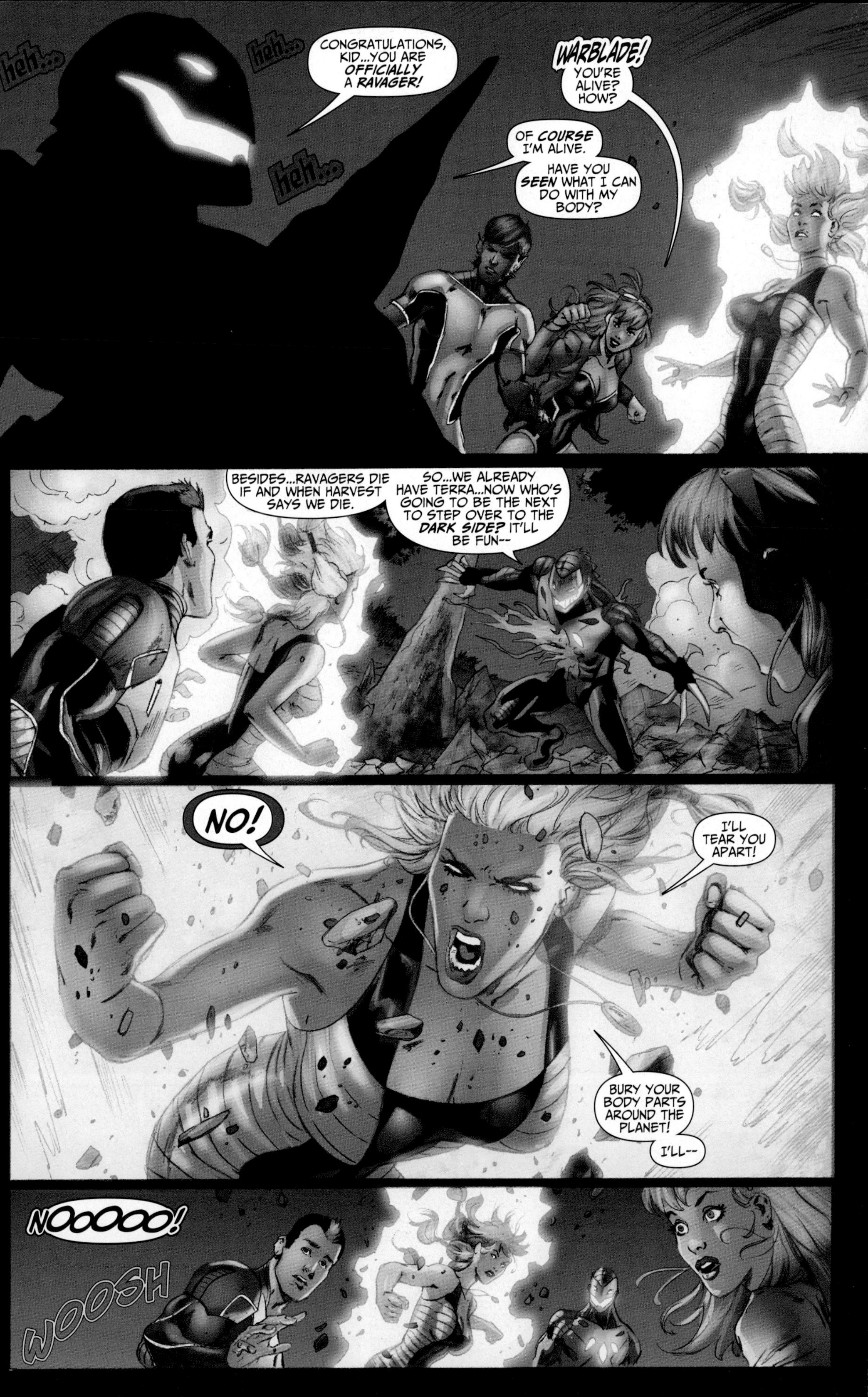
heh...
heh...
heh...
CONGRATULATIONS, KID...YOU ARE OFFICIALLY A RAVAGER!
WARBLADE! YOU'RE ALIVE? HOW?
OF COURSE I'M ALIVE.
HAVE YOU SEEN WHAT I CAN DO WITH MY BODY?
BESIDES...RAVAGERS DIE IF AND WHEN HARVEST SAYS WE DIE.
SO...WE ALREADY HAVE TERRA...NOW WHO'S GOING TO BE THE NEXT TO STEP OVER TO THE DARK SIDE? IT'LL BE FUN--
NO!
I'LL TEAR YOU APART!
BURY YOUR BODY PARTS AROUND THE PLANET!
I'LL--
NOOOOO!
WOOSH

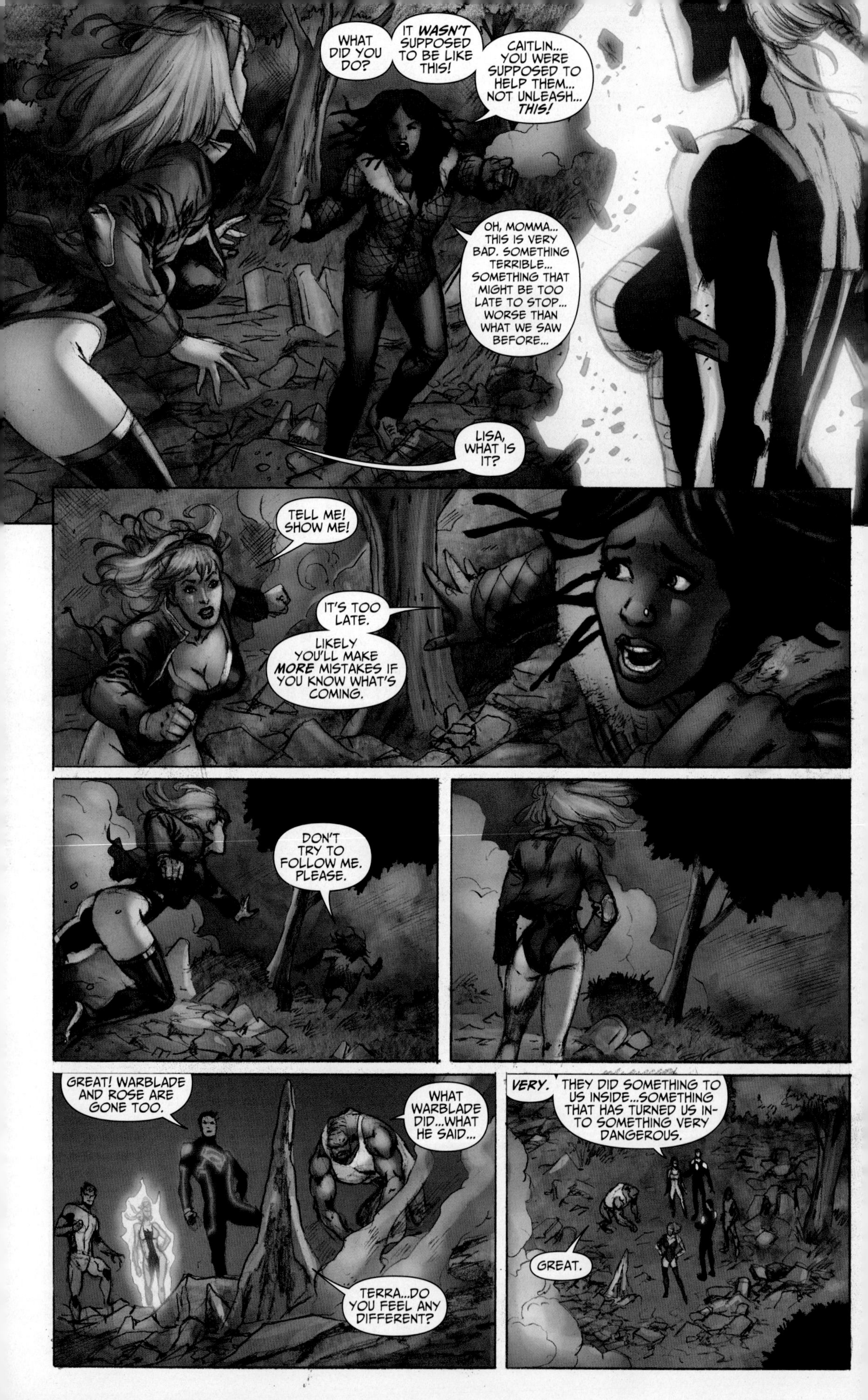
WHAT DID YOU DO?
IT WASN'T SUPPOSED TO BE LIKE THIS!
CAITLIN... YOU WERE SUPPOSED TO HELP THEM... NOT UNLEASH... THIS!
OH, MOMMA... THIS IS VERY BAD. SOMETHING TERRIBLE... SOMETHING THAT MIGHT BE TOO LATE TO STOP... WORSE THAN WHAT WE SAW BEFORE...
LISA, WHAT IS IT?
TELL ME! SHOW ME!
IT'S TOO LATE.
LIKELY YOU'LL MAKE MORE MISTAKES IF YOU KNOW WHAT'S COMING.
DON'T TRY TO FOLLOW ME. PLEASE.
GREAT! WARBLADE AND ROSE ARE GONE TOO.
WHAT WARBLADE DID...WHAT HE SAID...
TERRA...DO YOU FEEL ANY DIFFERENT?
VERY.
THEY DID SOMETHING TO US INSIDE...SOMETHING THAT HAS TURNED US IN-TO SOMETHING VERY DANGEROUS.
GREAT.

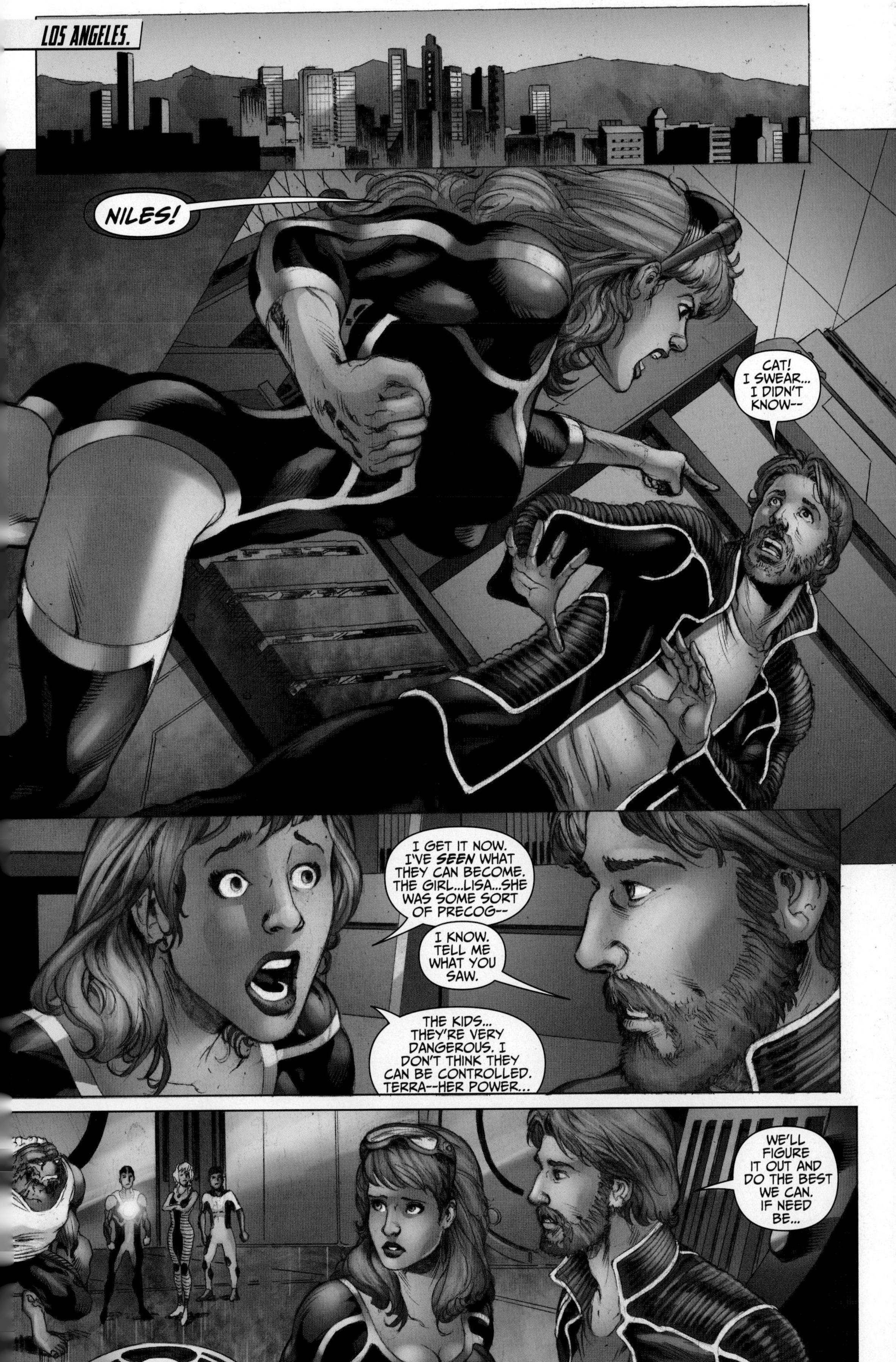
LOS ANGELES.
NILES!
CAT! I SWEAR... I DIDN'T KNOW--
I GET IT NOW. I'VE SEEN WHAT THEY CAN BECOME. THE GIRL...LISA...SHE WAS SOME SORT OF PRECOG--
I KNOW. TELL ME WHAT YOU SAW.
THE KIDS... THEY'RE VERY DANGEROUS. I DON'T THINK THEY CAN BE CONTROLLED. TERRA--HER POWER...
WE'LL FIGURE IT OUT AND DO THE BEST WE CAN. IF NEED BE...

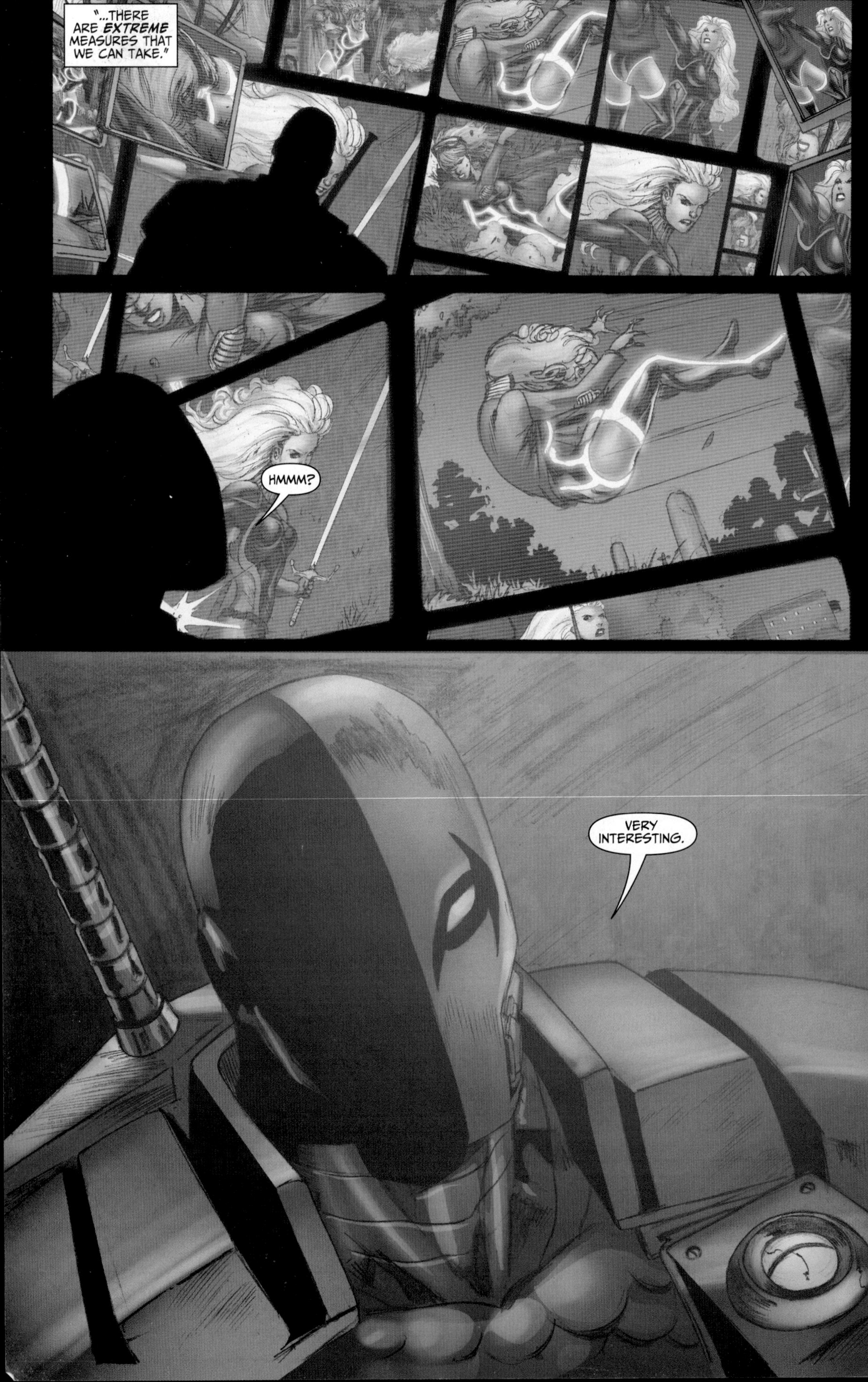
"...THERE ARE EXTREME MEASURES THAT WE CAN TAKE."
HMMM?
VERY INTERESTING.

THE RAVAGERS #1 VARIANT COVER
BY BRETT BOOTH with NORM RAPMUND & ANDREW DALHOUSE

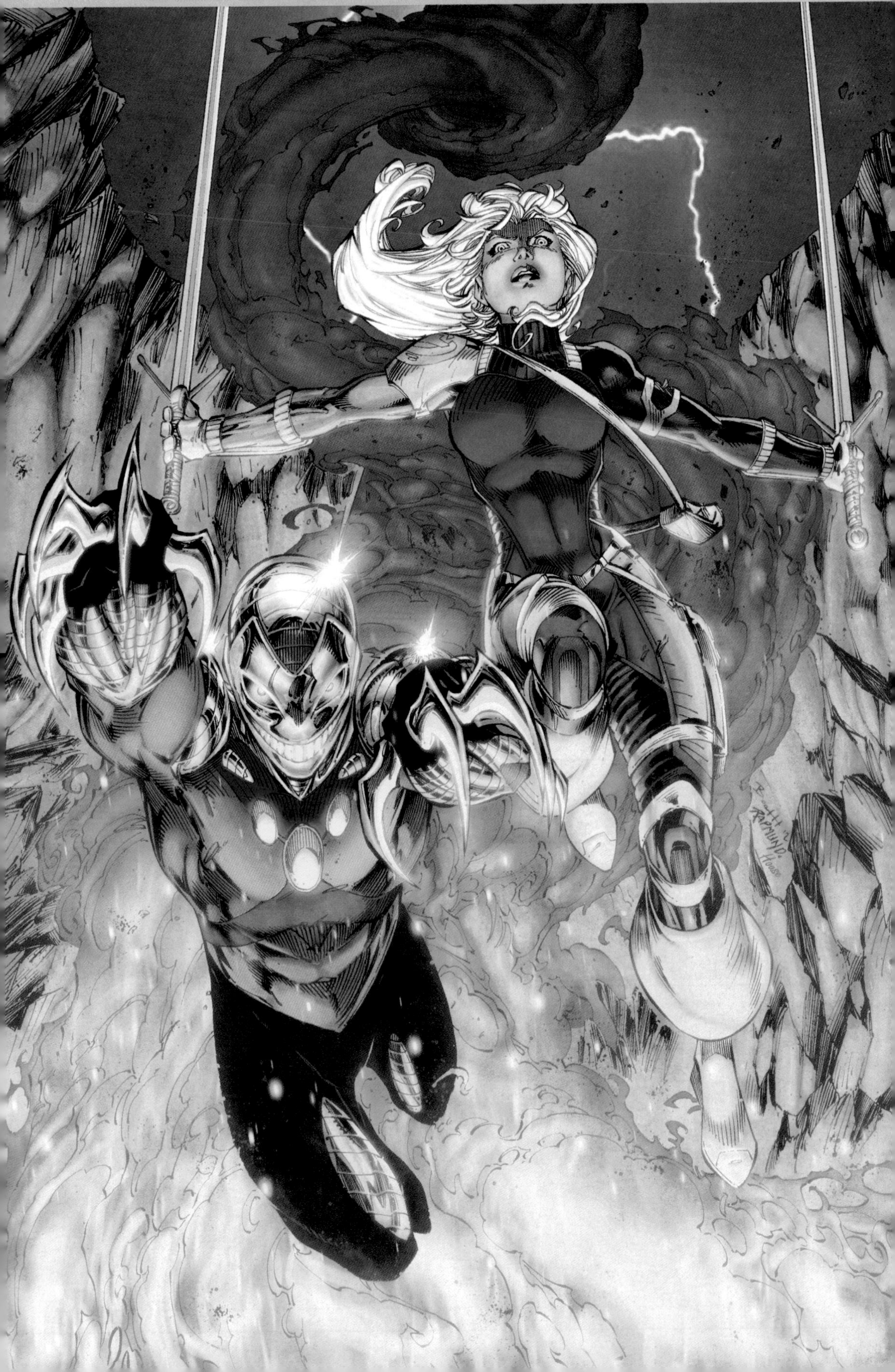

THE RAVAGERS #1
PAGES 16 & 17 PENCILS BY IAN CHURCHILL

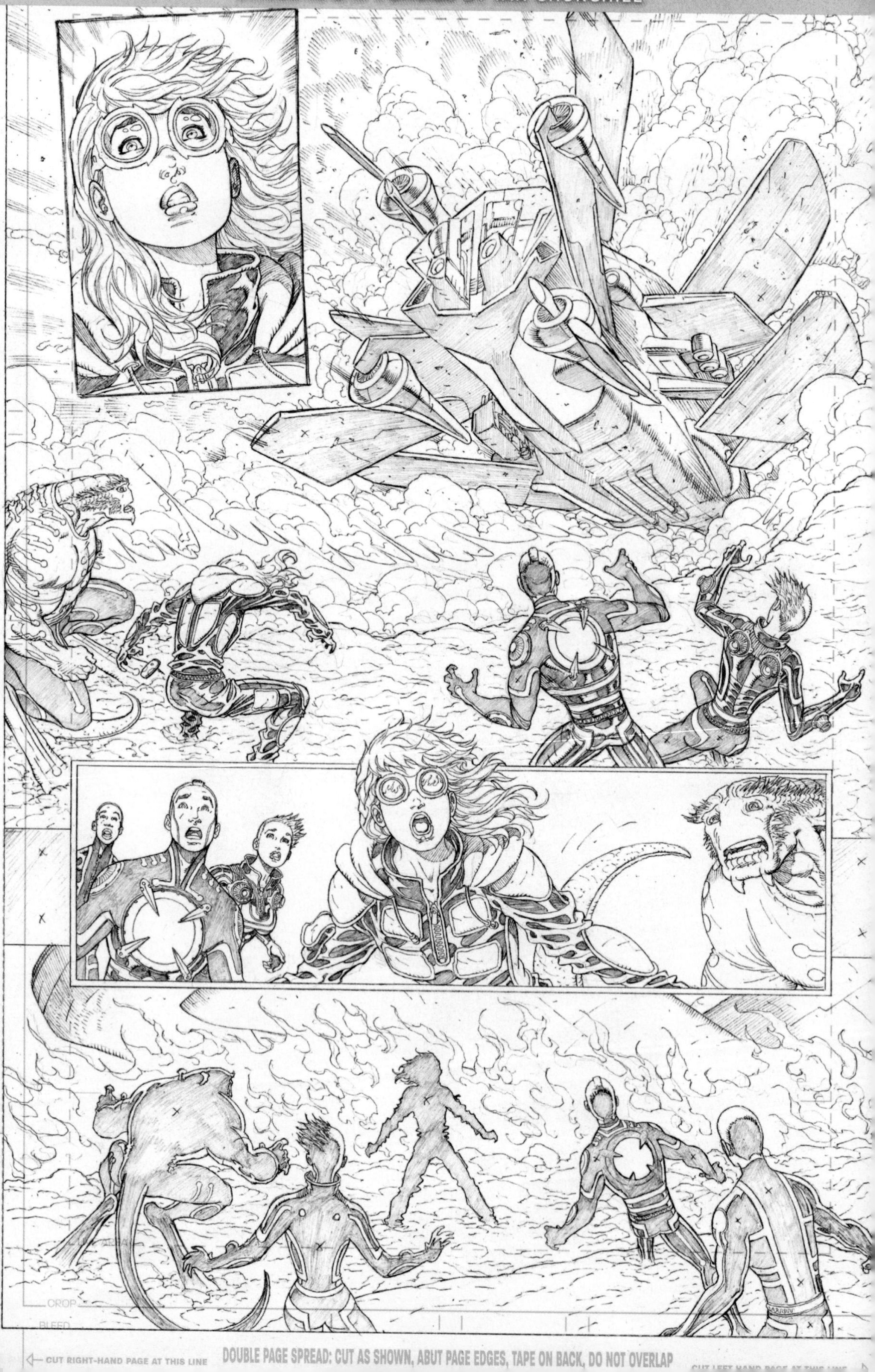
CROP
BLEED
CUT RIGHT-HAND PAGE AT THIS LINE
DOUBLE PAGE SPREAD: CUT AS SHOWN, ABUT PAGE EDGES, TAPE ON BACK, DO NOT OVERLAP

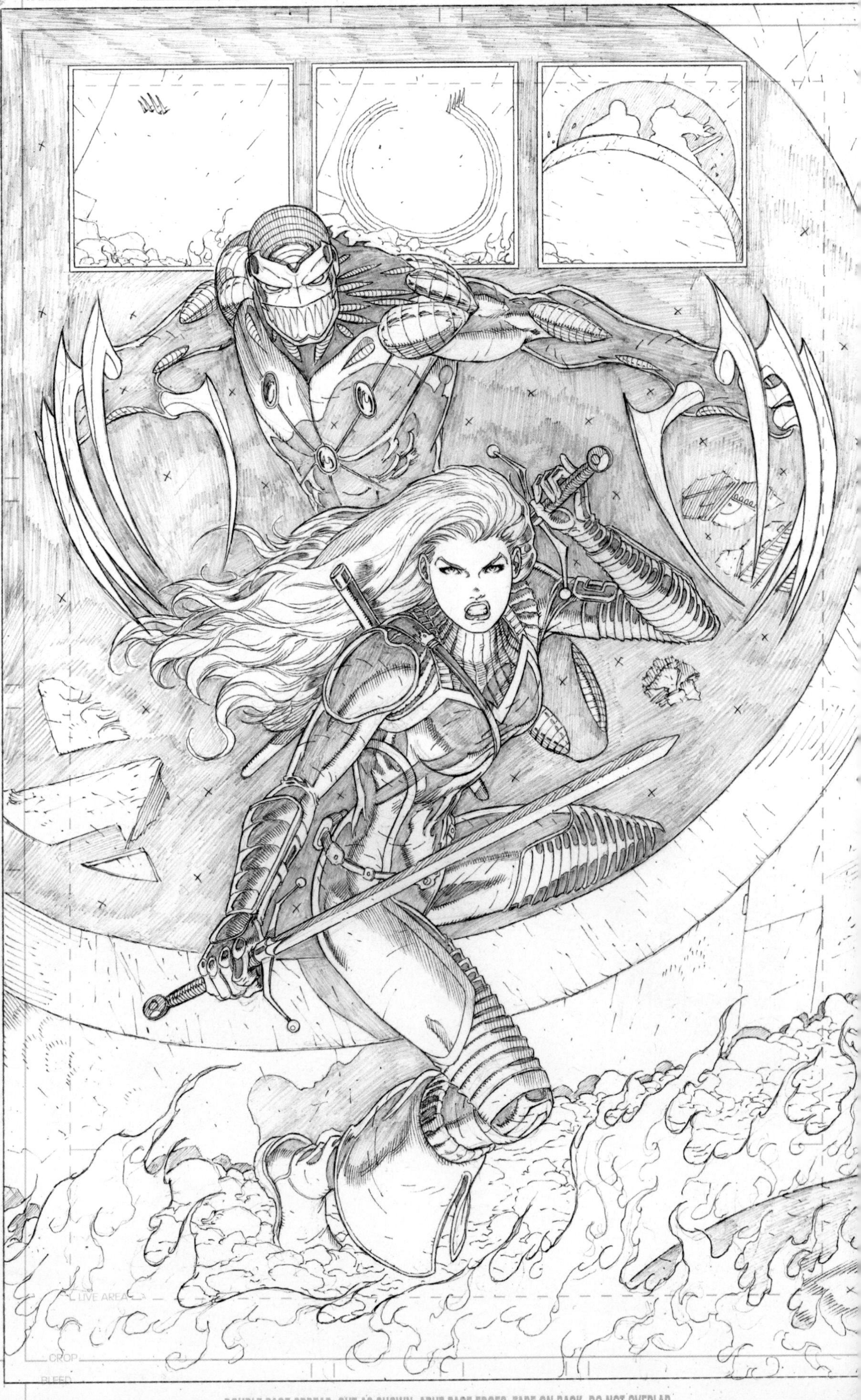
LIVE AREA
CROP
BLEED

Warblade character design by Jim Lee

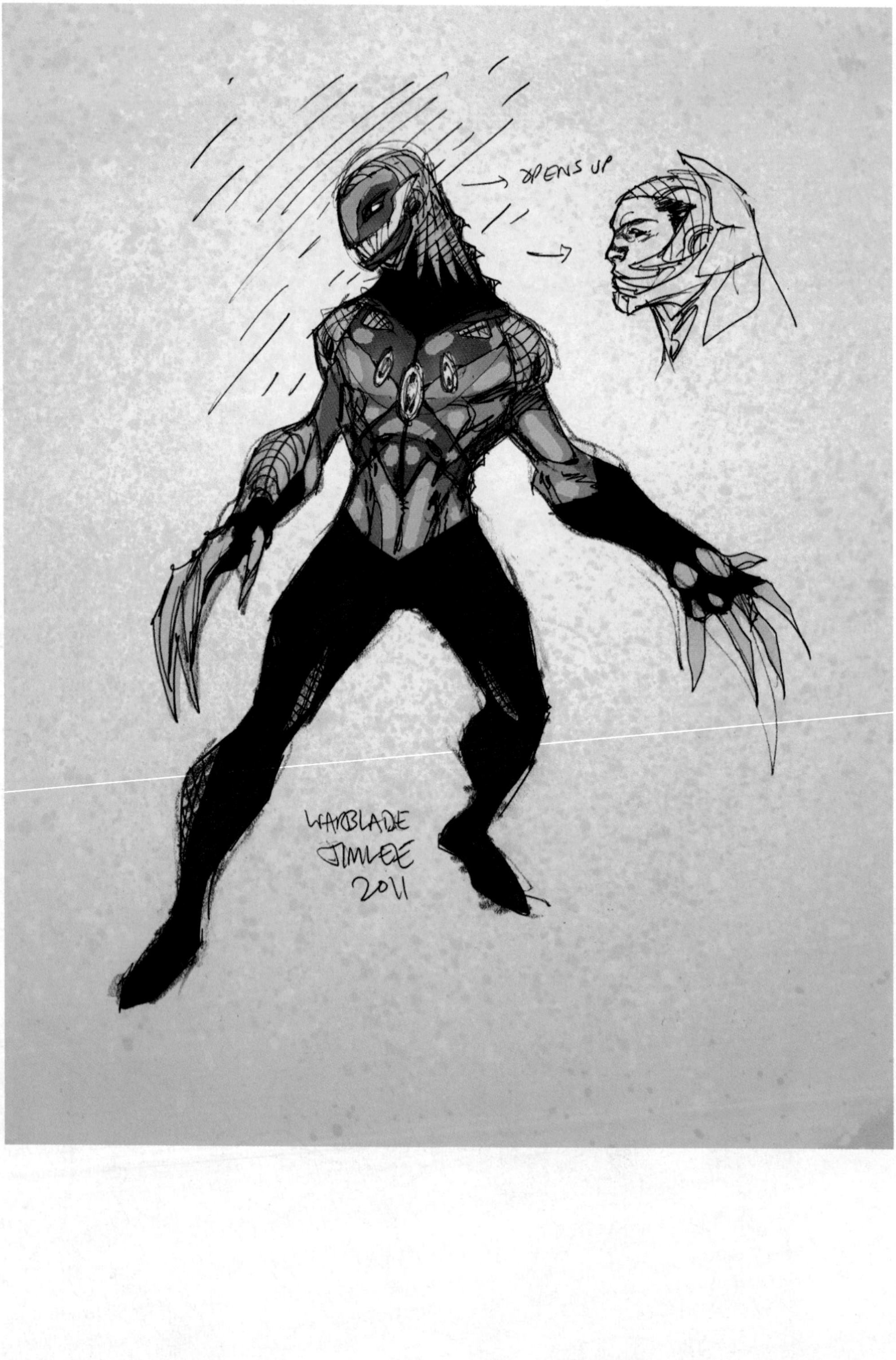
OPENS UP
WARBLADE
JIMLEE
2011

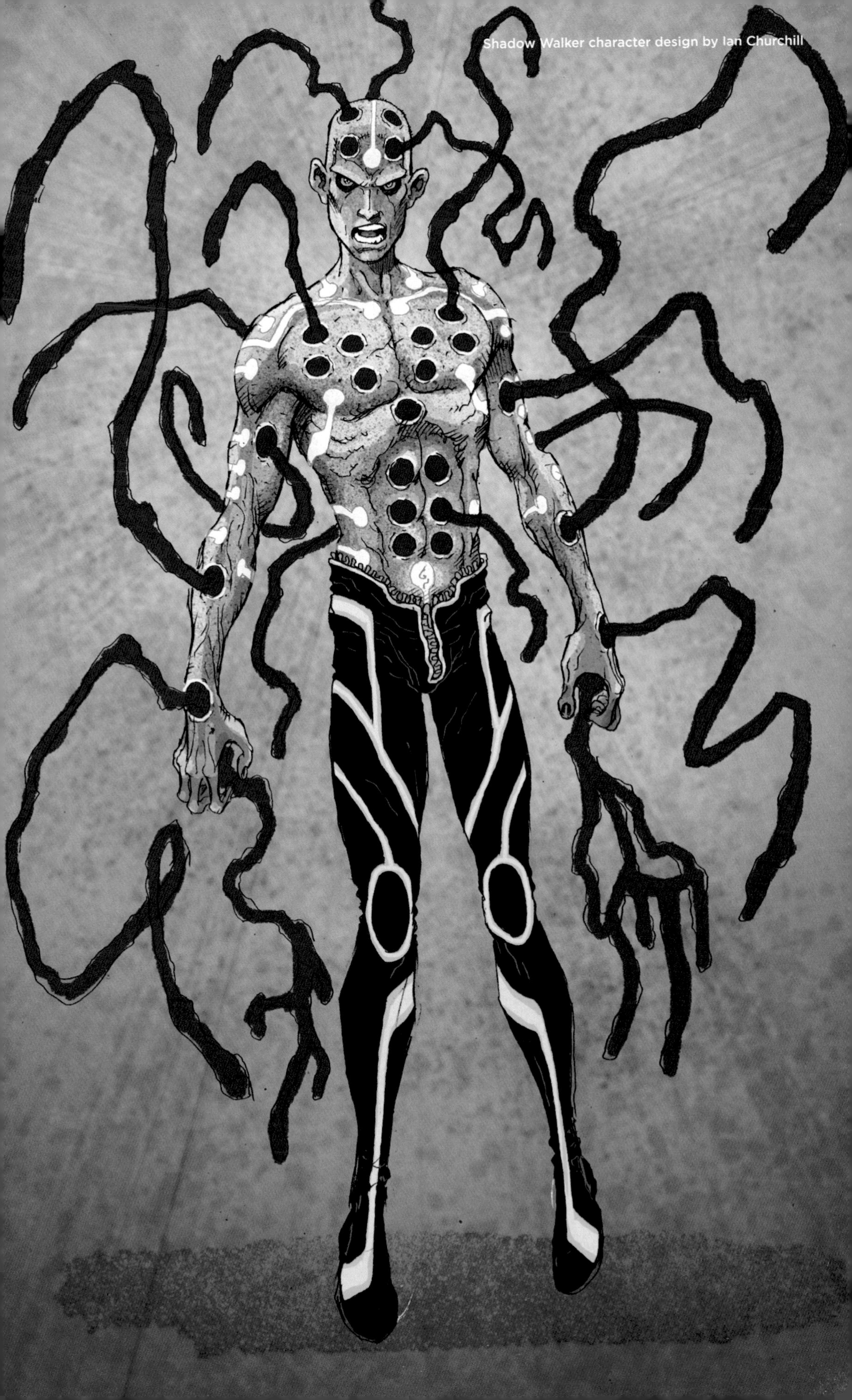

Shadow Walker character design by Ian Churchill

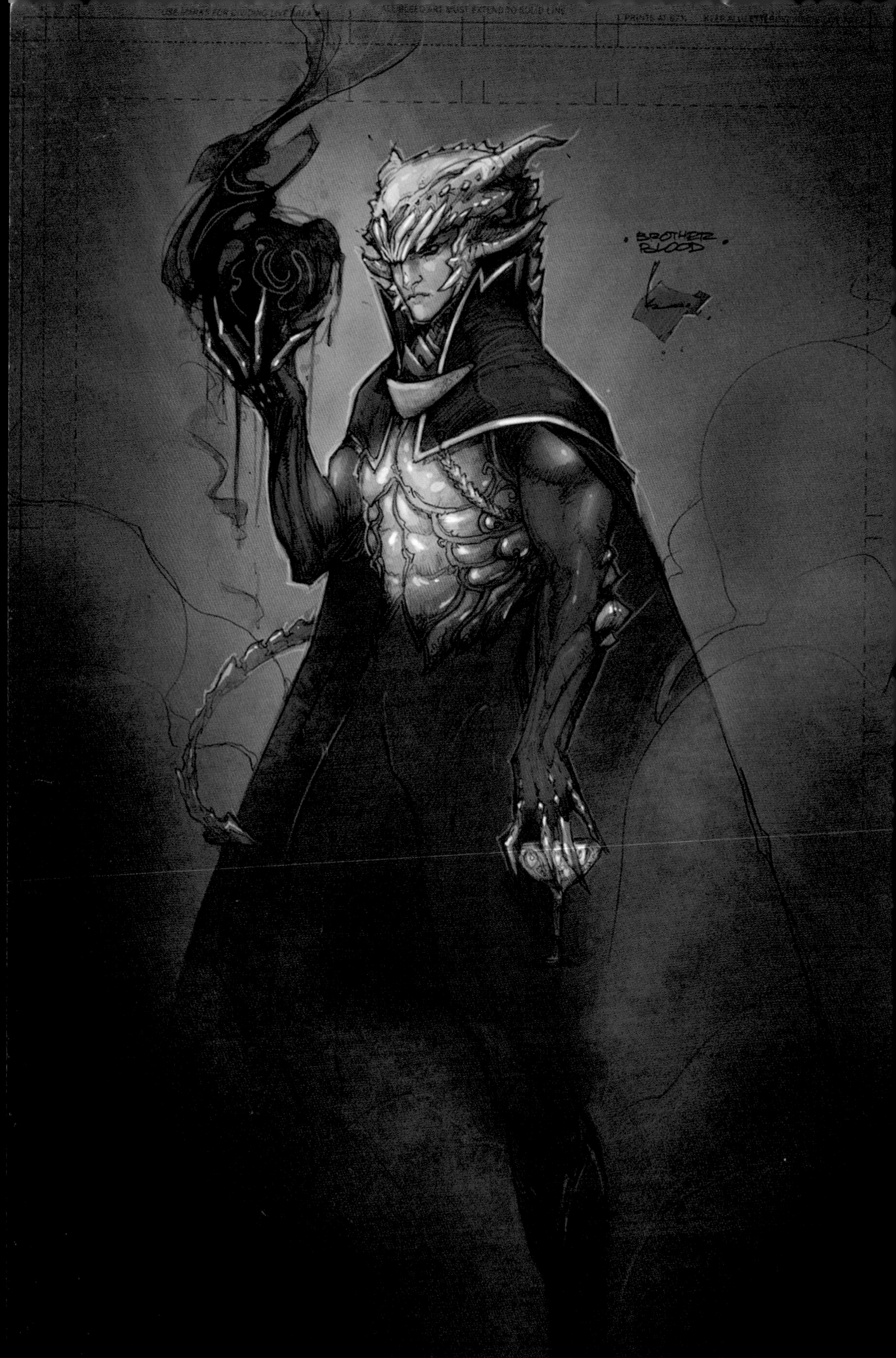
BROTHER BLOOD

Brother Blood character design by Kenneth Rocafort

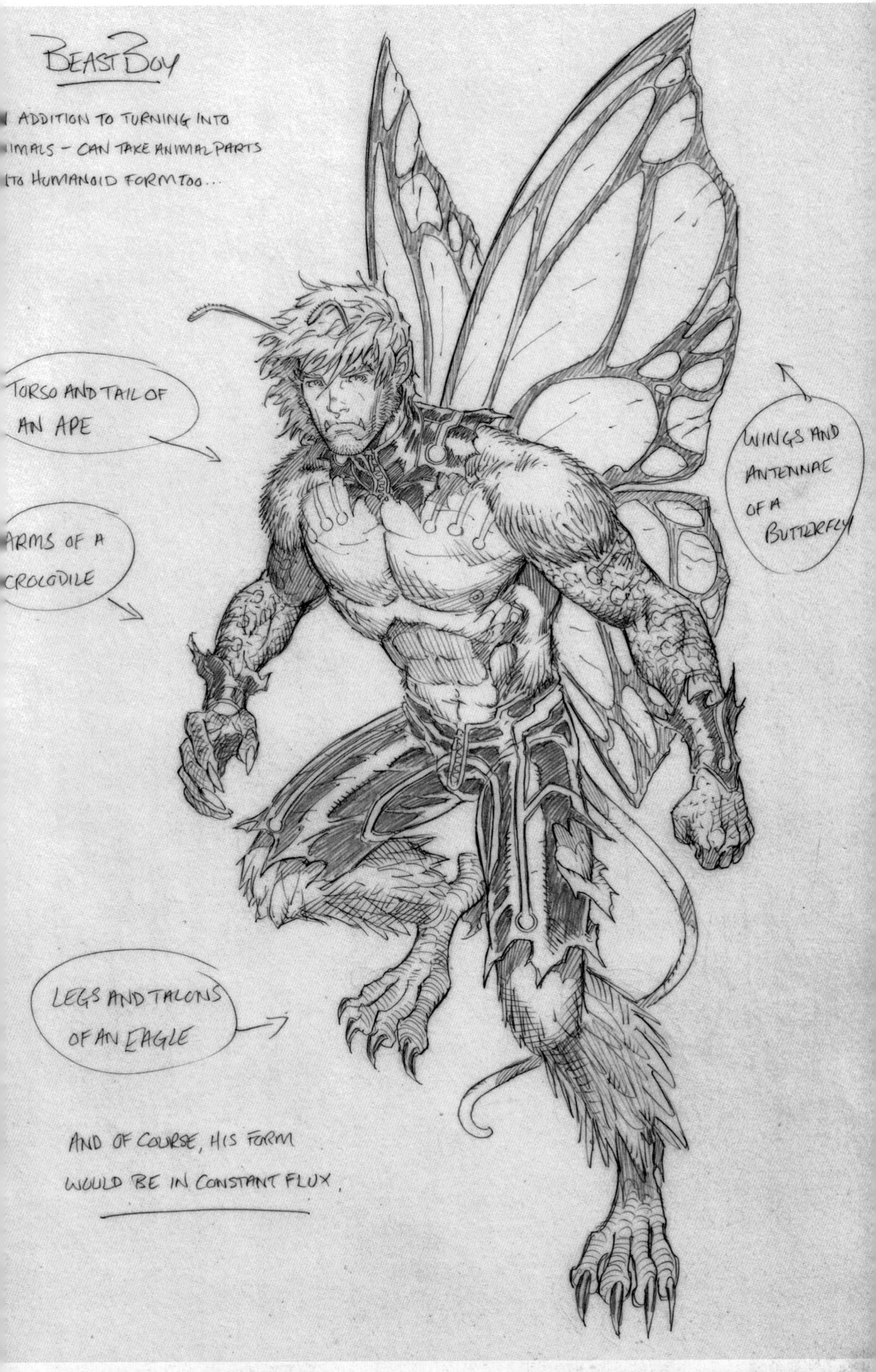
BEAST BOY
ADDITION TO TURNING INTO
IMALS – CAN TAKE ANIMAL PARTS
ITO HUMANOID FORM TOO...
TORSO AND TAIL OF AN APE
ARMS OF A CROCODILE
WINGS AND ANTENNAE OF A BUTTERFLY
LEGS AND TALONS OF AN EAGLE
AND OF COURSE, HIS FORM WOULD BE IN CONSTANT FLUX.

Beast Boy character design by Ian Churchill

Terra character design by Ian Churchill

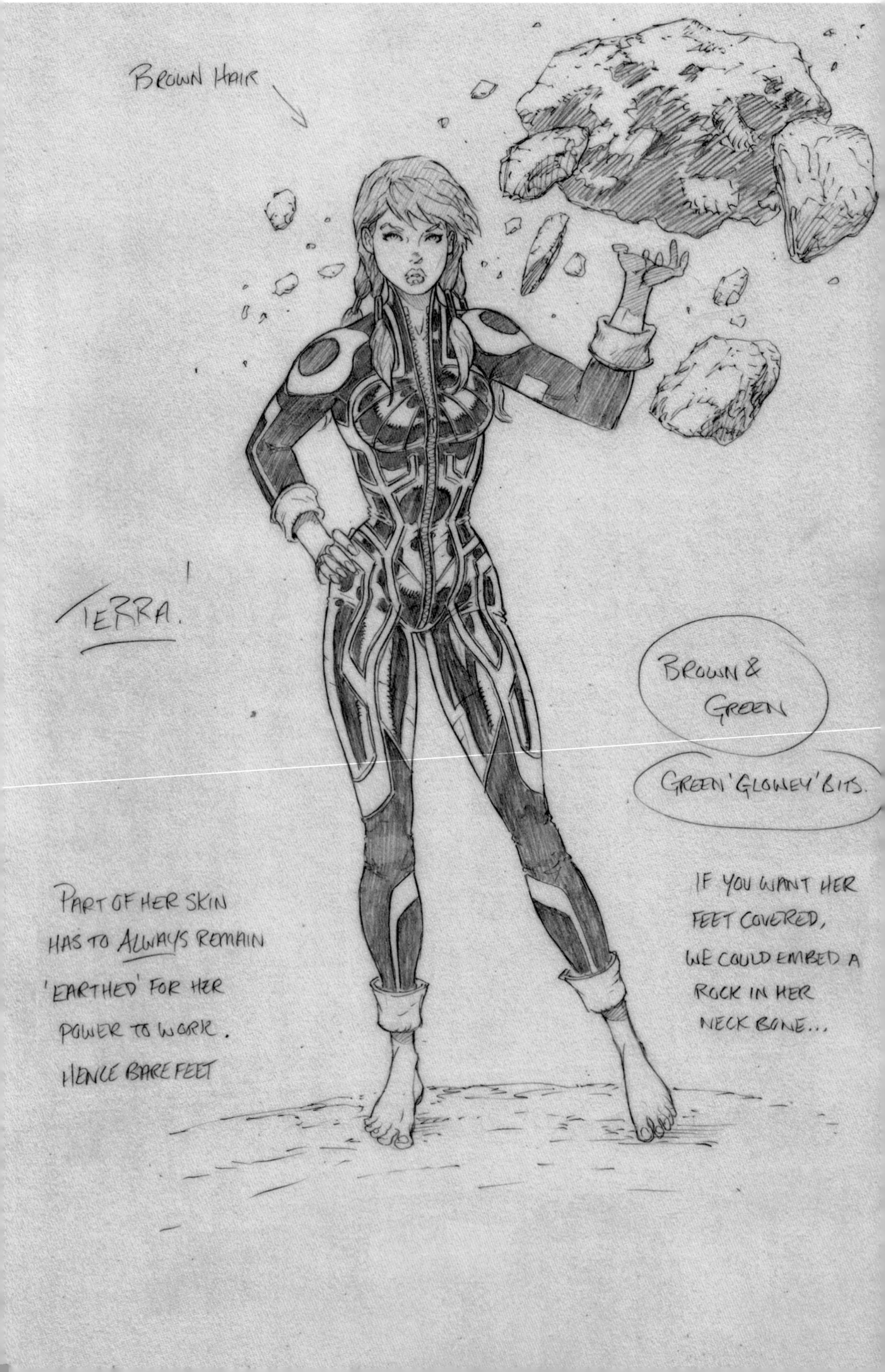
BROWN HAIR
TERRA!
BROWN & GREEN
GREEN 'GLOWEY' BITS.
PART OF HER SKIN HAS TO ALWAYS REMAIN 'EARTHED' FOR HER POWER TO WORK. HENCE BARE FEET
IF YOU WANT HER FEET COVERED, WE COULD EMBED A ROCK IN HER NECK BONE...

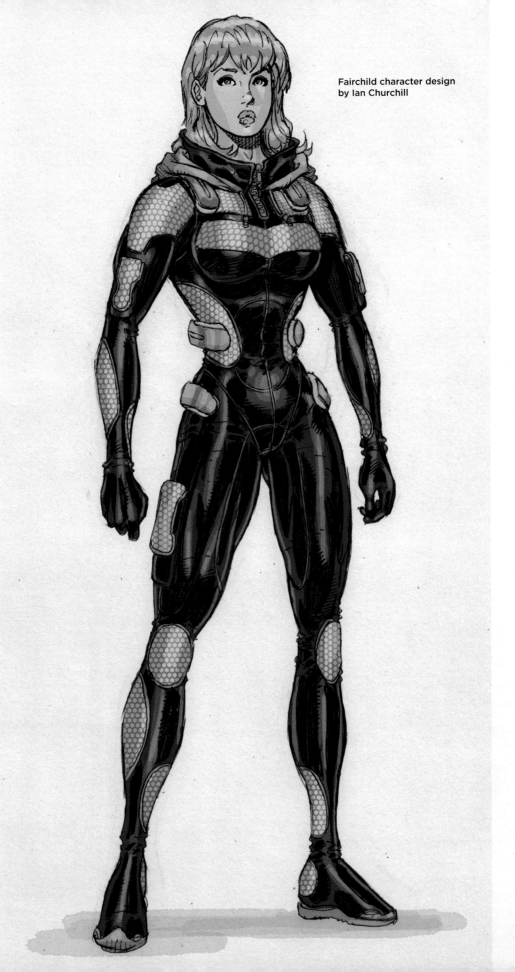

Fairchild character design
by Ian Churchill

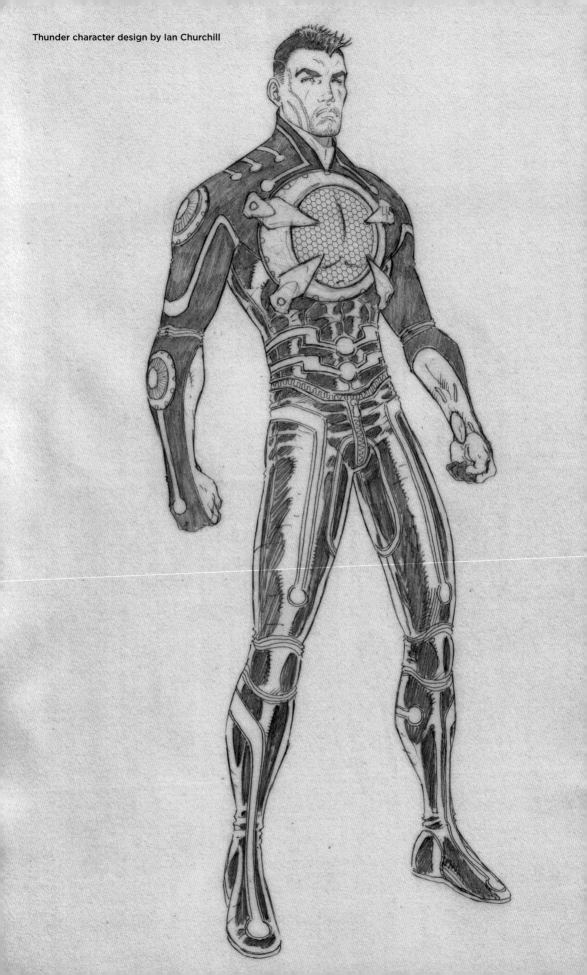

Thunder character design by Ian Churchill

Lightning character design by Ian Churchill

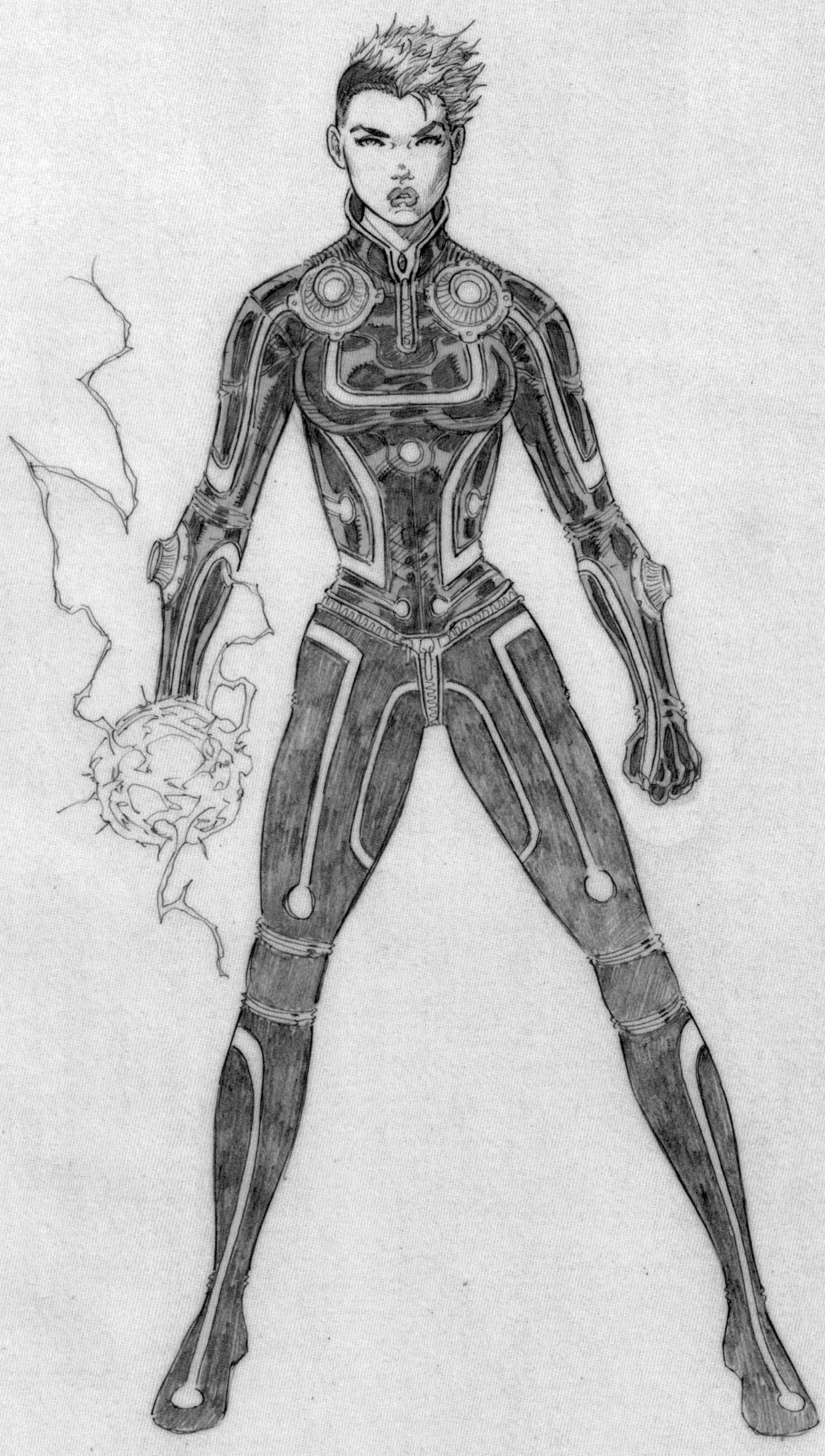

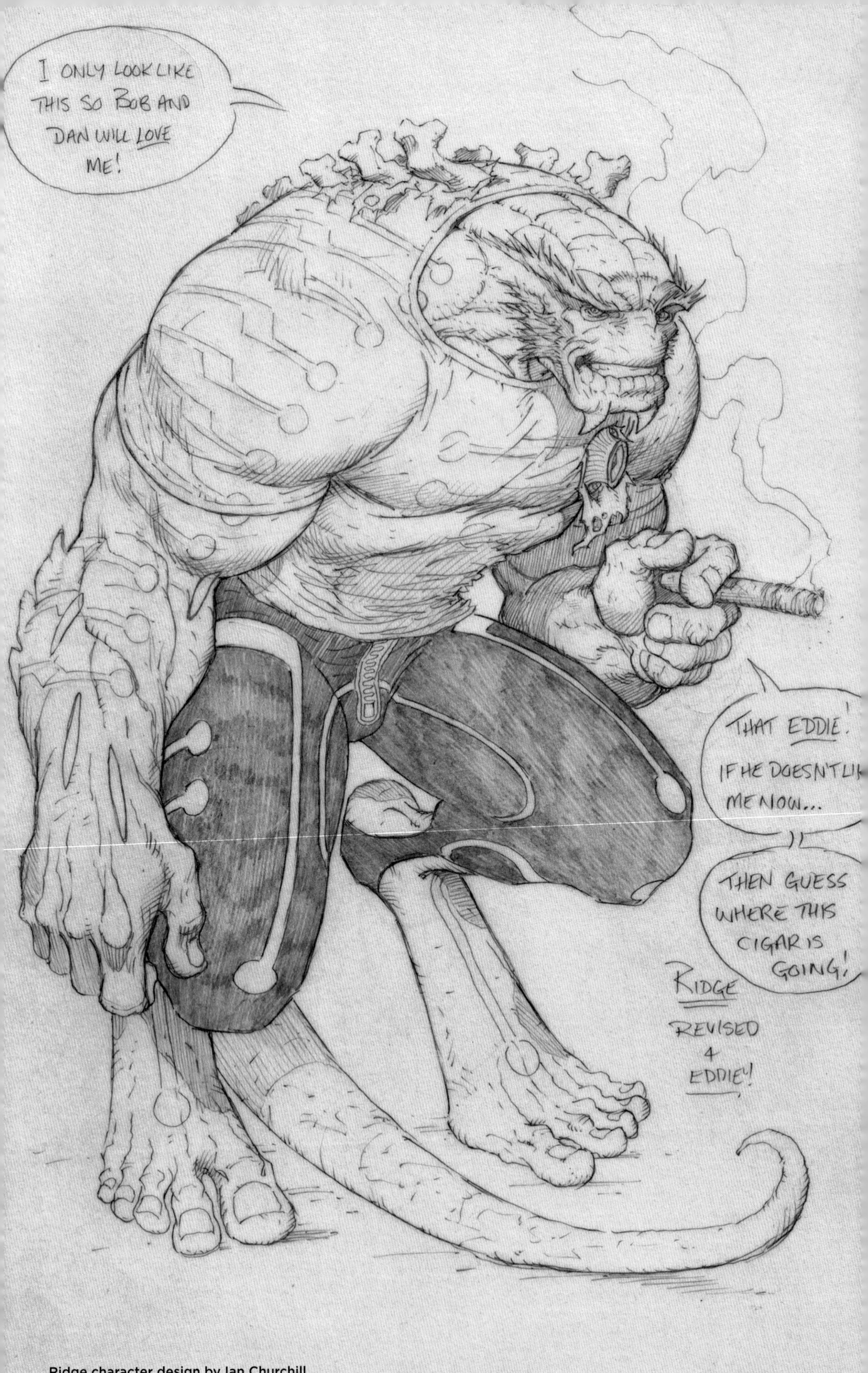
I ONLY LOOK LIKE THIS SO BOB AND DAN WILL LOVE ME!
THAT EDDIE! IF HE DOESN'T LI ME NOW...
THEN GUESS WHERE THIS CIGAR IS GOING!
RIDGE
REVISED 4 EDDIE!

Ridge character design by Ian Churchill

START AT THE BEGINNING!

TEEN TITANS VOLUME 1: IT'S OUR RIGHT TO FIGHT

LEGION OF SUPER-HEROES VOLUME 1: HOSTILE WORLD

LEGION LOST VOLUME 1: RUN FROM TOMORROW

STATIC SHOCK VOLUME 1: SUPERCHARGED

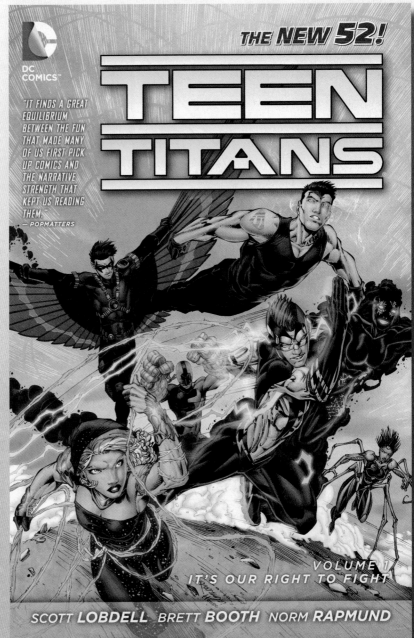

THE NEW 52!

TEEN TITANS

"IT FINDS A GREAT EQUILIBRIUM BETWEEN THE FUN THAT MADE MANY OF US FIRST PICK UP COMICS AND THE NARRATIVE STRENGTH THAT KEPT US READING THEM."
— POPMATTERS

VOLUME 1
IT'S OUR RIGHT TO FIGHT

SCOTT LOBDELL BRETT BOOTH NORM RAPMUND

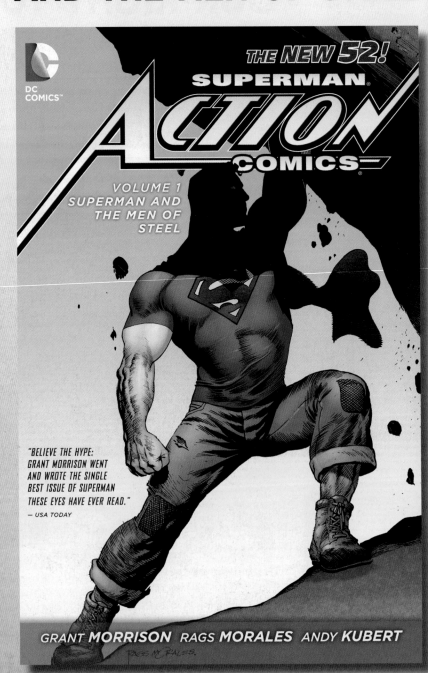

START AT THE BEGINNING!

WONDER WOMAN VOLUME 1: BLOOD

MR. TERRIFIC VOLUME 1: MIND GAMES

BLUE BEETLE VOLUME 1: METAMORPHOSIS

THE FURY OF FIRESTORM: THE NUCLEAR MEN VOLUME 1: GOD PARTICLE